RAGNARÖK

Other 100% Authentic Manga Available from TOKYOPOP®:

COWBOY BEBOP 1-3 (of 3)
All-new adventures of interstellar bounty hunting, based on the hit anime seen on Cartoon Network.

MARMALADE BOY 1-3 (of 8)
A tangled teen romance for the new millennium.

REAL BOUT HIGH SCHOOL 1-4 (of 4+)
At Daimon High, teachers don't break up fights…they grade them.

MARS 1-4 (of 15)
Biker Rei and artist Kira are as different as night and day, but fate binds them in this angst-filled romance.

GTO 1-6 (of 23+)
Biker gang member Onizuka is going back to school…as a teacher!

CHOBITS 1-3 (of 5+)
In the future, boys will be boys and girls will be…robots? The newest hit series from CLAMP!

SKULL MAN 1-3 (of 7+)
They took his family. They took his face. They took his soul. Now, he's going to take his revenge.

DRAGON KNIGHTS 1-4 (of 17)
Part dragon, part knight, ALL glam. The most inept knights on the block are out to kick some demon butt.

INITIAL D 1-3 (of 23+)
Delivery boy Tak has a gift for driving, but can he compete in the high-stakes world of street racing?

PARADISE KISS 1-3 (of 3+)
High fashion and deep passion collide in this hot new shojo series!

KODOCHA: Sana's Stage 1-3 (of 10)
There's a rumble in the jungle gym when child star Sana Kurata and bully Akito Hayama collide.

ANGELIC LAYER 1-2 (of 5)
In the future, the most popular game is Angelic Layer, where hand-raised robots battle for supremacy.

LOVE HINA 1-6 (of 14)
Can Keitaro handle living in a dorm with five cute girls…and still make it through school?

Also Available from TOKYOPOP®:

PRIEST 1-2 (of 10+)
The quick and the undead in one macabre manga.

RAGNAROK 1-3 (of 9+)
In the final battle between gods and men, only a small band of heroes stand
in the way of total annihilation.

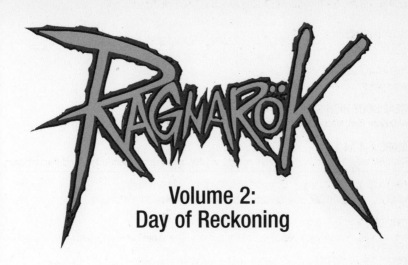

Volume 2:
Day of Reckoning

By
Myung-Jin Lee

English Version
by
Richard A. Knaak

Los Angeles • Tokyo

Translator - Lauren Na
Retouch & Lettering - Monalisa J.de Asis
Cover Layout - Anna Kernbaum

Senior Editor - Jake Forbes
Managing Editor - Jill Freshney
Production Coordinator - Antonio DePietro
Production Manager - Jennifer Miller
Art Director - Matthew Alford
Director of Editorial - Jeremy Ross
VP of Production & Manufacturing - Ron Klamert
President & C.O.O. - John Parker
Publisher - Stuart Levy

Email: editor@TOKYOPOP.com
Come visit us online at www.TOKYOPOP.com

A  Manga
TOKYOPOP® is an imprint of Mixx Entertainment, Inc.
5900 Wilshire Blvd. Suite 2000, Los Angeles, CA 90036

ISBN: 1-931514-74-7

First TOKYOPOP® printing: July 2002

10 9 8 7 6 5

Printed in the USA

RAGNARÖK

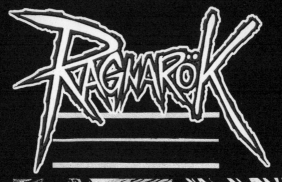

2

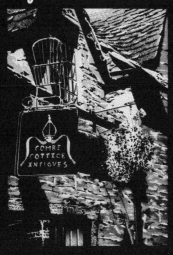

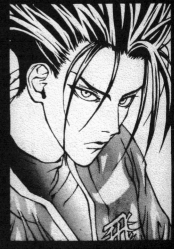

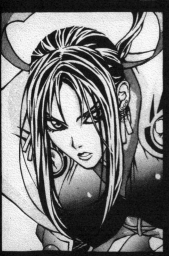

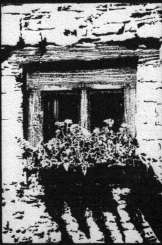

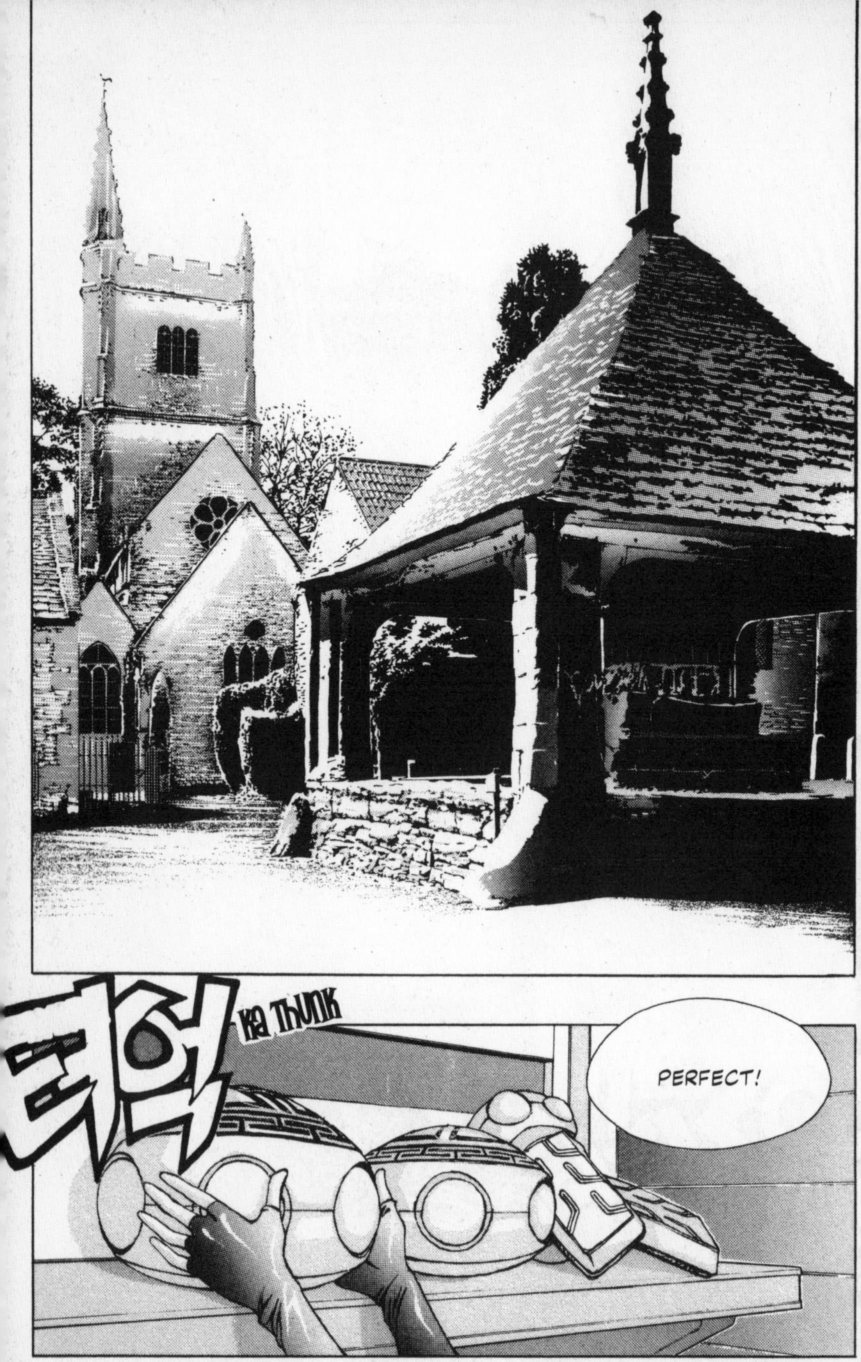

KA THUNK
PERFECT!

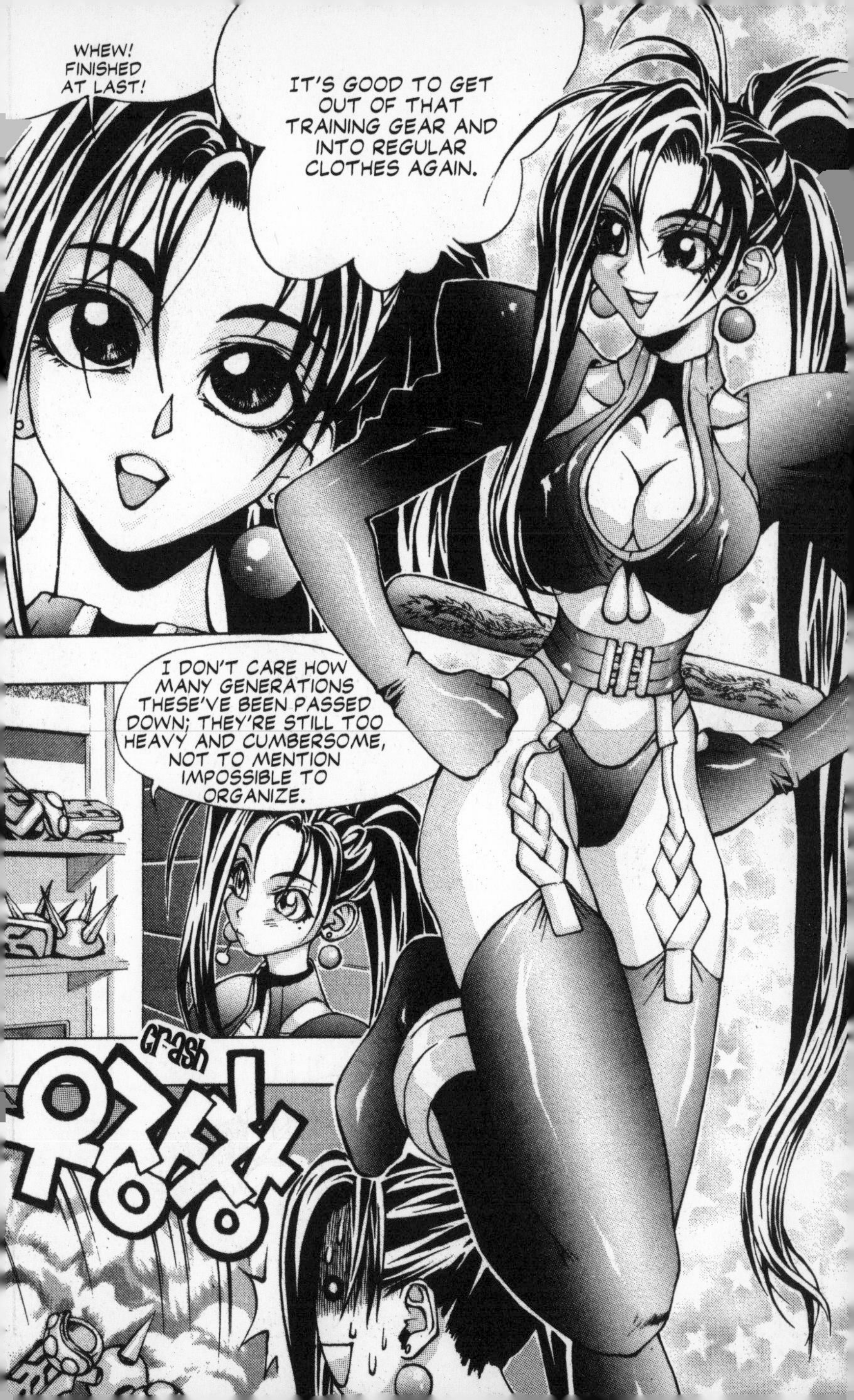
WHEW! FINISHED AT LAST!
IT'S GOOD TO GET OUT OF THAT TRAINING GEAR AND INTO REGULAR CLOTHES AGAIN.
I DON'T CARE HOW MANY GENERATIONS THESE'VE BEEN PASSED DOWN; THEY'RE STILL TOO HEAVY AND CUMBERSOME, NOT TO MENTION IMPOSSIBLE TO ORGANIZE.
crash
와창

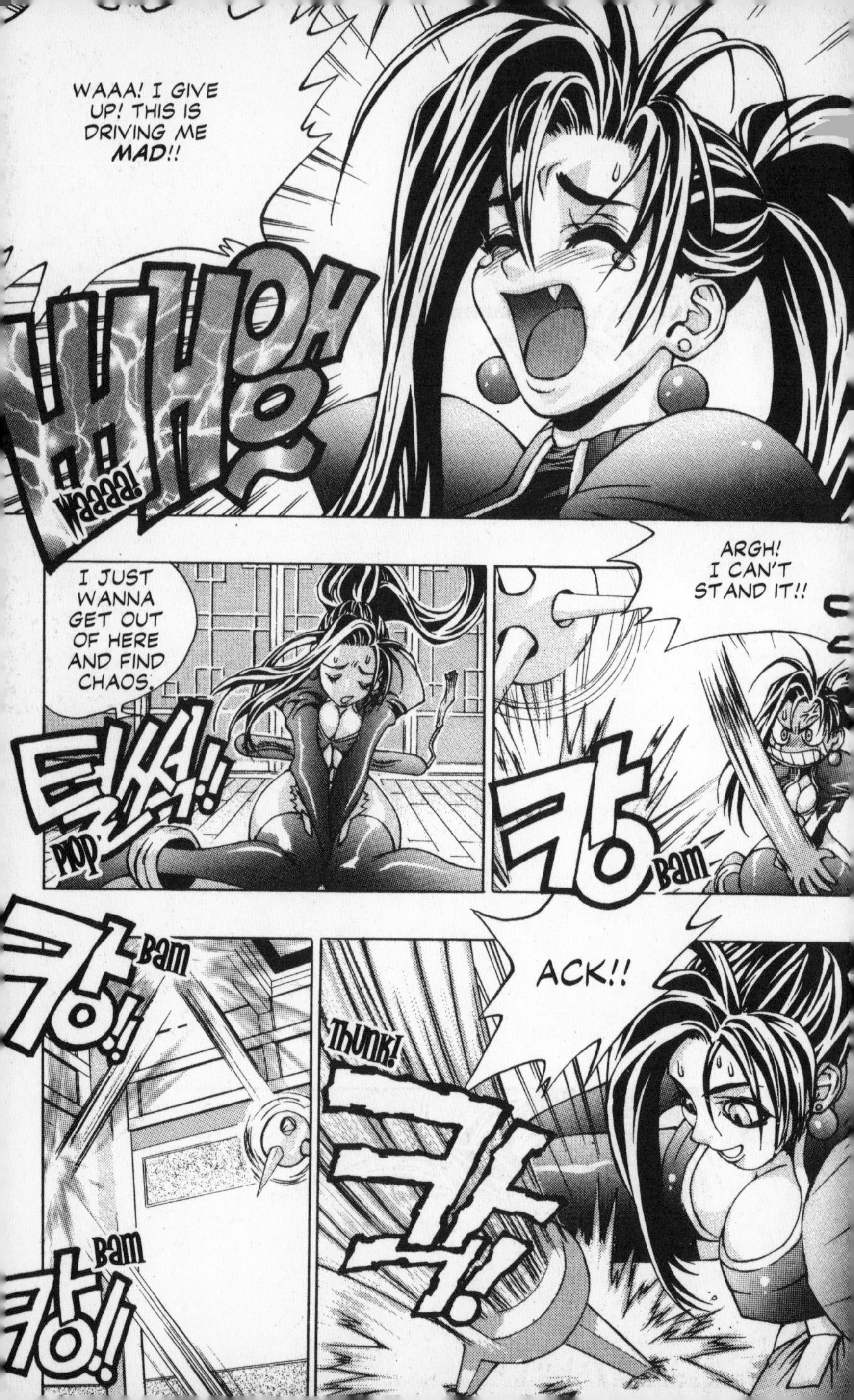
WAAA! I GIVE UP! THIS IS DRIVING ME MAD!!
WAAAA!
I JUST WANNA GET OUT OF HERE AND FIND CHAOS.
PLOP
ARGH! I CAN'T STAND IT!!
BAM
BAM
BAM
ACK!!
THUNK!

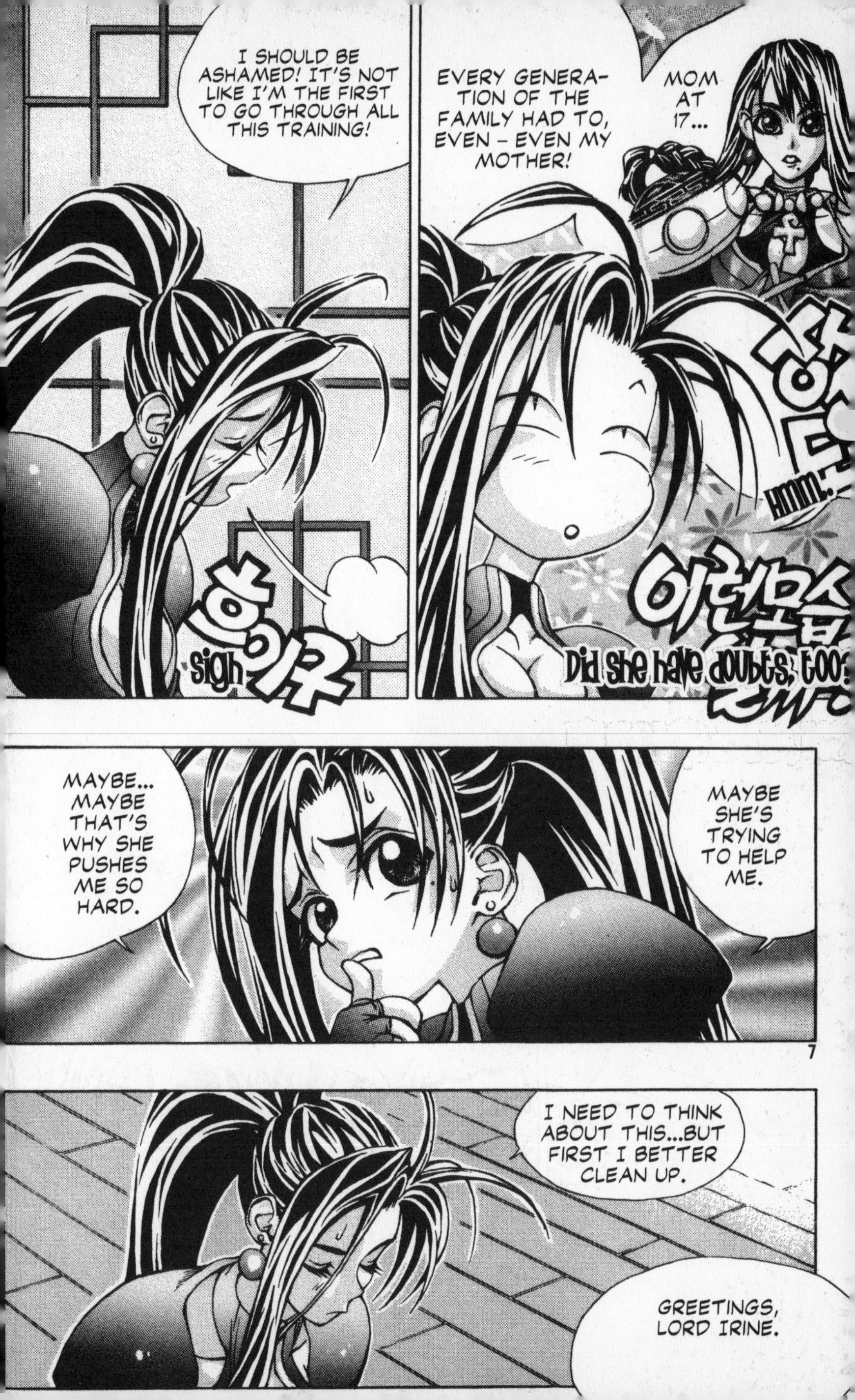

I SHOULD BE ASHAMED! IT'S NOT LIKE I'M THE FIRST TO GO THROUGH ALL THIS TRAINING!
sigh
EVERY GENERATION OF THE FAMILY HAD TO, EVEN – EVEN MY MOTHER!
MOM AT 17...
HMM.
Did she have doubts, too?
MAYBE... MAYBE THAT'S WHY SHE PUSHES ME SO HARD.
MAYBE SHE'S TRYING TO HELP ME.
I NEED TO THINK ABOUT THIS...BUT FIRST I BETTER CLEAN UP.
GREETINGS, LORD IRINE.

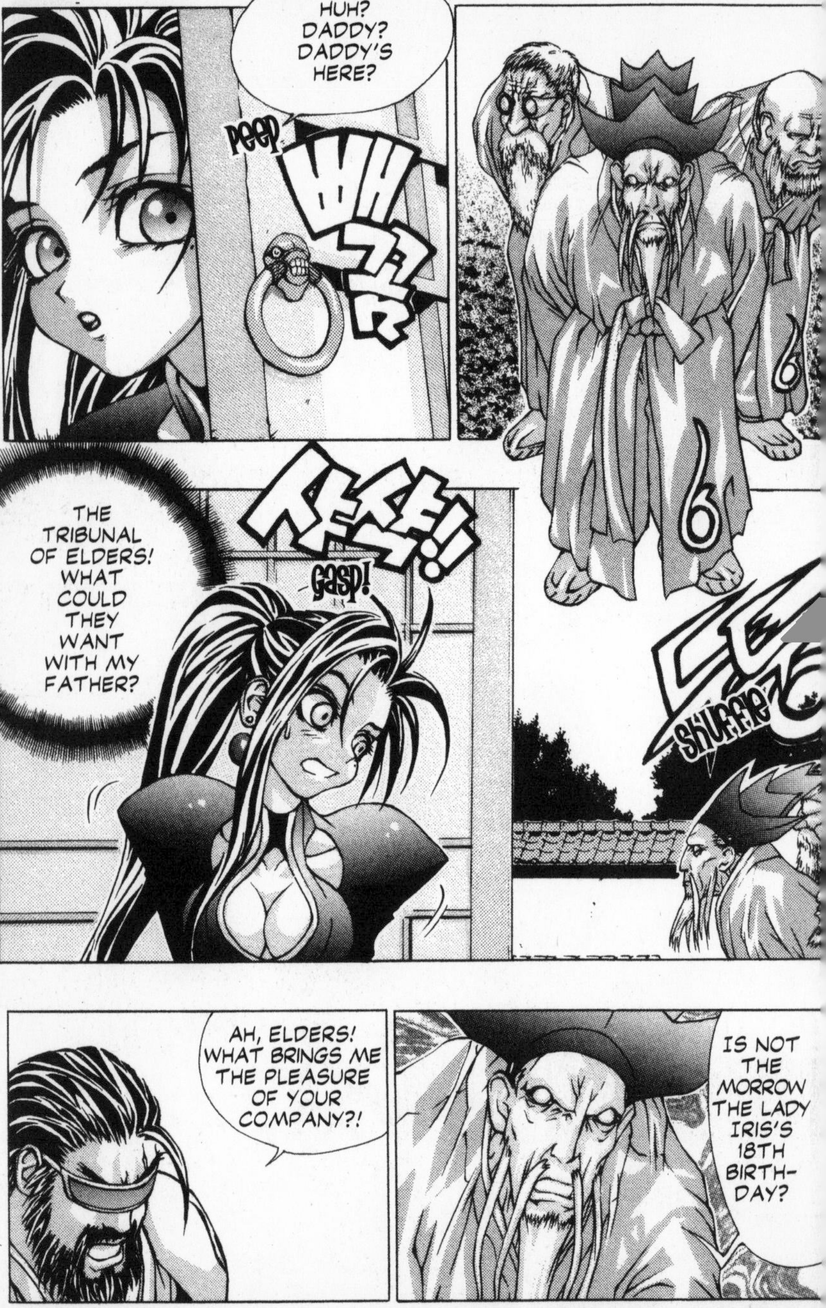
HUH? DADDY? DADDY'S HERE?
PEEP
THE TRIBUNAL OF ELDERS! WHAT COULD THEY WANT WITH MY FATHER?
GASP!
SHUFFLE
AH, ELDERS! WHAT BRINGS ME THE PLEASURE OF YOUR COMPANY?!
IS NOT THE MORROW THE LADY IRIS'S 18TH BIRTH-DAY?

BUT MY DAUGHTER STILL HAS NOT RECEIVED THE BLESSINGS OF THE FOUR CONSTELLATIONS. SHE CANNOT BE FORMALLY RECOGNIZED AS HEIR WITHOUT THEM. BESIDES, HER TRAINING--

PARDON, MY LORD, BUT WE ALL KNOW THE BLESSINGS ARE ONLY *RITUAL*.

THE CONSTELLATIONS LOOK OVER US IN NAME ONLY NOW.

YOU OF ALL PEOPLE SHOULD KNOW WHY...

...THEY NO LONGER LOOK DOWN AT US WITH FAVOR.

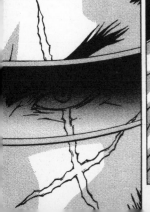

THINK BACK, MY LORD. 12 YEARS AGO. THAT NIGHT. THE "INCIDENT" AND THE CHILD WHO ESCAPED...

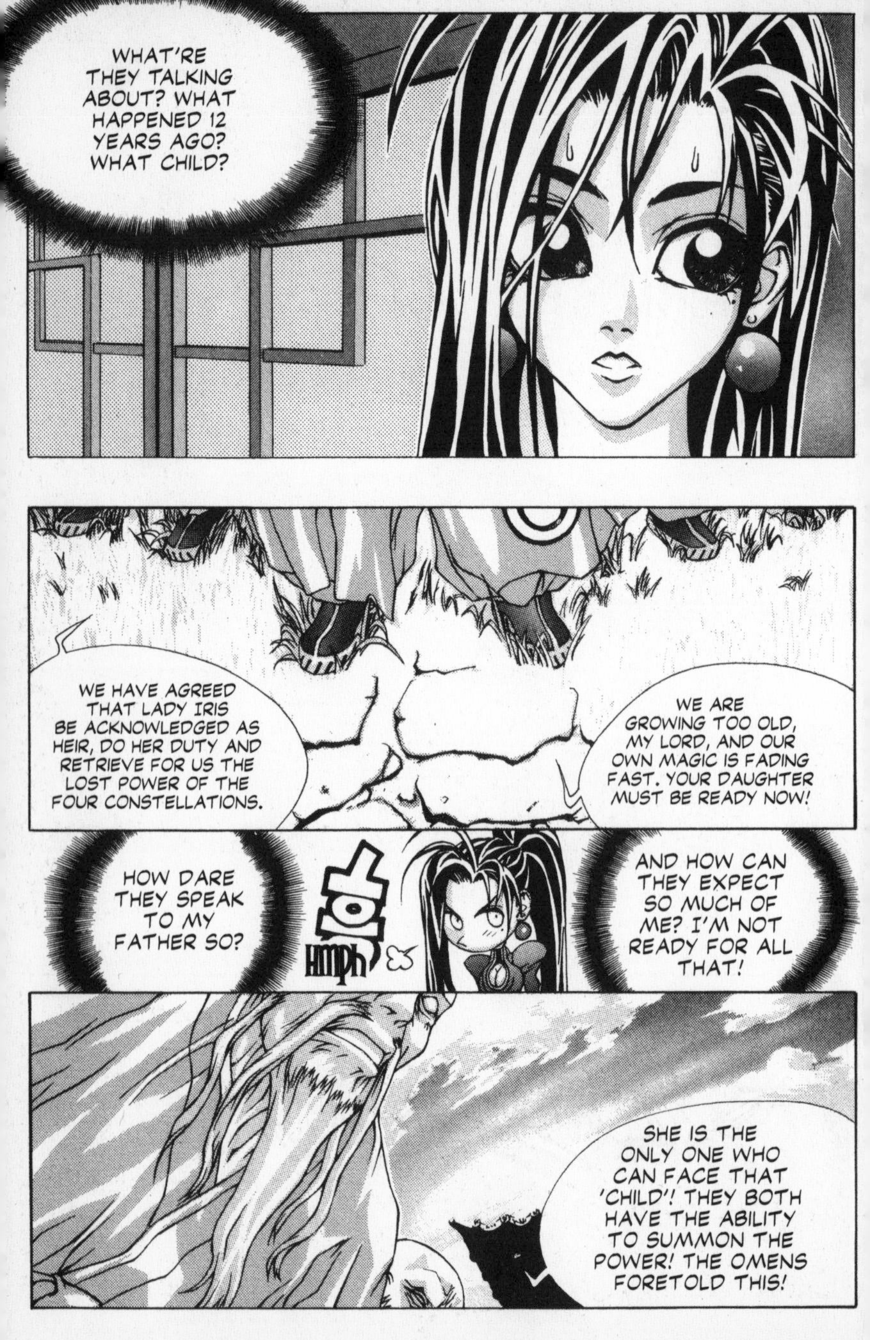
WHAT'RE THEY TALKING ABOUT? WHAT HAPPENED 12 YEARS AGO? WHAT CHILD?
WE HAVE AGREED THAT LADY IRIS BE ACKNOWLEDGED AS HEIR, DO HER DUTY AND RETRIEVE FOR US THE LOST POWER OF THE FOUR CONSTELLATIONS.
WE ARE GROWING TOO OLD, MY LORD, AND OUR OWN MAGIC IS FADING FAST. YOUR DAUGHTER MUST BE READY NOW!
HOW DARE THEY SPEAK TO MY FATHER SO?
HMPH
AND HOW CAN THEY EXPECT SO MUCH OF ME? I'M NOT READY FOR ALL THAT!
SHE IS THE ONLY ONE WHO CAN FACE THAT 'CHILD'! THEY BOTH HAVE THE ABILITY TO SUMMON THE POWER! THE OMENS FORETOLD THIS!

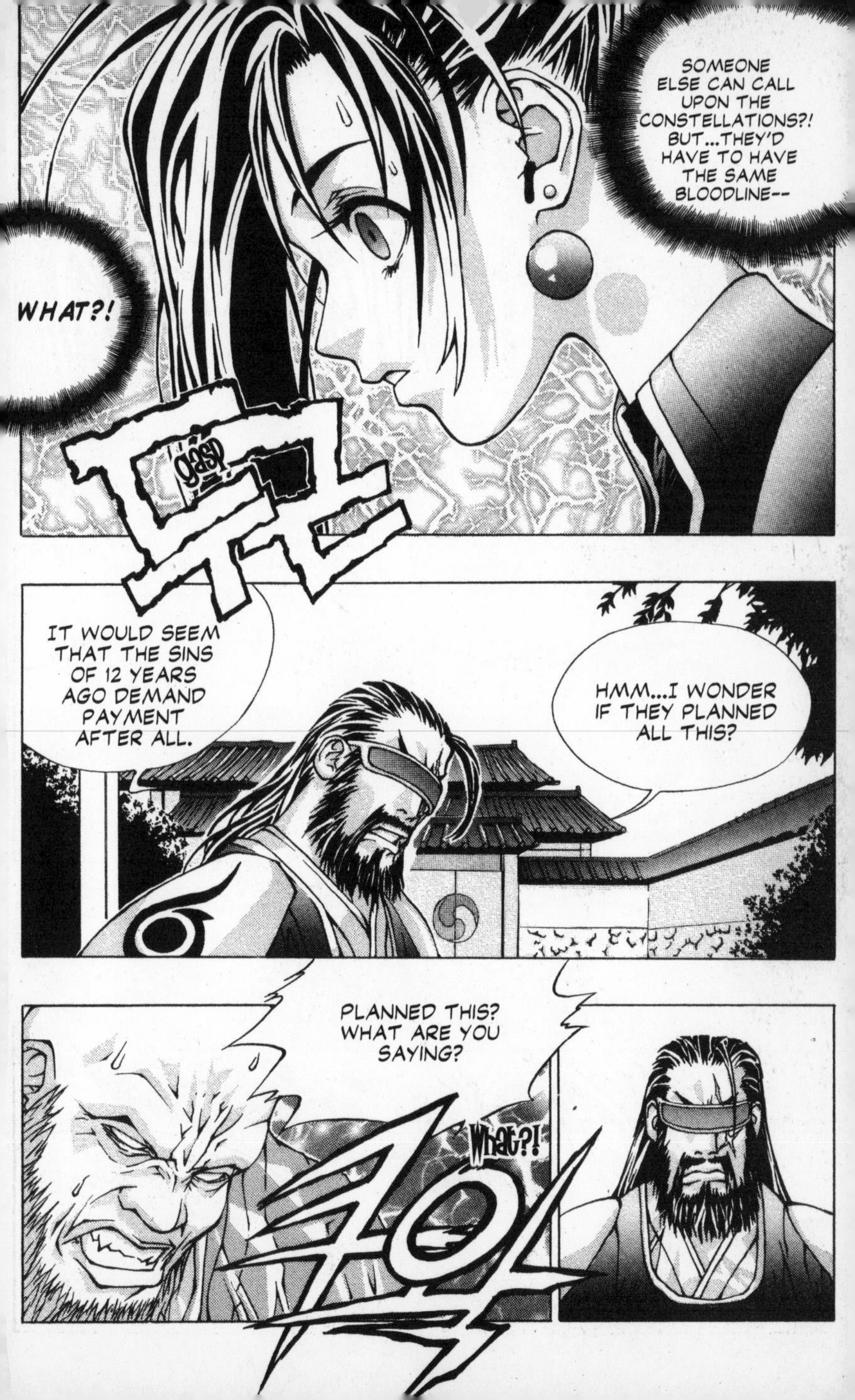
SOMEONE ELSE CAN CALL UPON THE CONSTELLATIONS?! BUT...THEY'D HAVE TO HAVE THE SAME BLOODLINE--
WHAT?!
gasp
IT WOULD SEEM THAT THE SINS OF 12 YEARS AGO DEMAND PAYMENT AFTER ALL.
HMM...I WONDER IF THEY PLANNED ALL THIS?
PLANNED THIS? WHAT ARE YOU SAYING?
What?!

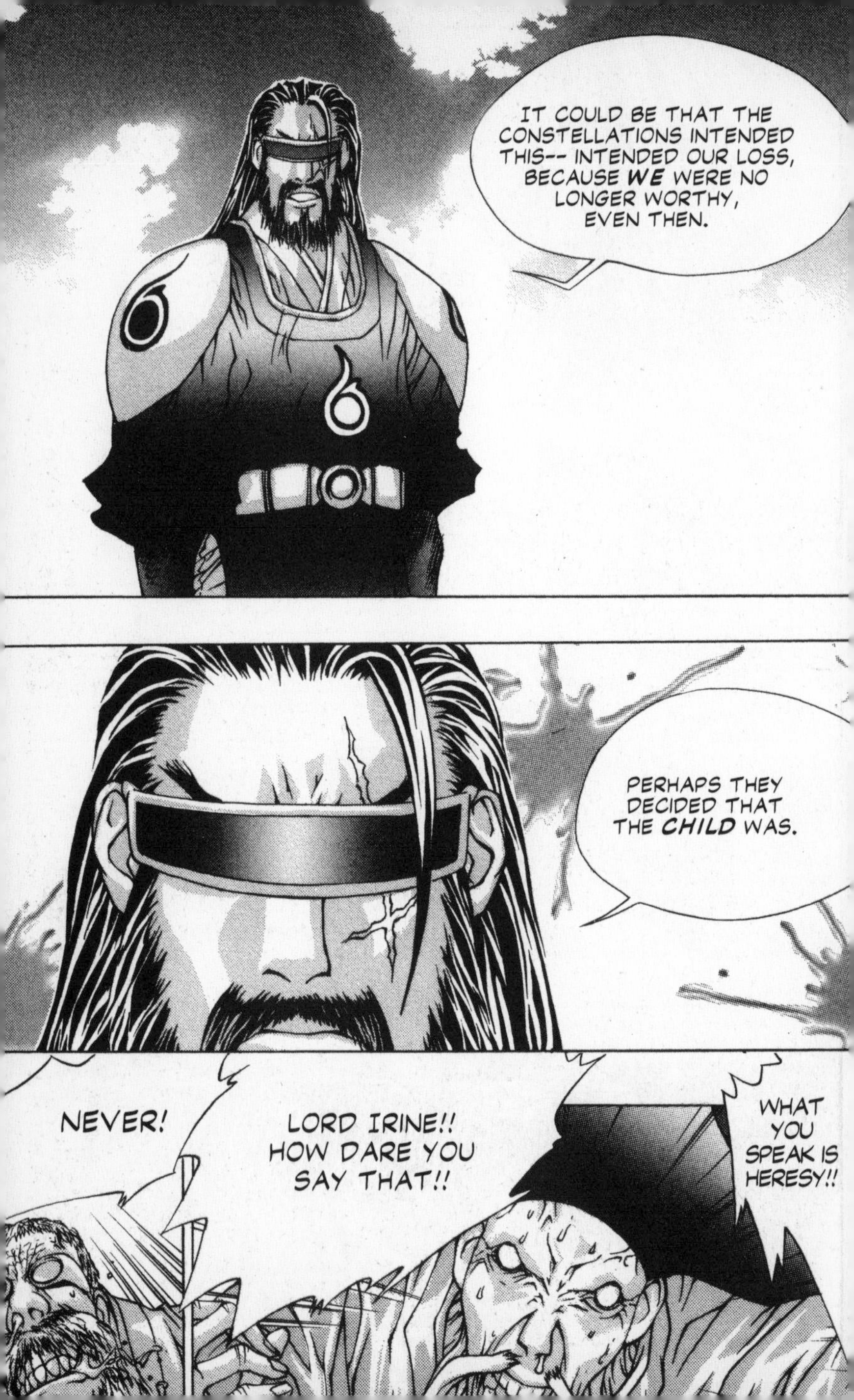
IT COULD BE THAT THE CONSTELLATIONS INTENDED THIS-- INTENDED OUR LOSS, BECAUSE *WE* WERE NO LONGER WORTHY, EVEN THEN.
PERHAPS THEY DECIDED THAT THE *CHILD* WAS.
NEVER!
LORD IRINE!! HOW DARE YOU SAY THAT!!
WHAT YOU SPEAK IS HERESY!!

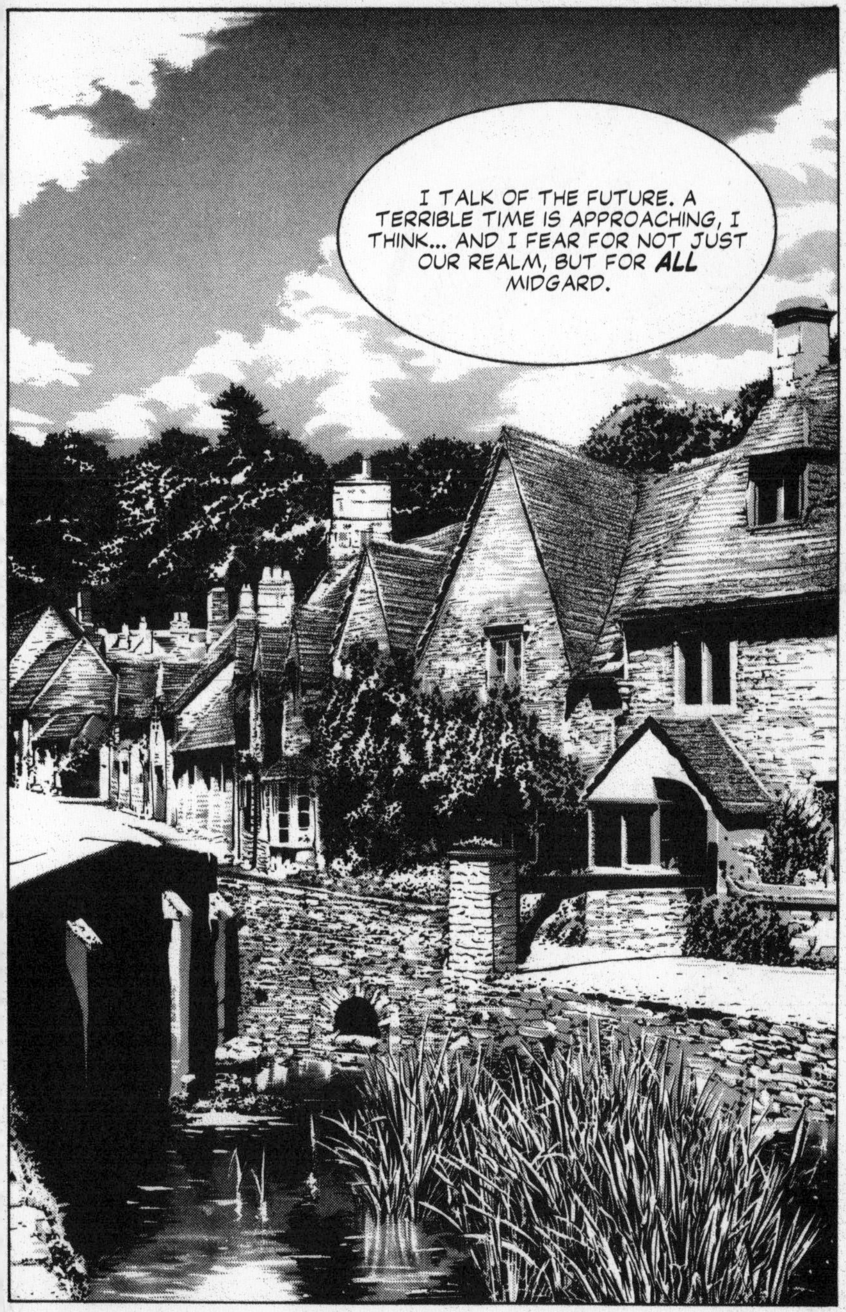
I TALK OF THE FUTURE. A TERRIBLE TIME IS APPROACHING, I THINK... AND I FEAR FOR NOT JUST OUR REALM, BUT FOR ALL MIDGARD.

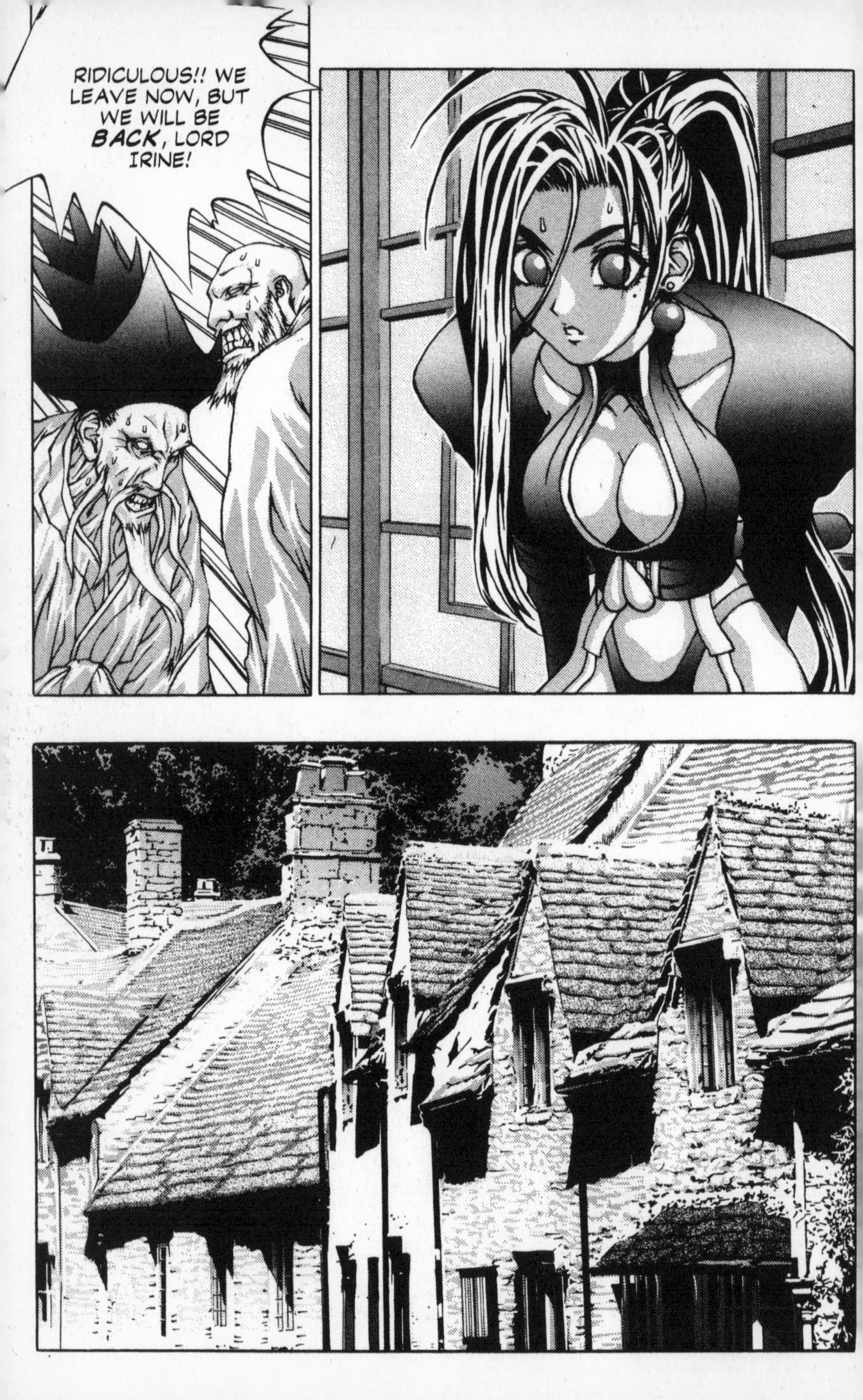
RIDICULOUS!! WE LEAVE NOW, BUT WE WILL BE BACK, LORD IRINE!

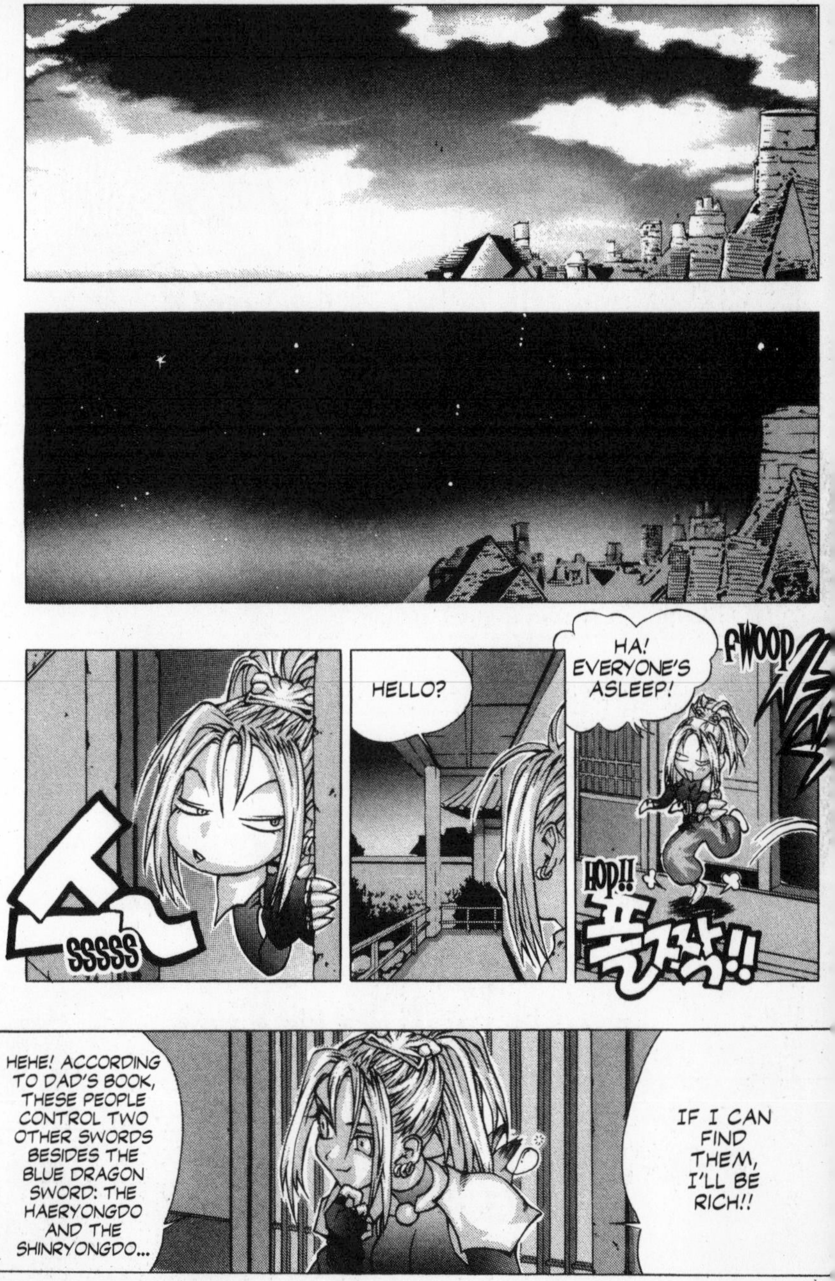
SSSSS
HELLO?
HA! EVERYONE'S ASLEEP!
FWOOP
HOP!!
HEHE! ACCORDING TO DAD'S BOOK, THESE PEOPLE CONTROL TWO OTHER SWORDS BESIDES THE BLUE DRAGON SWORD: THE HAERYONGDO AND THE SHINRYONGDO...
IF I CAN FIND THEM, I'LL BE RICH!!

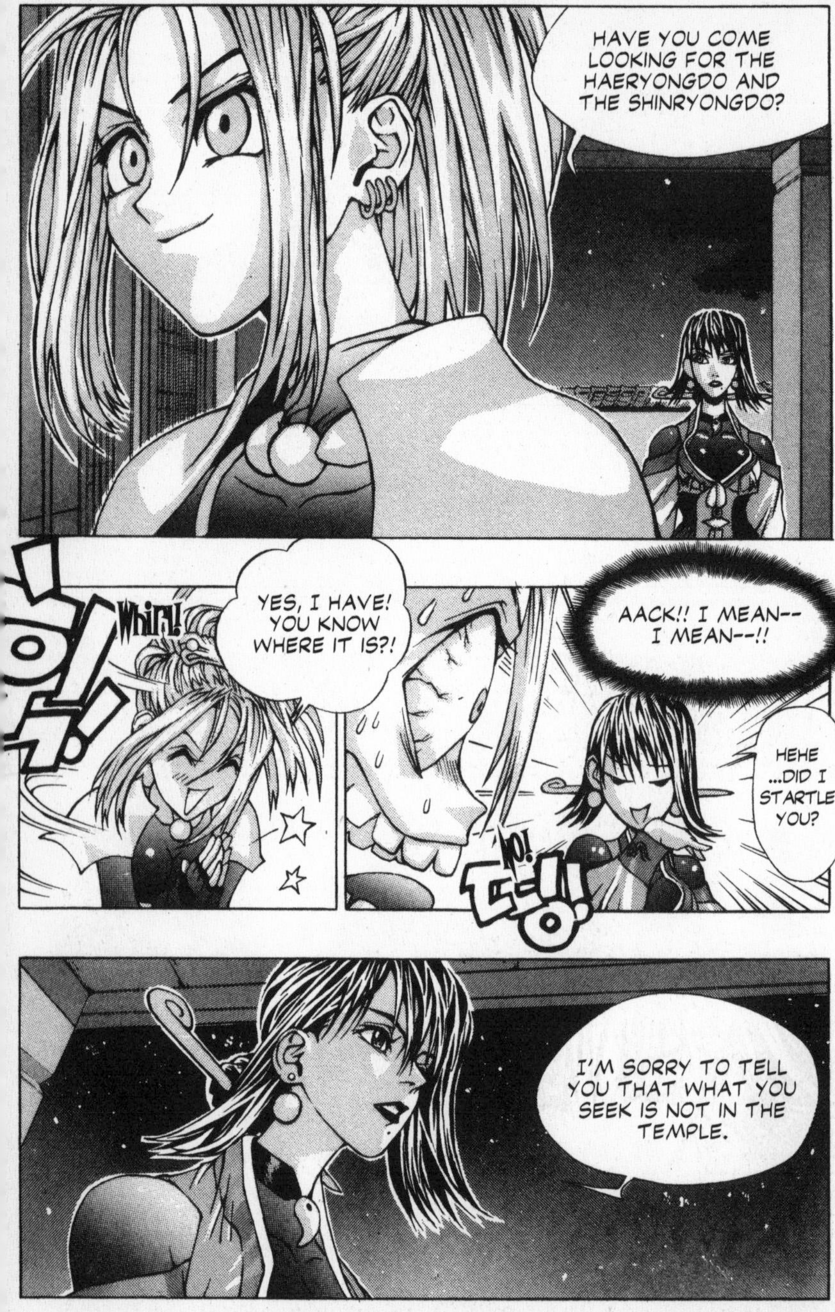
HAVE YOU COME LOOKING FOR THE HAERYONGDO AND THE SHINRYONGDO?
Whirl!
YES, I HAVE! YOU KNOW WHERE IT IS?!
AACK!! I MEAN-- I MEAN--!!
HEHE ...DID I STARTLE YOU?
HO!
I'M SORRY TO TELL YOU THAT WHAT YOU SEEK IS NOT IN THE TEMPLE.

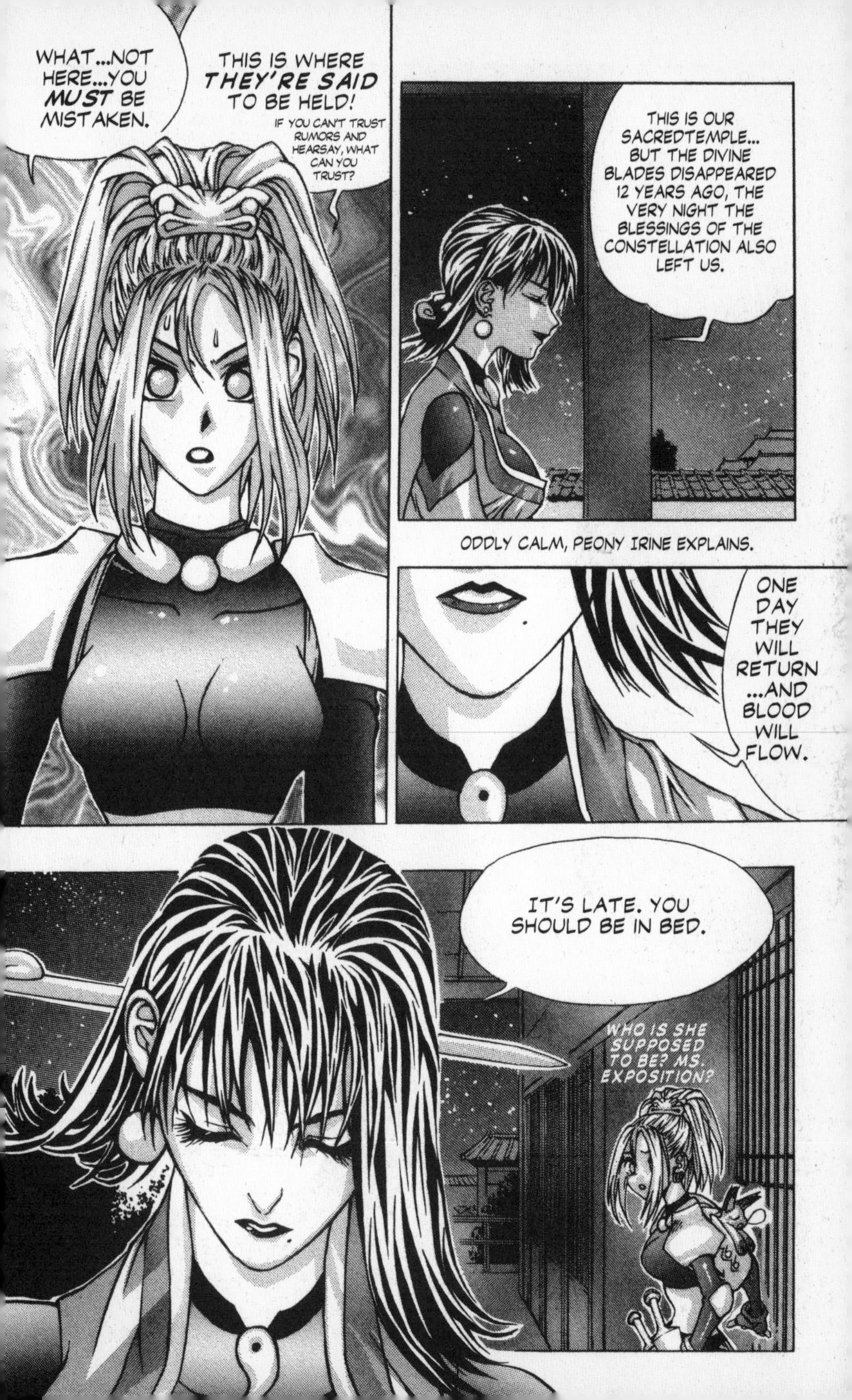
WHAT...NOT HERE...YOU MUST BE MISTAKEN.
THIS IS WHERE THEY'RE SAID TO BE HELD!
IF YOU CAN'T TRUST RUMORS AND HEARSAY, WHAT CAN YOU TRUST?
THIS IS OUR SACREDTEMPLE... BUT THE DIVINE BLADES DISAPPEARED 12 YEARS AGO, THE VERY NIGHT THE BLESSINGS OF THE CONSTELLATION ALSO LEFT US.
ODDLY CALM, PEONY IRINE EXPLAINS.
ONE DAY THEY WILL RETURN ...AND BLOOD WILL FLOW.
IT'S LATE. YOU SHOULD BE IN BED.
WHO IS SHE SUPPOSED TO BE? MS. EXPOSITION?

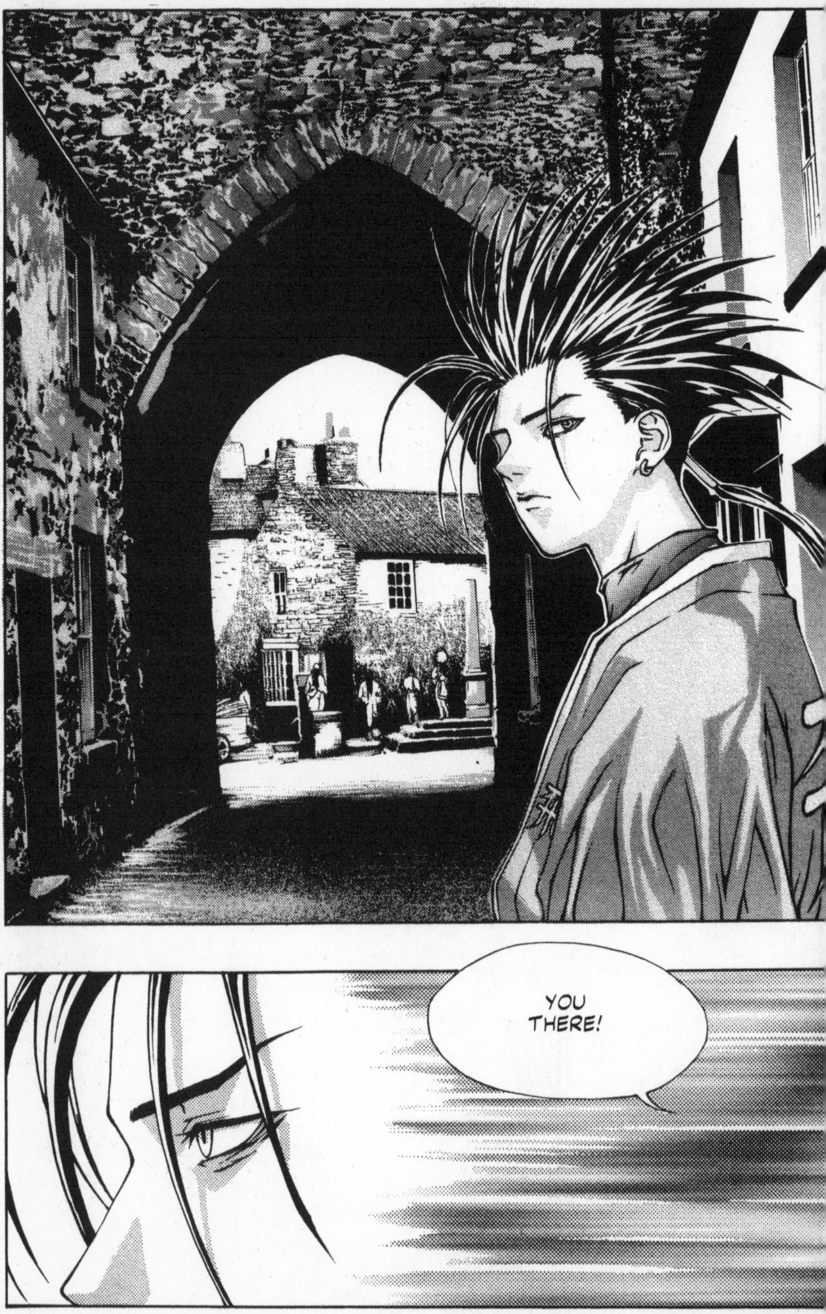
YOU THERE!

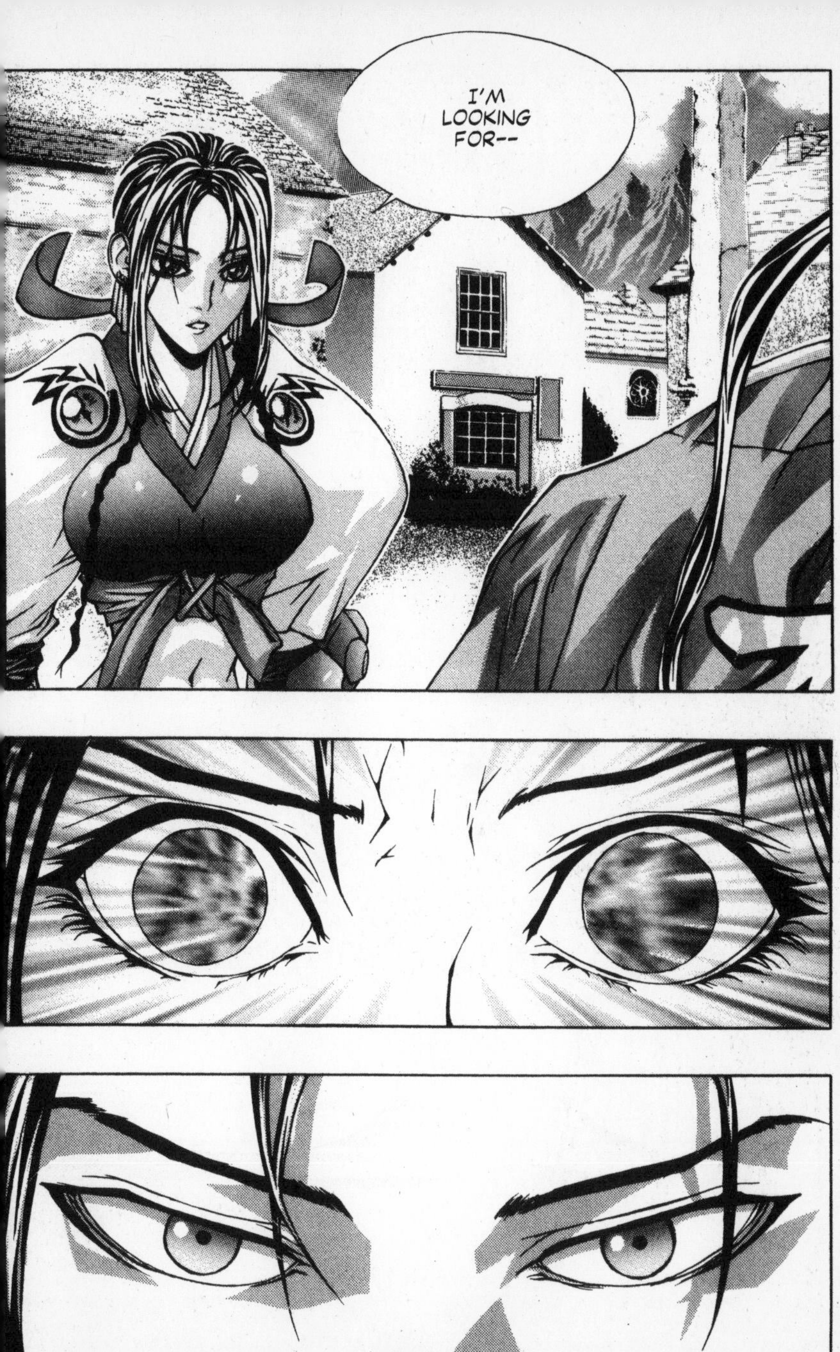
I'M LOOKING FOR--

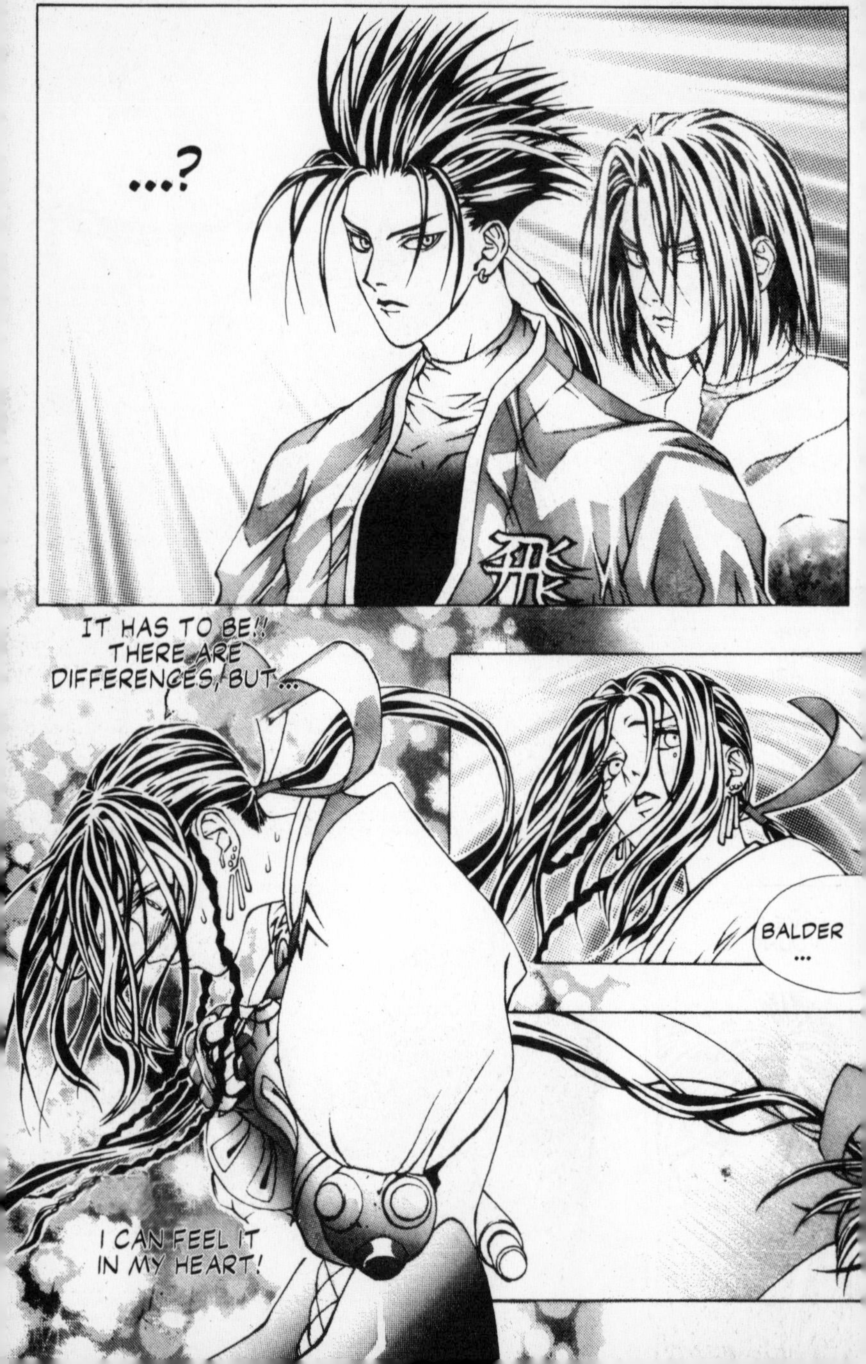
...?
IT HAS TO BE!! THERE ARE DIFFERENCES, BUT...
BALDER ...
I CAN FEEL IT IN MY HEART!

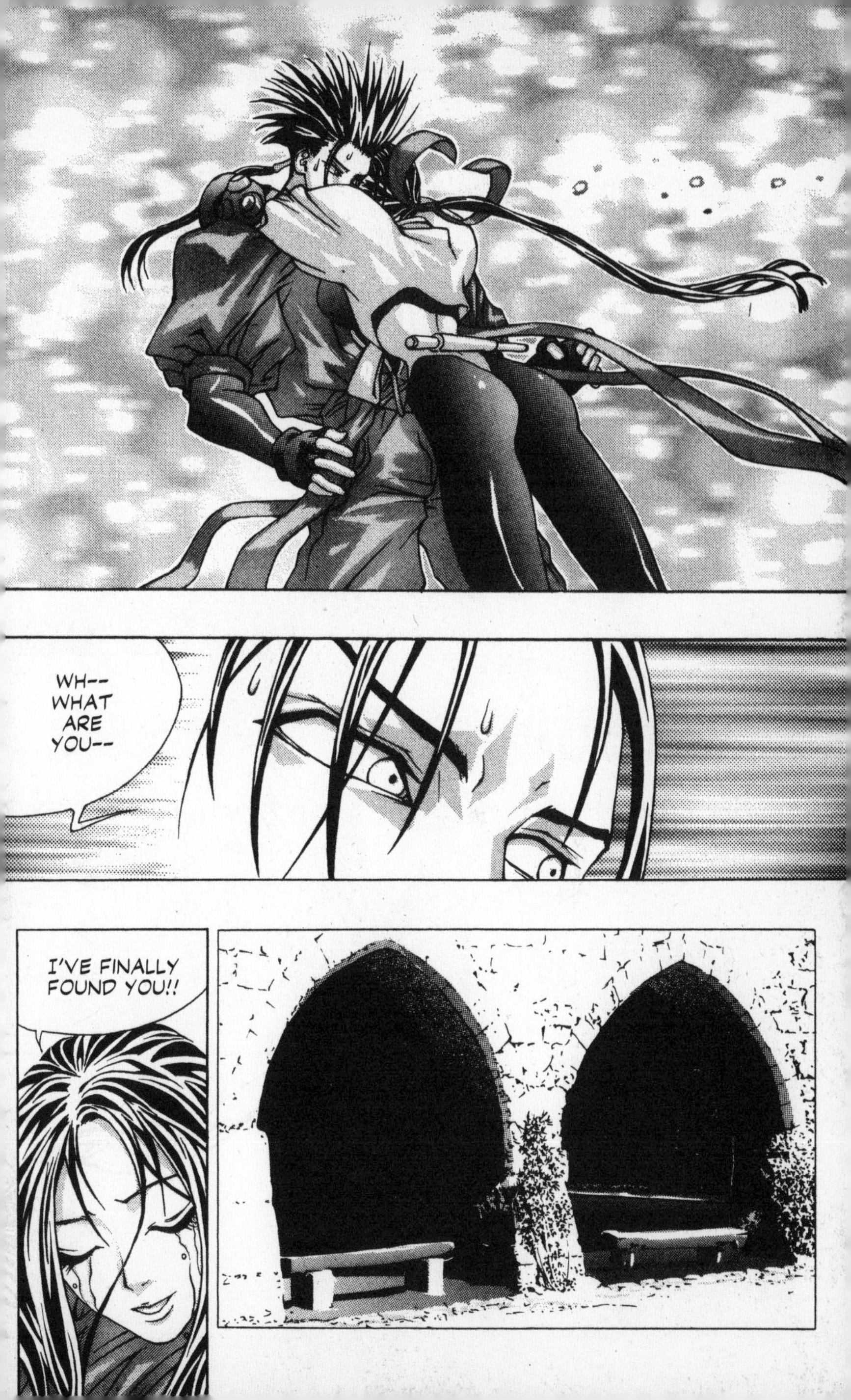
WH-- WHAT ARE YOU--
I'VE FINALLY FOUND YOU!!

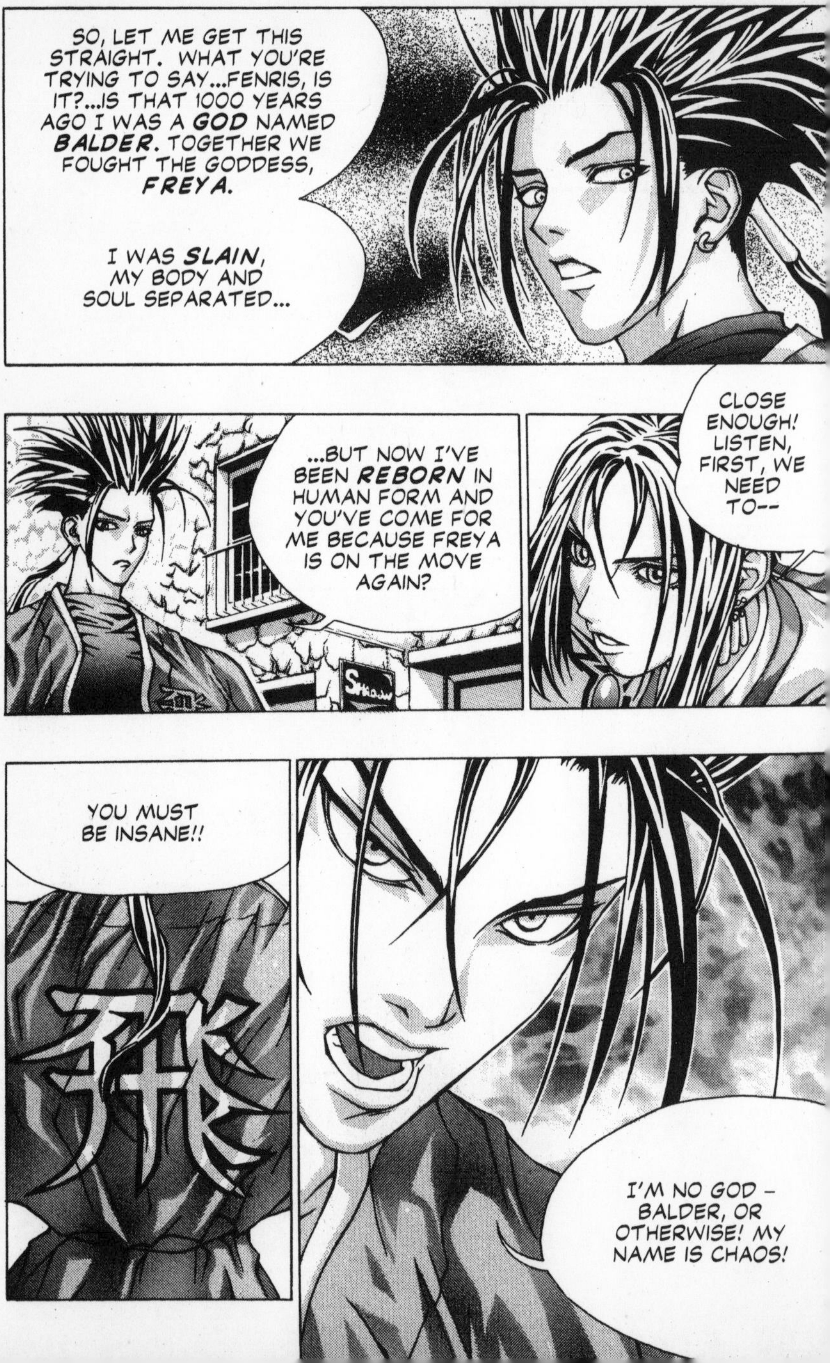
SO, LET ME GET THIS STRAIGHT. WHAT YOU'RE TRYING TO SAY...FENRIS, IS IT?...IS THAT 1000 YEARS AGO I WAS A ***GOD*** NAMED ***BALDER***. TOGETHER WE FOUGHT THE GODDESS, ***FREYA***.
I WAS ***SLAIN***, MY BODY AND SOUL SEPARATED...
...BUT NOW I'VE BEEN ***REBORN*** IN HUMAN FORM AND YOU'VE COME FOR ME BECAUSE FREYA IS ON THE MOVE AGAIN?
CLOSE ENOUGH! LISTEN, FIRST, WE NEED TO--
YOU MUST BE INSANE!!
I'M NO GOD – BALDER, OR OTHERWISE! MY NAME IS CHAOS!

RAGNAROK
라그나로크
INTO THE ABYSS

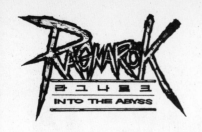

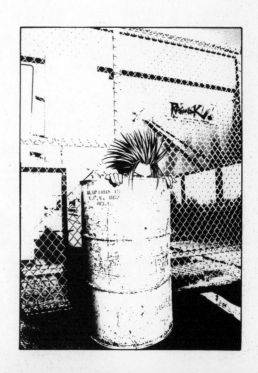

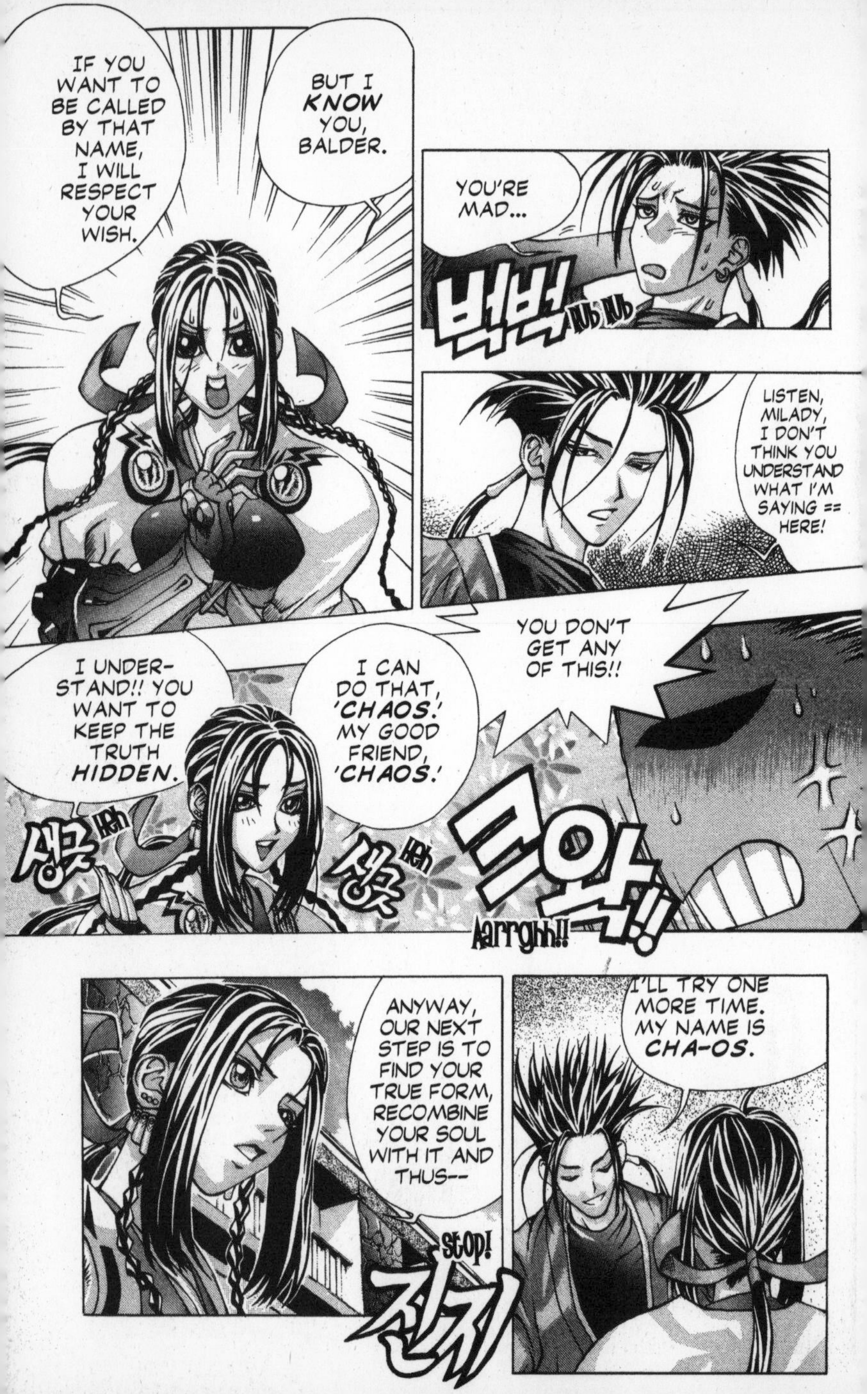
IF YOU WANT TO BE CALLED BY THAT NAME, I WILL RESPECT YOUR WISH.
BUT I KNOW YOU, BALDER.
YOU'RE MAD...
벅벅 RUB RUB
LISTEN, MILADY, I DON'T THINK YOU UNDERSTAND WHAT I'M SAYING == HERE!
I UNDER-STAND!! YOU WANT TO KEEP THE TRUTH HIDDEN.
씽긋 HEH
I CAN DO THAT, 'CHAOS.' MY GOOD FRIEND, 'CHAOS.'
씽긋 HEH
YOU DON'T GET ANY OF THIS!!
크악!! Aarrghh!!
ANYWAY, OUR NEXT STEP IS TO FIND YOUR TRUE FORM, RECOMBINE YOUR SOUL WITH IT AND THUS--
정지 STOP!
I'LL TRY ONE MORE TIME. MY NAME IS CHA-OS.

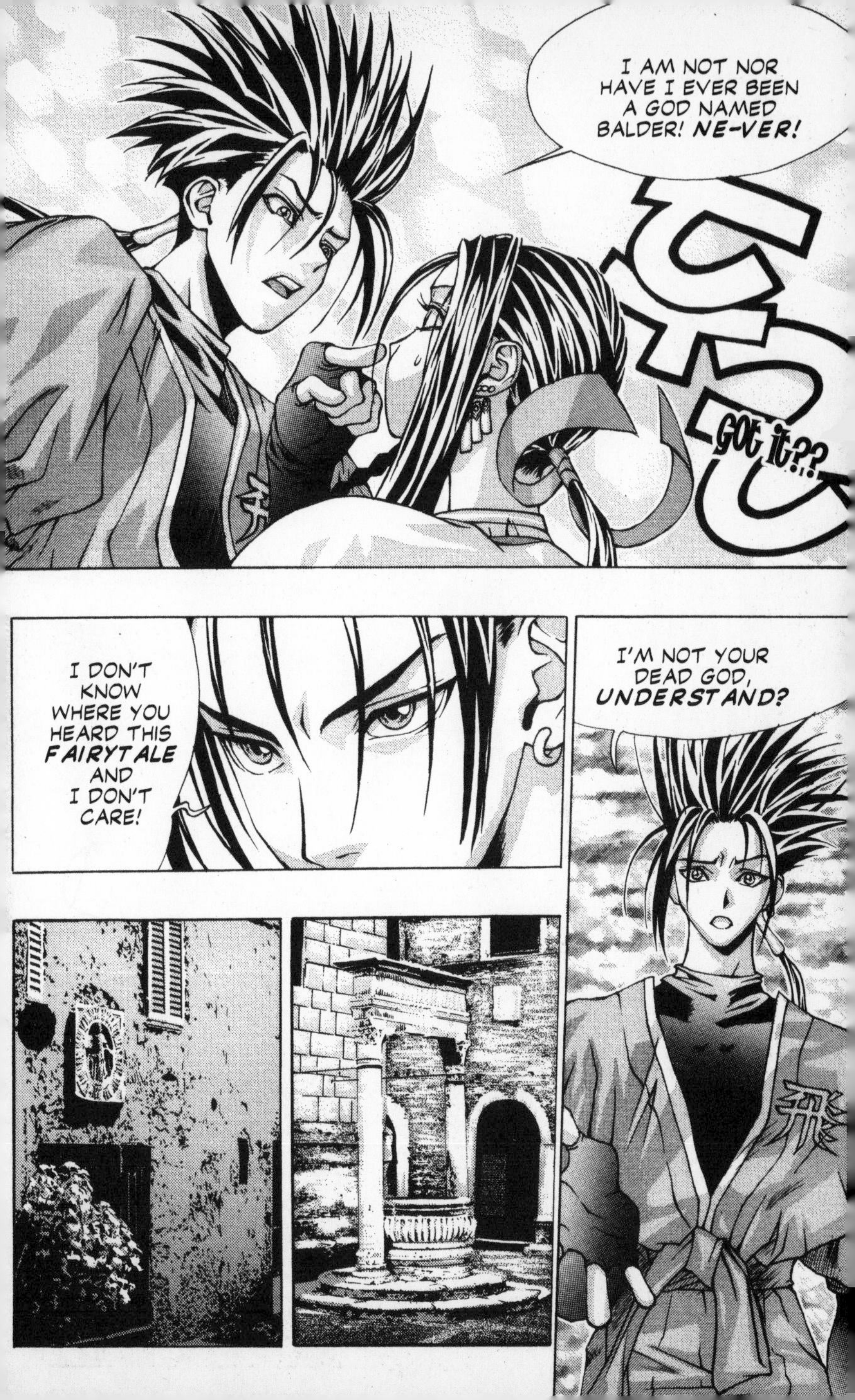
I AM NOT NOR HAVE I EVER BEEN A GOD NAMED BALDER! NE-VER!
GOT IT??
I DON'T KNOW WHERE YOU HEARD THIS FAIRYTALE AND I DON'T CARE!
I'M NOT YOUR DEAD GOD, UNDERSTAND?

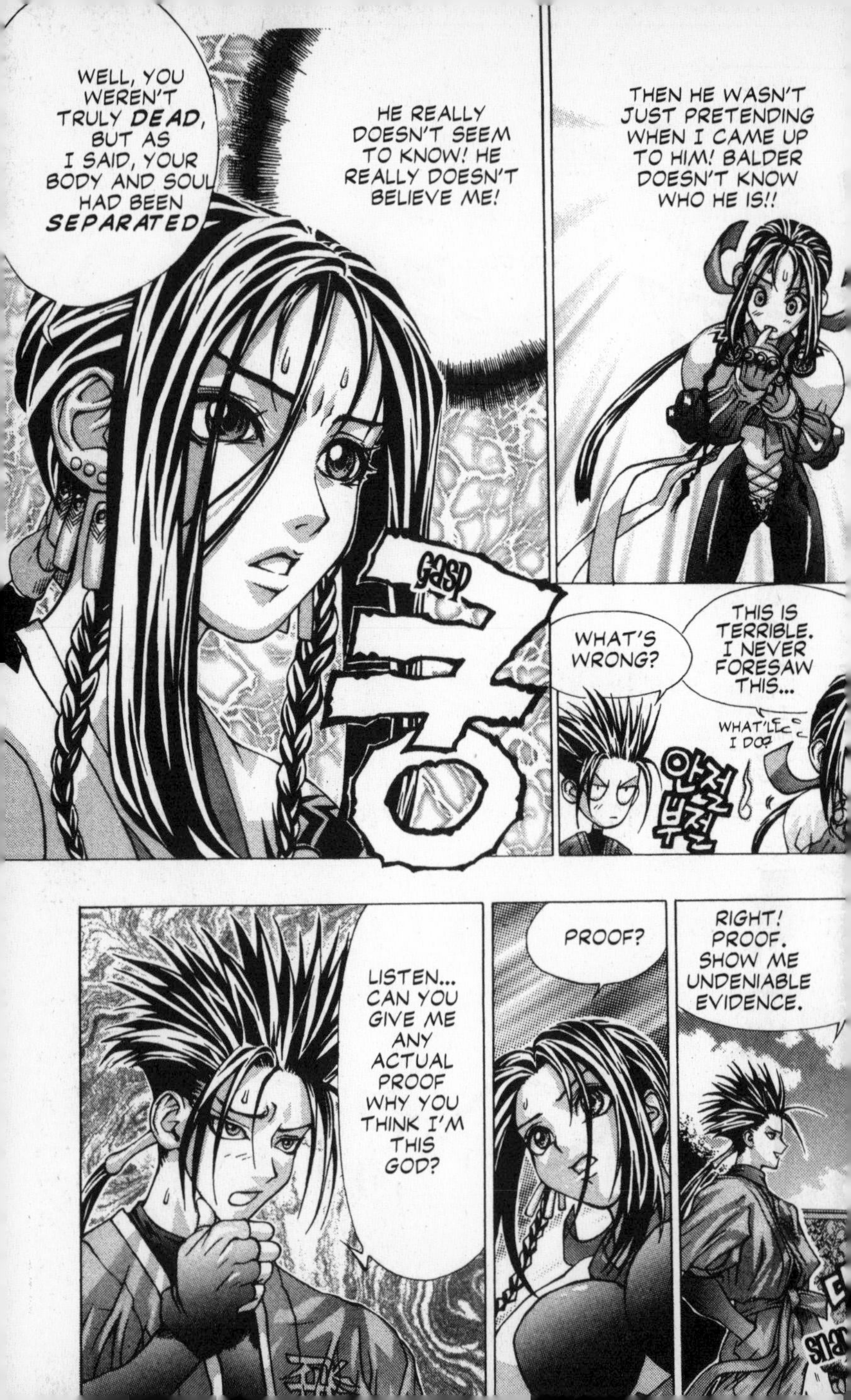

WELL, YOU WEREN'T TRULY **DEAD**, BUT AS I SAID, YOUR BODY AND SOUL HAD BEEN **SEPARATED**
HE REALLY DOESN'T SEEM TO KNOW! HE REALLY DOESN'T BELIEVE ME!
GASP
THEN HE WASN'T JUST PRETENDING WHEN I CAME UP TO HIM! BALDER DOESN'T KNOW WHO HE IS!!
WHAT'S WRONG?
THIS IS TERRIBLE. I NEVER FORESAW THIS...
WHAT'LL I DO?
안절부절
LISTEN... CAN YOU GIVE ME ANY ACTUAL PROOF WHY YOU THINK I'M THIS GOD?
PROOF?
RIGHT! PROOF. SHOW ME UNDENIABLE EVIDENCE.

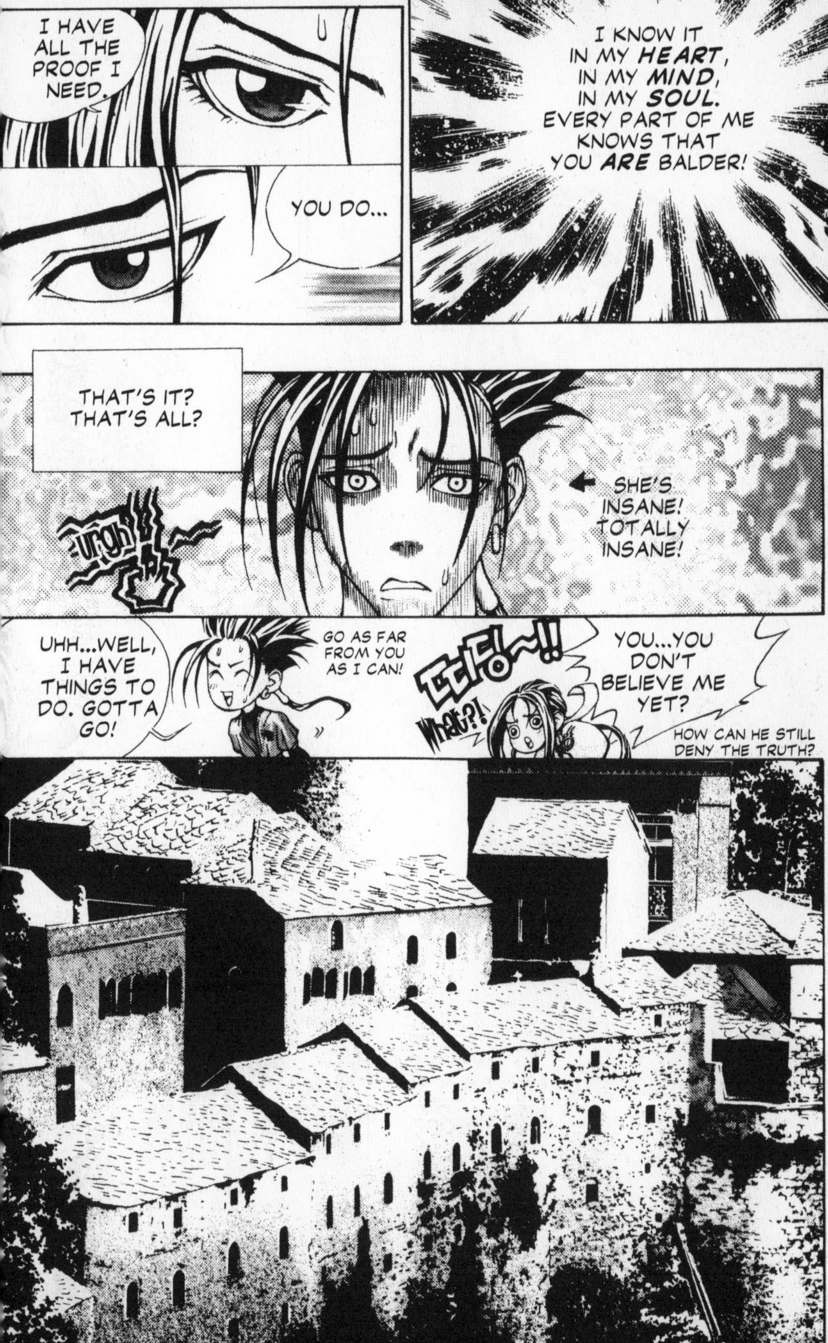

I HAVE ALL THE PROOF I NEED.
YOU DO...
I KNOW IT IN MY **HEART**, IN MY **MIND**, IN MY **SOUL**. EVERY PART OF ME KNOWS THAT YOU **ARE** BALDER!
THAT'S IT? THAT'S ALL?
urgh
SHE'S INSANE! TOTALLY INSANE!
UHH...WELL, I HAVE THINGS TO DO. GOTTA GO!
GO AS FAR FROM YOU AS I CAN!
What?!
YOU...YOU DON'T BELIEVE ME YET?
HOW CAN HE STILL DENY THE TRUTH?

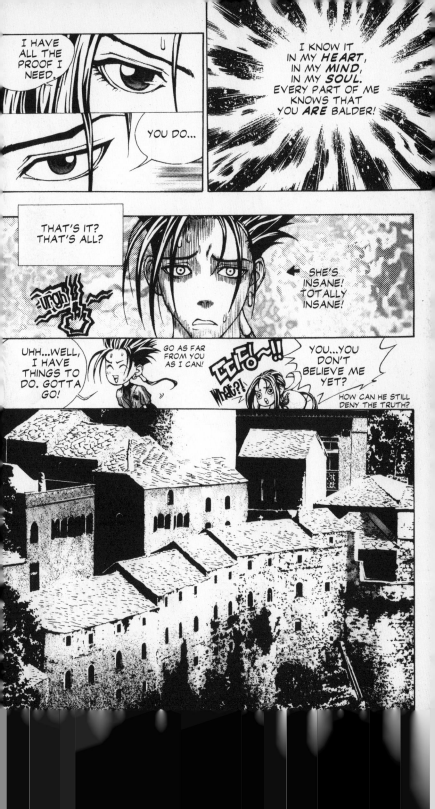

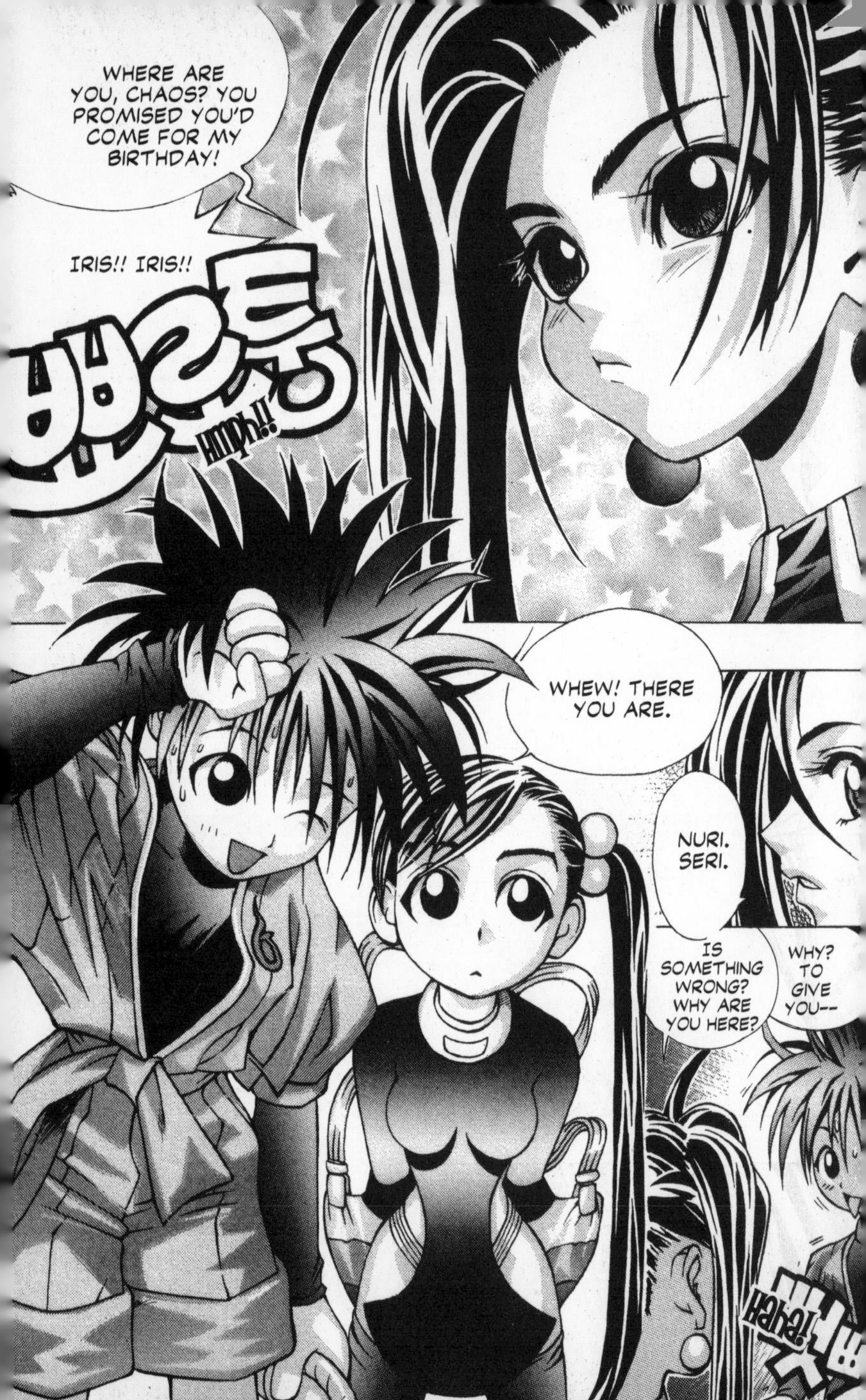
WHERE ARE YOU, CHAOS? YOU PROMISED YOU'D COME FOR MY BIRTHDAY!
IRIS!! IRIS!!
HMPH!!
WHEW! THERE YOU ARE.
NURI. SERI.
IS SOMETHING WRONG? WHY ARE YOU HERE?
WHY? TO GIVE YOU--

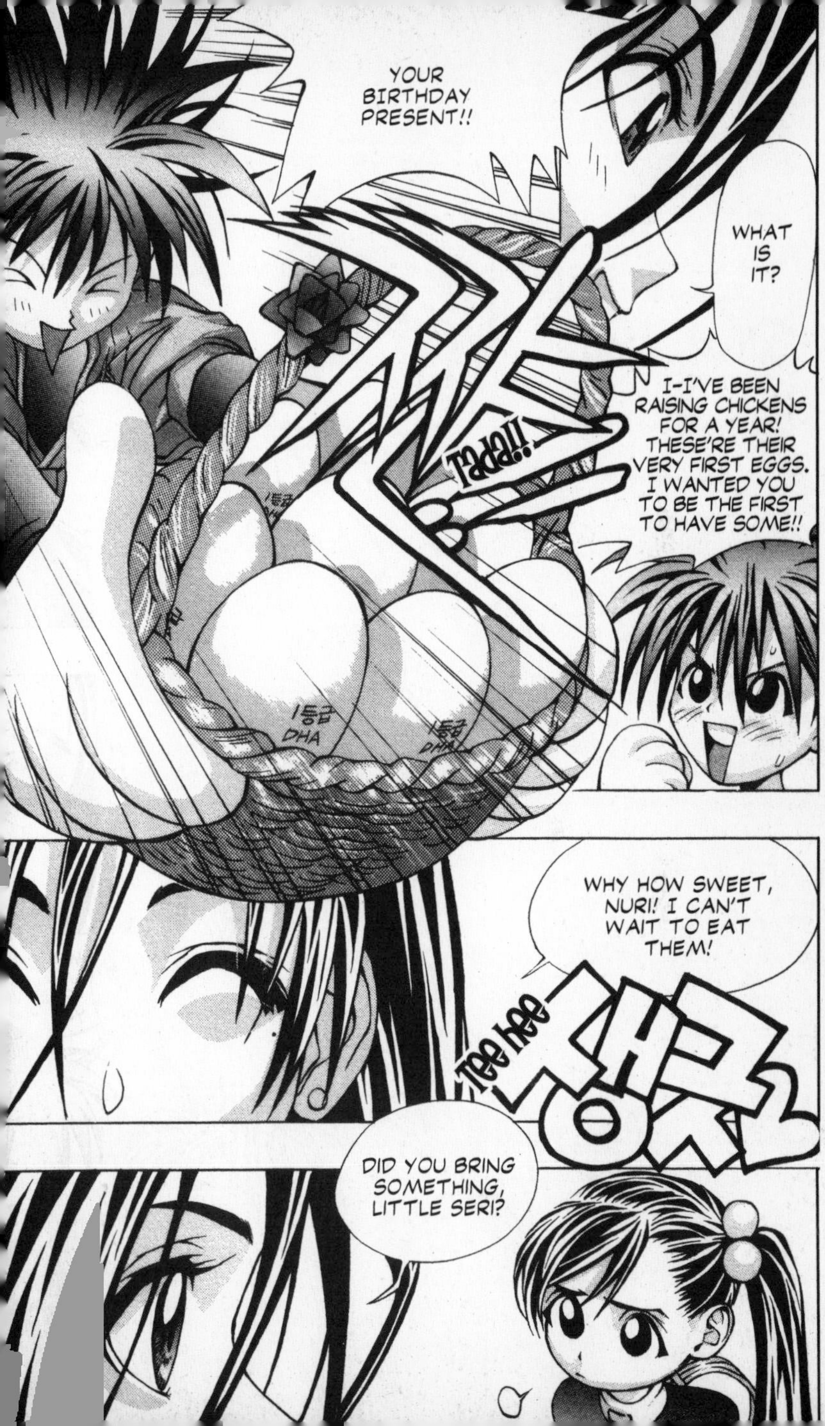
YOUR BIRTHDAY PRESENT!!
WHAT IS IT?
TADA!!
I-I'VE BEEN RAISING CHICKENS FOR A YEAR! THESE'RE THEIR VERY FIRST EGGS. I WANTED YOU TO BE THE FIRST TO HAVE SOME!!
WHY HOW SWEET, NURI! I CAN'T WAIT TO EAT THEM!
TEE HEE
DID YOU BRING SOMETHING, LITTLE SERI?

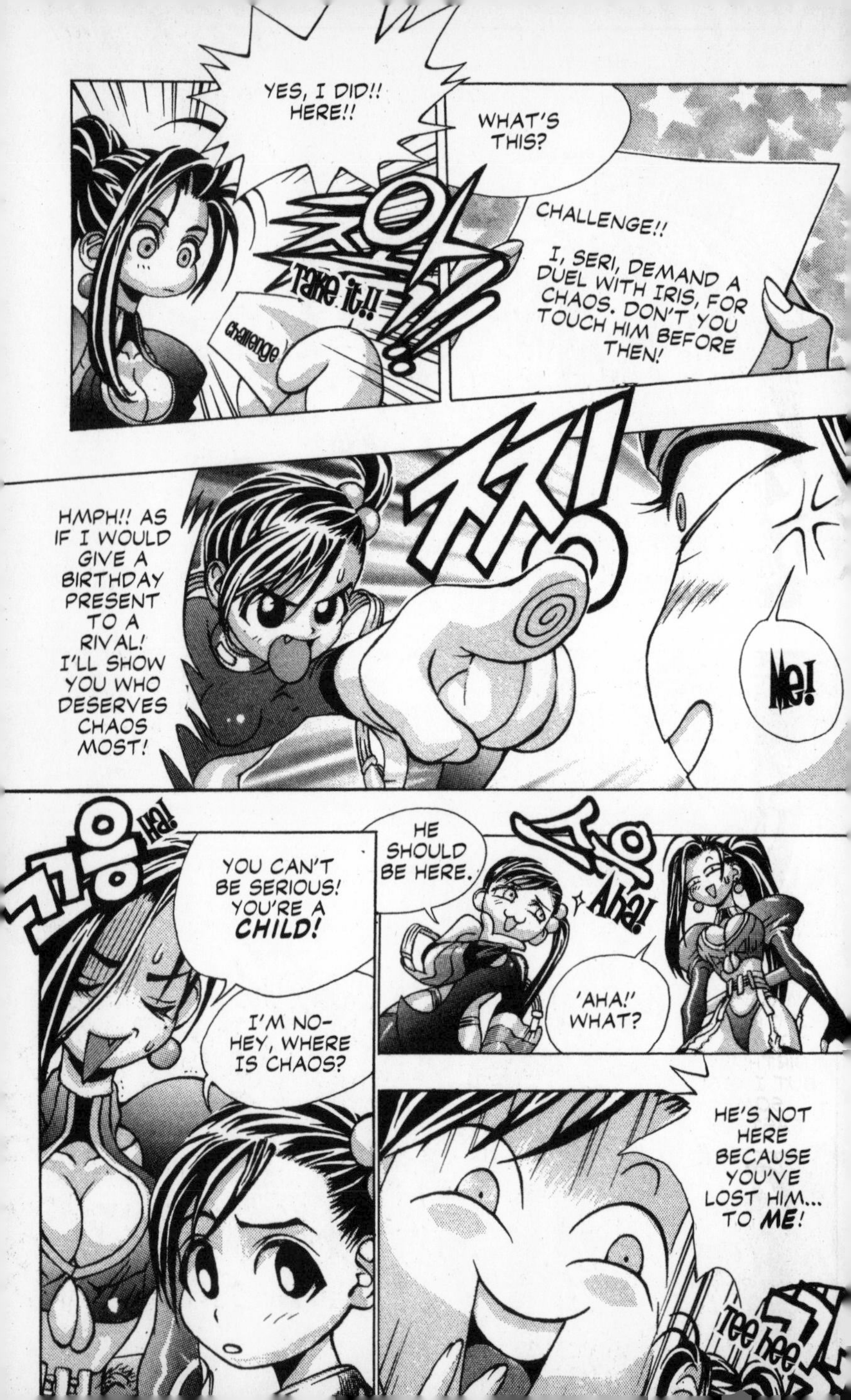
YES, I DID!! HERE!!
WHAT'S THIS?
Take it!!
Challenge
CHALLENGE!!
I, SERI, DEMAND A DUEL WITH IRIS, FOR CHAOS. DON'T YOU TOUCH HIM BEFORE THEN!
HMPH!! AS IF I WOULD GIVE A BIRTHDAY PRESENT TO A RIVAL! I'LL SHOW YOU WHO DESERVES CHAOS MOST!
Me!
Ha!
YOU CAN'T BE SERIOUS! YOU'RE A ***CHILD!***
I'M NO- HEY, WHERE IS CHAOS?
HE SHOULD BE HERE.
Aha!
'AHA!' WHAT?
HE'S NOT HERE BECAUSE YOU'VE LOST HIM... TO ***ME!***
Tee hee

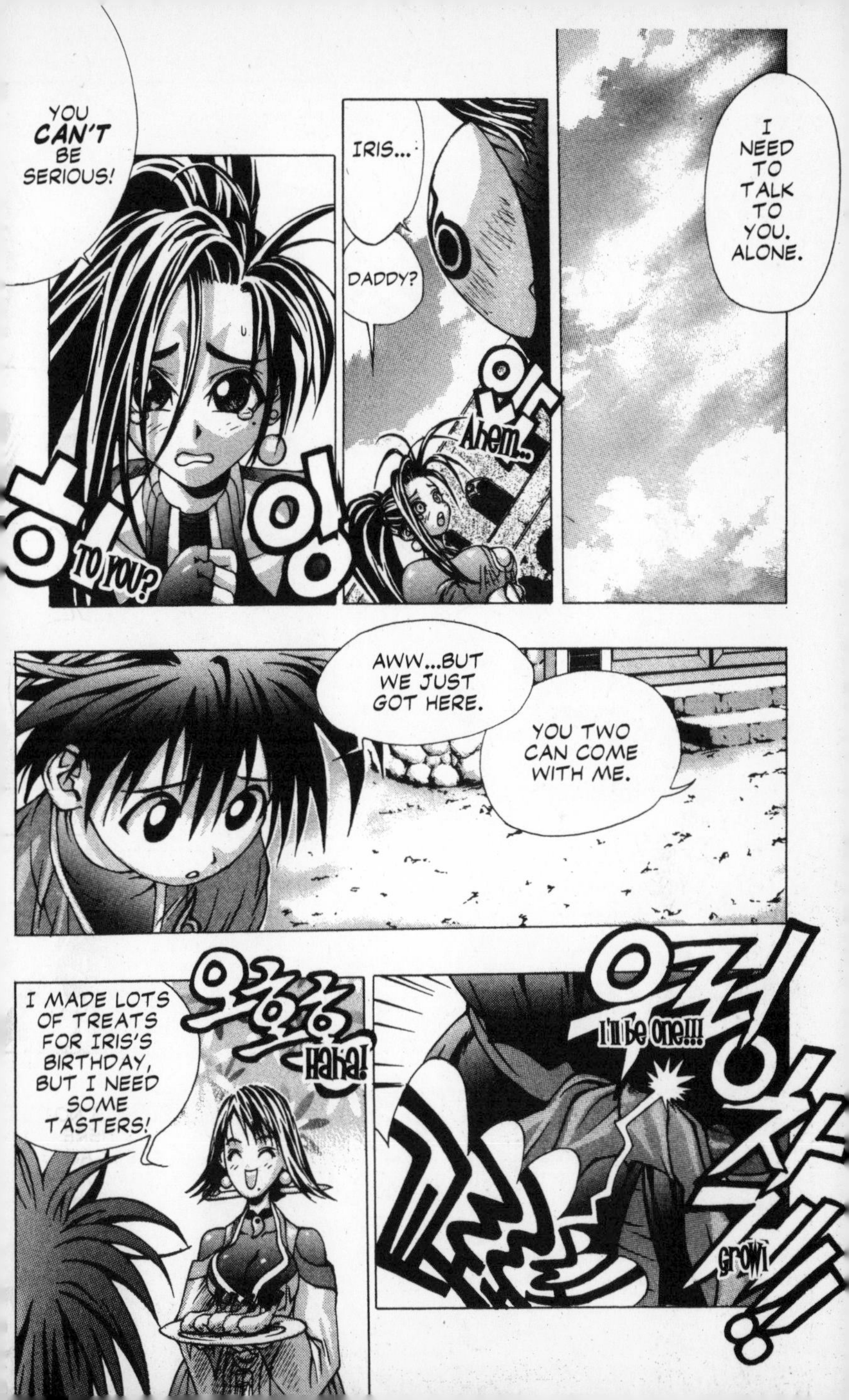
YOU CAN'T BE SERIOUS!
TO YOU?
IRIS...
DADDY?
Ahem...
I NEED TO TALK TO YOU. ALONE.
AWW...BUT WE JUST GOT HERE.
YOU TWO CAN COME WITH ME.
I MADE LOTS OF TREATS FOR IRIS'S BIRTHDAY, BUT I NEED SOME TASTERS!
Haha!
I'll be one!!!
Growl

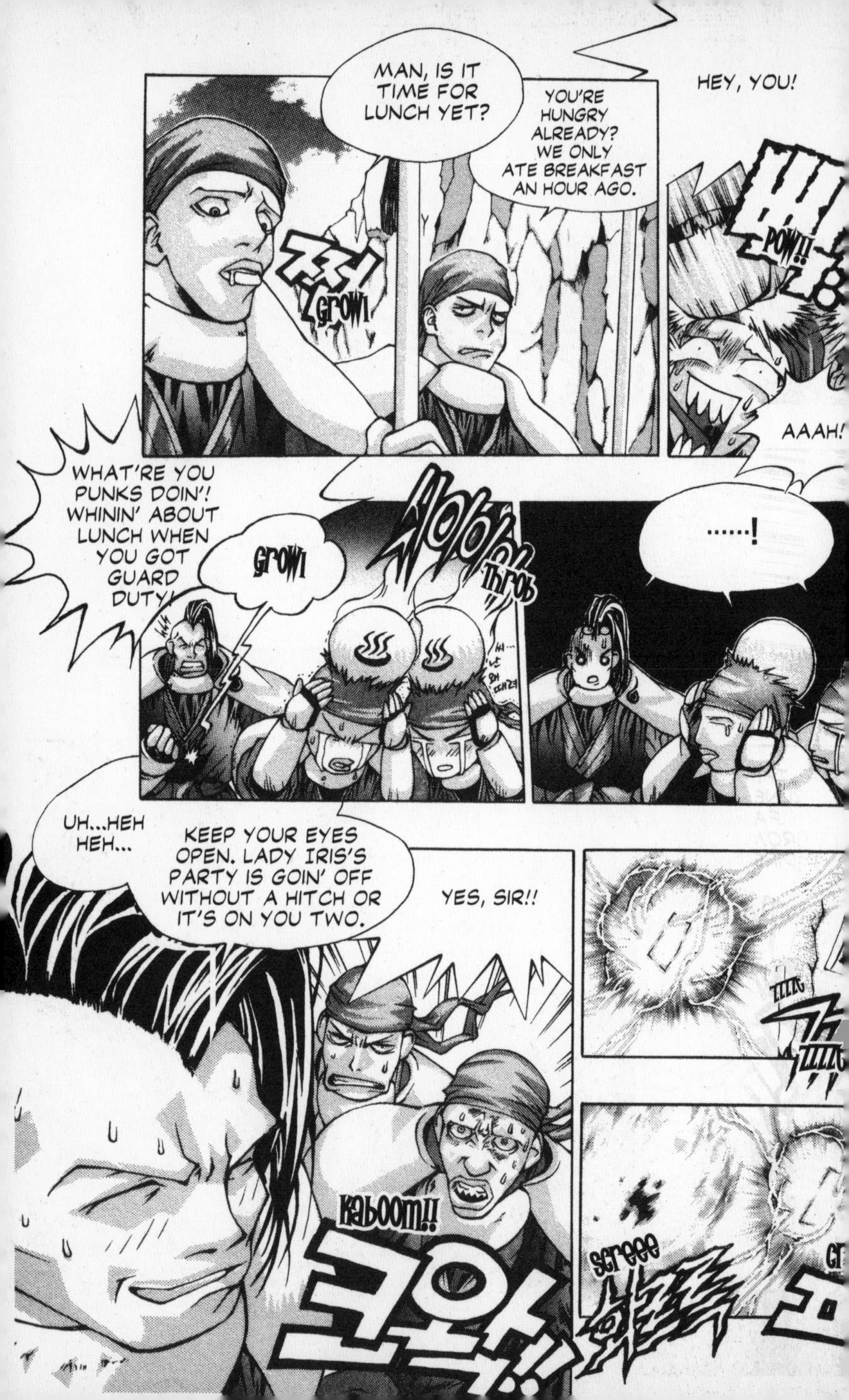

MAN, IS IT TIME FOR LUNCH YET?
GROWL
YOU'RE HUNGRY ALREADY? WE ONLY ATE BREAKFAST AN HOUR AGO.
HEY, YOU!
POW!!
AAAH!
WHAT'RE YOU PUNKS DOIN'! WHININ' ABOUT LUNCH WHEN YOU GOT GUARD DUTY!
GROWL
THROB
......!
UH...HEH HEH...
KEEP YOUR EYES OPEN. LADY IRIS'S PARTY IS GOIN' OFF WITHOUT A HITCH OR IT'S ON YOU TWO.
YES, SIR!!
KABOOM!!
SCREEE

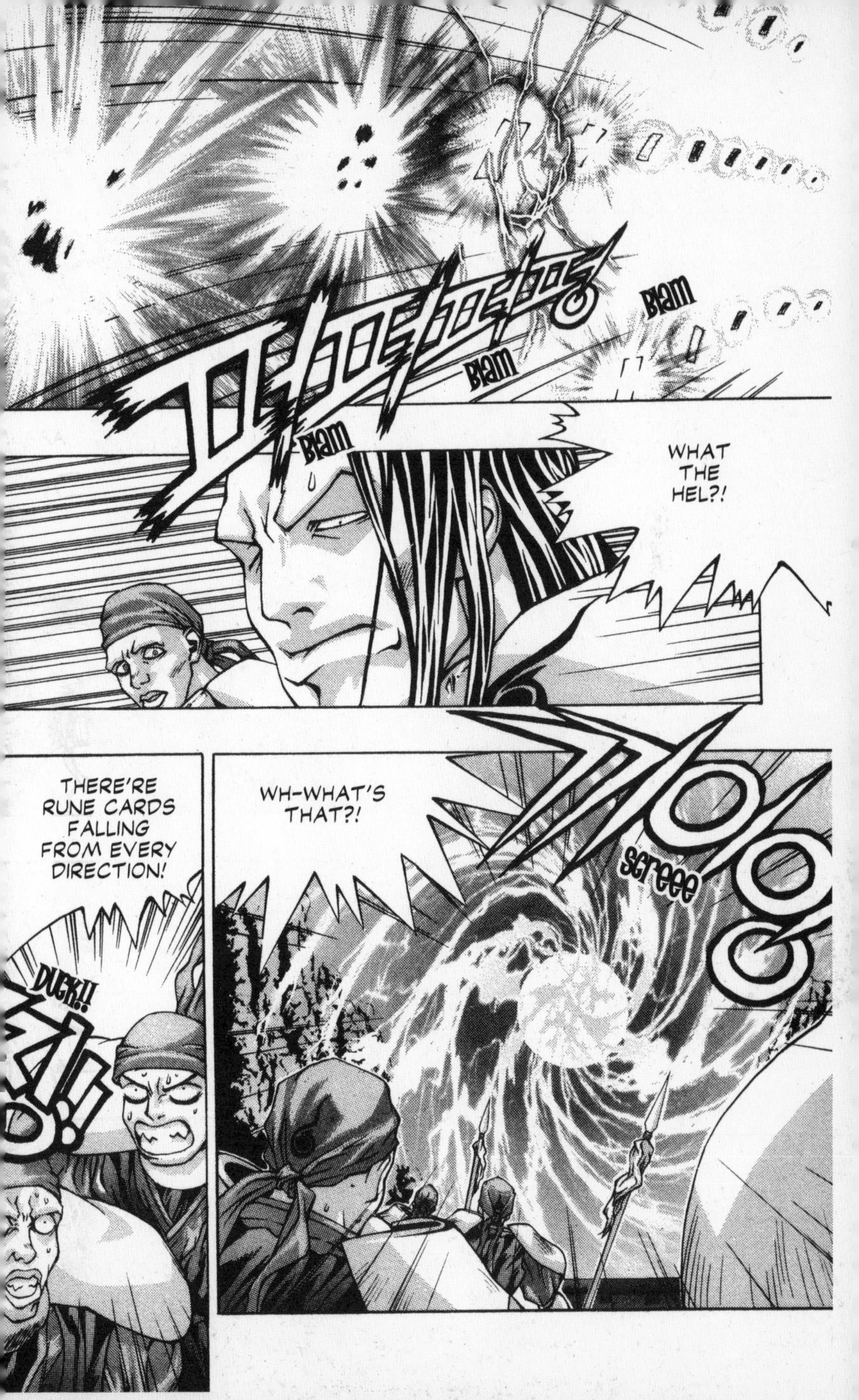

BLAM
BLAM
BLAM
WHAT THE HEL?!
BLAM
THERE'RE RUNE CARDS FALLING FROM EVERY DIRECTION!
DUCK!!
WH-WHAT'S THAT?!
SCREEE

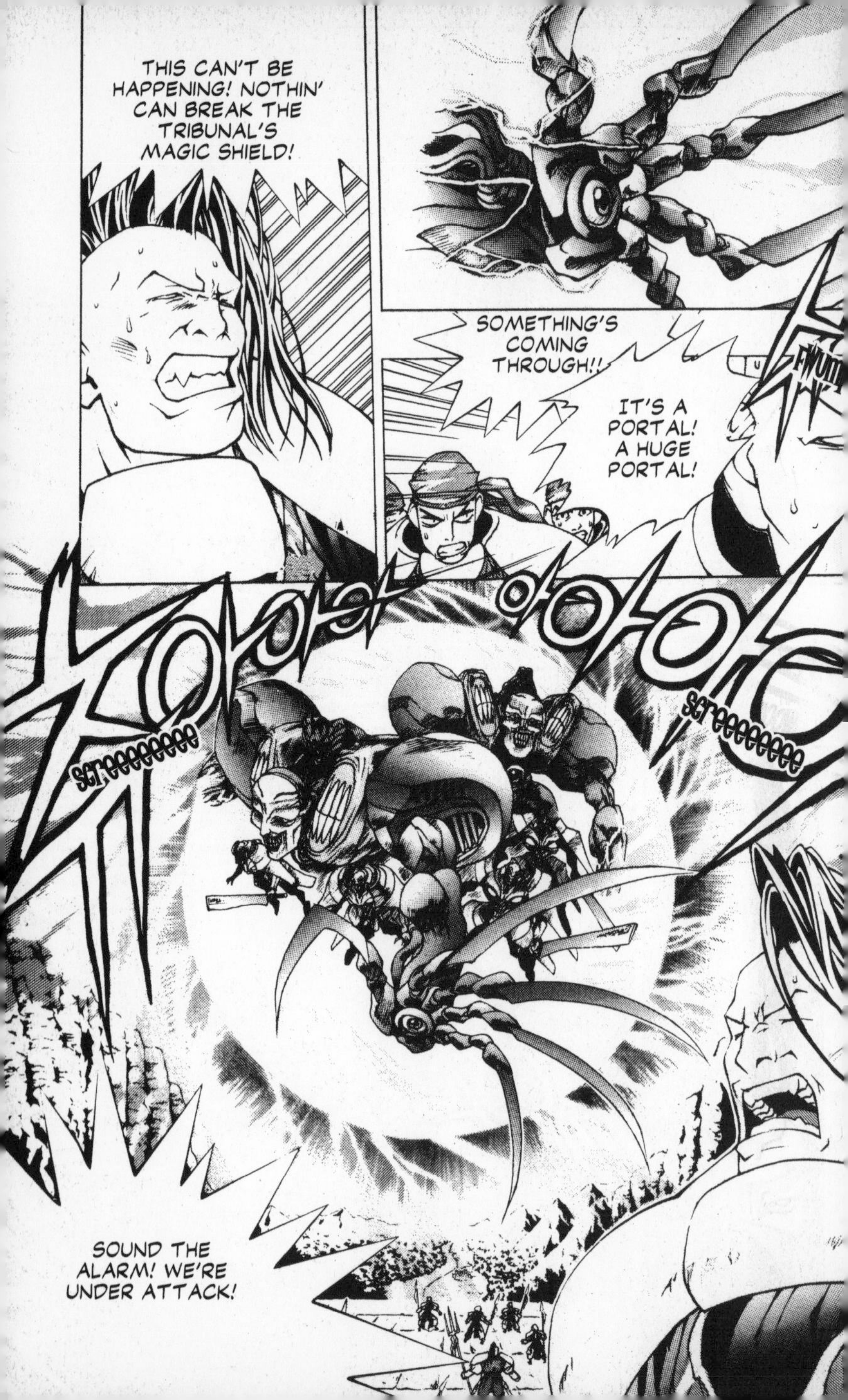
THIS CAN'T BE HAPPENING! NOTHIN' CAN BREAK THE TRIBUNAL'S MAGIC SHIELD!
SOMETHING'S COMING THROUGH!!
FWUM
IT'S A PORTAL! A HUGE PORTAL!
screeeeeeeee
screeeeeeeee
SOUND THE ALARM! WE'RE UNDER ATTACK!

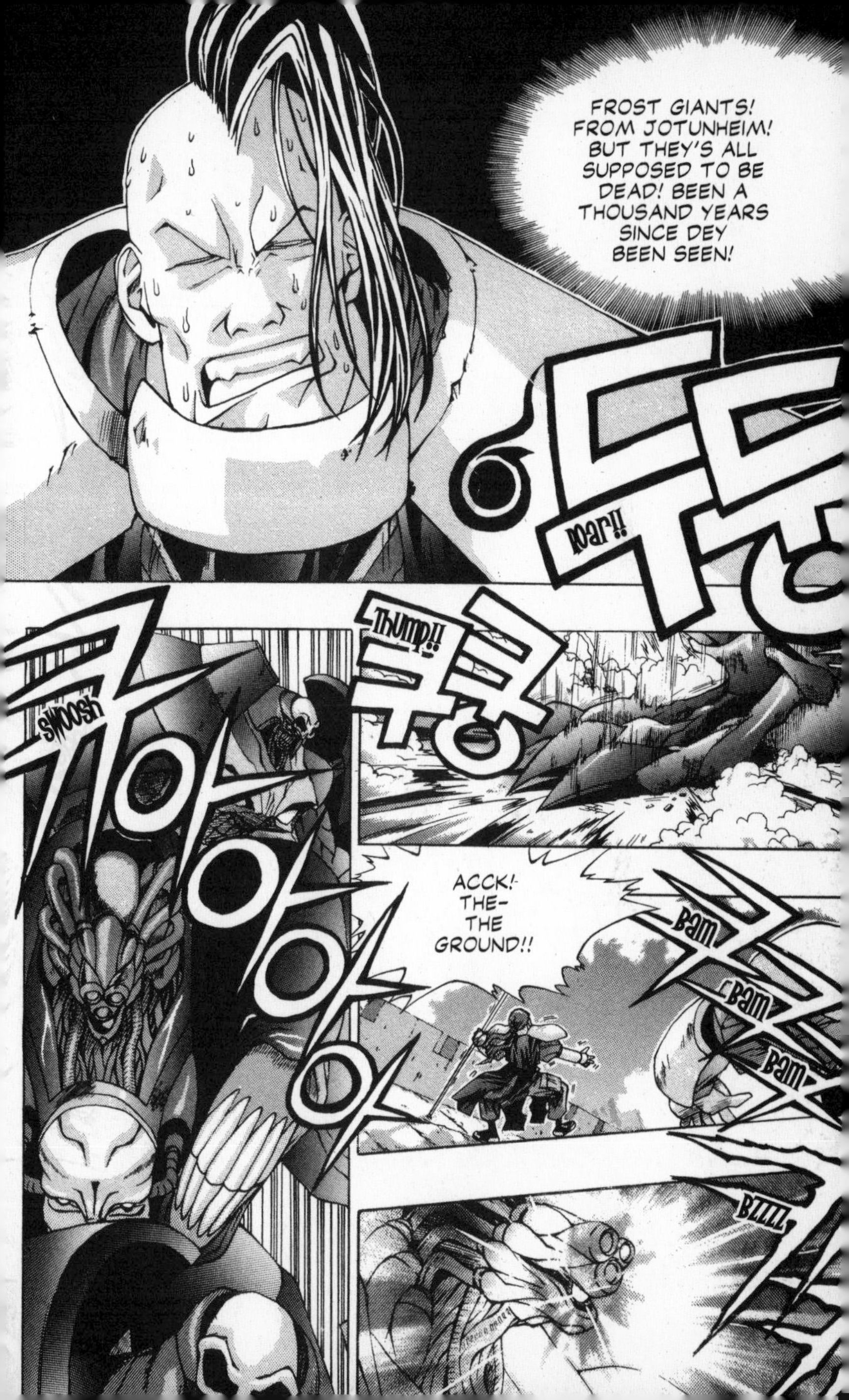

FROST GIANTS! FROM JOTUNHEIM! BUT THEY'S ALL SUPPOSED TO BE DEAD! BEEN A THOUSAND YEARS SINCE DEY BEEN SEEN!
ROAR!!
SWOOSH
THUMP!!
ACCK!- THE- THE GROUND!!
BAM
BAM
BAM
BZZZZ

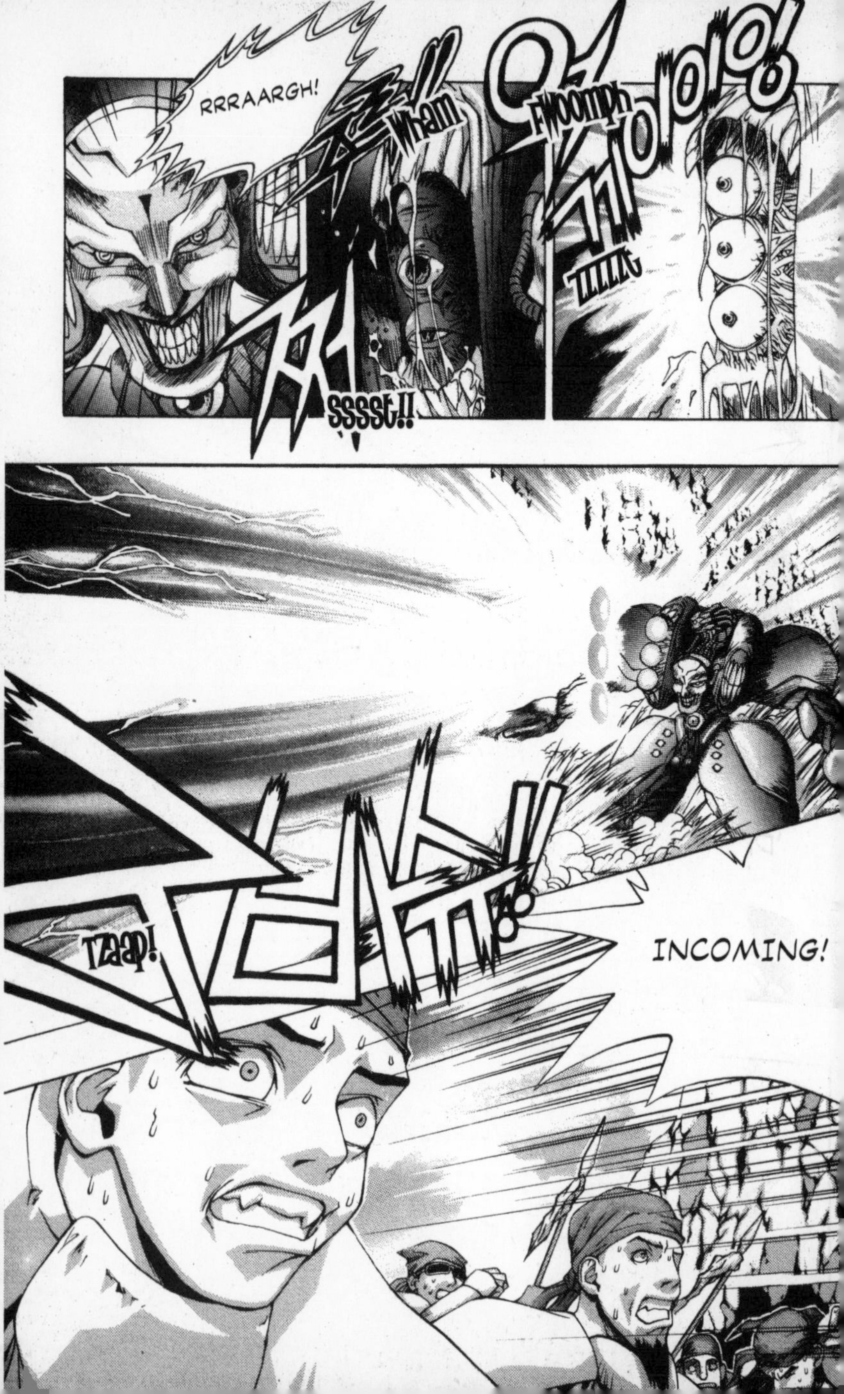
RRRAARGH!
Wham
sssst!!
FWOOMPH
Tzaap!
INCOMING!

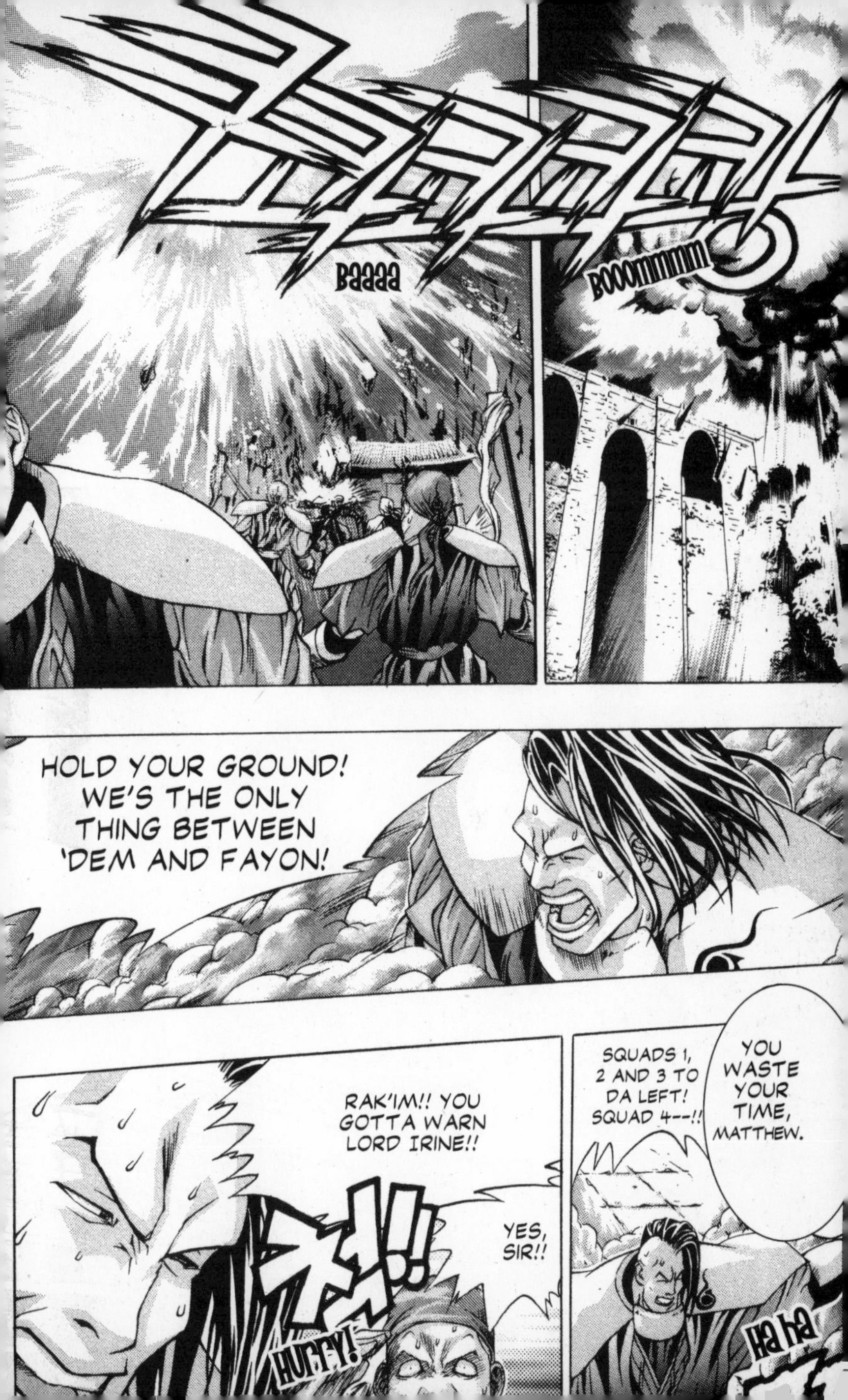
BAAAA
BOOOMMMM
HOLD YOUR GROUND! WE'S THE ONLY THING BETWEEN 'DEM AND FAYON!
RAK'IM!! YOU GOTTA WARN LORD IRINE!!
YES, SIR!!
HURRY!
SQUADS 1, 2 AND 3 TO DA LEFT! SQUAD 4--!!
YOU WASTE YOUR TIME, MATTHEW.
HA HA

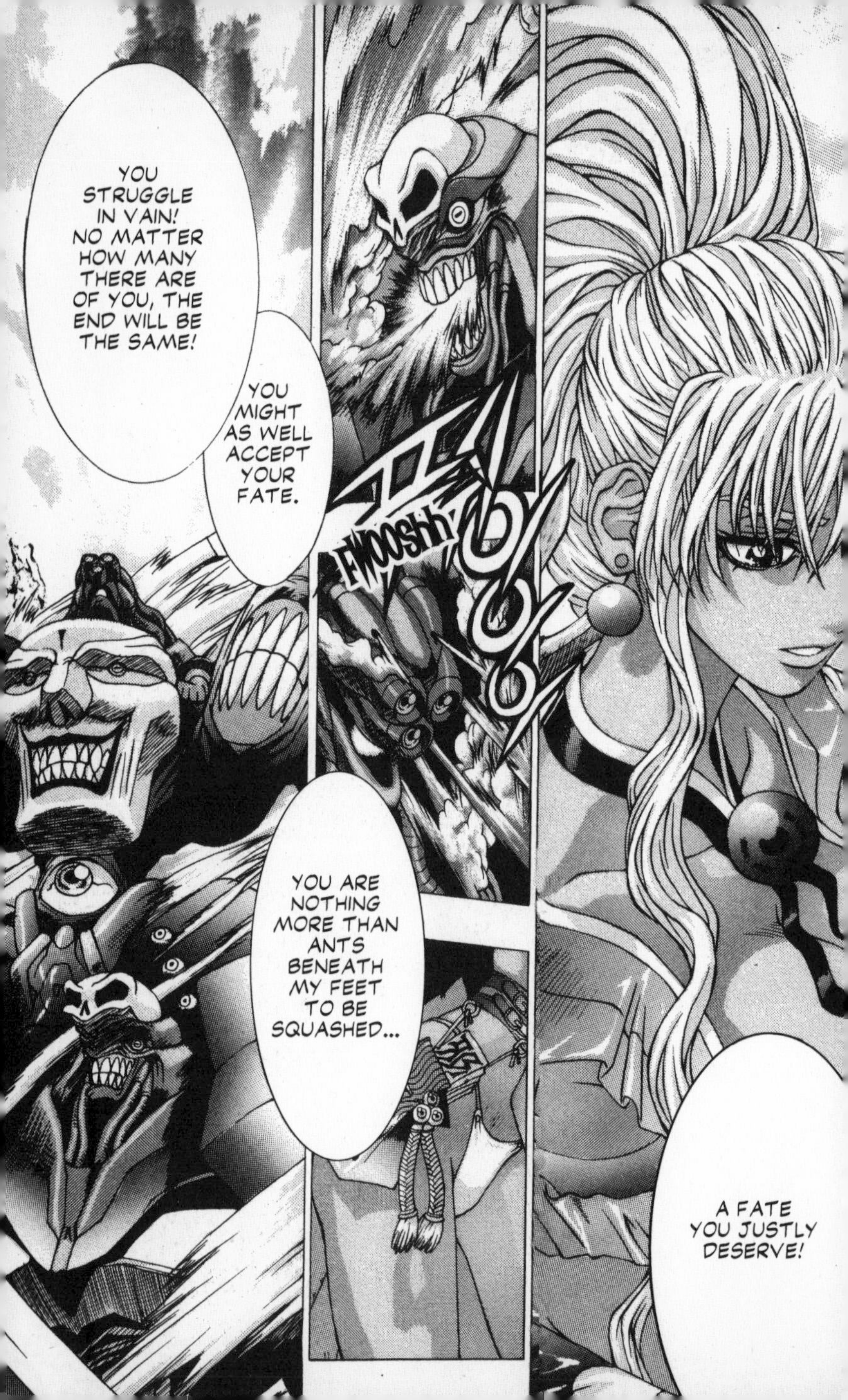

YOU STRUGGLE IN VAIN! NO MATTER HOW MANY THERE ARE OF YOU, THE END WILL BE THE SAME!
YOU MIGHT AS WELL ACCEPT YOUR FATE.
FWOOSHH
YOU ARE NOTHING MORE THAN ANTS BENEATH MY FEET TO BE SQUASHED...
A FATE YOU JUSTLY DESERVE!

RAGNAROK
라그나로크
INTO THE ABYSS

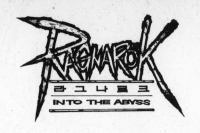

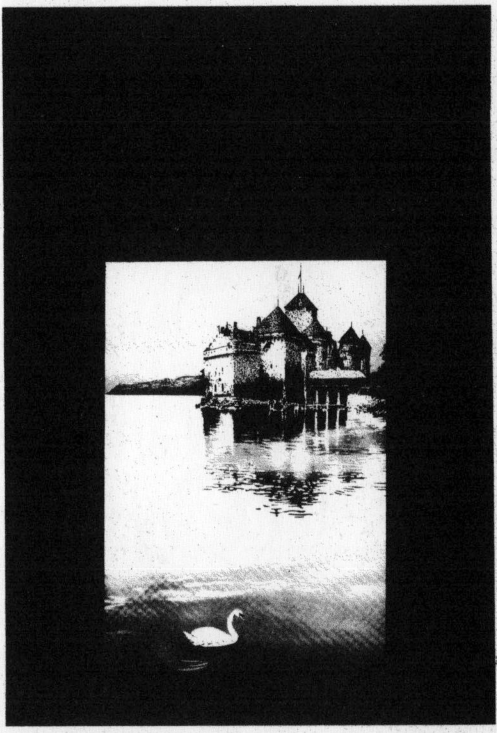

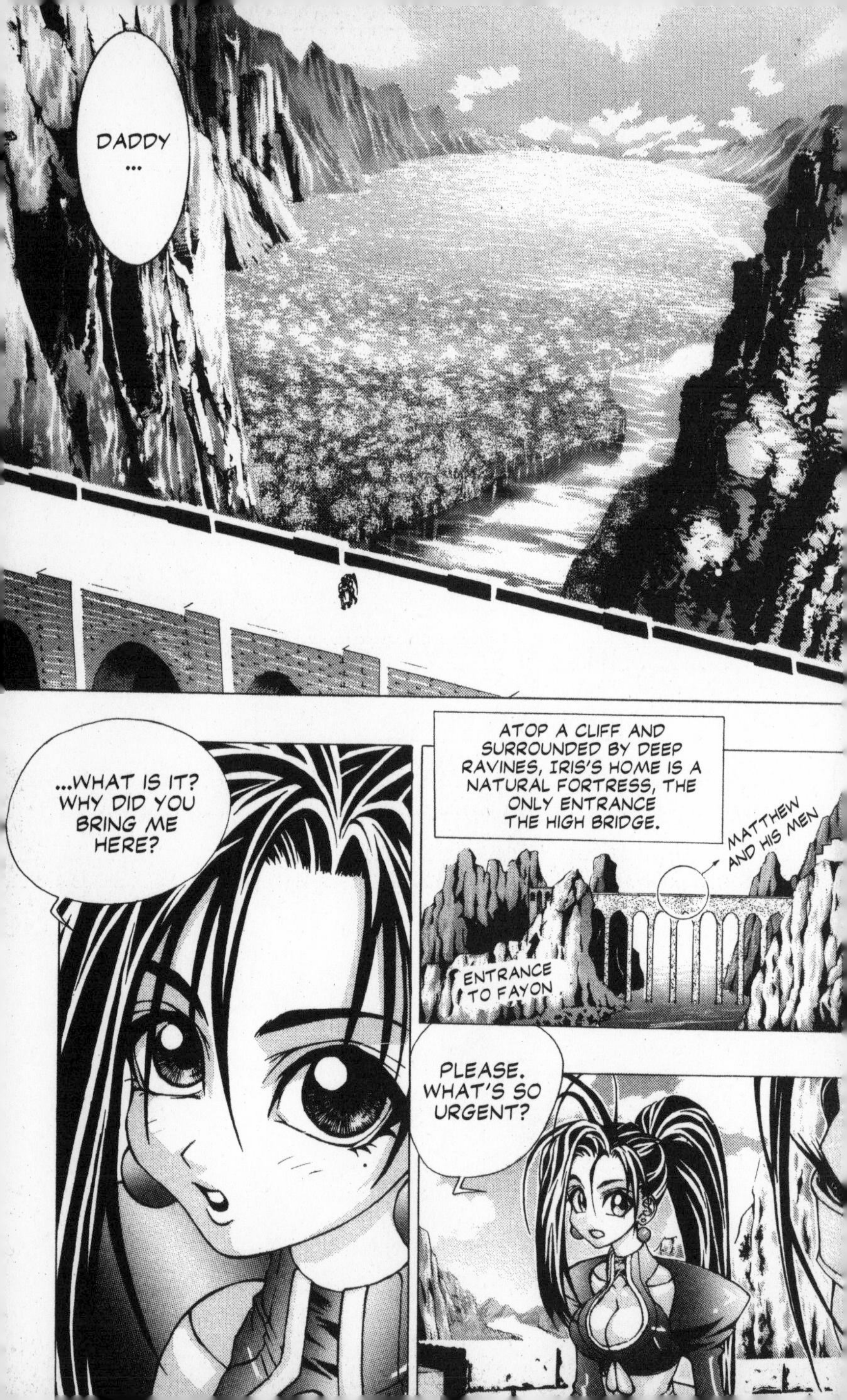
DADDY ...
...WHAT IS IT? WHY DID YOU BRING ME HERE?
ATOP A CLIFF AND SURROUNDED BY DEEP RAVINES, IRIS'S HOME IS A NATURAL FORTRESS, THE ONLY ENTRANCE THE HIGH BRIDGE.
MATTHEW AND HIS MEN
ENTRANCE TO FAYON
PLEASE. WHAT'S SO URGENT?

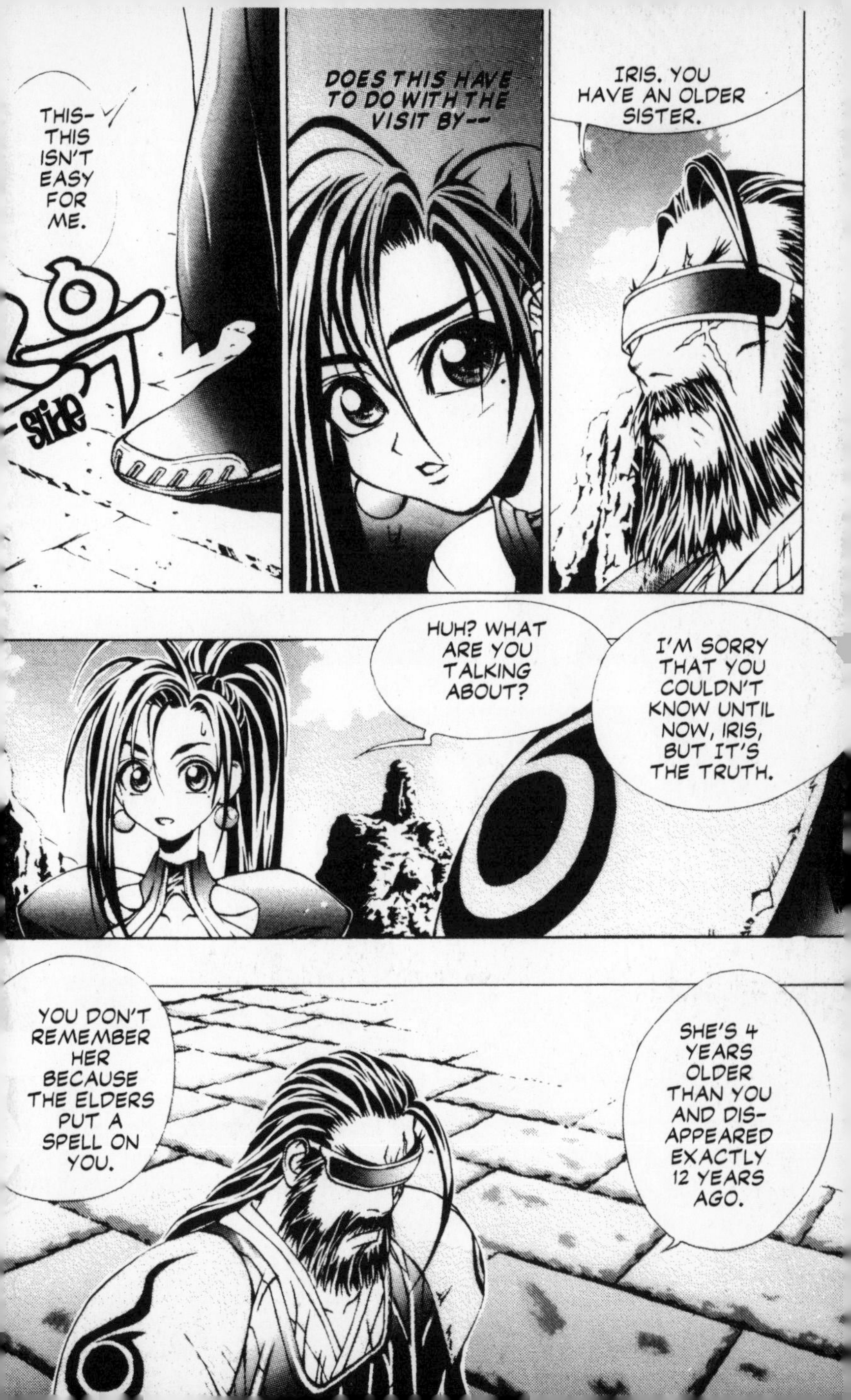
THIS- THIS ISN'T EASY FOR ME.
SLIDE
DOES THIS HAVE TO DO WITH THE VISIT BY--
IRIS. YOU HAVE AN OLDER SISTER.
HUH? WHAT ARE YOU TALKING ABOUT?
I'M SORRY THAT YOU COULDN'T KNOW UNTIL NOW, IRIS, BUT IT'S THE TRUTH.
YOU DON'T REMEMBER HER BECAUSE THE ELDERS PUT A SPELL ON YOU.
SHE'S 4 YEARS OLDER THAN YOU AND DIS-APPEARED EXACTLY 12 YEARS AGO.

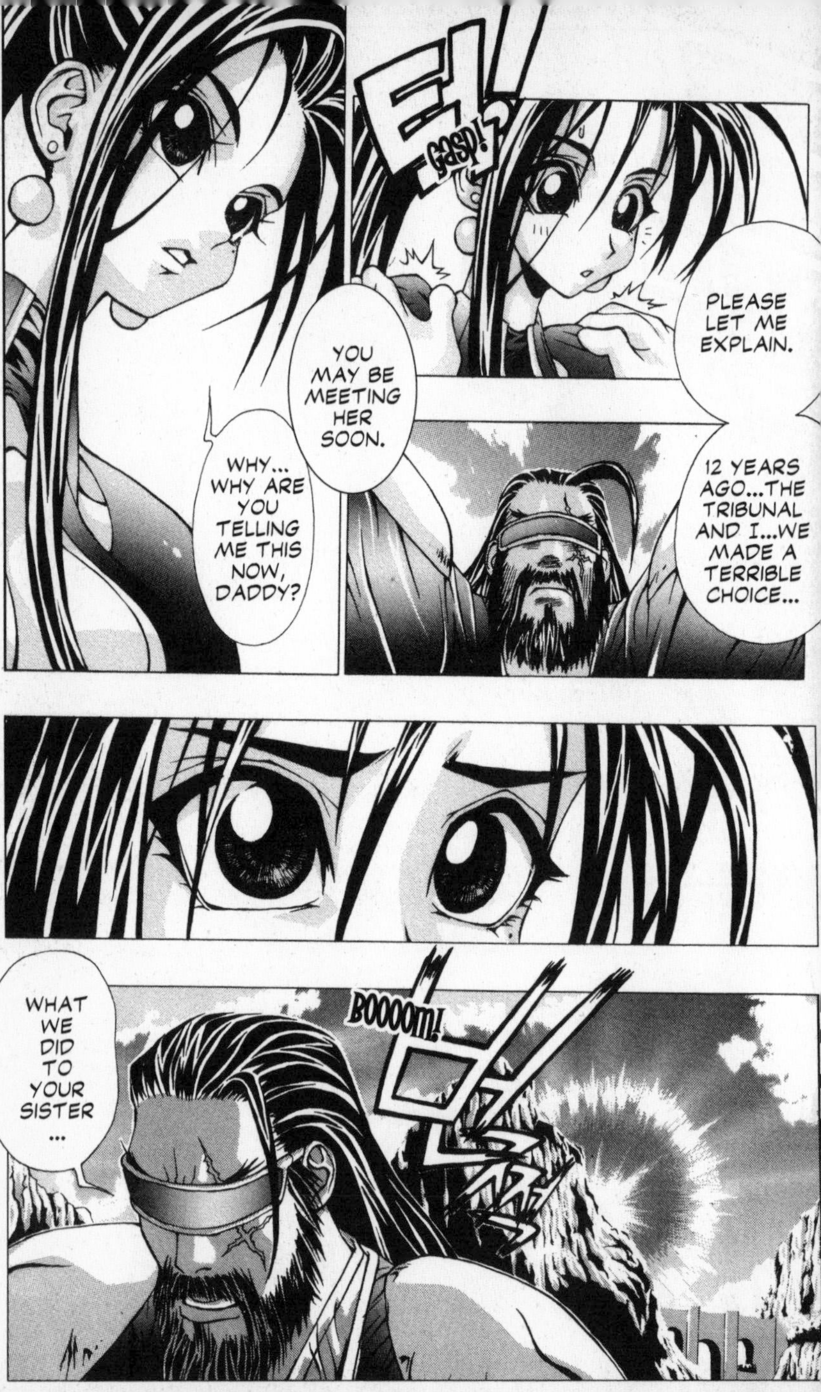
YOU MAY BE MEETING HER SOON.
WHY... WHY ARE YOU TELLING ME THIS NOW, DADDY?
GASP!
PLEASE LET ME EXPLAIN.
12 YEARS AGO...THE TRIBUNAL AND I...WE MADE A TERRIBLE CHOICE...
WHAT WE DID TO YOUR SISTER ...
BOOOOM!

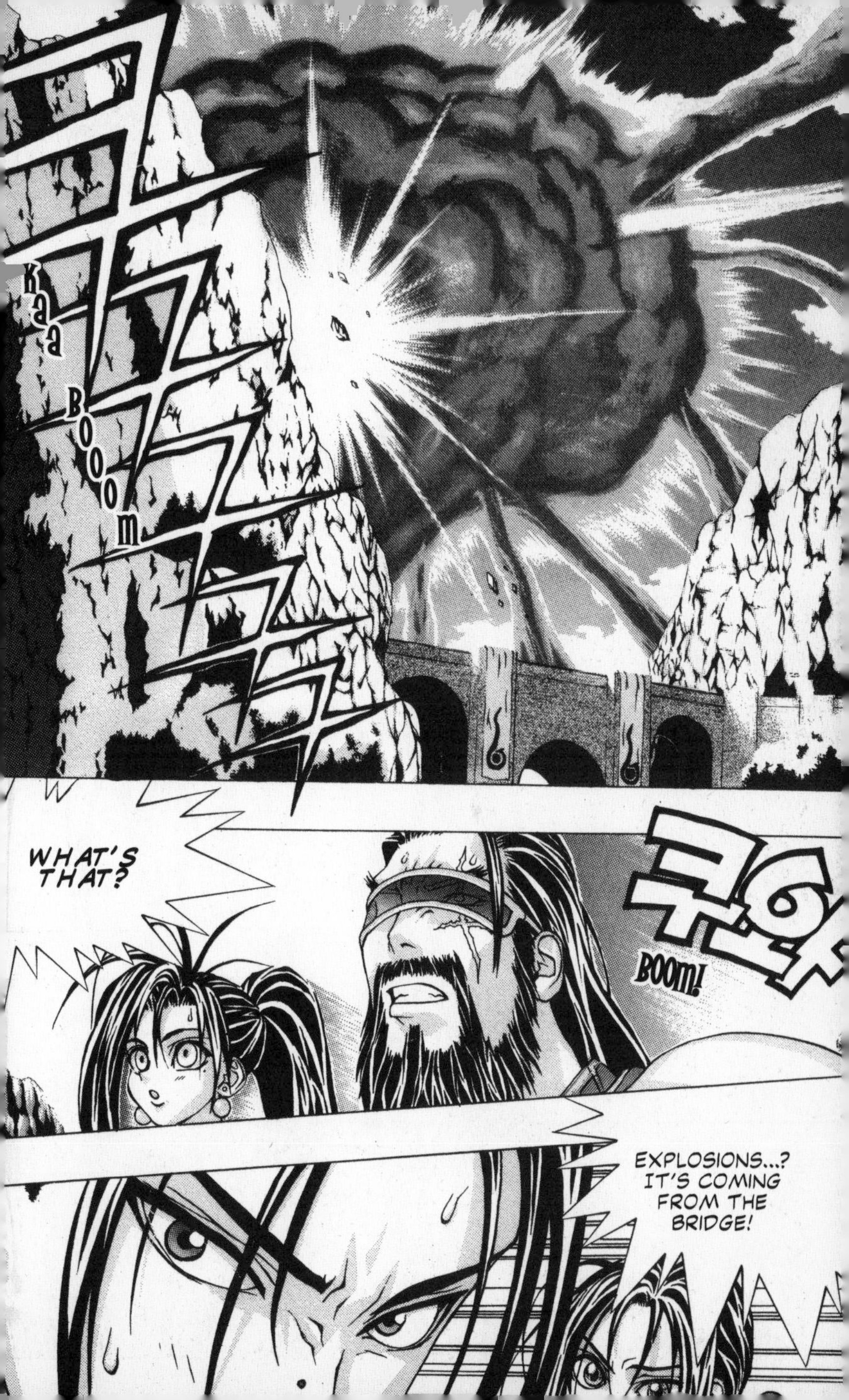
Kaaa BOOOOm
WHAT'S THAT?
BOOM!
EXPLOSIONS...? IT'S COMING FROM THE BRIDGE!

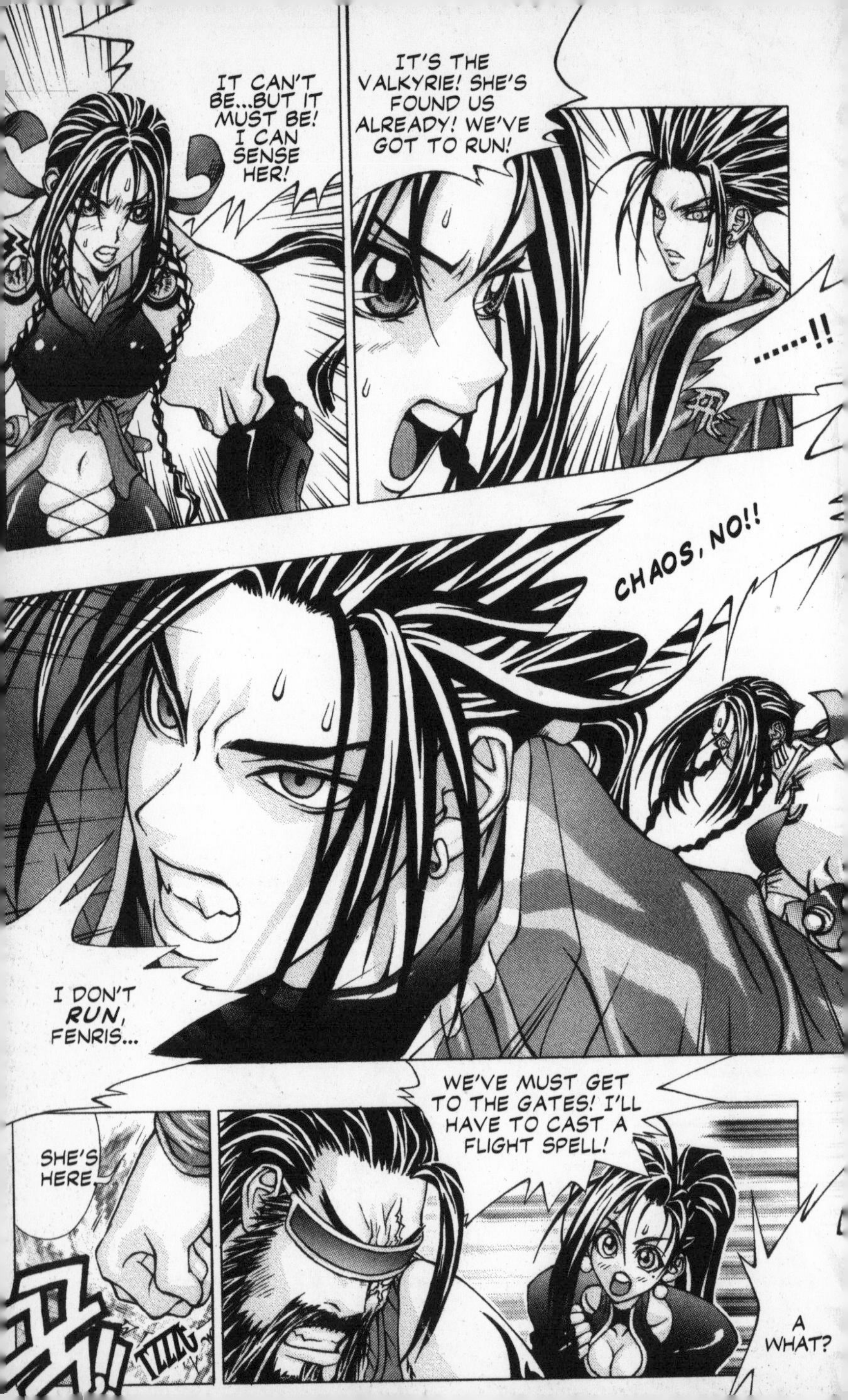
IT CAN'T BE...BUT IT MUST BE! I CAN SENSE HER!
IT'S THE VALKYRIE! SHE'S FOUND US ALREADY! WE'VE GOT TO RUN!
......!!
CHAOS, NO!!
I DON'T *RUN*, FENRIS...
SHE'S HERE.
WE'VE MUST GET TO THE GATES! I'LL HAVE TO CAST A FLIGHT SPELL!
A WHAT?

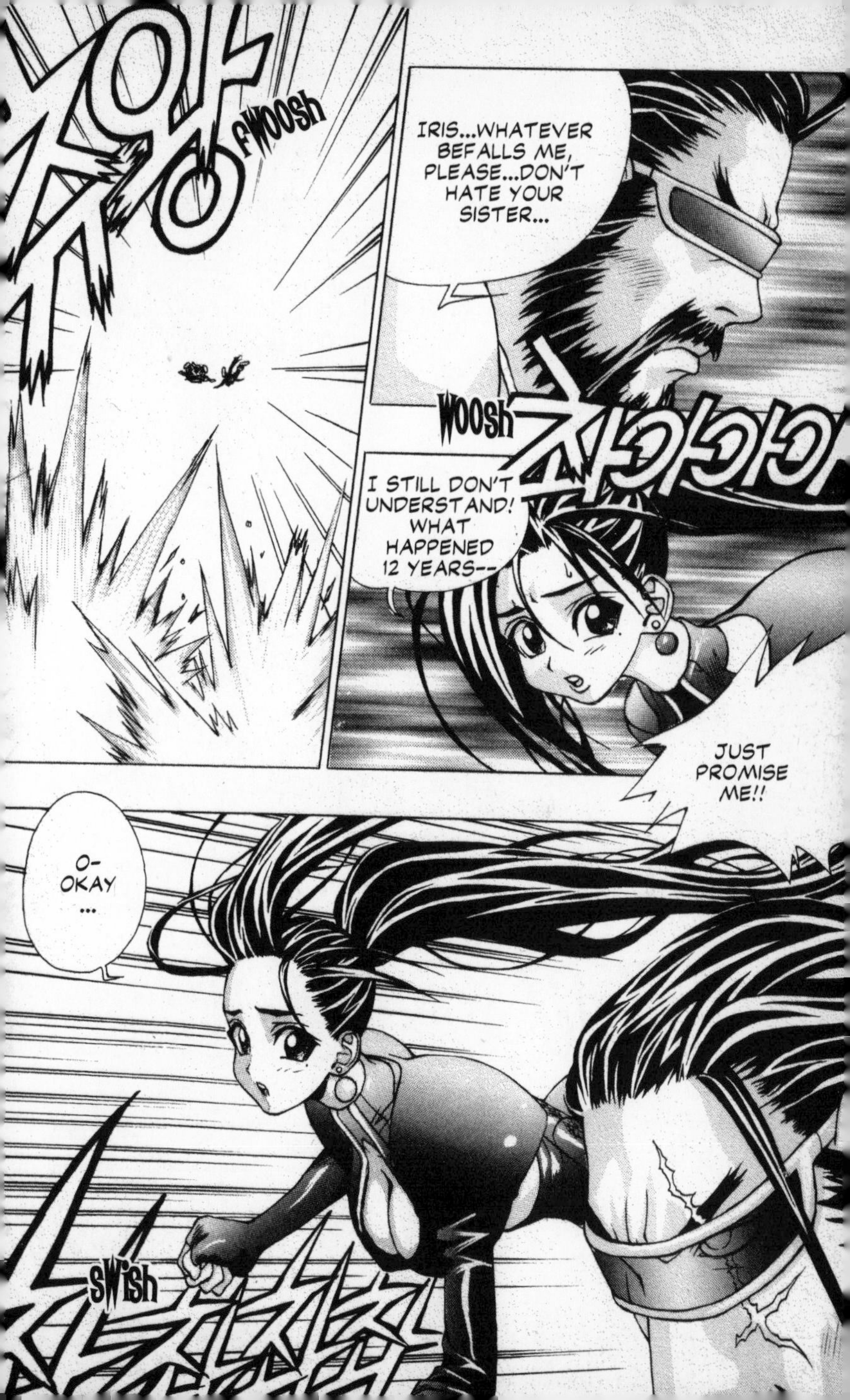
FWOOSH
IRIS...WHATEVER BEFALLS ME, PLEASE...DON'T HATE YOUR SISTER...
WOOSH
I STILL DON'T UNDERSTAND! WHAT HAPPENED 12 YEARS--
JUST PROMISE ME!!
O-OKAY ...
SWISH

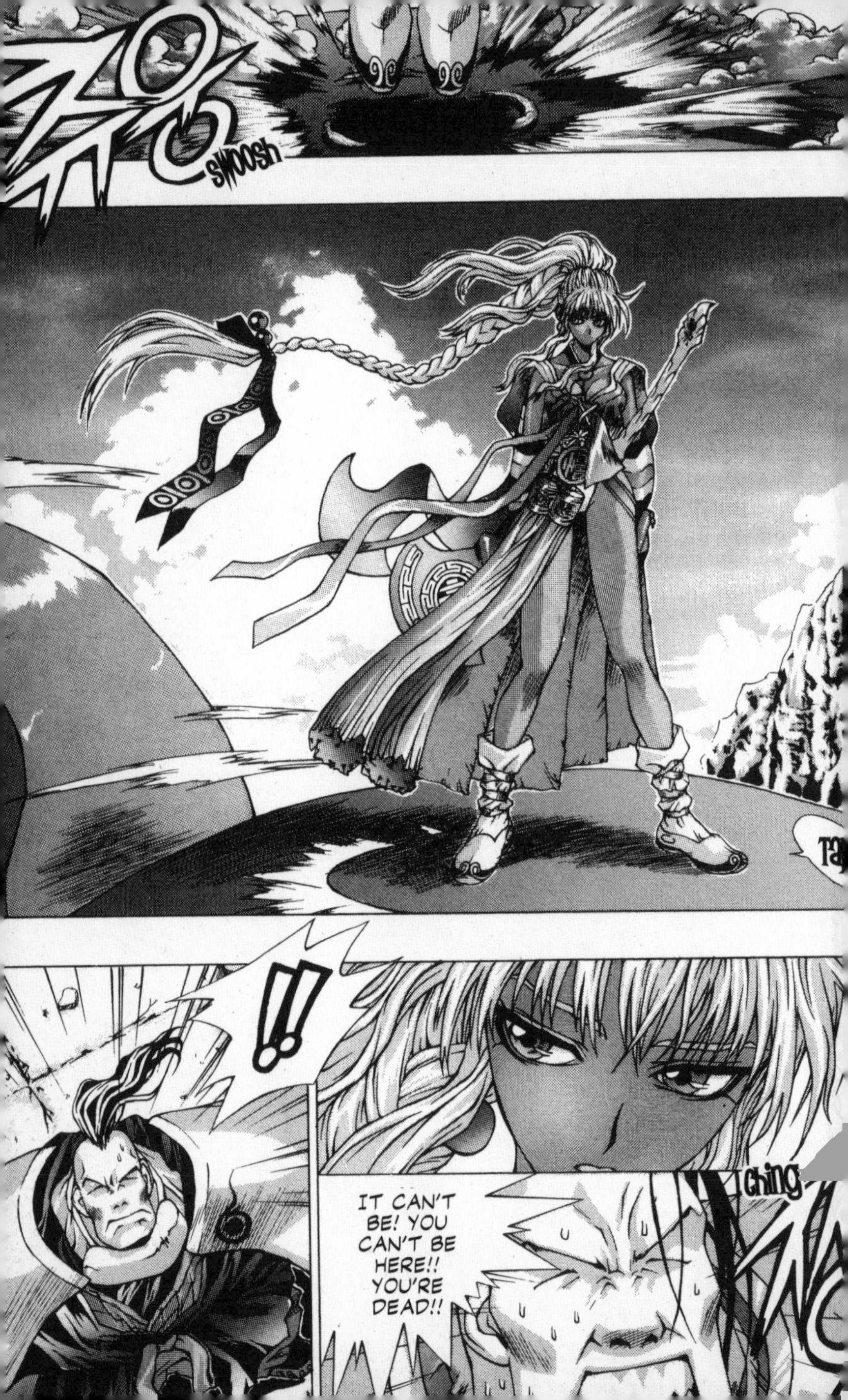
SWOOSH
Ta
!!
Ching
IT CAN'T BE! YOU CAN'T BE HERE!! YOU'RE DEAD!!

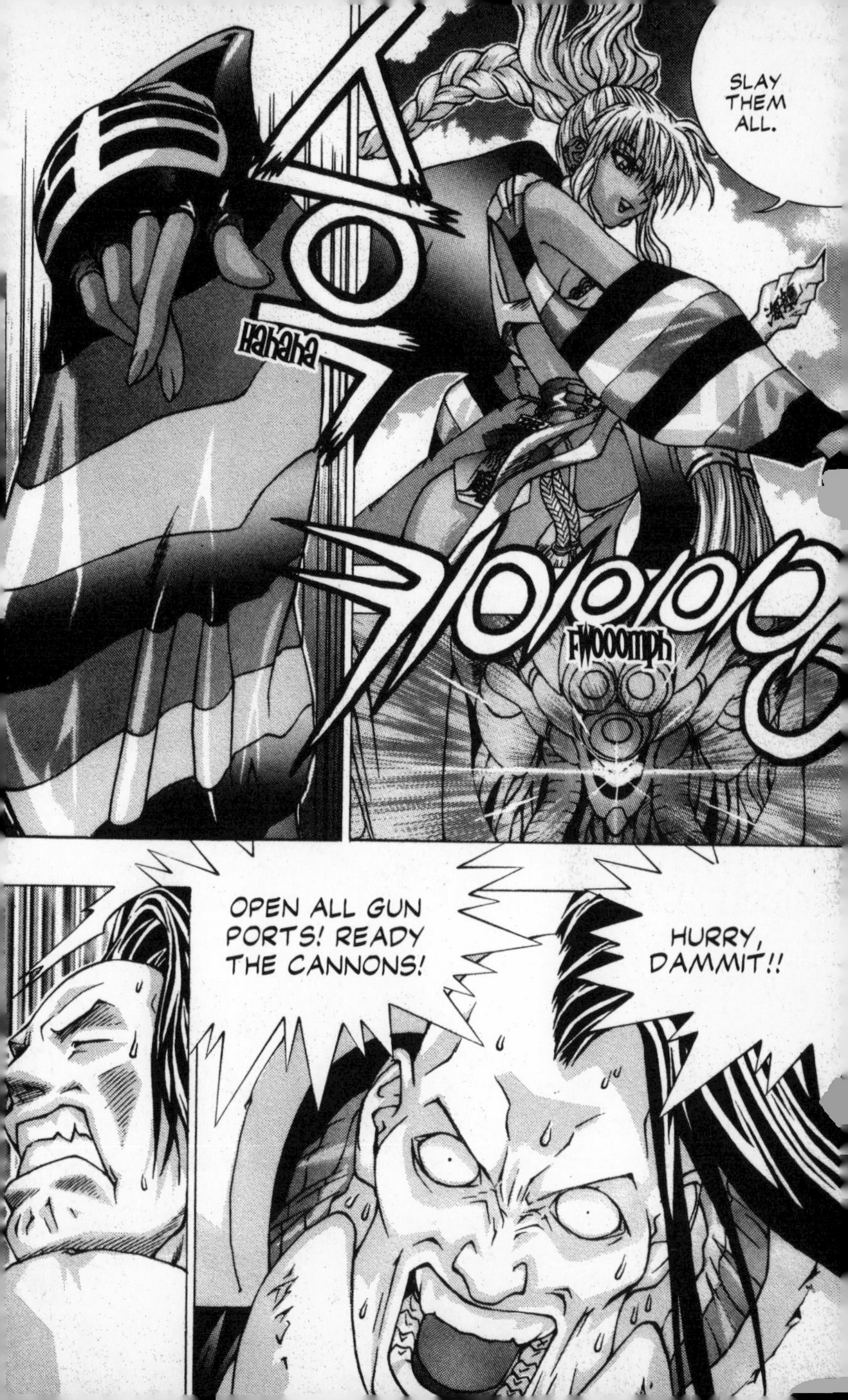
HAHAHA
SLAY THEM ALL.
FWOOOMPH
OPEN ALL GUN PORTS! READY THE CANNONS!
HURRY, DAMMIT!!

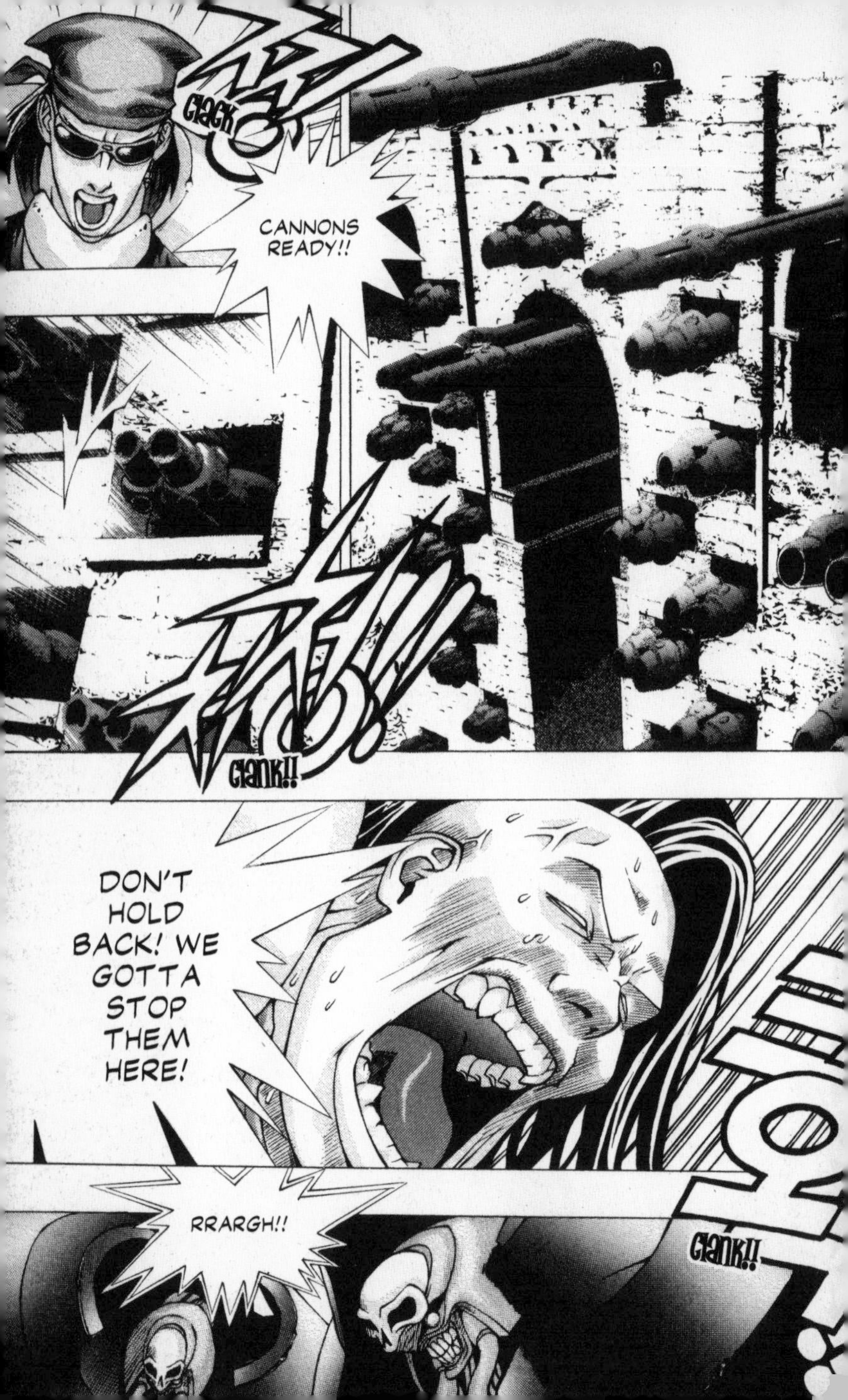
CLACK
CANNONS READY!!
CLANK!!
DON'T HOLD BACK! WE GOTTA STOP THEM HERE!
RRARGH!!
CLANK!!

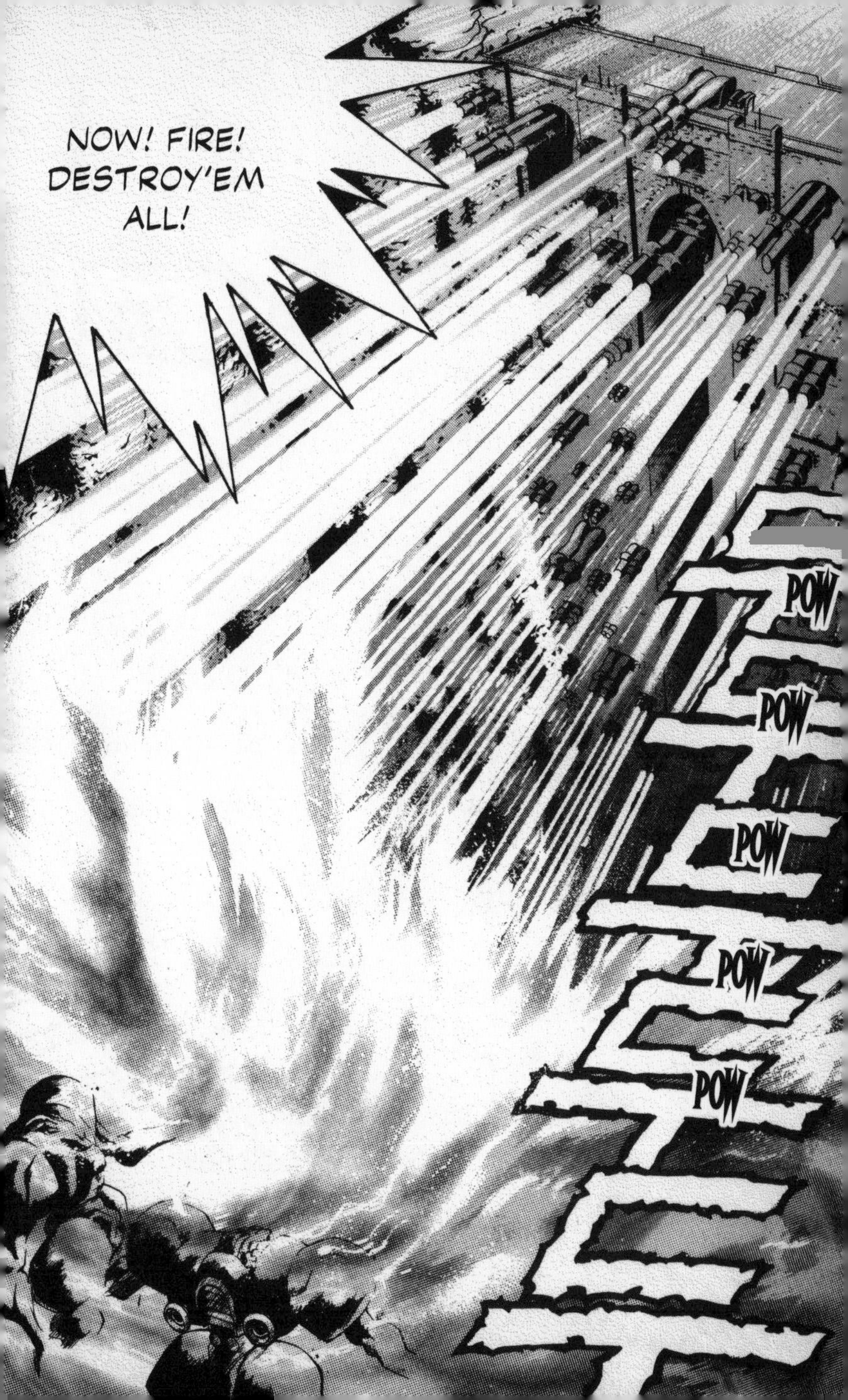
NOW! FIRE! DESTROY'EM ALL!
POW
POW
POW
POW
POW

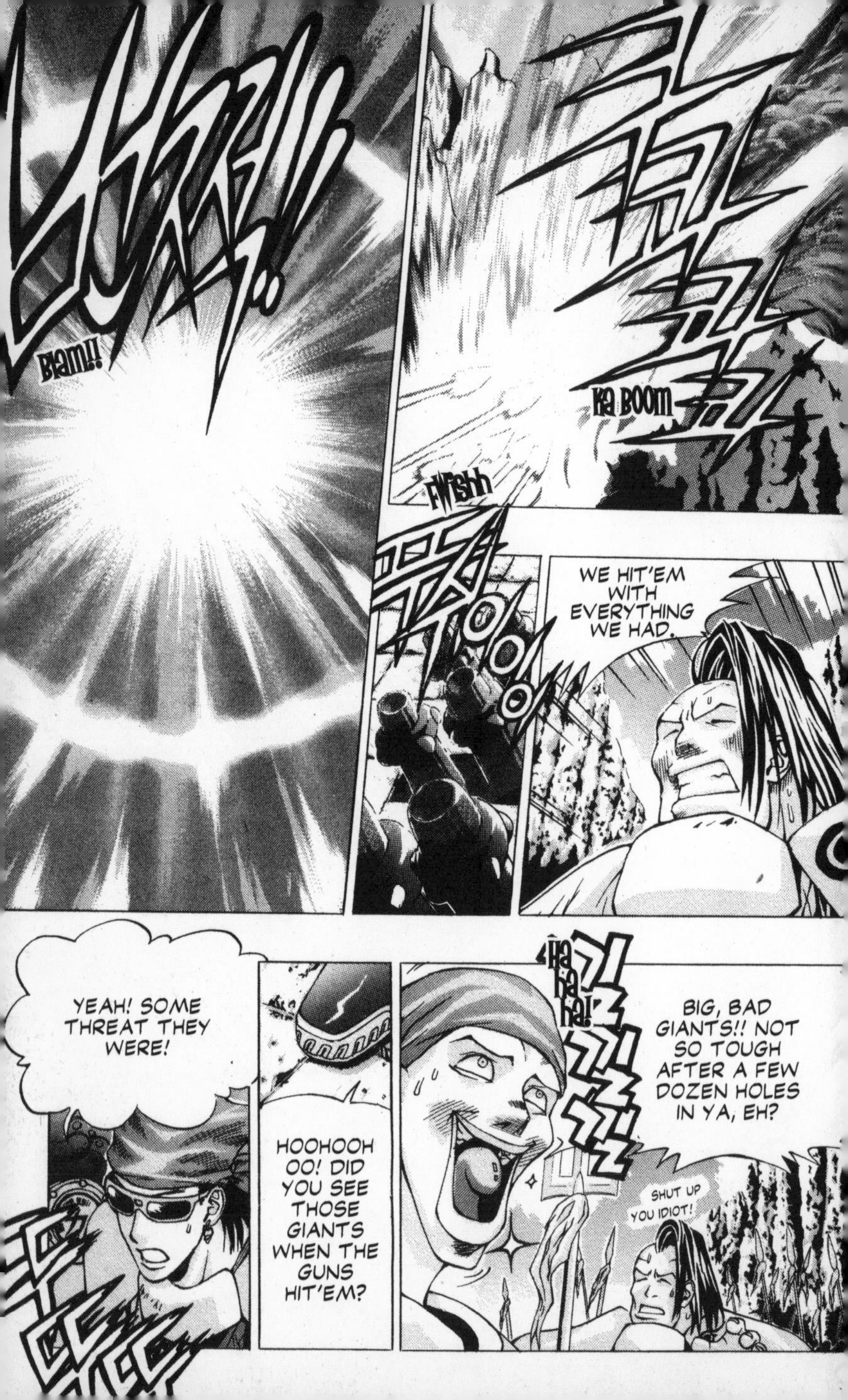
BLAM!!
FWISHH
KA BOOM
WE HIT'EM WITH EVERYTHING WE HAD.
YEAH! SOME THREAT THEY WERE!
HOOHOOHOOO! DID YOU SEE THOSE GIANTS WHEN THE GUNS HIT'EM?
HA HA HA!
BIG, BAD GIANTS!! NOT SO TOUGH AFTER A FEW DOZEN HOLES IN YA, EH?
SHUT UP YOU IDIOT!

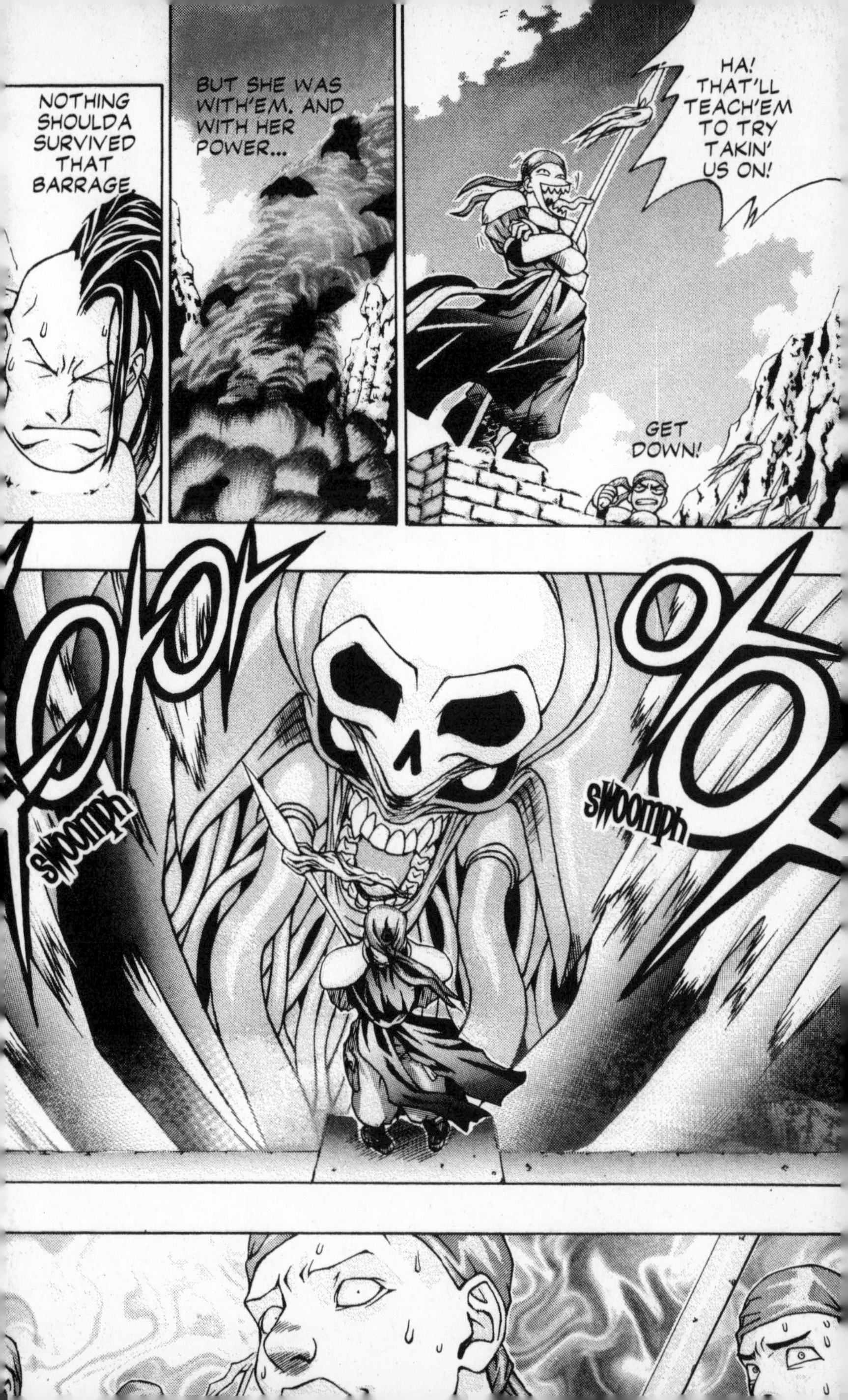
NOTHING SHOULDA SURVIVED THAT BARRAGE.
BUT SHE WAS WITH'EM. AND WITH HER POWER...
HA! THAT'LL TEACH'EM TO TRY TAKIN' US ON!
GET DOWN!
swoomph
swoomph

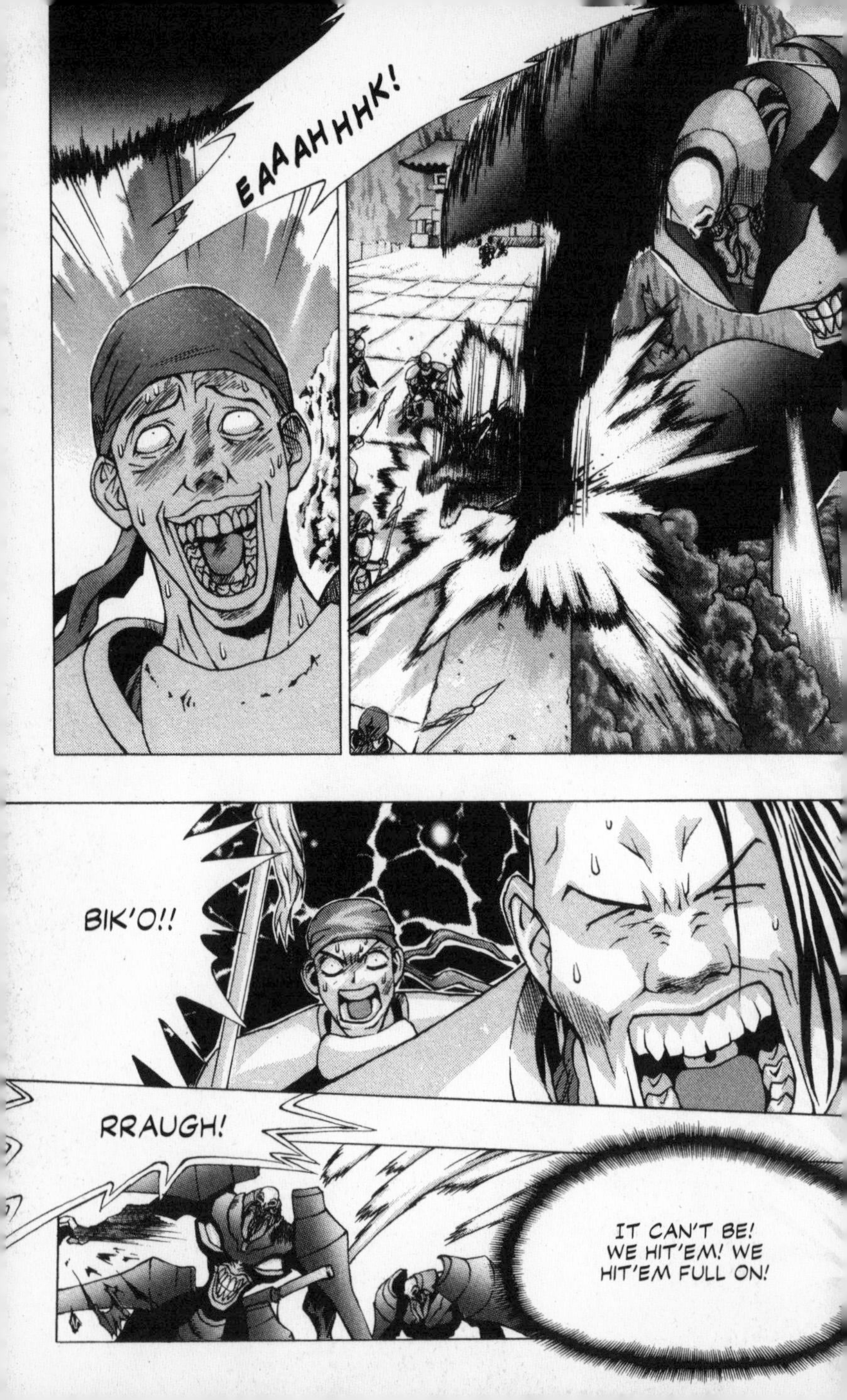
EAAAHHHK!
BIK'O!!
RRAUGH!
IT CAN'T BE! WE HIT'EM! WE HIT'EM FULL ON!

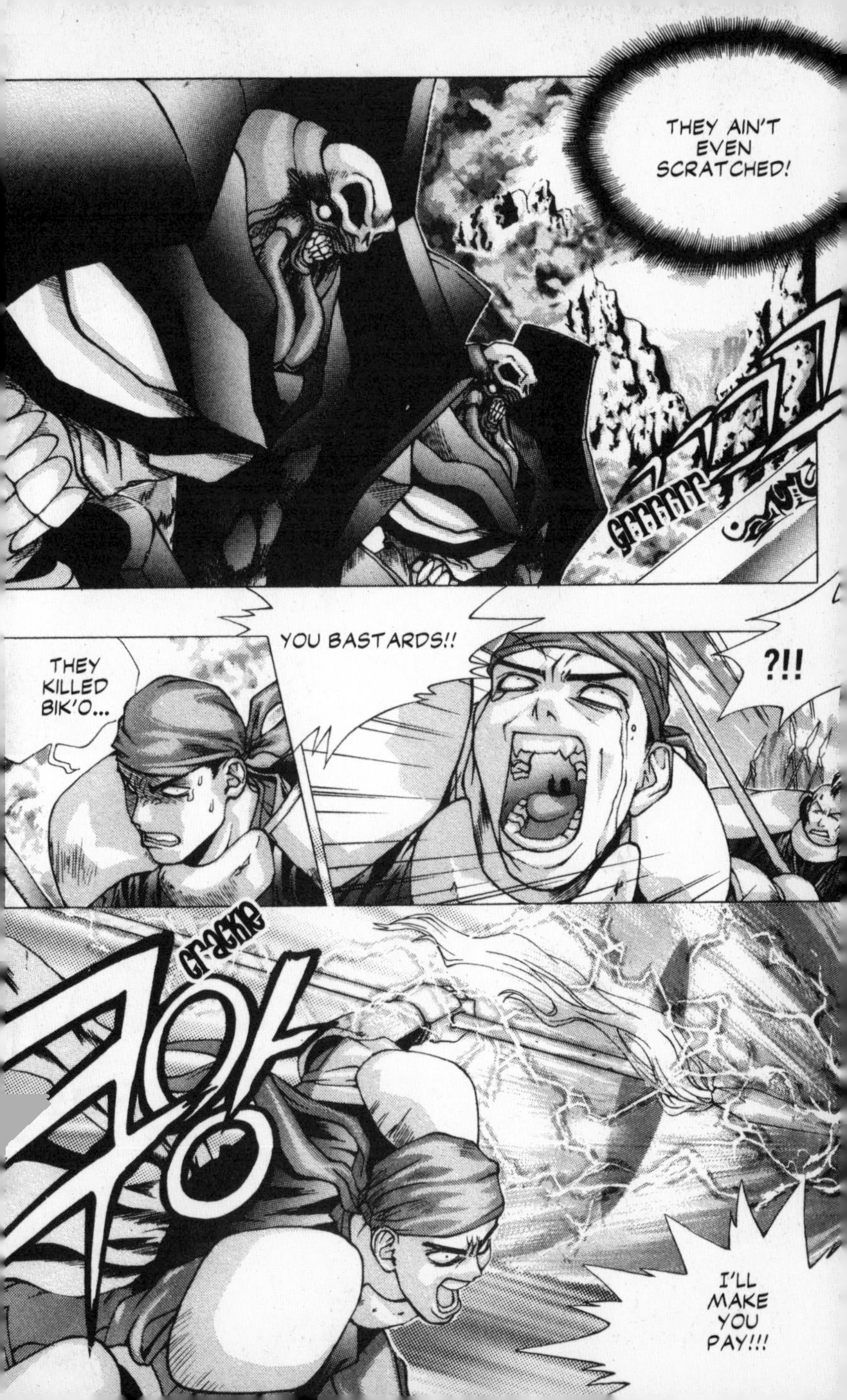
THEY AIN'T EVEN SCRATCHED!
GRRRRRR
THEY KILLED BIK'O...
YOU BASTARDS!!
?!!
CRACKLE
ZOK
I'LL MAKE YOU PAY!!!

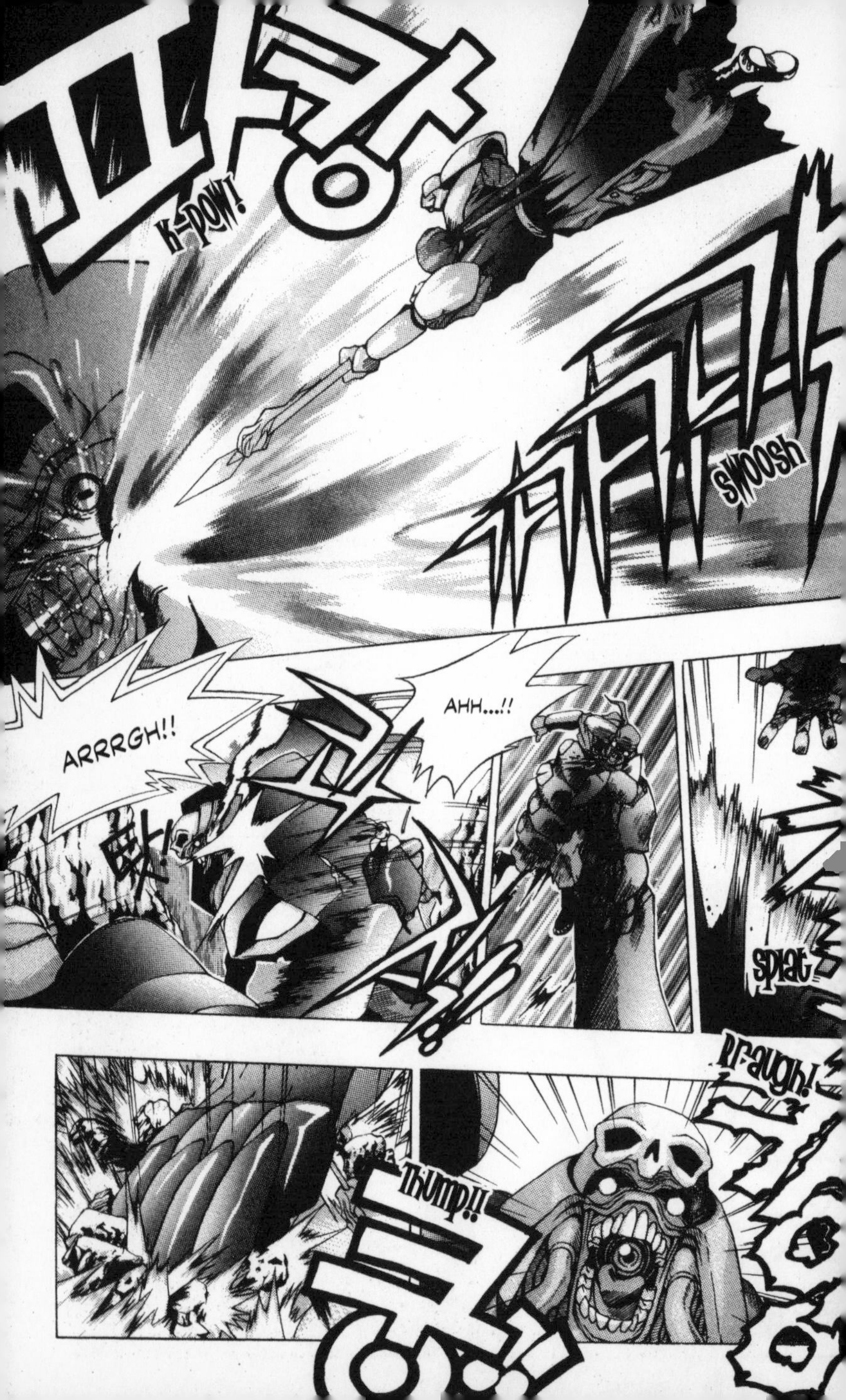
K-POW!
SWOOSH
ARRRGH!!
AHH...!!
splat
THUMP!!
Rr-augh!

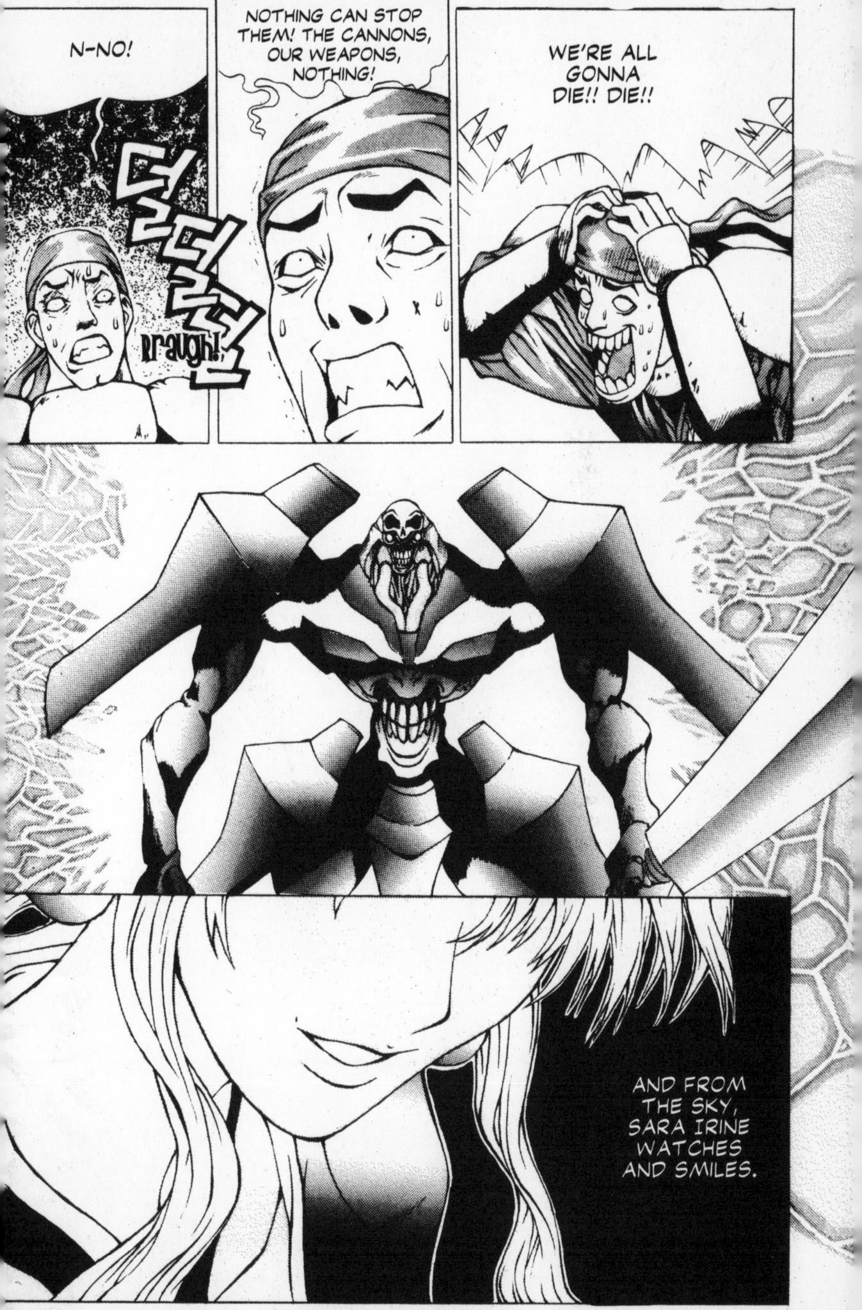
N-NO!
Brraugh!
NOTHING CAN STOP THEM! THE CANNONS, OUR WEAPONS, NOTHING!
WE'RE ALL GONNA DIE!! DIE!!
AND FROM THE SKY, SARA IRINE WATCHES AND SMILES.

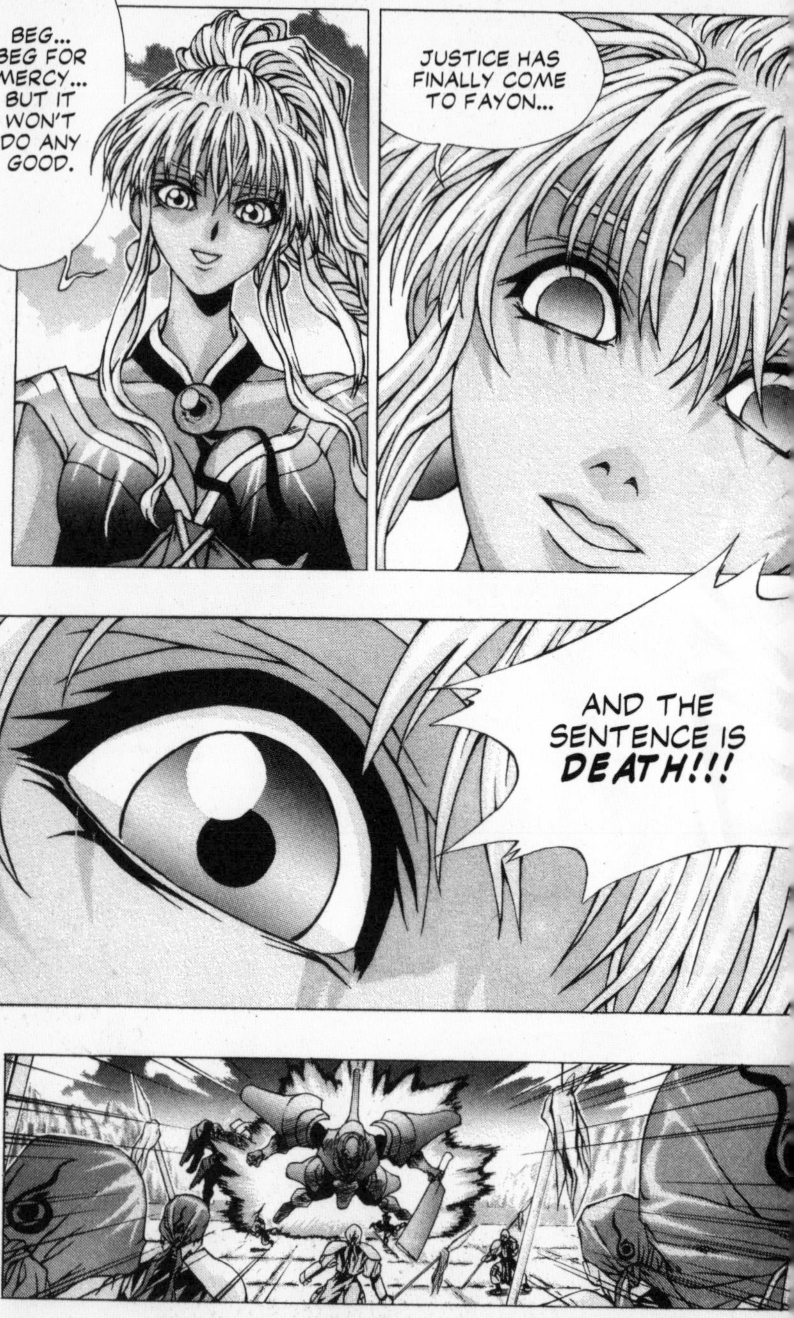
BEG... BEG FOR MERCY... BUT IT WON'T DO ANY GOOD.
JUSTICE HAS FINALLY COME TO FAYON...
AND THE SENTENCE IS **DEATH!!!**

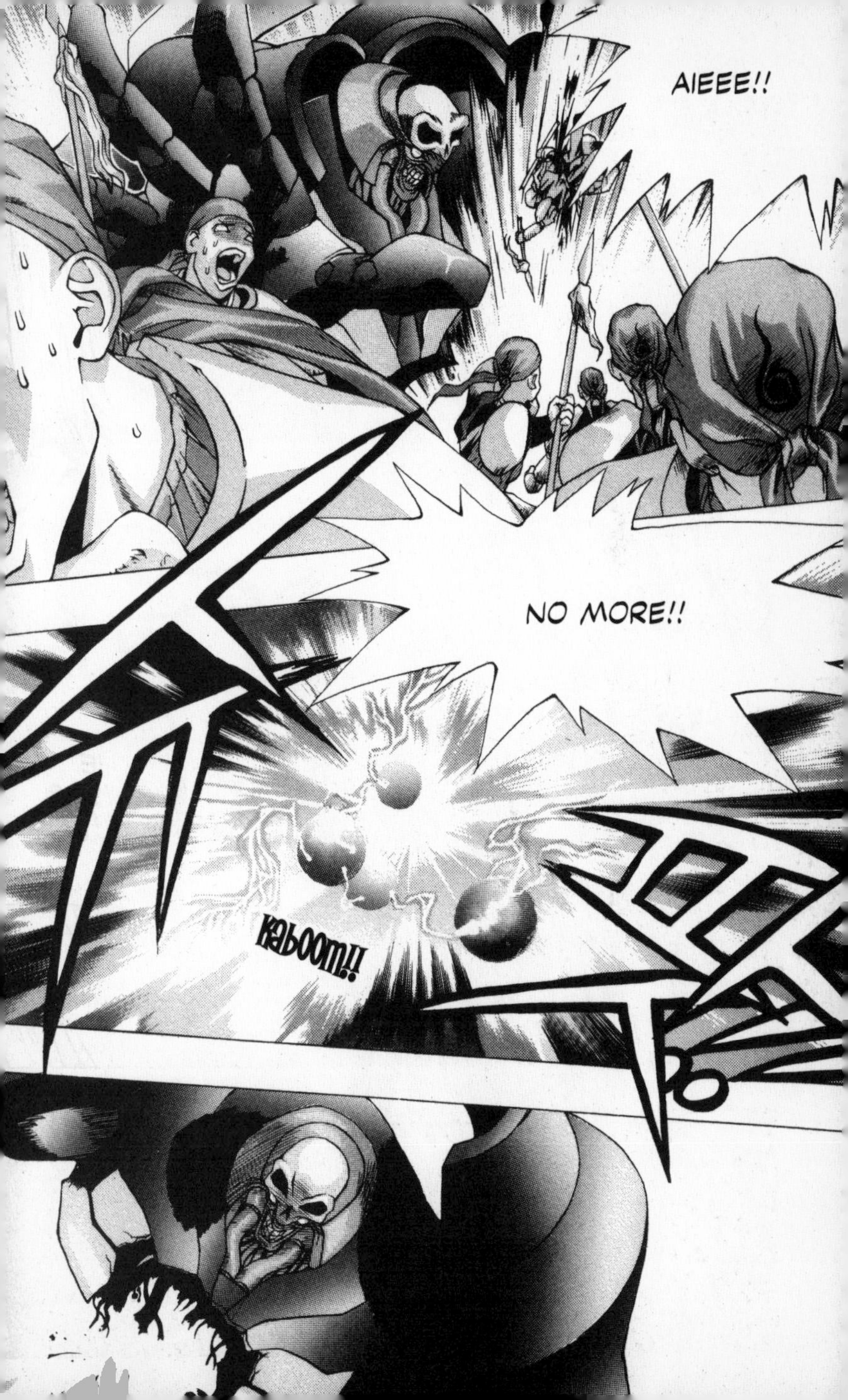
AIEEE!!
NO MORE!!
KAPOOM!!

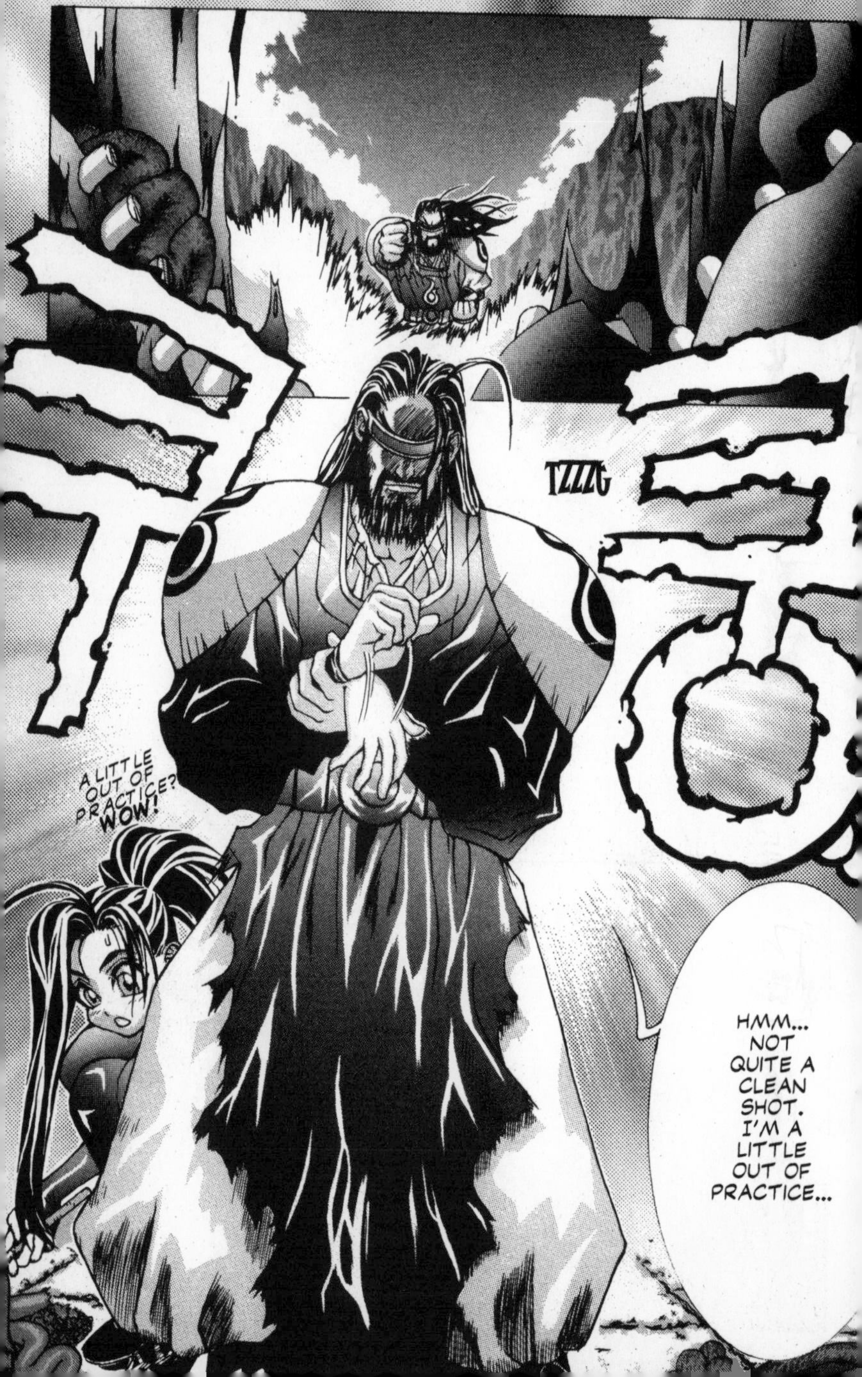
TZZZG
A LITTLE OUT OF PRACTICE? WOW!
HMM... NOT QUITE A CLEAN SHOT. I'M A LITTLE OUT OF PRACTICE...

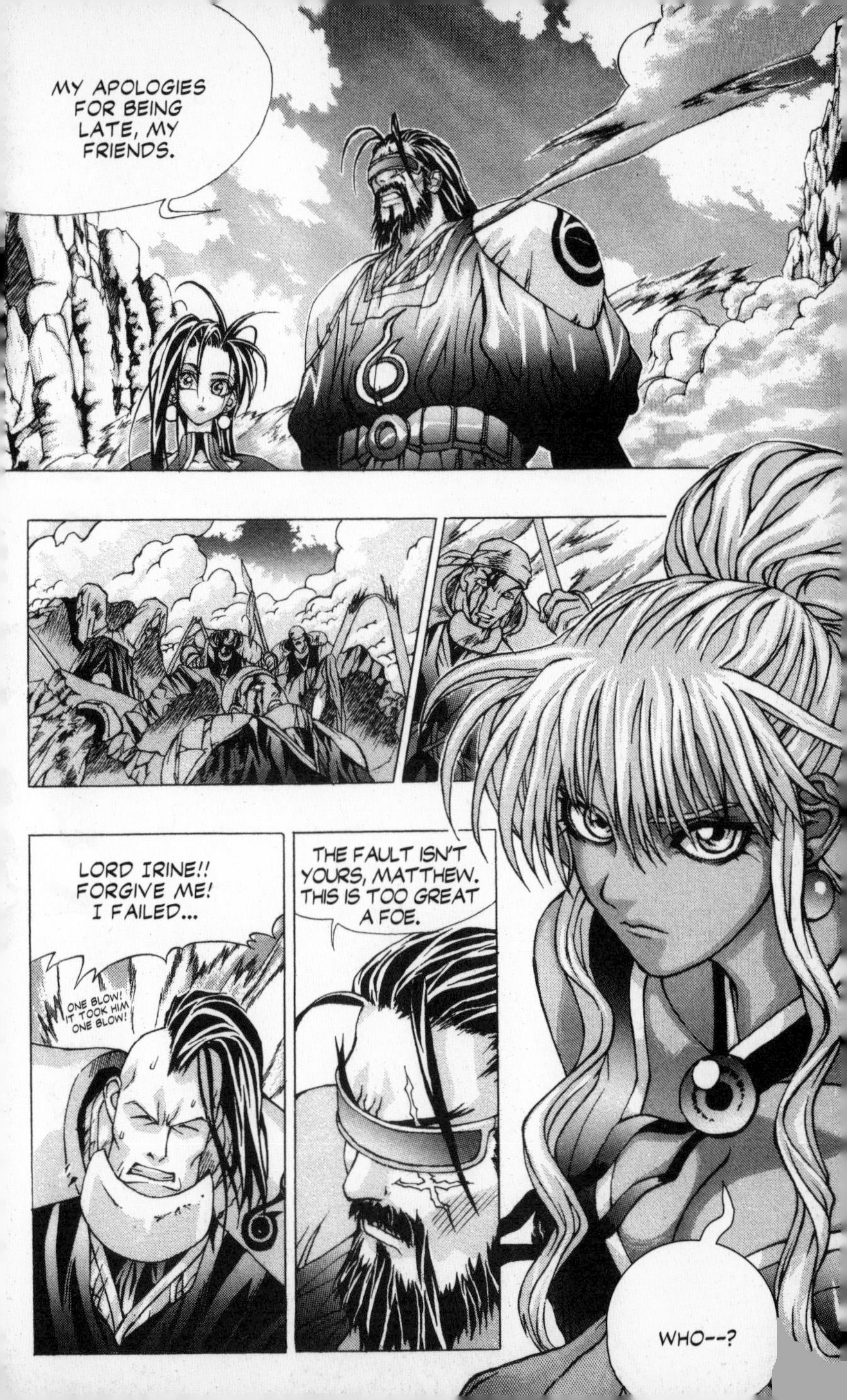
MY APOLOGIES FOR BEING LATE, MY FRIENDS.
LORD IRINE!! FORGIVE ME! I FAILED...
ONE BLOW! IT TOOK HIM ONE BLOW!
THE FAULT ISN'T YOURS, MATTHEW. THIS IS TOO GREAT A FOE.
WHO--?

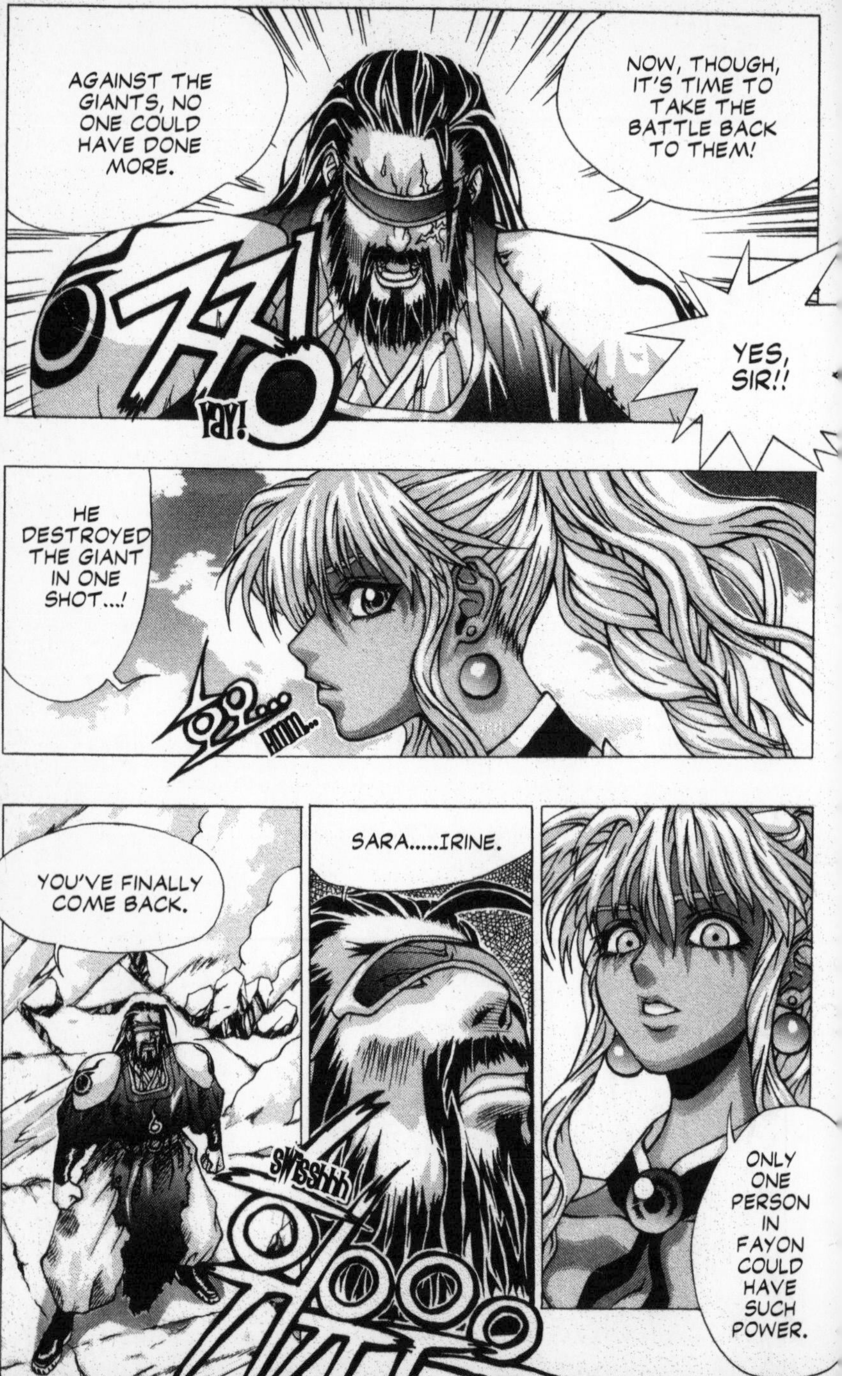
AGAINST THE GIANTS, NO ONE COULD HAVE DONE MORE.
NOW, THOUGH, IT'S TIME TO TAKE THE BATTLE BACK TO THEM!
YAY!
YES, SIR!!
HE DESTROYED THE GIANT IN ONE SHOT...!
HMM...
YOU'VE FINALLY COME BACK.
SARA......IRINE.
SWISHHH
ONLY ONE PERSON IN FAYON COULD HAVE SUCH POWER.

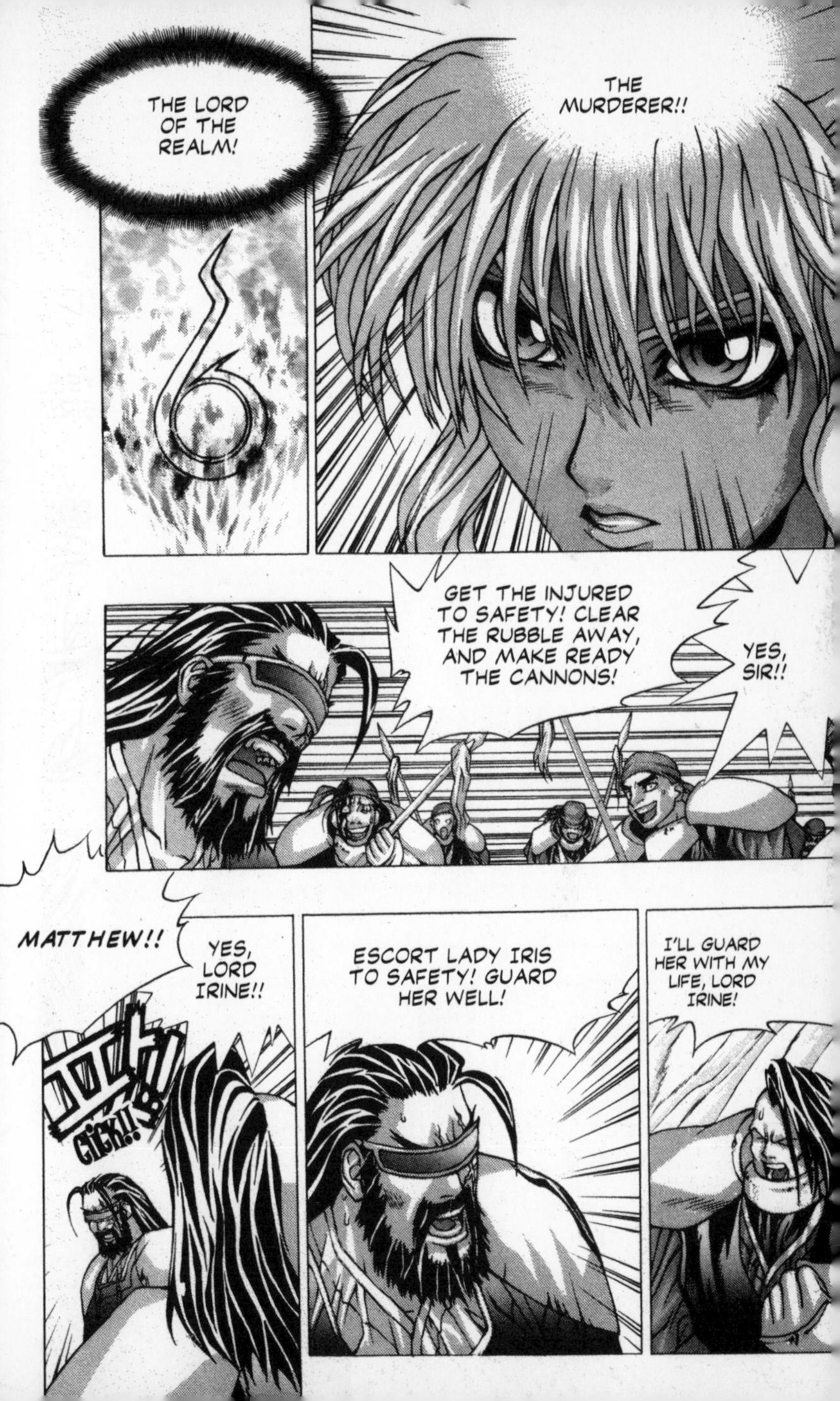
THE LORD OF THE REALM!
THE MURDERER!!
GET THE INJURED TO SAFETY! CLEAR THE RUBBLE AWAY, AND MAKE READY THE CANNONS!
YES, SIR!!
MATTHEW!!
YES, LORD IRINE!!
CLICK!!
ESCORT LADY IRIS TO SAFETY! GUARD HER WELL!
I'LL GUARD HER WITH MY LIFE, LORD IRINE!

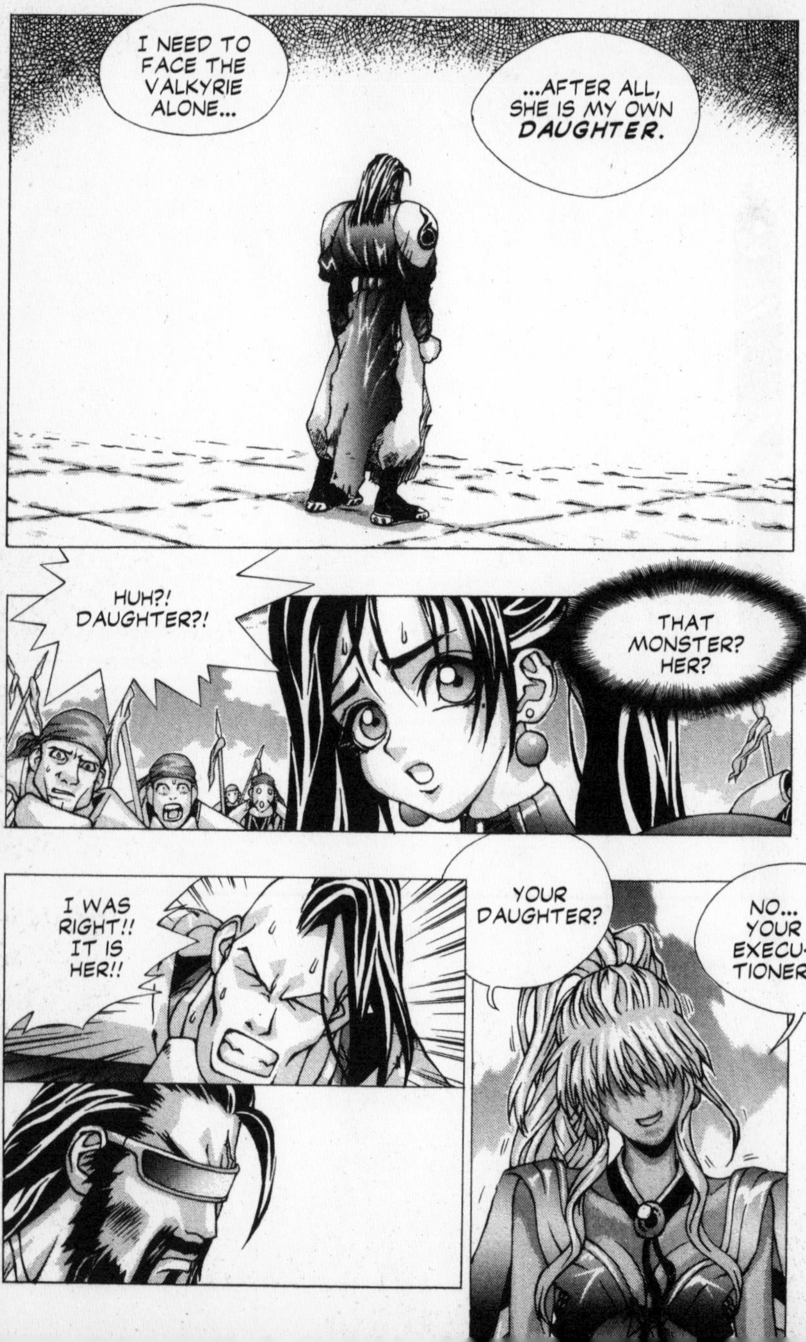

I NEED TO FACE THE VALKYRIE ALONE...
...AFTER ALL, SHE IS MY OWN DAUGHTER.
HUH?! DAUGHTER?!
THAT MONSTER? HER?
I WAS RIGHT!! IT IS HER!!
YOUR DAUGHTER?
NO... YOUR EXECU- TIONER.

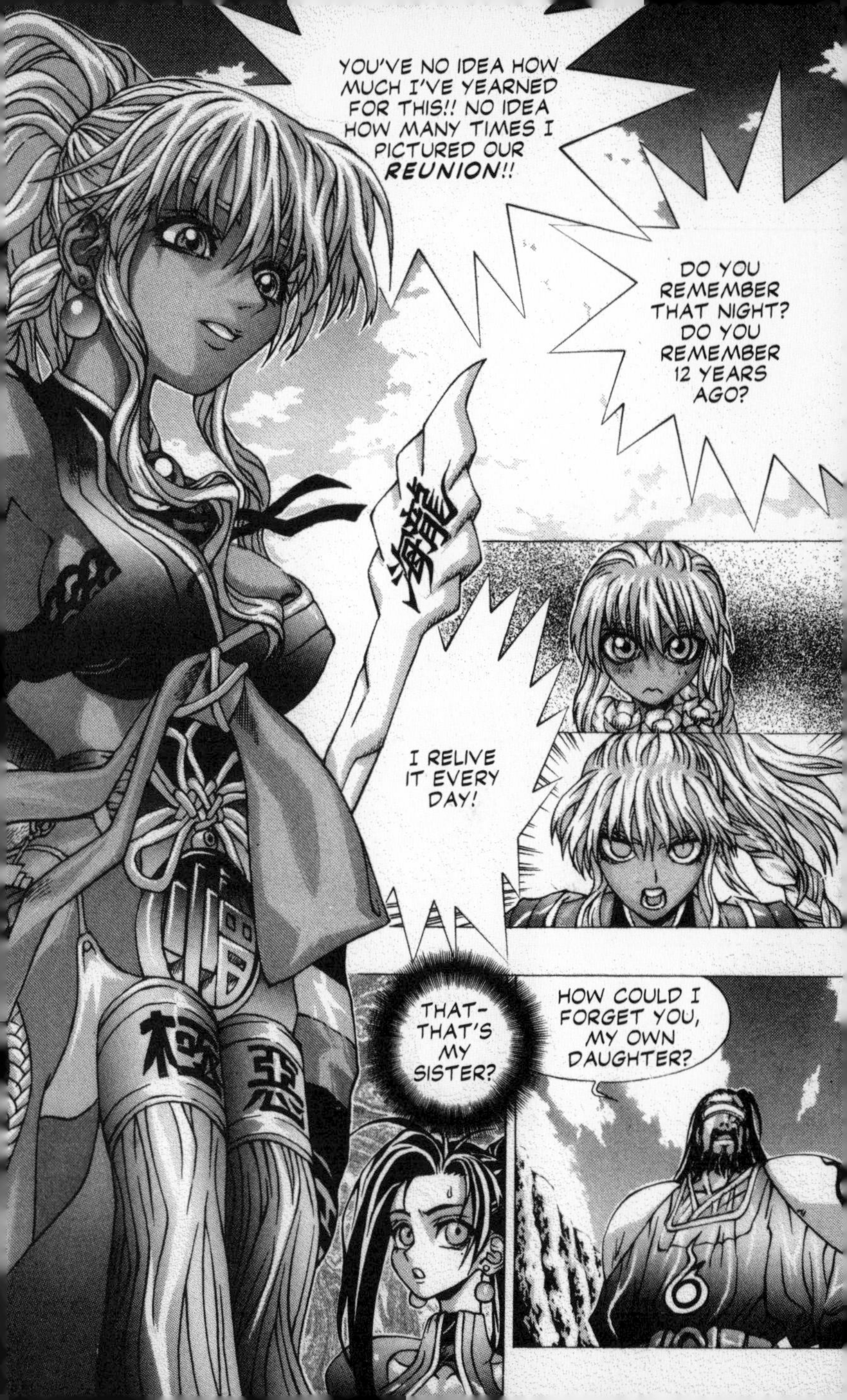
YOU'VE NO IDEA HOW MUCH I'VE YEARNED FOR THIS!! NO IDEA HOW MANY TIMES I PICTURED OUR **REUNION**!!
DO YOU REMEMBER THAT NIGHT? DO YOU REMEMBER 12 YEARS AGO?
I RELIVE IT EVERY DAY!
THAT-THAT'S MY SISTER?
HOW COULD I FORGET YOU, MY OWN DAUGHTER?

RAGNAROK

라그나로크

INTO THE ABYSS

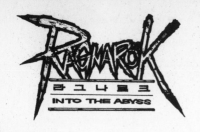

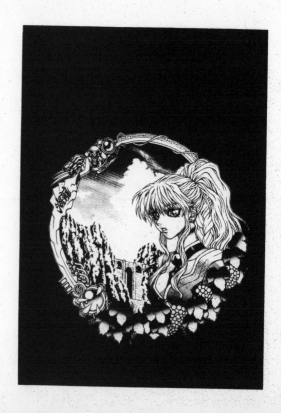

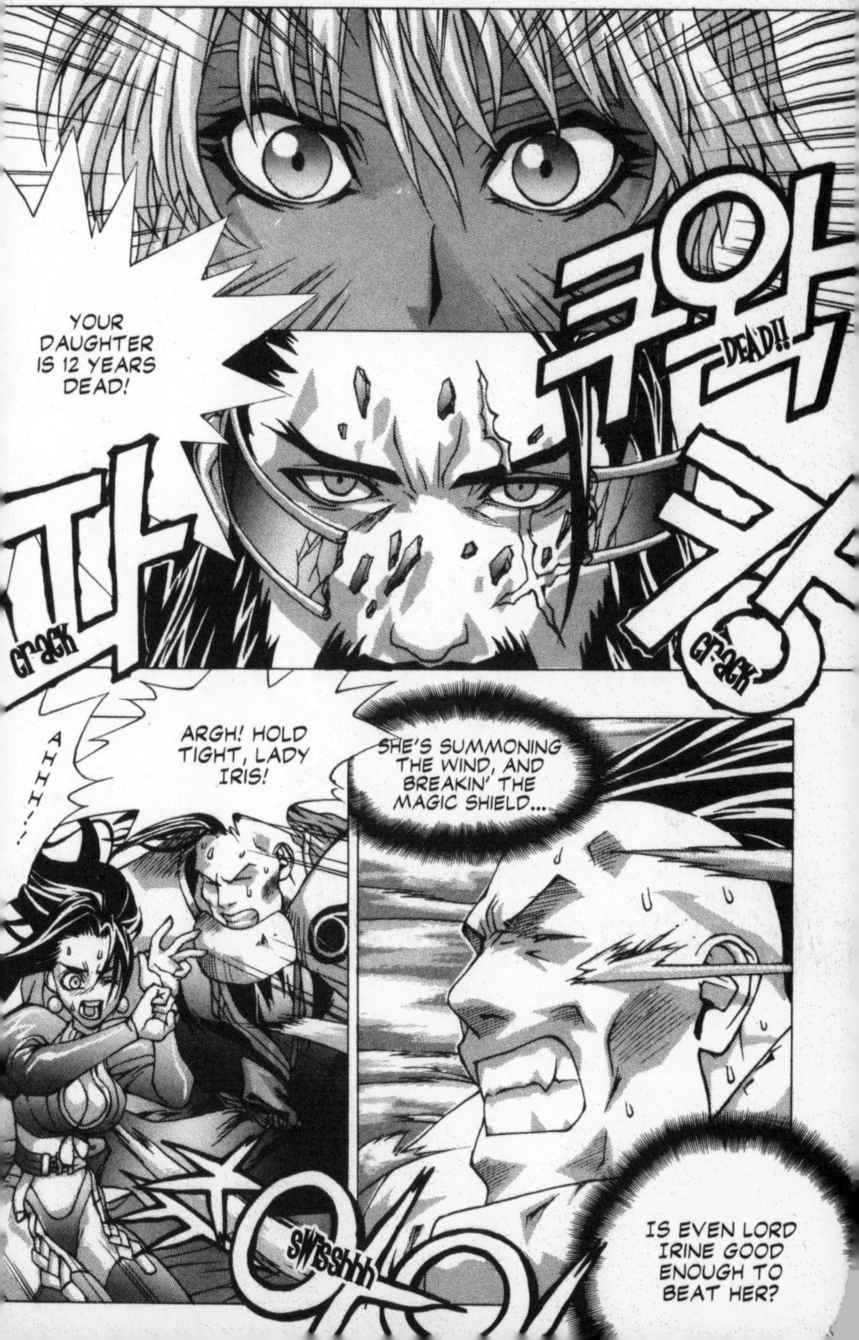
YOUR DAUGHTER IS 12 YEARS DEAD!
DEAD!!
crack
crack
AHHH!!
ARGH! HOLD TIGHT, LADY IRIS!
SHE'S SUMMONING THE WIND, AND BREAKIN' THE MAGIC SHIELD...
SWISSHHH
IS EVEN LORD IRINE GOOD ENOUGH TO BEAT HER?

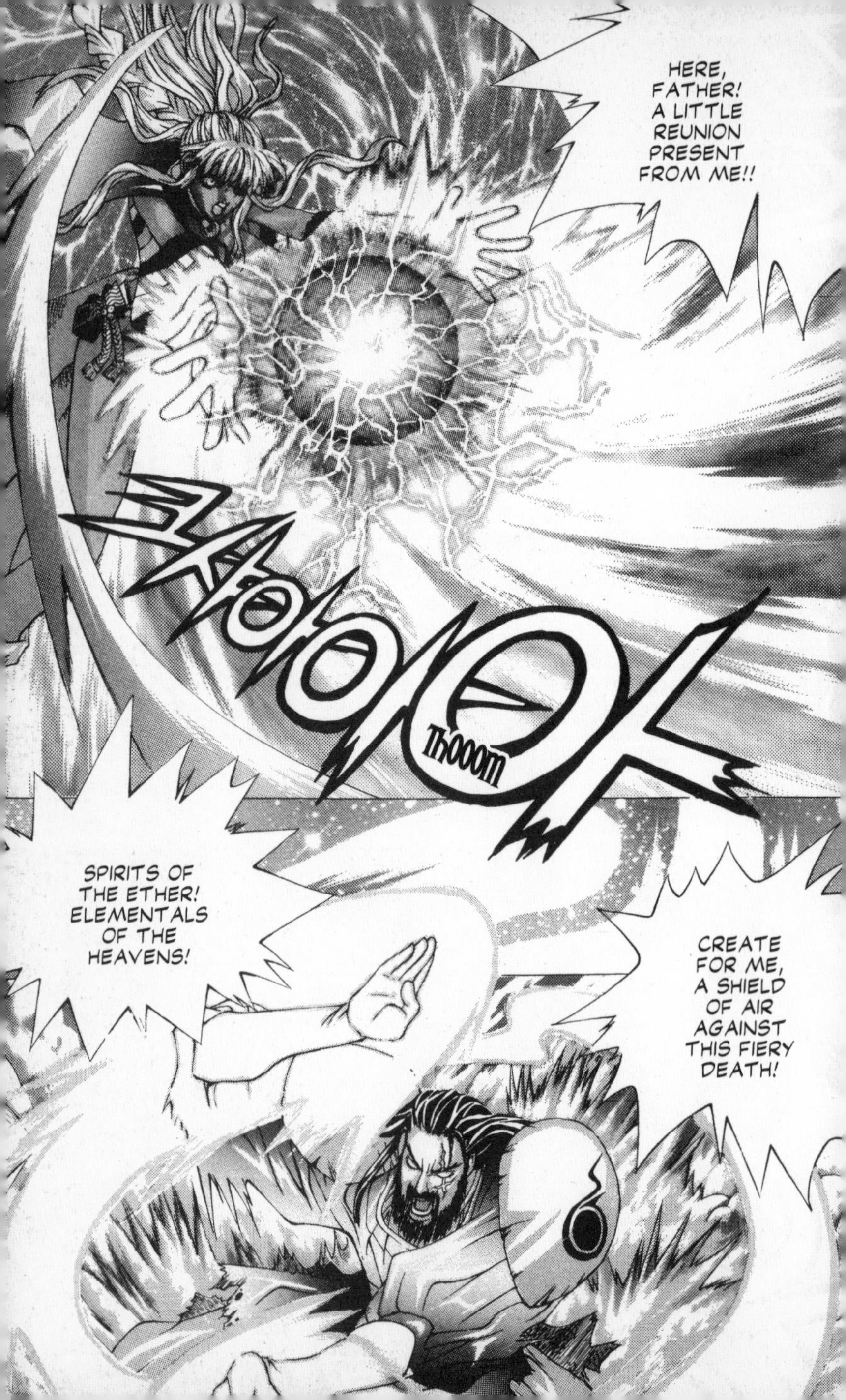
HERE, FATHER! A LITTLE REUNION PRESENT FROM ME!!
THOOOM
SPIRITS OF THE ETHER! ELEMENTALS OF THE HEAVENS!
CREATE FOR ME, A SHIELD OF AIR AGAINST THIS FIERY DEATH!

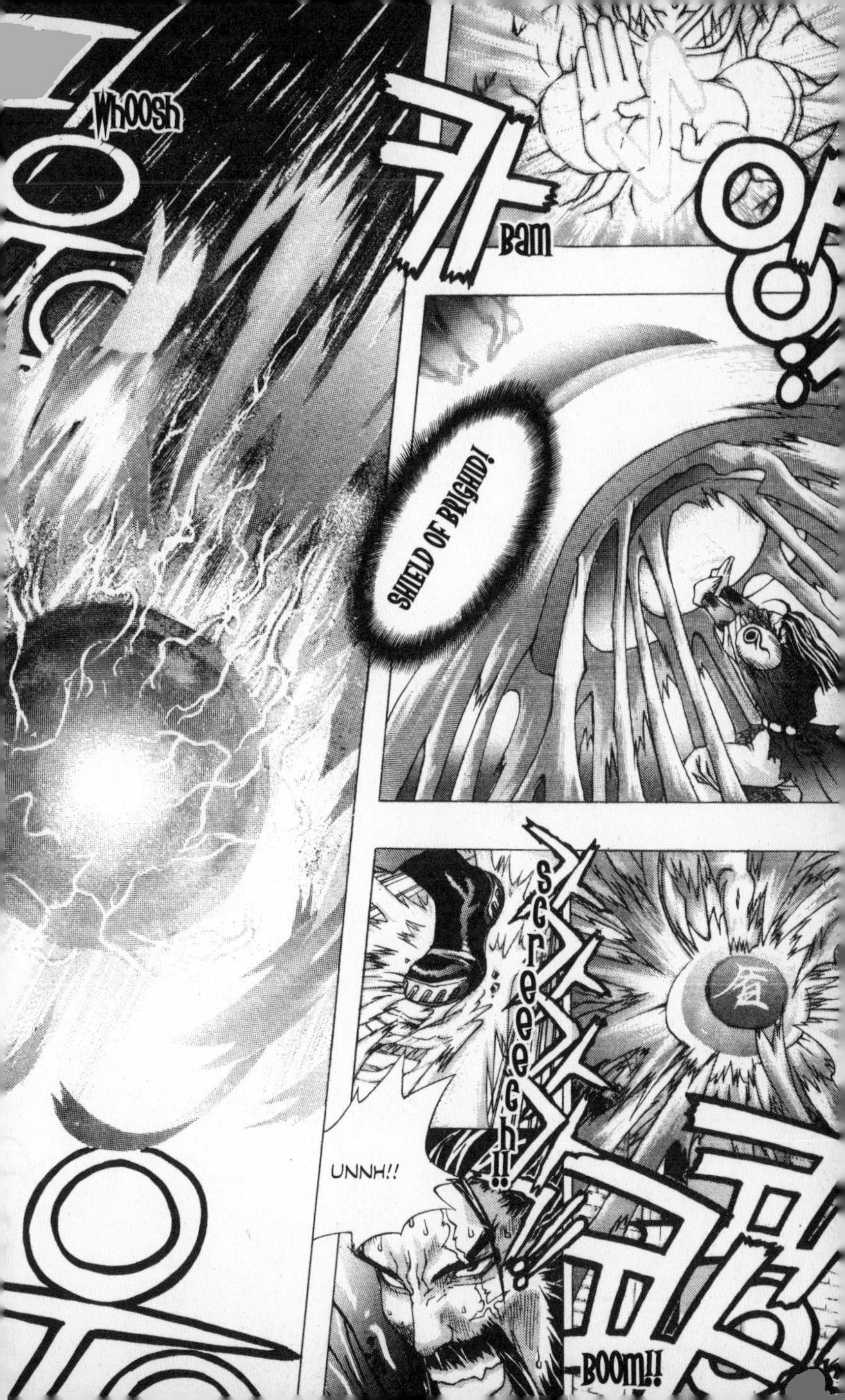
BAM
SHIELD OF BRIGHID!
WHOOSH
SCREEEECH!!
UNNH!!
BOOM!!

YOU CAST THAT TOO QUICKLY! YOU HAD IT PREPARED ALL THE TIME!

I ALWAYS KNEW IN MY HEART THAT YOU WOULD ONE DAY RETURN...

SARA, IT'S MY LIFE YOU SEEK. THERE IS NO REASON TO INVOLVE INNOCENTS.

INNOCENT? THERE ARE NO INNOCENTS...

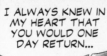

MOMMY... MOMMY...

DON'T LOSE HER!!

HUFF.

HUFF.

THAT WAY!!

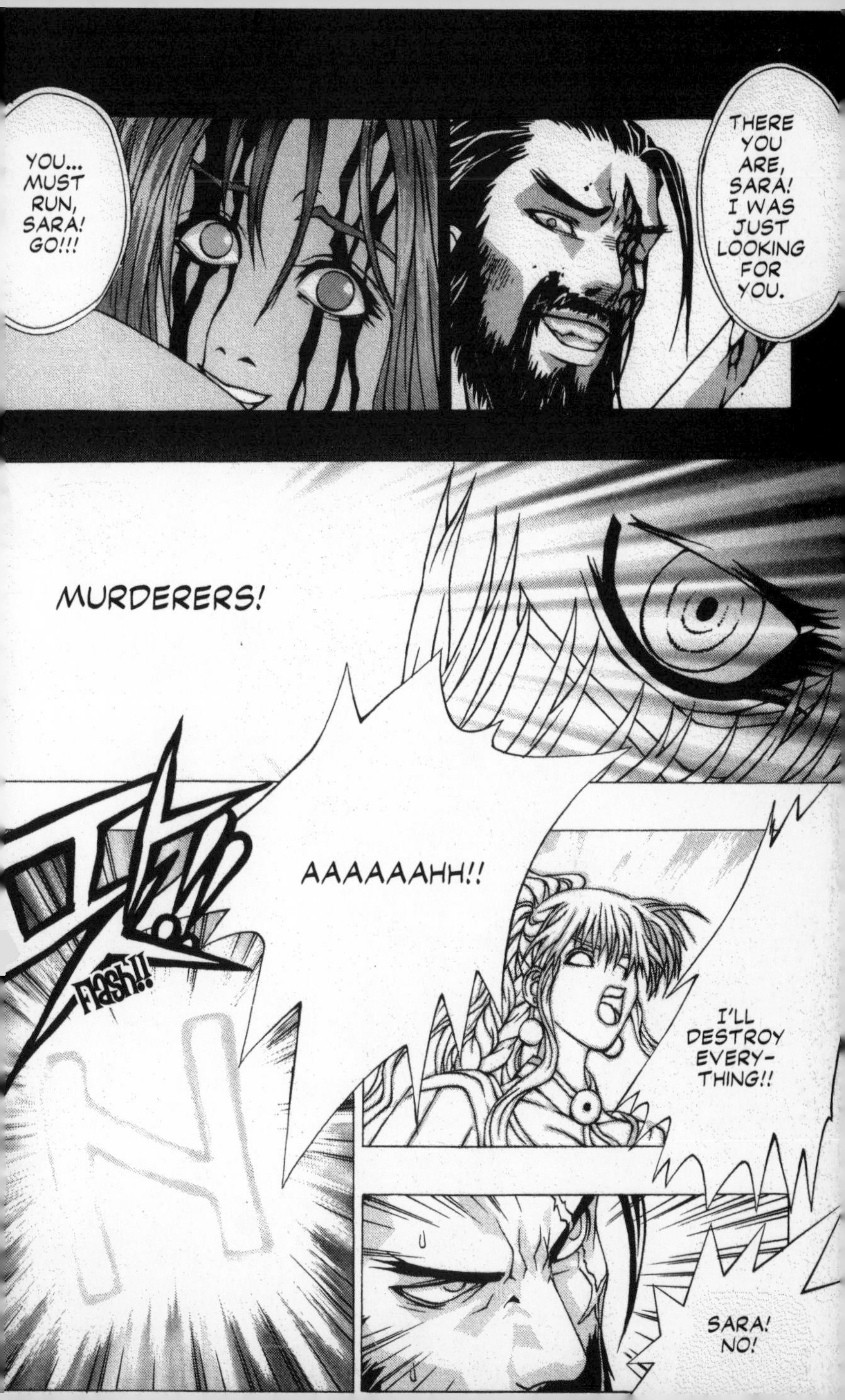
YOU... MUST RUN, SARA! GO!!!
THERE YOU ARE, SARA! I WAS JUST LOOKING FOR YOU.
MURDERERS!
FLASH!!
AAAAAAHH!!
I'LL DESTROY EVERY-THING!!
SARA! NO!

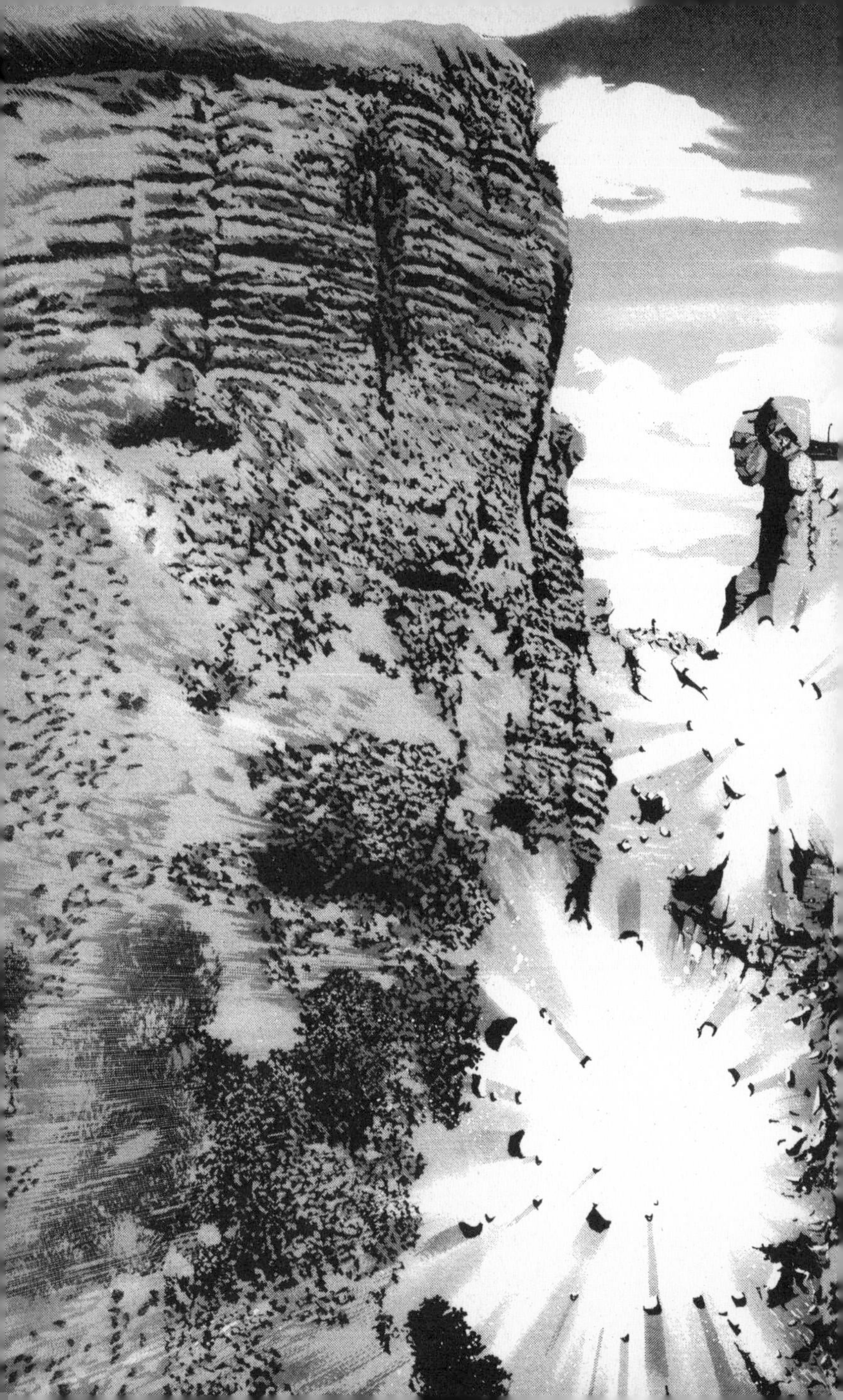

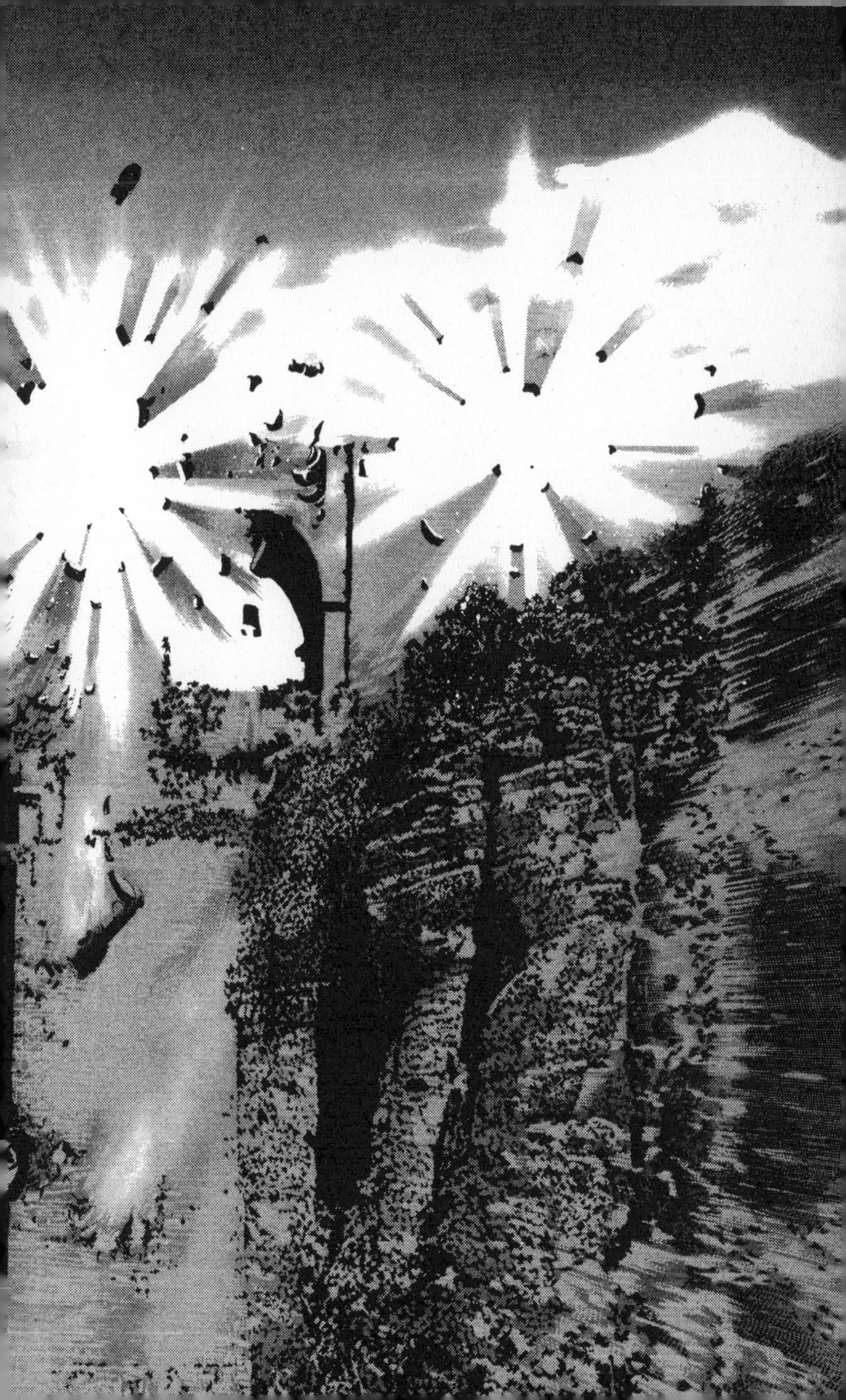

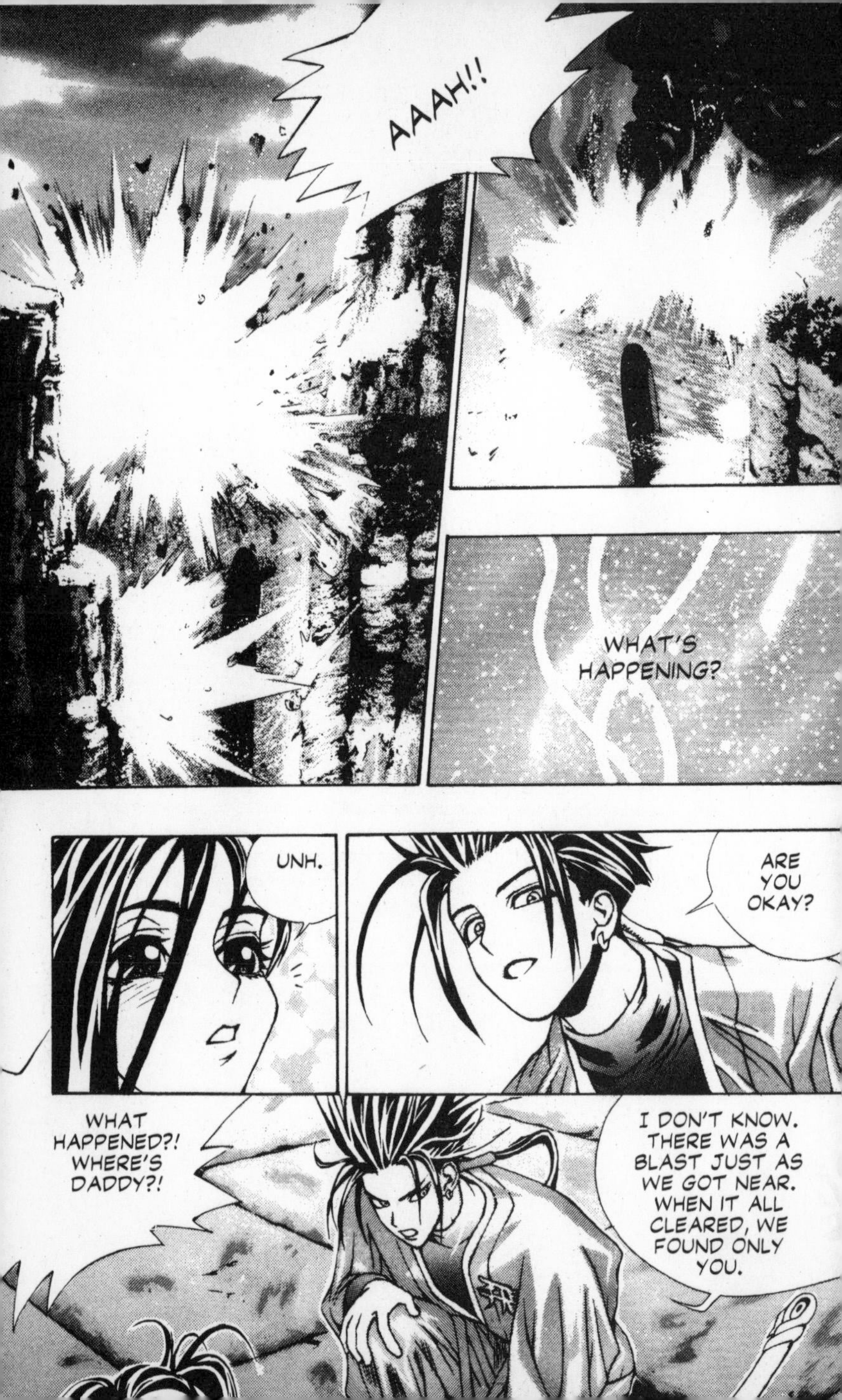
AAAH!!
WHAT'S HAPPENING?
UNH.
ARE YOU OKAY?
WHAT HAPPENED?! WHERE'S DADDY?!
I DON'T KNOW. THERE WAS A BLAST JUST AS WE GOT NEAR. WHEN IT ALL CLEARED, WE FOUND ONLY YOU.

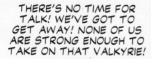

THERE'S NO TIME FOR TALK! WE'VE GOT TO GET AWAY! NONE OF US ARE STRONG ENOUGH TO TAKE ON THAT VALKYRIE!

A VALKYRIE? HER?

RIGHT! ONE OF THE 12 POWERFUL SERVANTS OF THE RESURRECTED GODDESS, FREYA!

THERE'S SOMETHING FAMILIAR...

GEO!! GASP!!

WHO ARE YOU, ANYWAY?

NO TIME! AFTER WE ESCAPE, WE CAN TALK ALL YOU WANT!

BUT CHAOS!! WHAT ABOUT THE OTHERS?!

IRIS...IT LOOKS LIKE...

WHY WON'T YOU LISTEN?

I'M AFRAID YOU'D BETTER EXPECT THE WORST. THAT EXPLOSION...

HEY! SOMEONE'S COMING FROM FAYON!

HUFF HUFF HUFF

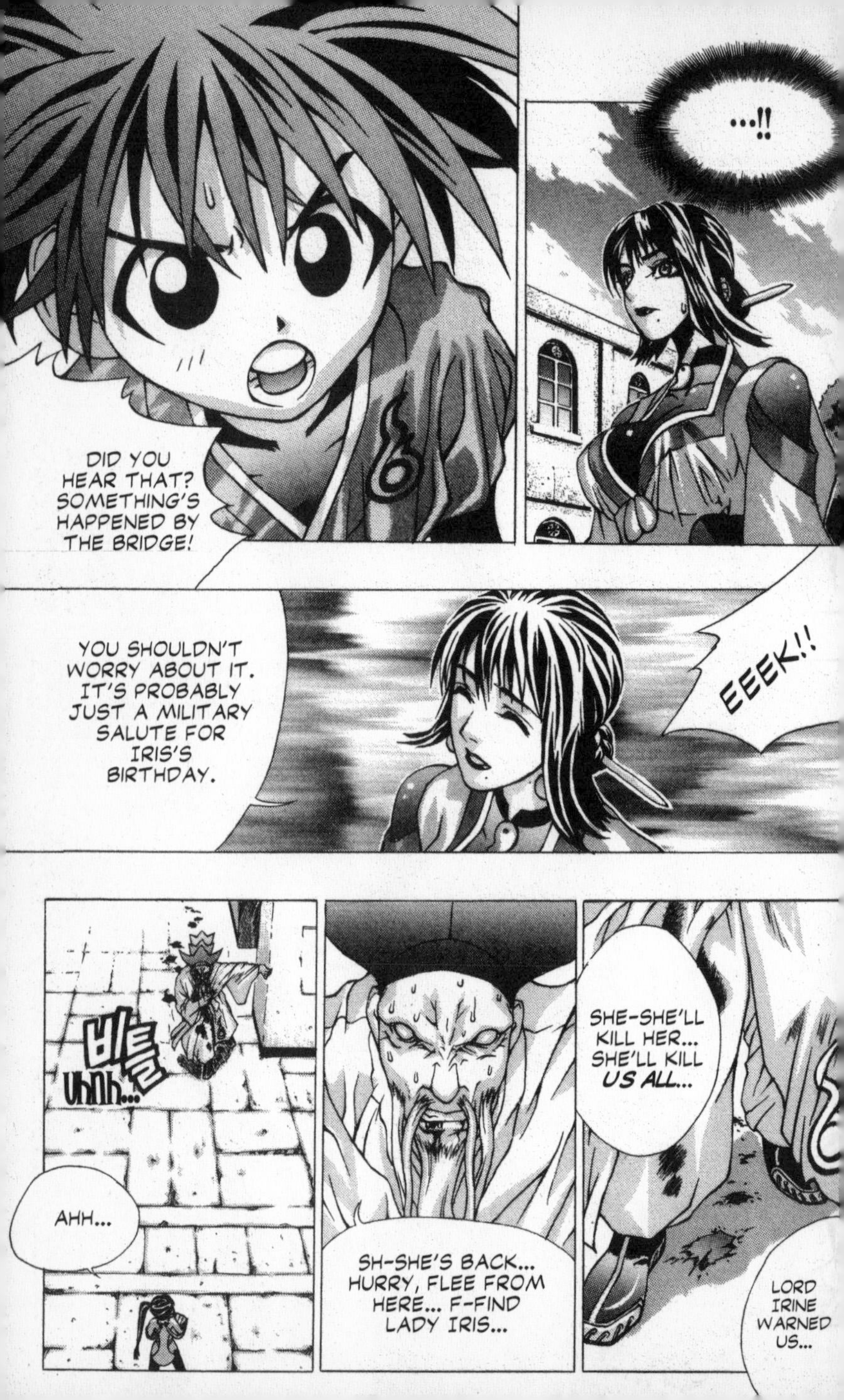
DID YOU HEAR THAT? SOMETHING'S HAPPENED BY THE BRIDGE!
...!!
YOU SHOULDN'T WORRY ABOUT IT. IT'S PROBABLY JUST A MILITARY SALUTE FOR IRIS'S BIRTHDAY.
EEEK!!
비틀
Uhnh...
AHH...
SH-SHE'S BACK... HURRY, FLEE FROM HERE... F-FIND LADY IRIS...
SHE-SHE'LL KILL HER... SHE'LL KILL US ALL...
LORD IRINE WARNED US...

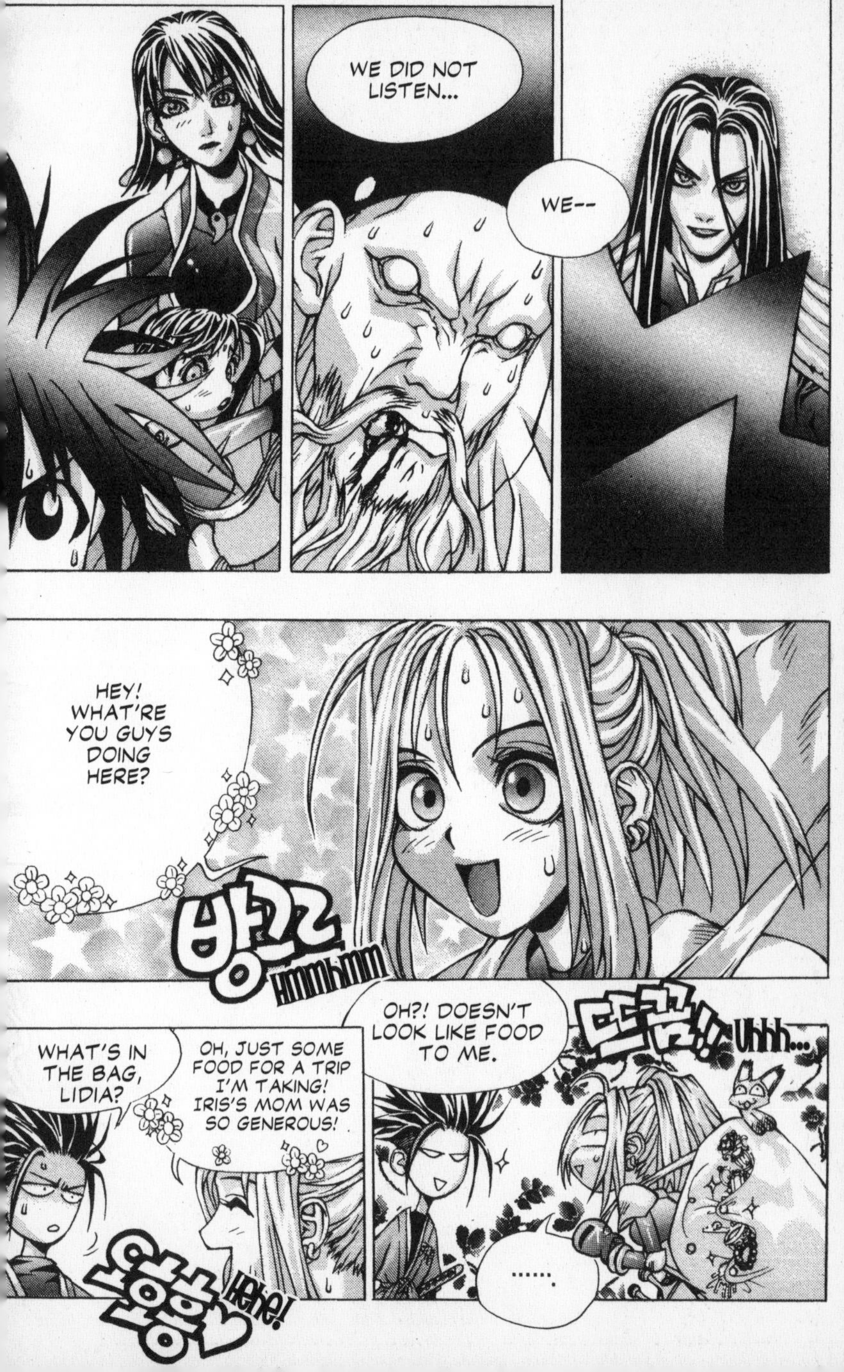
WE DID NOT LISTEN...
WE--
HEY! WHAT'RE YOU GUYS DOING HERE?
HMMHMM
WHAT'S IN THE BAG, LIDIA?
OH, JUST SOME FOOD FOR A TRIP I'M TAKING! IRIS'S MOM WAS SO GENEROUS!
Hehe!
OH?! DOESN'T LOOK LIKE FOOD TO ME.
Uhhh...
....

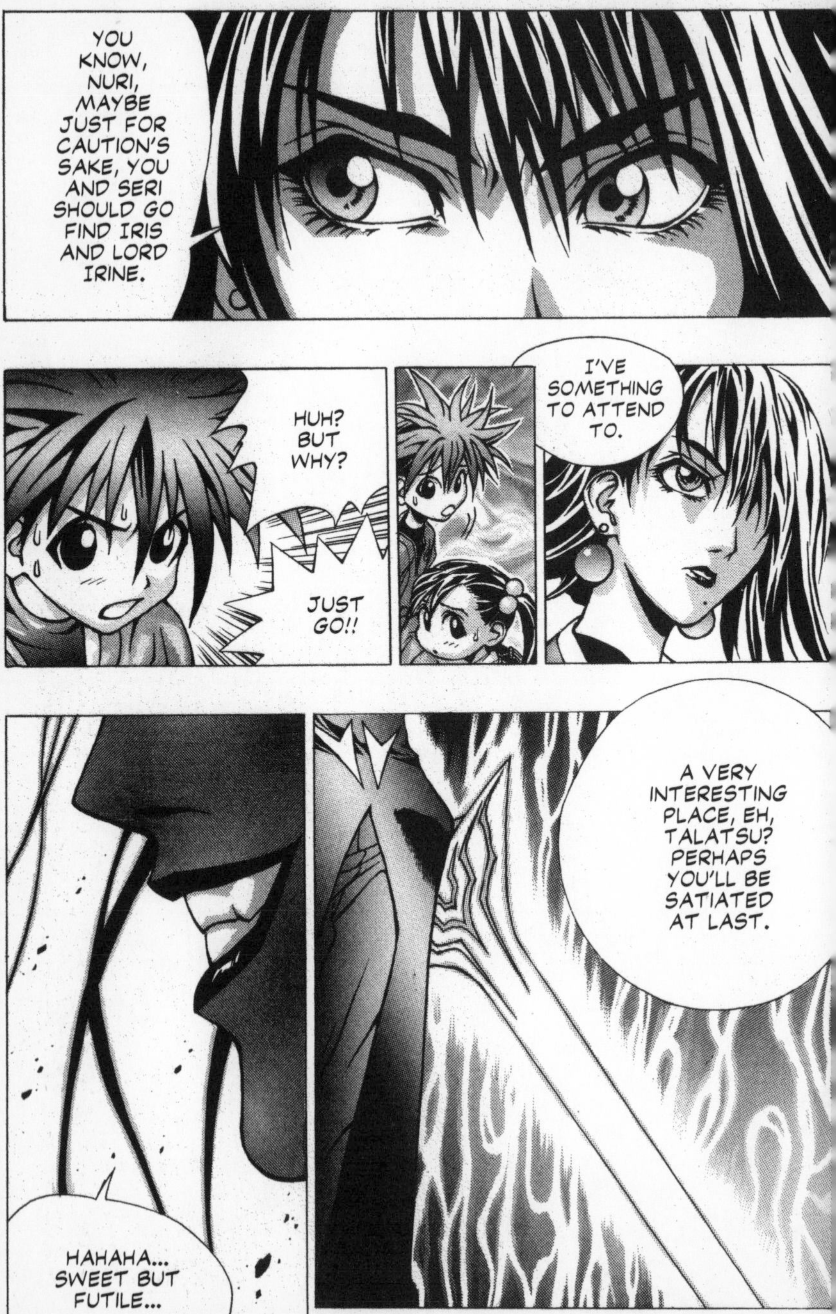
YOU KNOW, NURI, MAYBE JUST FOR CAUTION'S SAKE, YOU AND SERI SHOULD GO FIND IRIS AND LORD IRINE.
HUH? BUT WHY?
JUST GO!!
I'VE SOMETHING TO ATTEND TO.
HAHAHA... SWEET BUT FUTILE...
A VERY INTERESTING PLACE, EH, TALATSU? PERHAPS YOU'LL BE SATIATED AT LAST.

RAGNAROK

라그나로크

INTO THE ABYSS

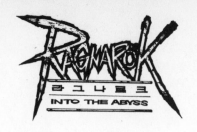

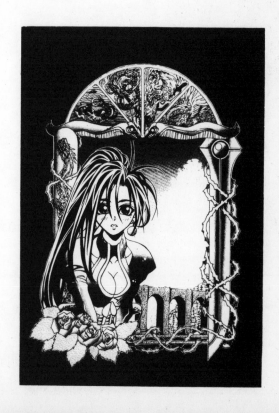

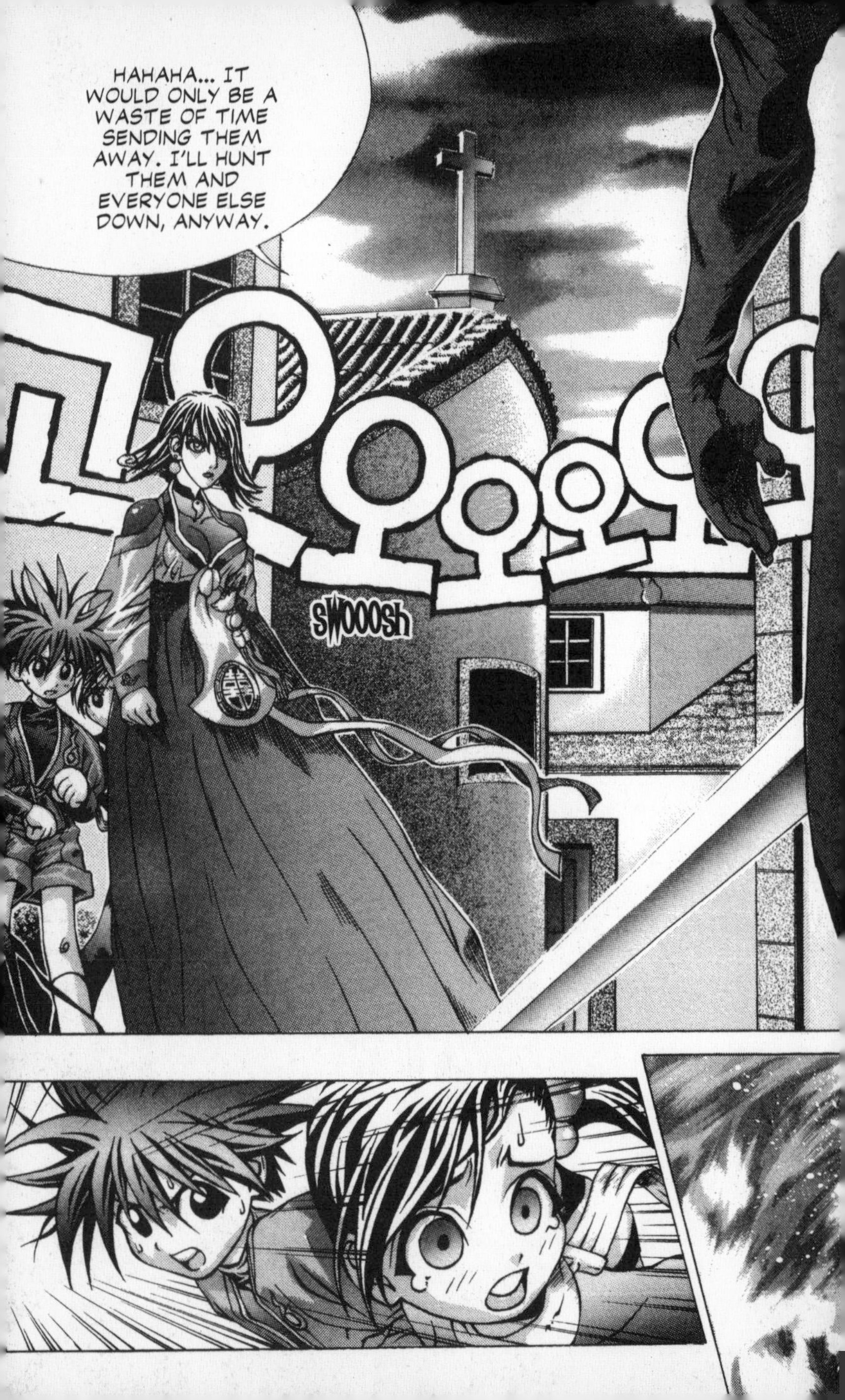
HAHAHA... IT WOULD ONLY BE A WASTE OF TIME SENDING THEM AWAY. I'LL HUNT THEM AND EVERYONE ELSE DOWN, ANYWAY.
SWOOOSH

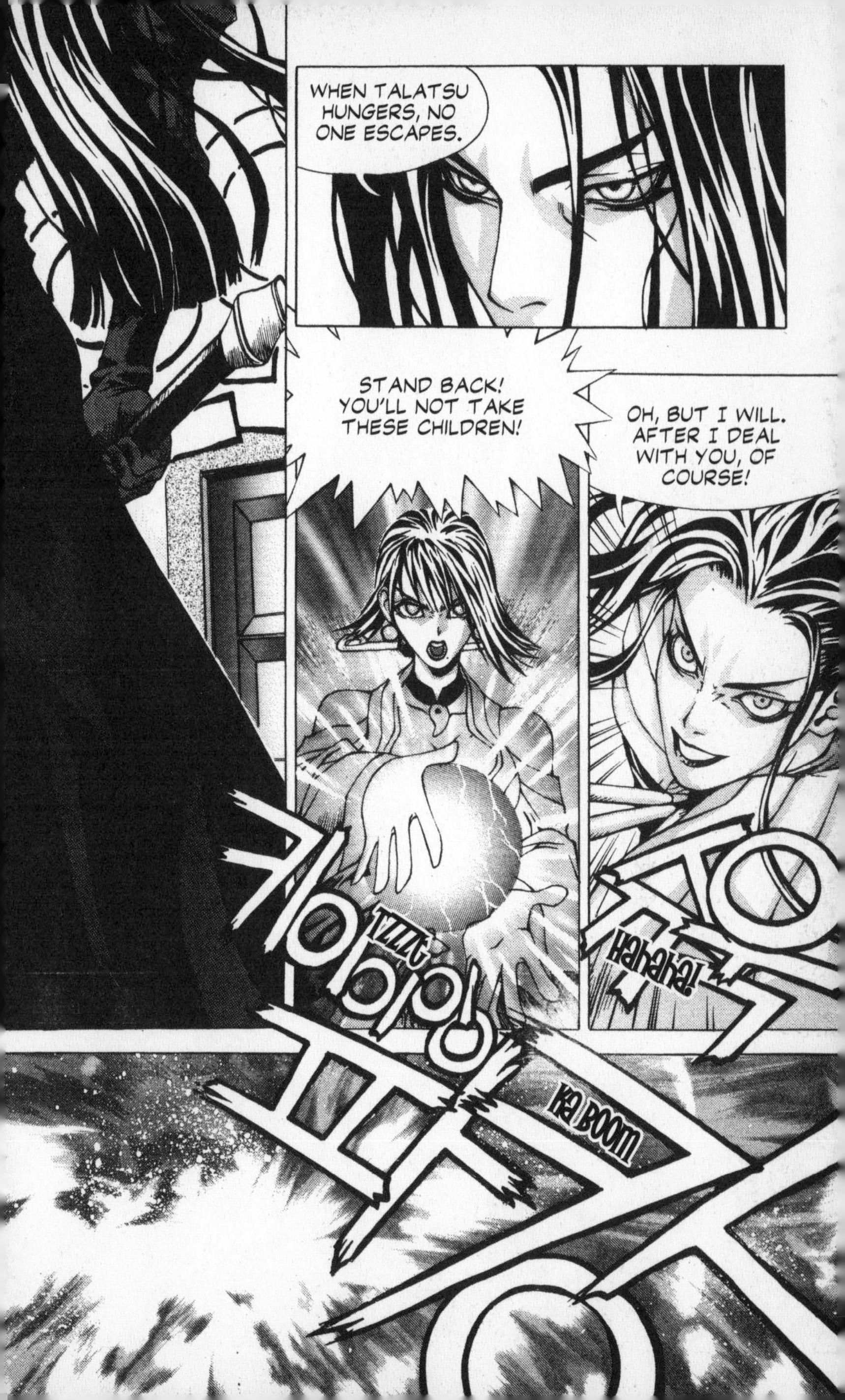
WHEN TALATSU HUNGERS, NO ONE ESCAPES.
STAND BACK! YOU'LL NOT TAKE THESE CHILDREN!
TZZZT
OH, BUT I WILL. AFTER I DEAL WITH YOU, OF COURSE!
HAHAHA!
KA BOOM

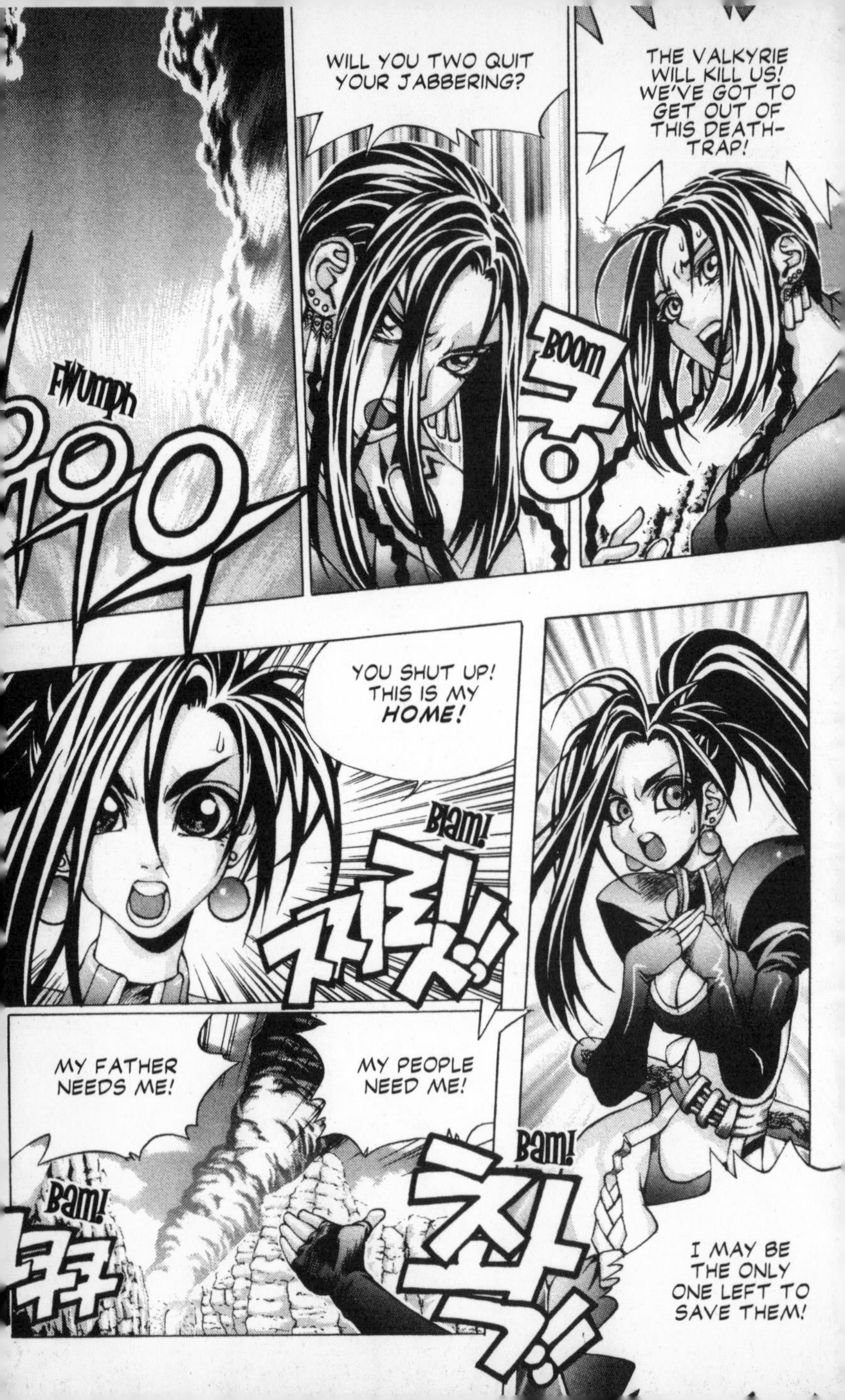
FWUMPH
WILL YOU TWO QUIT YOUR JABBERING?
THE VALKYRIE WILL KILL US! WE'VE GOT TO GET OUT OF THIS DEATH-TRAP!
BOOM
YOU SHUT UP! THIS IS MY HOME!
BLAM!
MY FATHER NEEDS ME!
MY PEOPLE NEED ME!
BAM!
BAM!
I MAY BE THE ONLY ONE LEFT TO SAVE THEM!

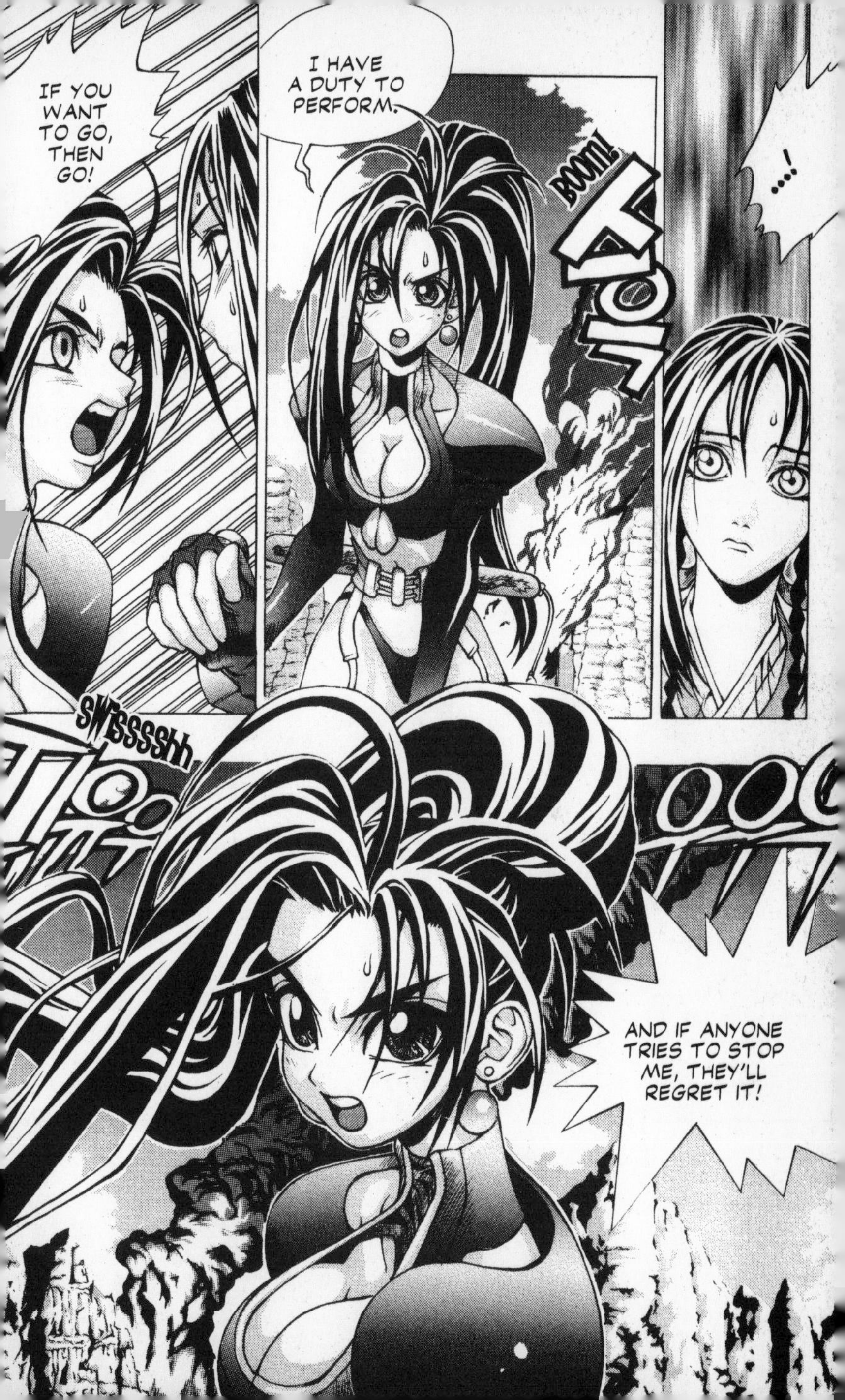
IF YOU WANT TO GO, THEN GO!
I HAVE A DUTY TO PERFORM.
BOOM!
...!
SWISSSSHH
AND IF ANYONE TRIES TO STOP ME, THEY'LL REGRET IT!

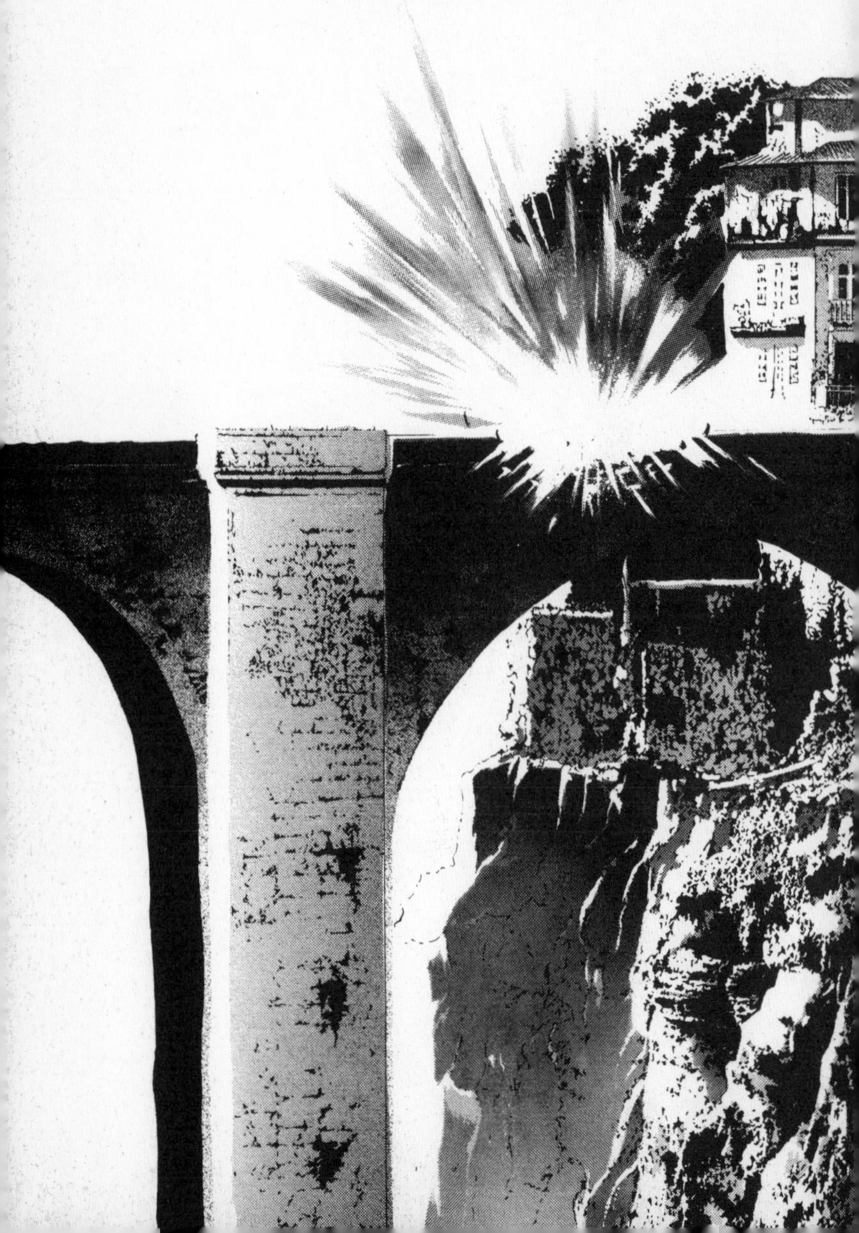

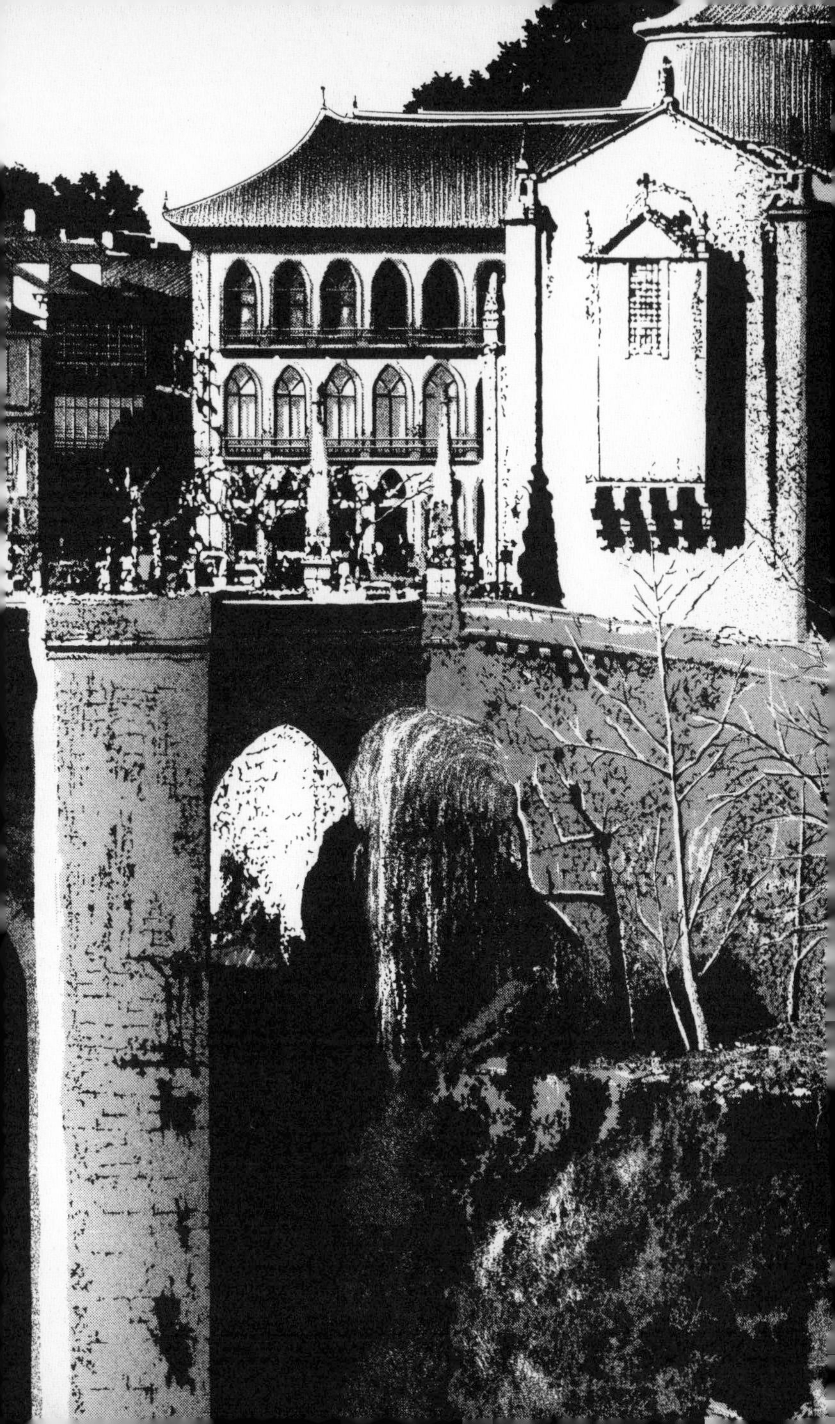

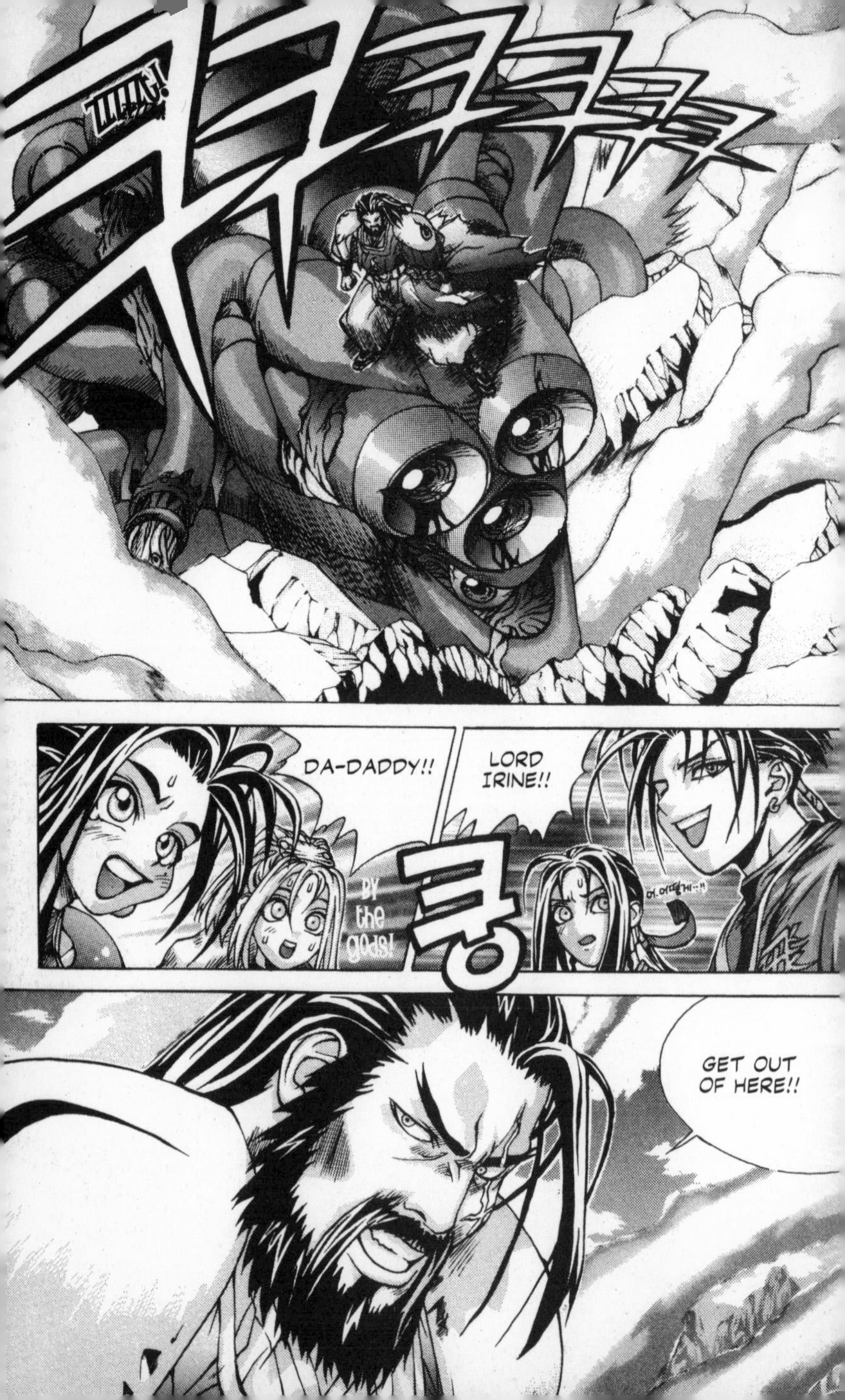
ZIIING!
DA-DADDY!!
BY the gods!
LORD IRINE!!
쿵
어.어떻게··!!
GET OUT OF HERE!!

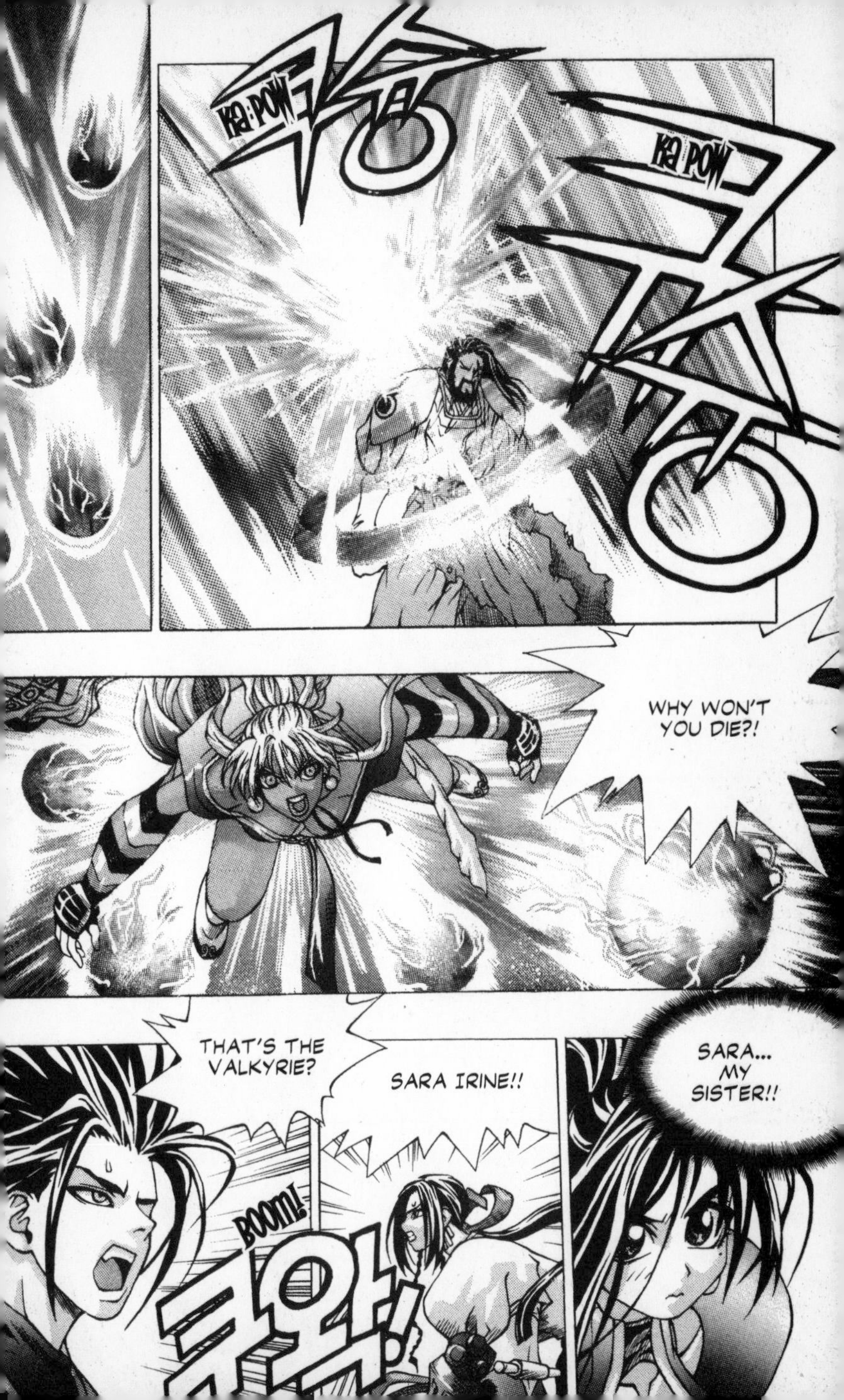
KA-POW
KA-POW
WHY WON'T YOU DIE?!
THAT'S THE VALKYRIE?
SARA IRINE!!
BOOM!
SARA... MY SISTER!!

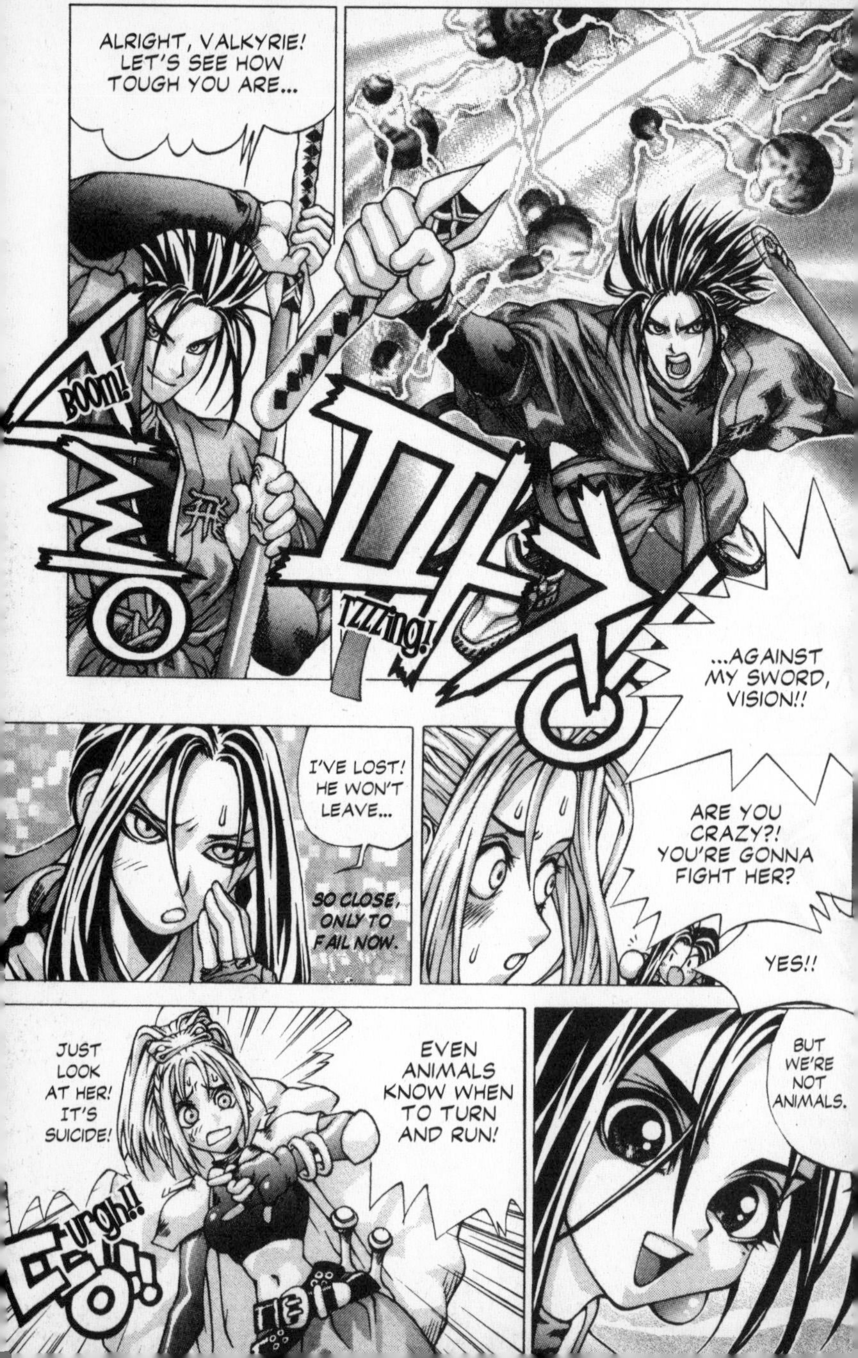
ALRIGHT, VALKYRIE! LET'S SEE HOW TOUGH YOU ARE...
BOOM!
TZZZing!
...AGAINST MY SWORD, VISION!!
I'VE LOST! HE WON'T LEAVE...
SO CLOSE, ONLY TO FAIL NOW.
ARE YOU CRAZY?! YOU'RE GONNA FIGHT HER?
YES!!
JUST LOOK AT HER! IT'S SUICIDE!
EVEN ANIMALS KNOW WHEN TO TURN AND RUN!
urgh!!
BUT WE'RE NOT ANIMALS.

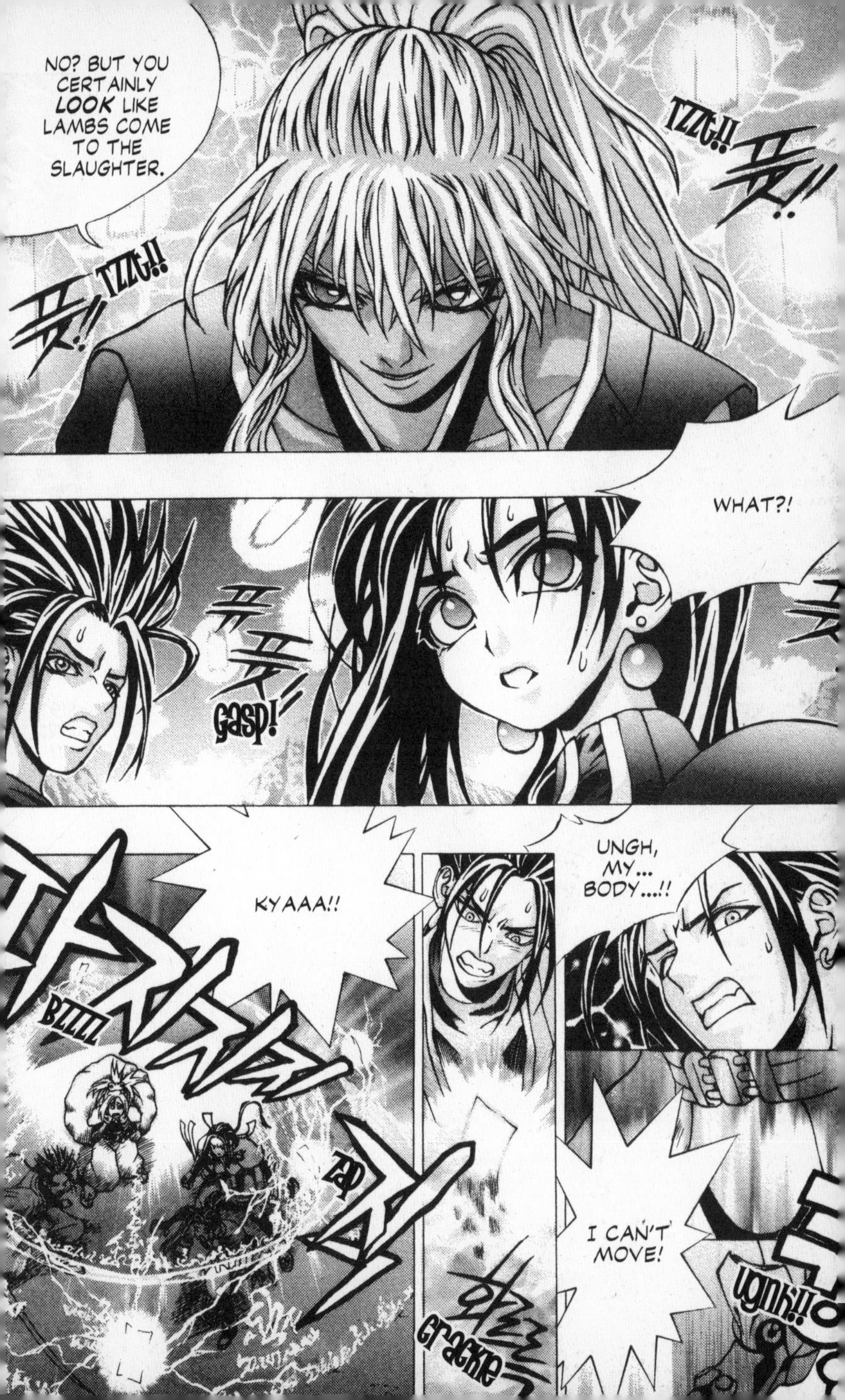
NO? BUT YOU CERTAINLY **LOOK** LIKE LAMBS COME TO THE SLAUGHTER.
TZZT!!
TZZT!!
WHAT?!
GASP!
KYAAA!!
BZZZZ
ZAP
UNGH, MY... BODY...!!
I CAN'T MOVE!
CRACKLE
UGNH!!

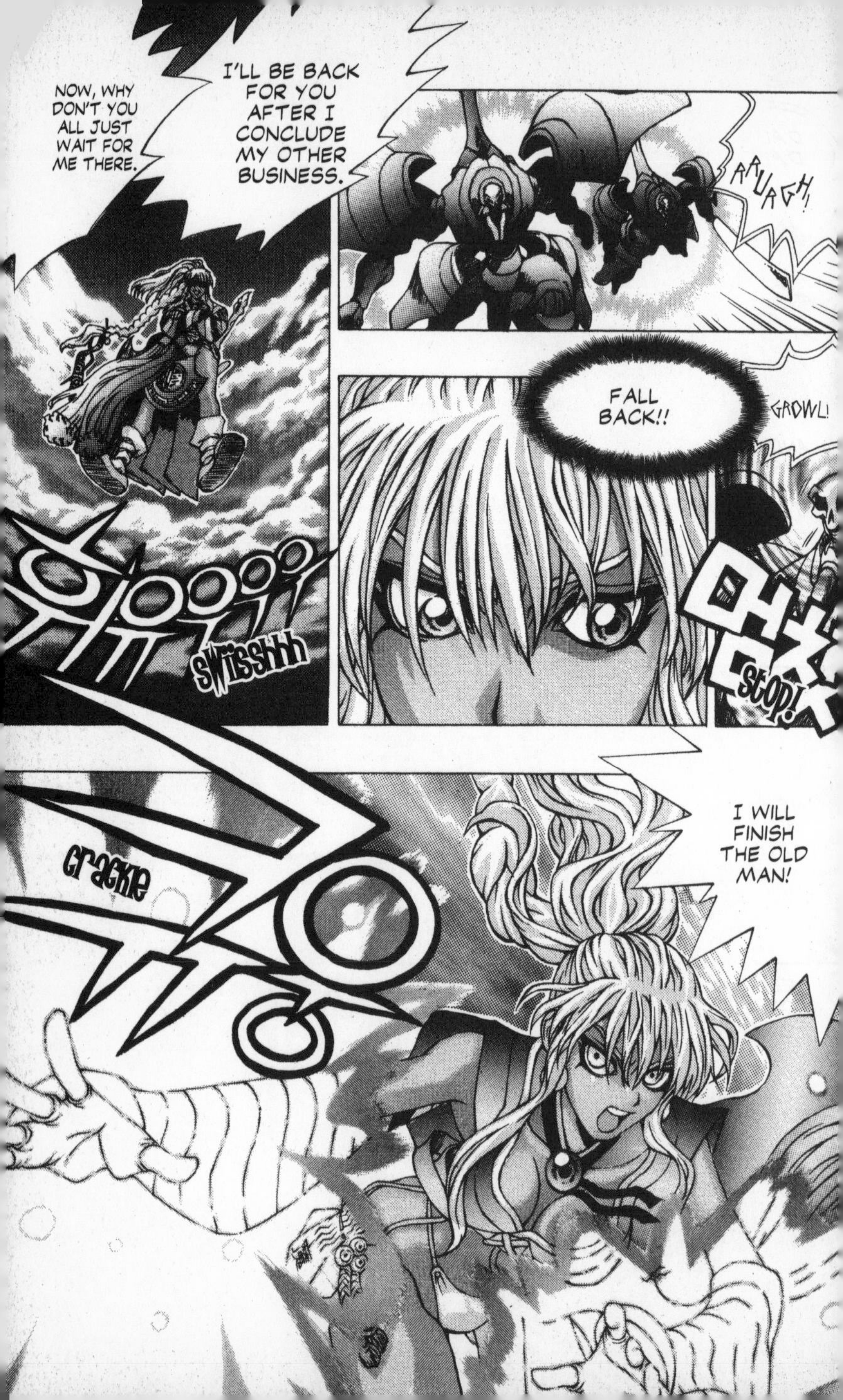
NOW, WHY DON'T YOU ALL JUST WAIT FOR ME THERE.
I'LL BE BACK FOR YOU AFTER I CONCLUDE MY OTHER BUSINESS.
SWISSHHH
RRURGH!
FALL BACK!!
GROWL!
STOP!
CRACKLE
I WILL FINISH THE OLD MAN!

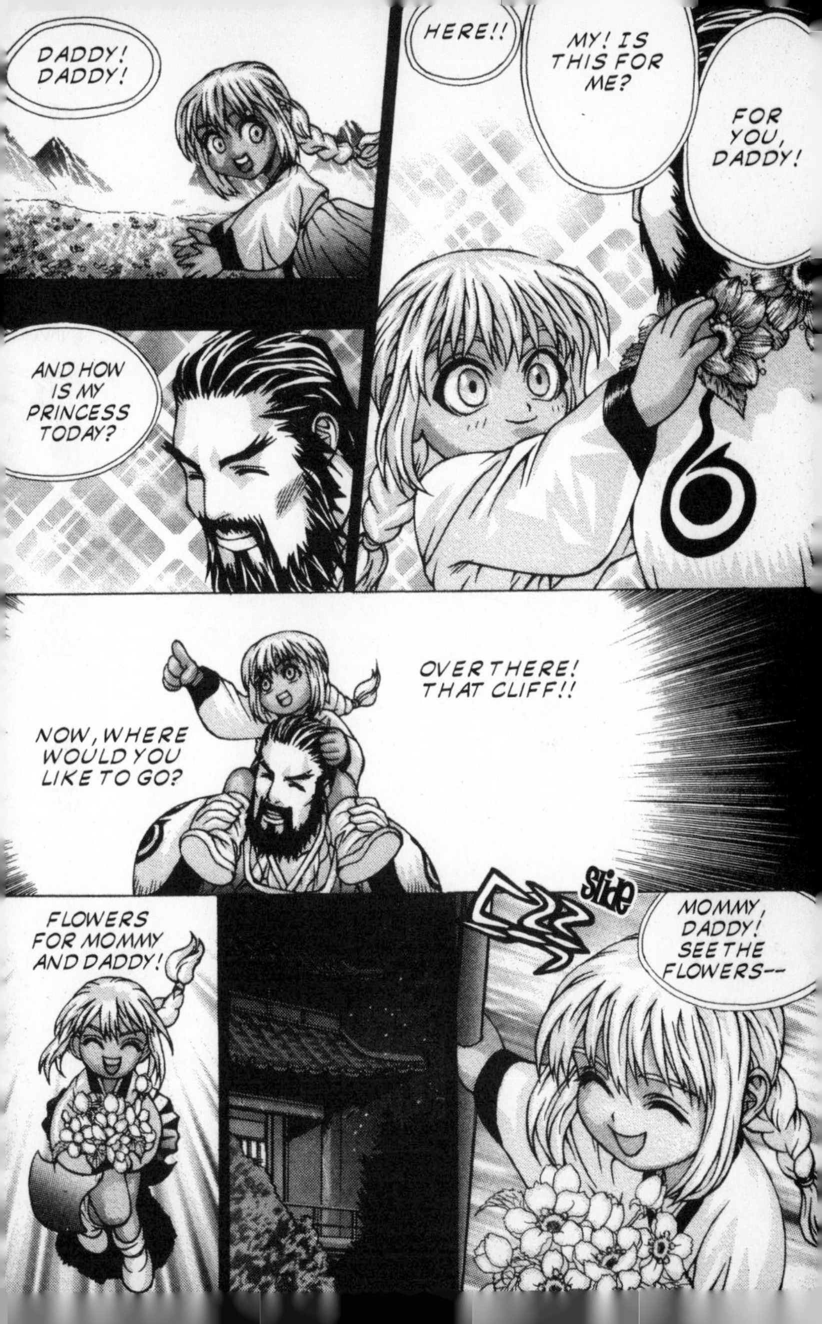
DADDY! DADDY!
AND HOW IS MY PRINCESS TODAY?
HERE!!
MY! IS THIS FOR ME?
FOR YOU, DADDY!
NOW, WHERE WOULD YOU LIKE TO GO?
OVER THERE! THAT CLIFF!!
FLOWERS FOR MOMMY AND DADDY!
slide
MOMMY, DADDY! SEE THE FLOWERS--

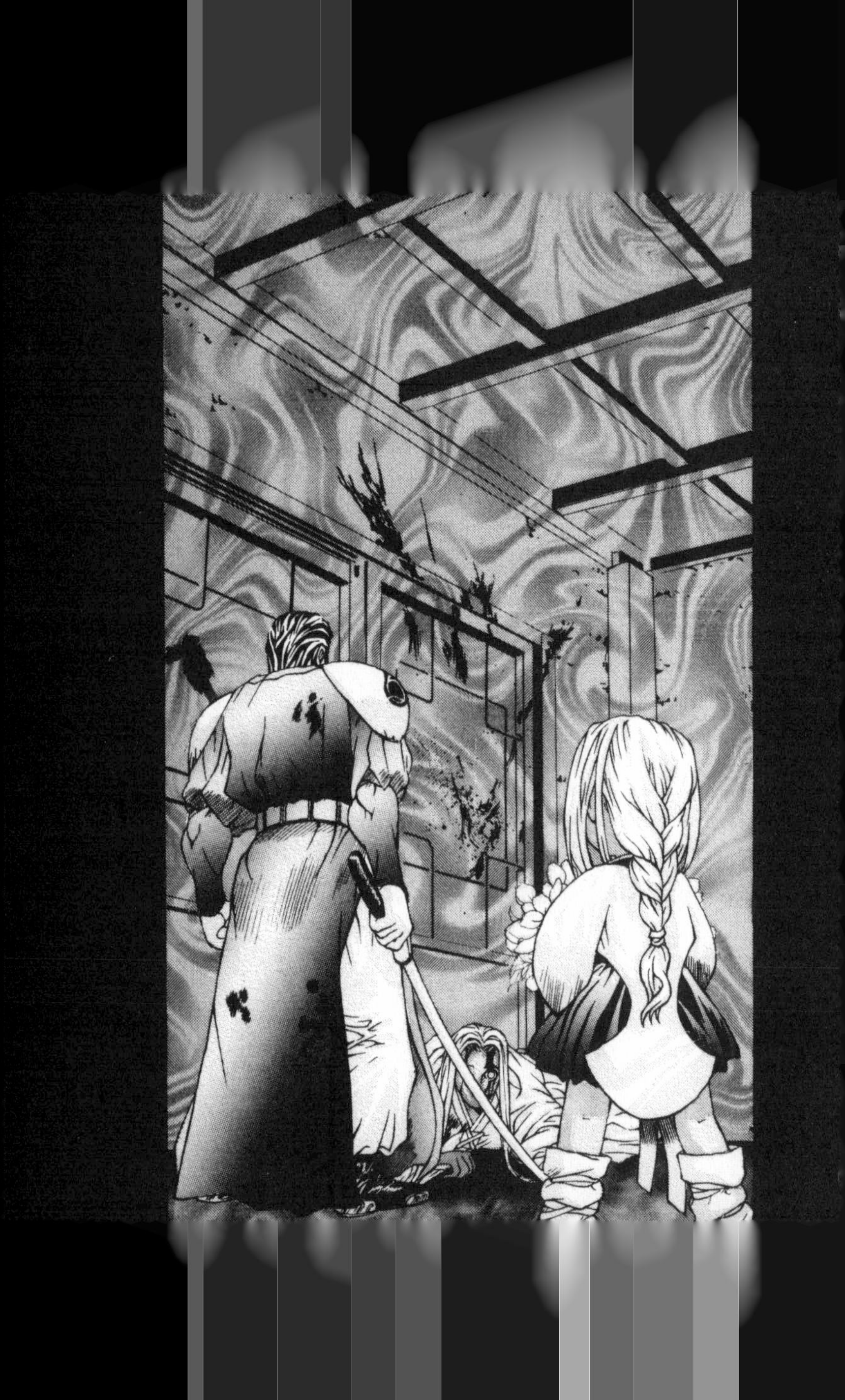

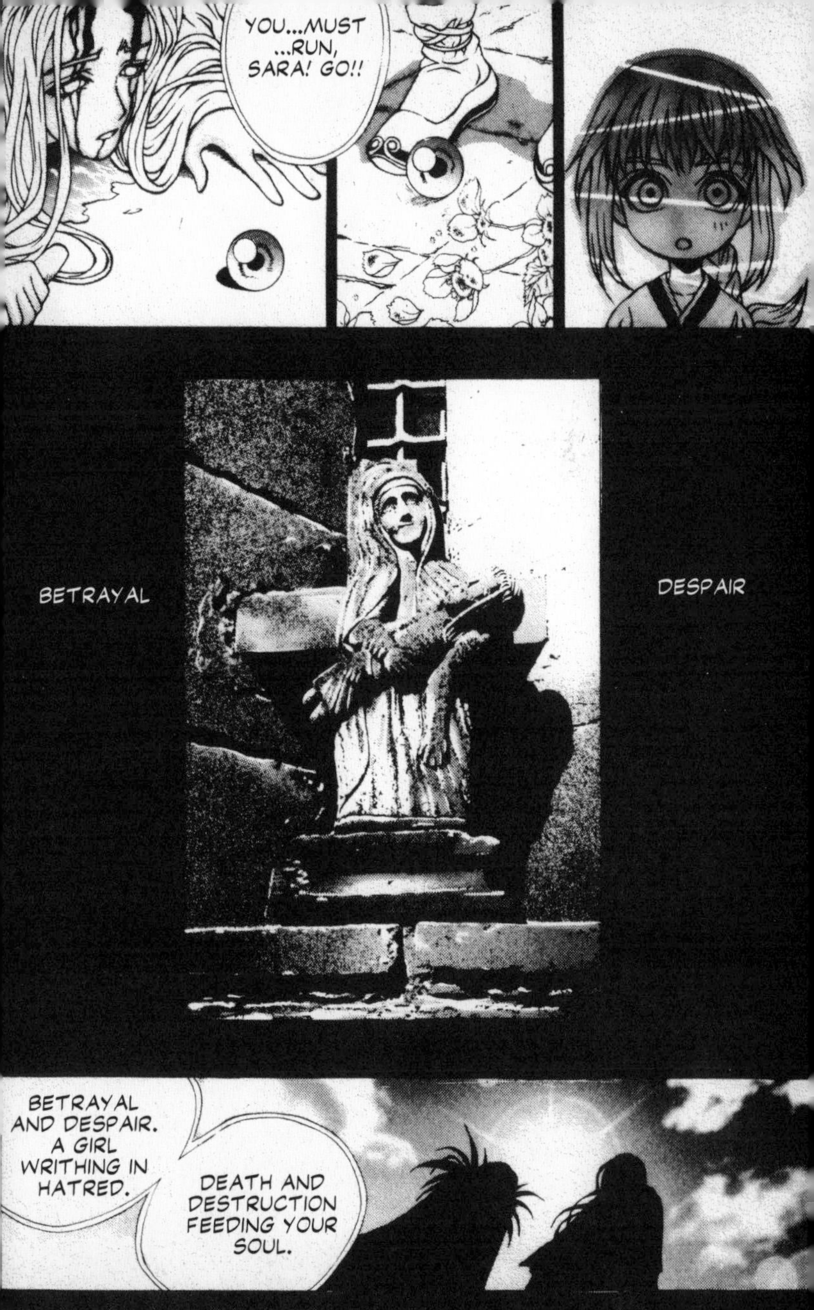
YOU...MUST ...RUN, SARA! GO!!
BETRAYAL
DESPAIR
BETRAYAL AND DESPAIR. A GIRL WRITHING IN HATRED.
DEATH AND DESTRUCTION FEEDING YOUR SOUL.

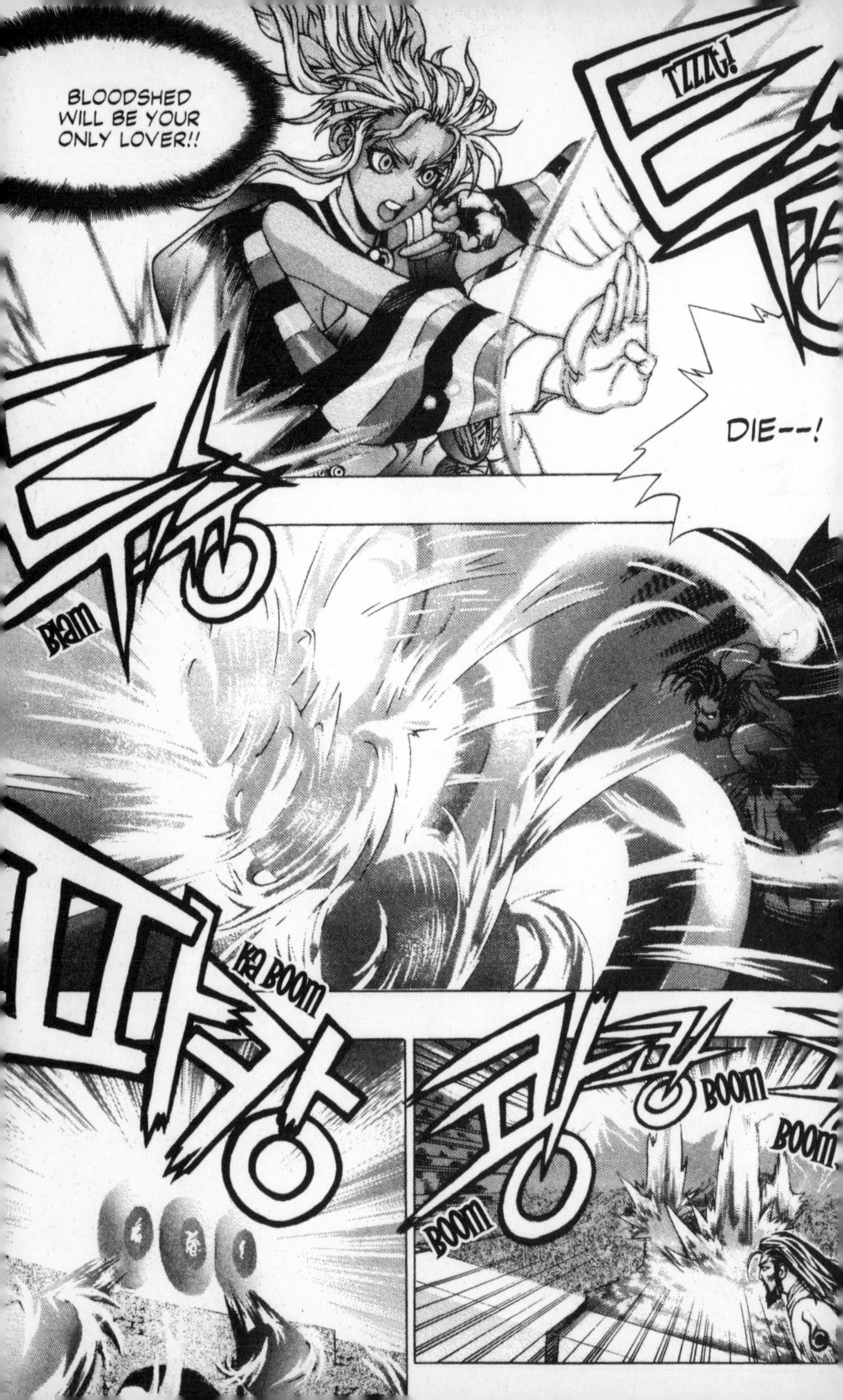
TZZZG!
BLOODSHED WILL BE YOUR ONLY LOVER!!
DIE--!
BLAM
KA BOOM
BOOM
BOOM
BOOM

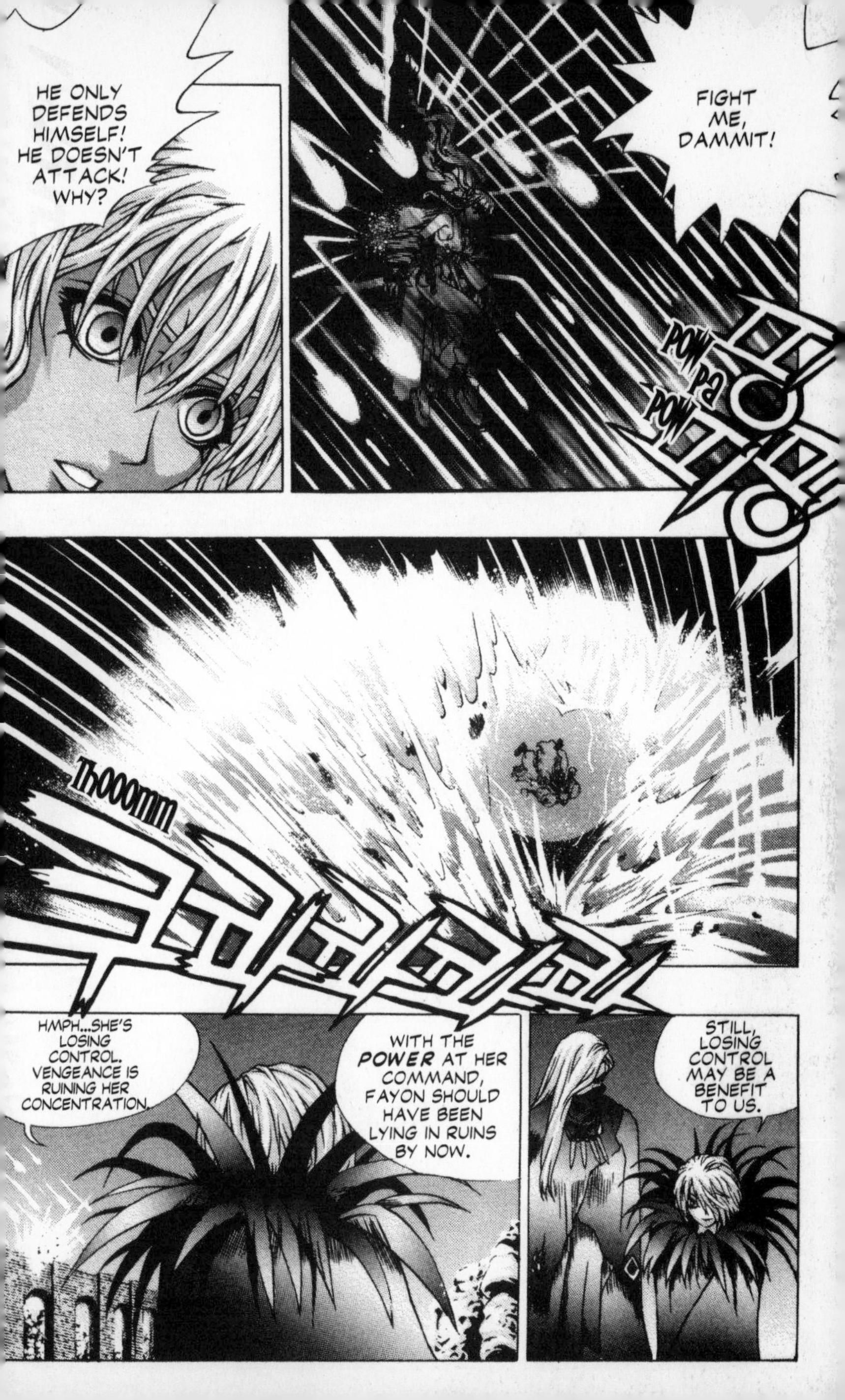
HE ONLY DEFENDS HIMSELF! HE DOESN'T ATTACK! WHY?
FIGHT ME, DAMMIT!
POW PA POW
THOOOMM
HMPH...SHE'S LOSING CONTROL. VENGEANCE IS RUINING HER CONCENTRATION.
WITH THE POWER AT HER COMMAND, FAYON SHOULD HAVE BEEN LYING IN RUINS BY NOW.
STILL, LOSING CONTROL MAY BE A BENEFIT TO US.

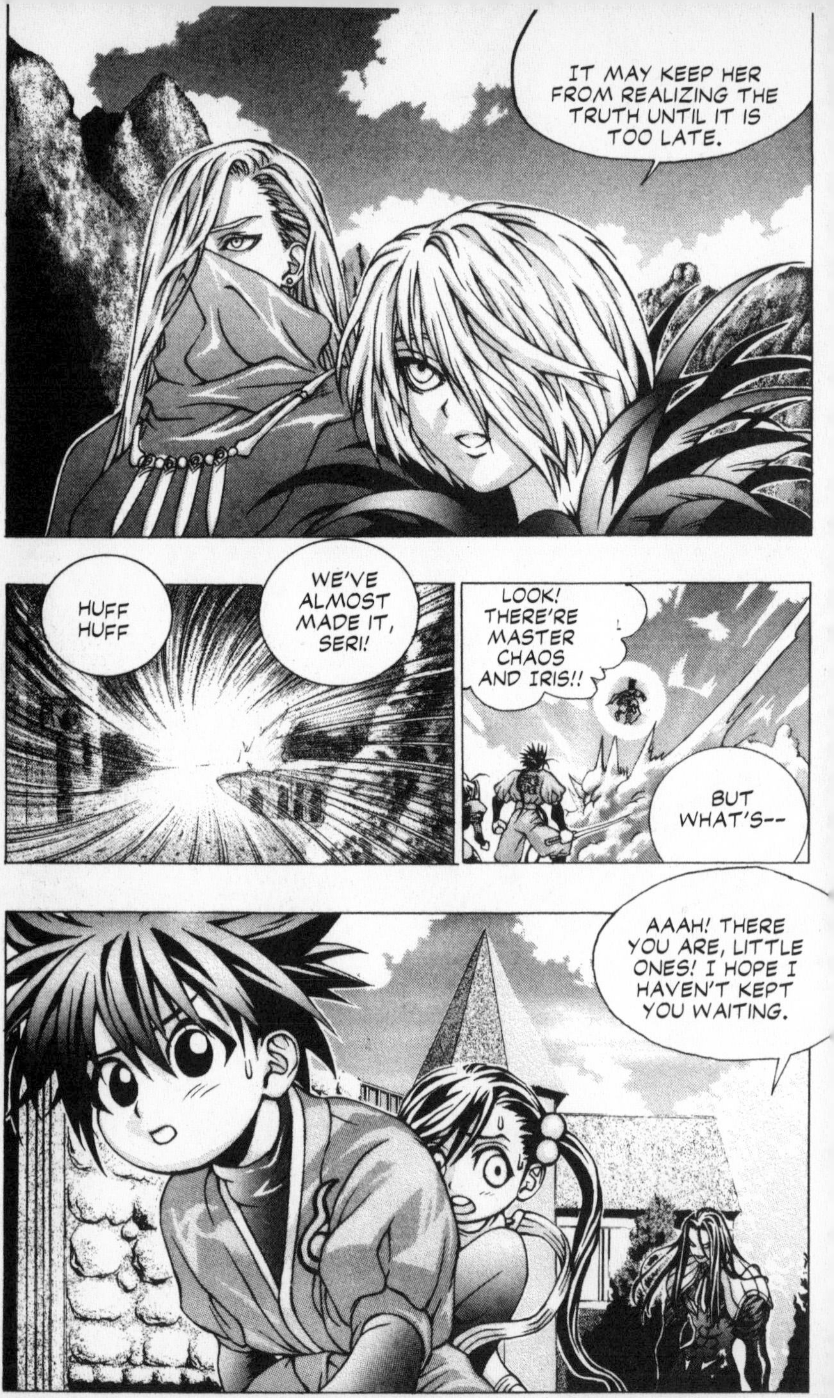
IT MAY KEEP HER FROM REALIZING THE TRUTH UNTIL IT IS TOO LATE.
HUFF HUFF
WE'VE ALMOST MADE IT, SERI!
LOOK! THERE'RE MASTER CHAOS AND IRIS!!
BUT WHAT'S--
AAAH! THERE YOU ARE, LITTLE ONES! I HOPE I HAVEN'T KEPT YOU WAITING.

RAGNAROK
라그나로크
INTO THE ABYSS

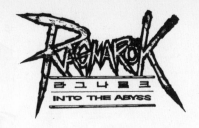

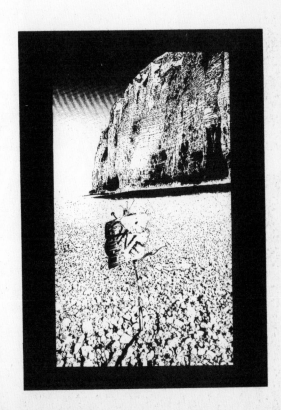

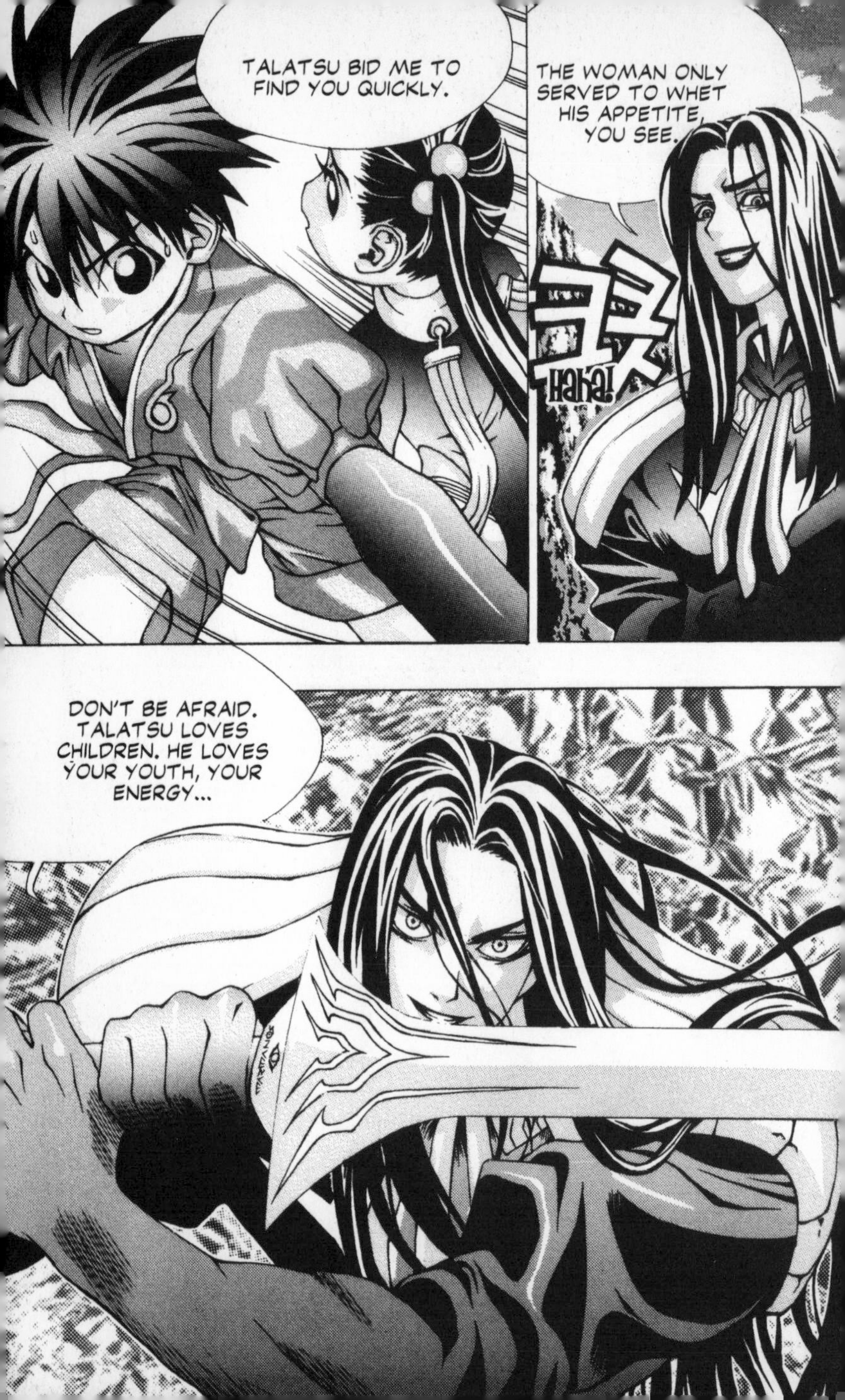
TALATSU BID ME TO FIND YOU QUICKLY.
THE WOMAN ONLY SERVED TO WHET HIS APPETITE, YOU SEE.
HAHA!
DON'T BE AFRAID. TALATSU LOVES CHILDREN. HE LOVES YOUR YOUTH, YOUR ENERGY...

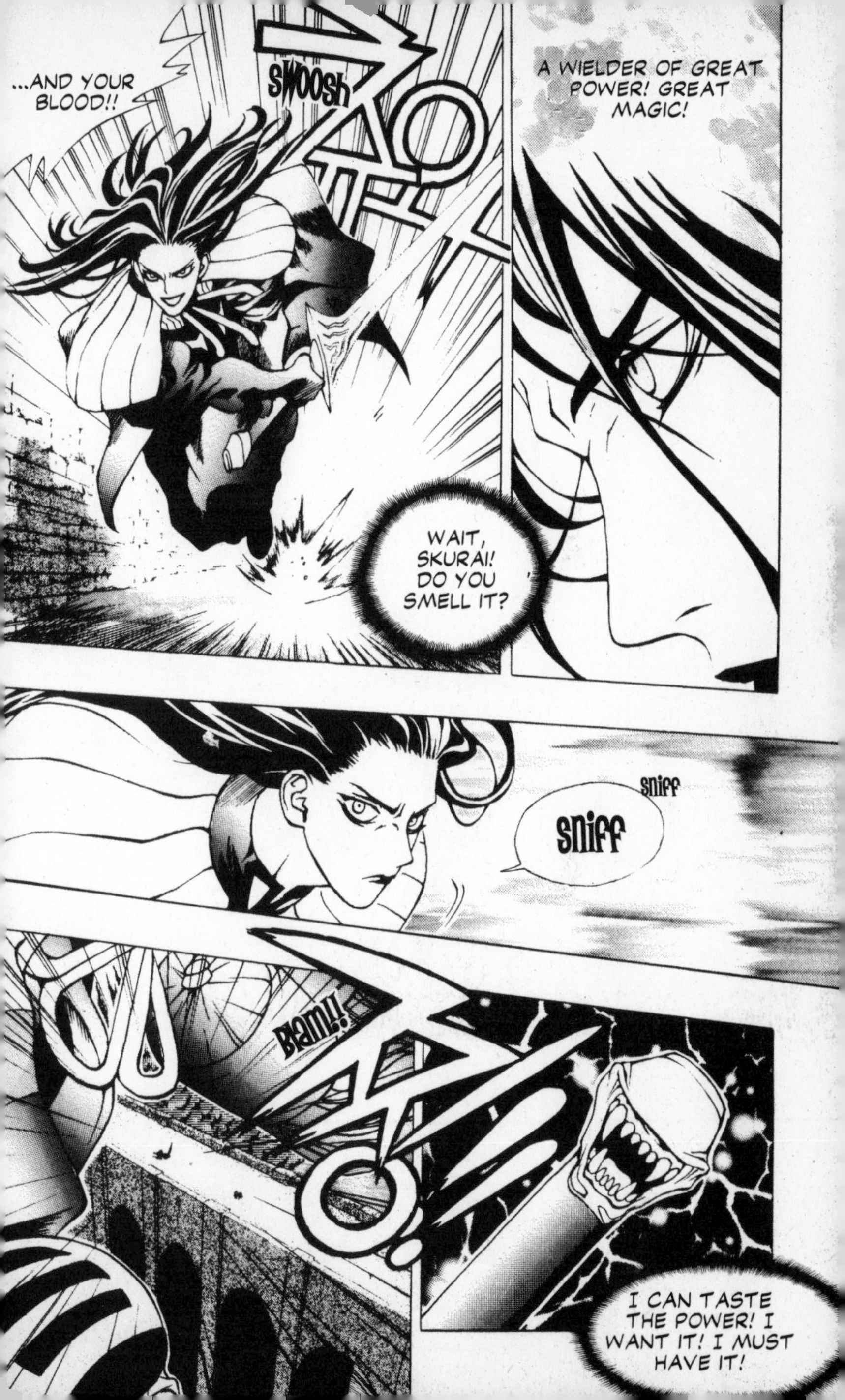
...AND YOUR BLOOD!!
SWOOSH
A WIELDER OF GREAT POWER! GREAT MAGIC!
WAIT, SKURAI! DO YOU SMELL IT?
SNIFF
SNIFF
BLAM!!
I CAN TASTE THE POWER! I WANT IT! I MUST HAVE IT!

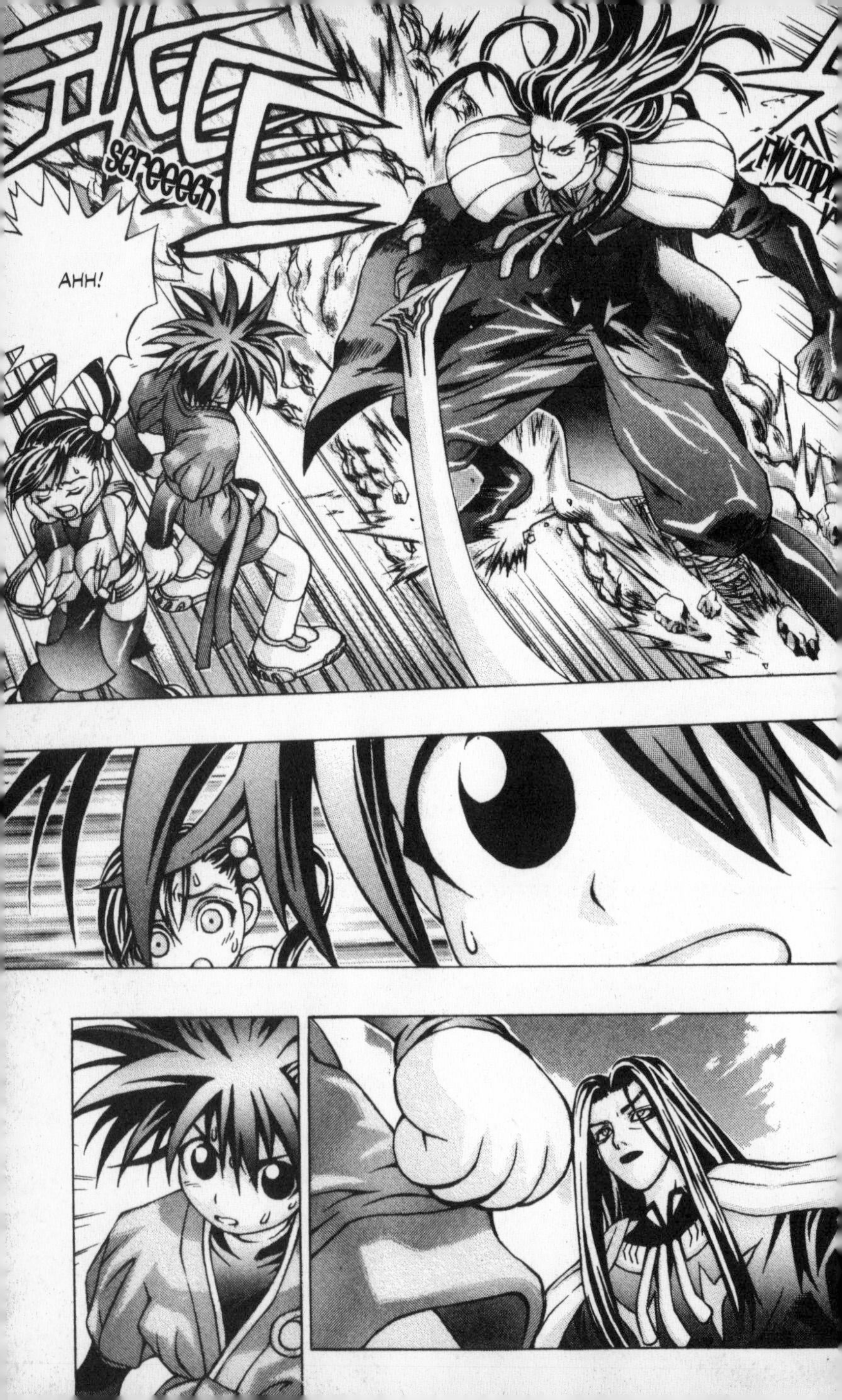
SCREEEECH
FWUMP
AHH!

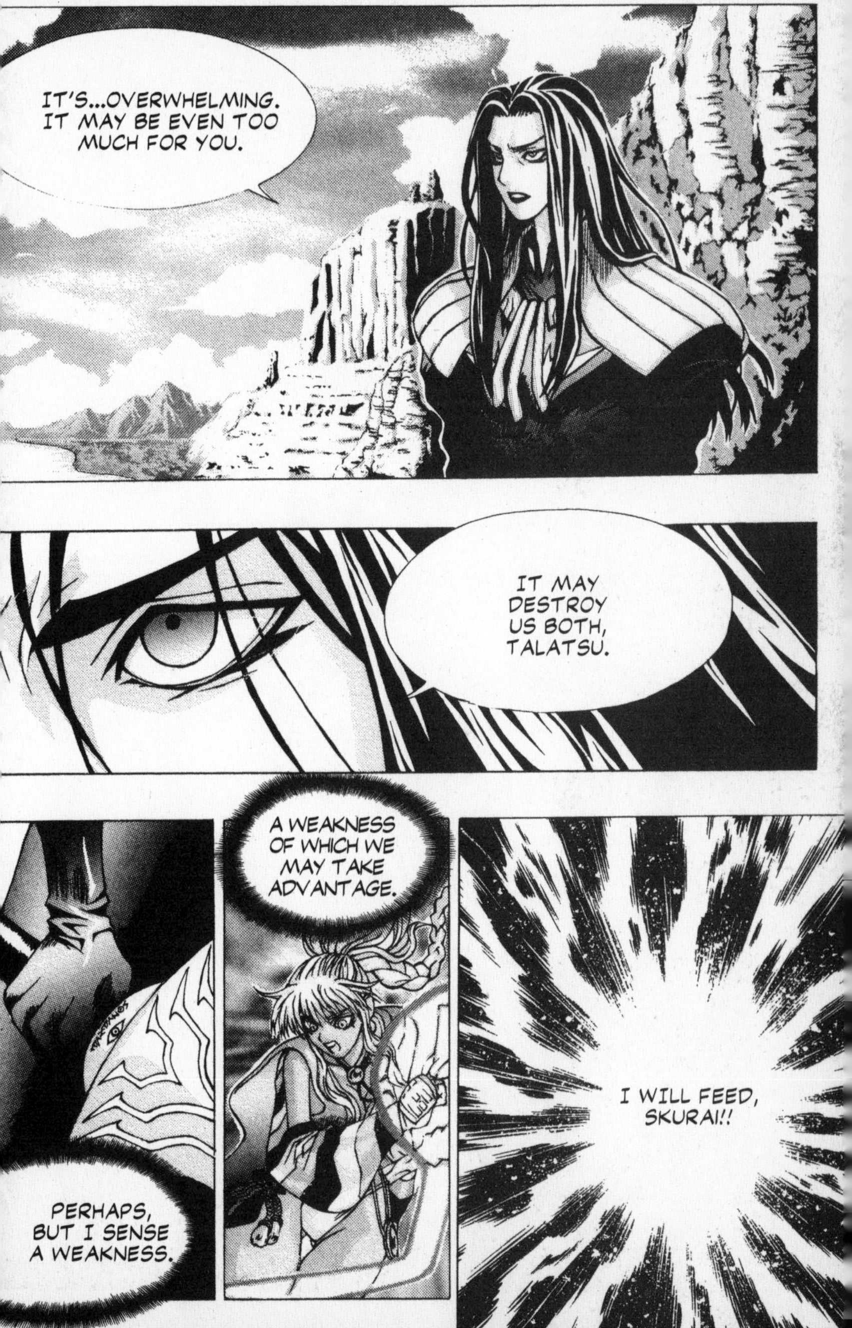
IT'S...OVERWHELMING. IT MAY BE EVEN TOO MUCH FOR YOU.
IT MAY DESTROY US BOTH, TALATSU.
PERHAPS, BUT I SENSE A WEAKNESS.
A WEAKNESS OF WHICH WE MAY TAKE ADVANTAGE.
I WILL FEED, SKURAI!!

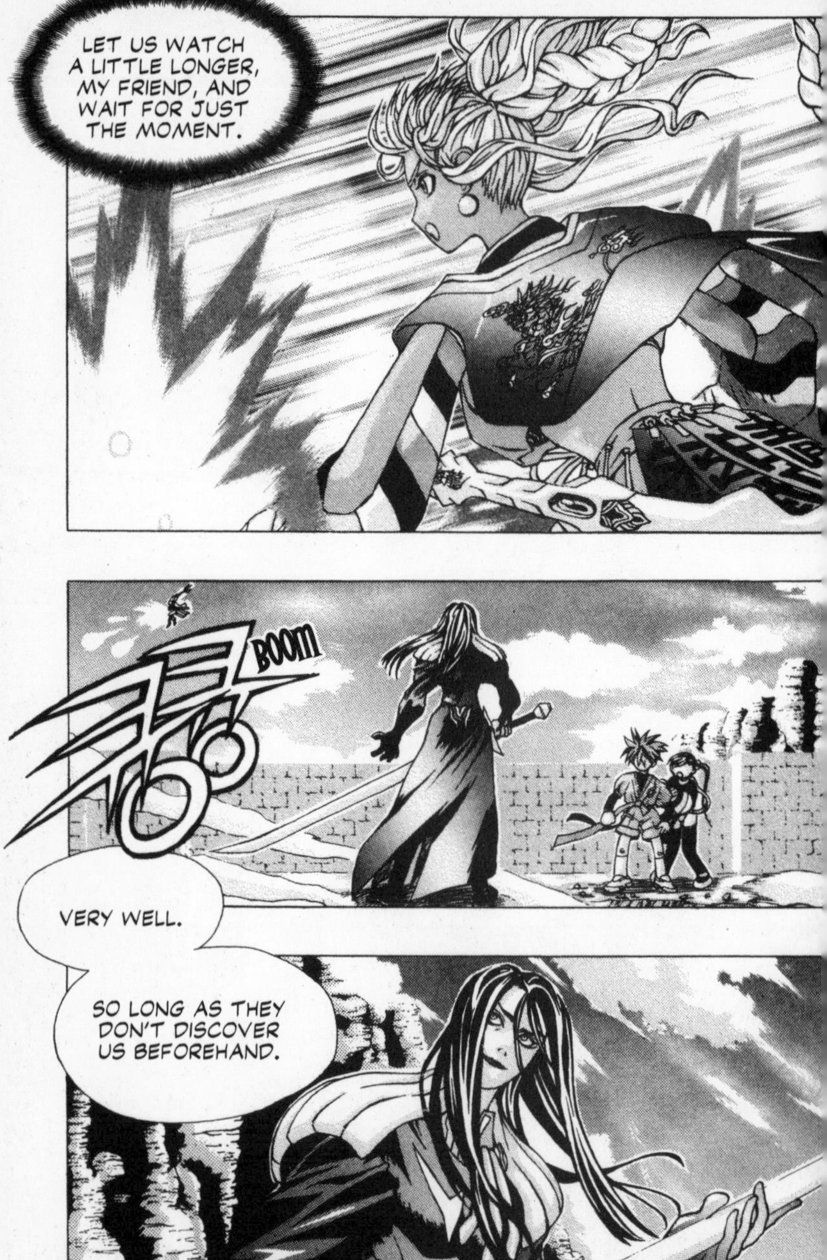
LET US WATCH A LITTLE LONGER, MY FRIEND, AND WAIT FOR JUST THE MOMENT.
BOOM
VERY WELL.
SO LONG AS THEY DON'T DISCOVER US BEFOREHAND.

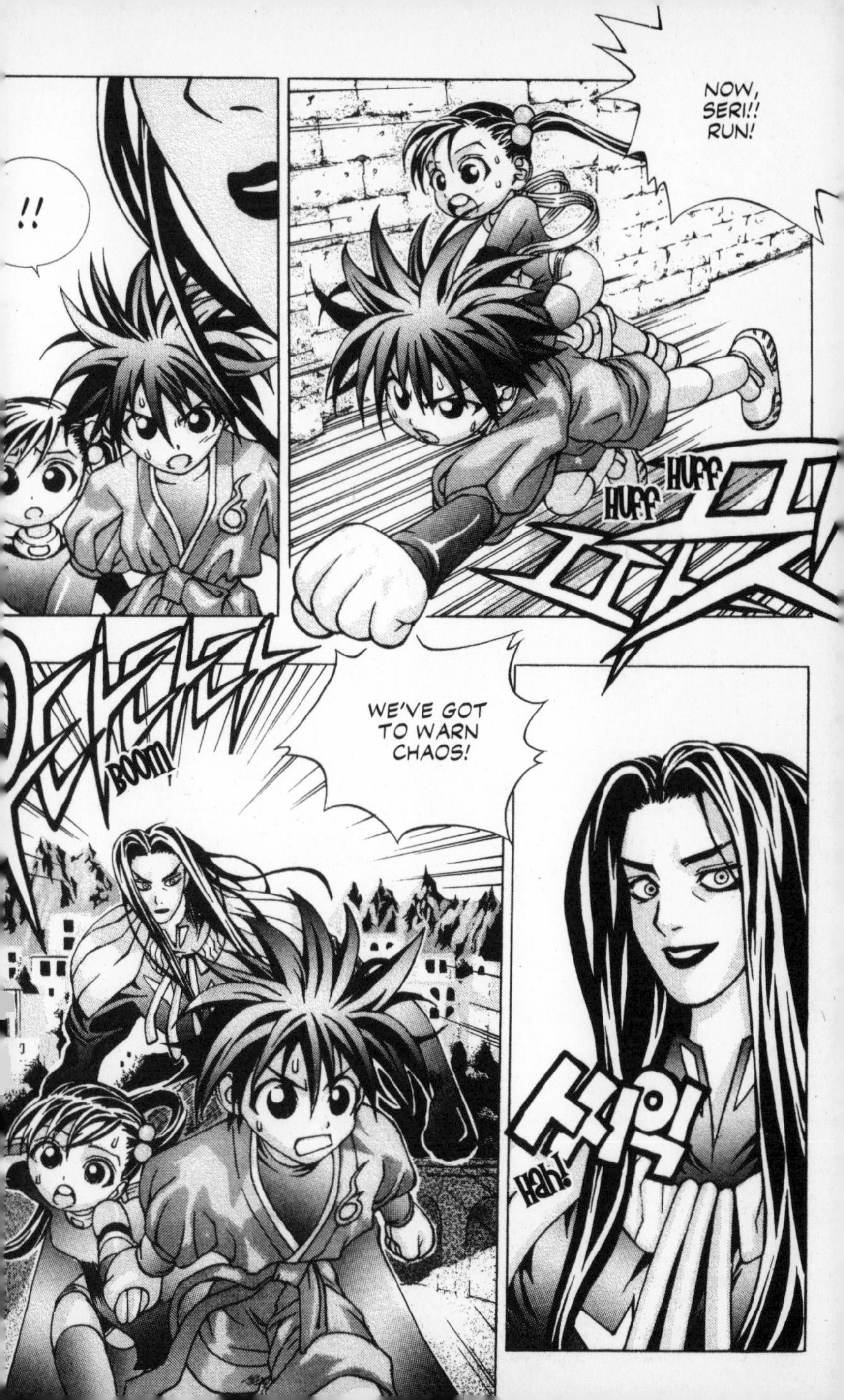
!!
NOW, SERI!! RUN!
HUFF
HUFF
BOOM
WE'VE GOT TO WARN CHAOS!
HAH!

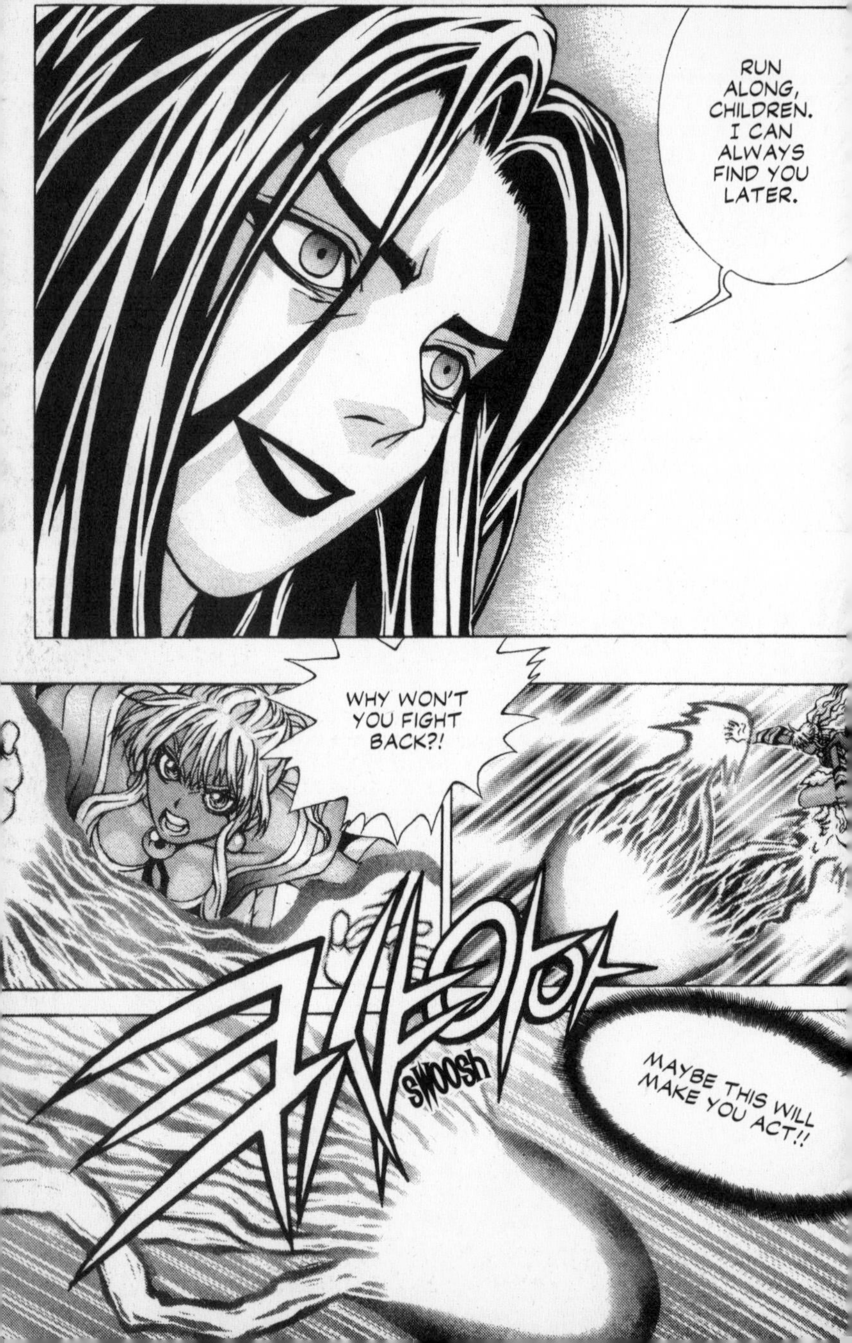
RUN ALONG, CHILDREN. I CAN ALWAYS FIND YOU LATER.
WHY WON'T YOU FIGHT BACK?!
SWOOSH
MAYBE THIS WILL MAKE YOU ACT!!

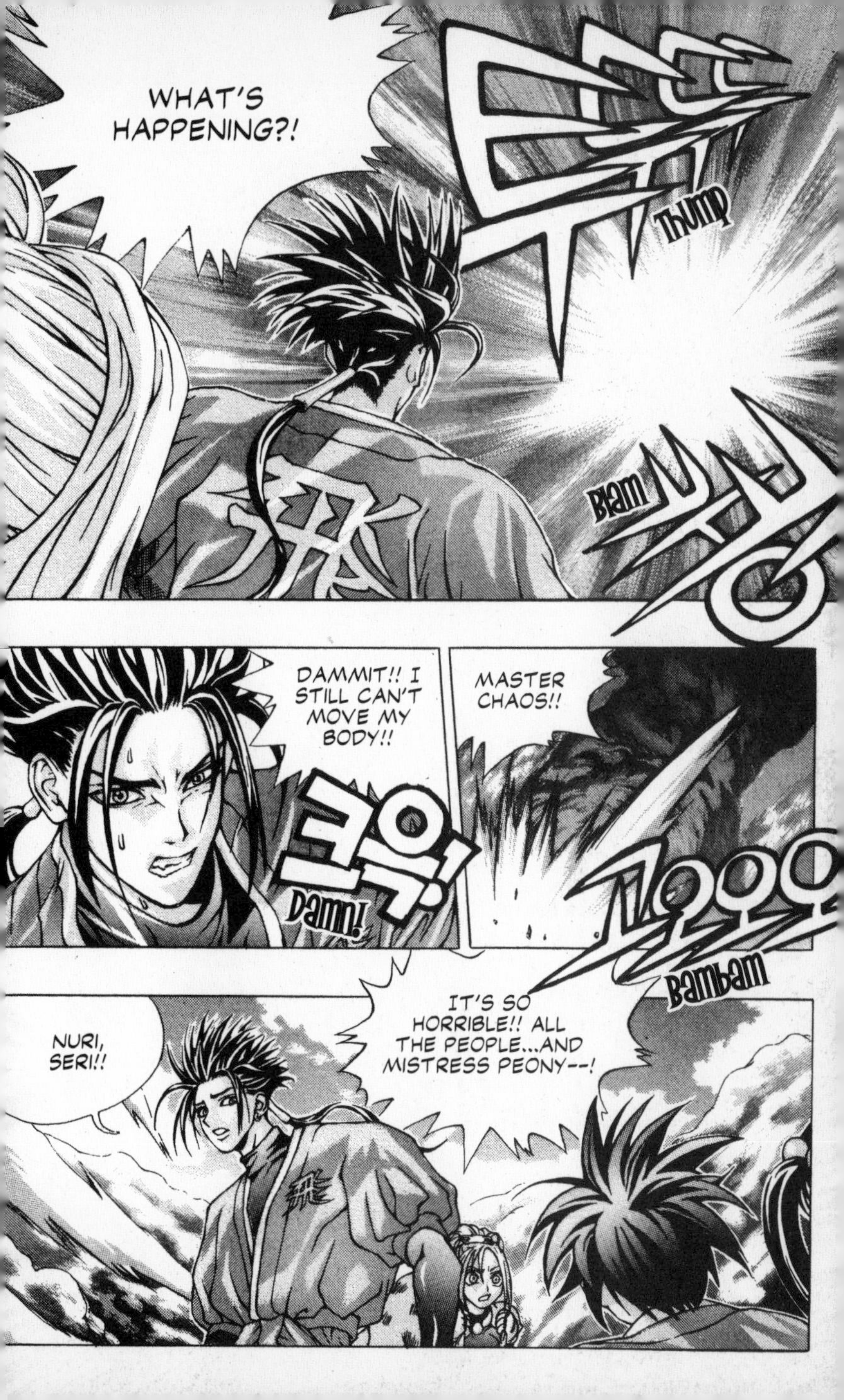
WHAT'S HAPPENING?!
THUMP
BLAM
DAMMIT!! I STILL CAN'T MOVE MY BODY!!
DAMN!
MASTER CHAOS!!
BAMBAM
NURI, SERI!!
IT'S SO HORRIBLE!! ALL THE PEOPLE...AND MISTRESS PEONY--!

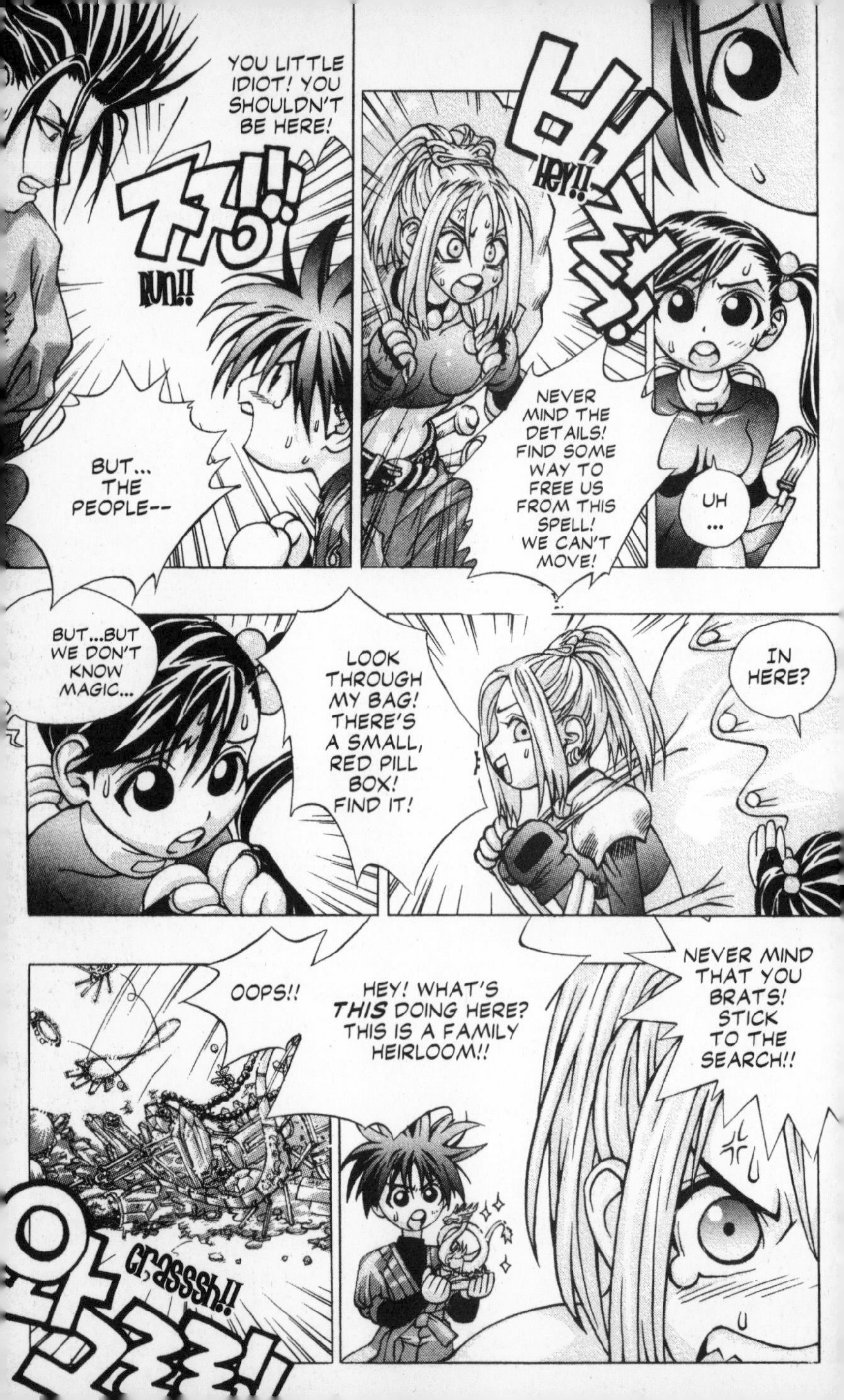
YOU LITTLE IDIOT! YOU SHOULDN'T BE HERE!
RUN!!
BUT... THE PEOPLE--
HEY!!
NEVER MIND THE DETAILS! FIND SOME WAY TO FREE US FROM THIS SPELL! WE CAN'T MOVE!
UH ...
BUT...BUT WE DON'T KNOW MAGIC...
LOOK THROUGH MY BAG! THERE'S A SMALL, RED PILL BOX! FIND IT!
IN HERE?
OOPS!!
cr,asssh!!
HEY! WHAT'S *THIS* DOING HERE? THIS IS A FAMILY HEIRLOOM!!
NEVER MIND THAT YOU BRATS! STICK TO THE SEARCH!!

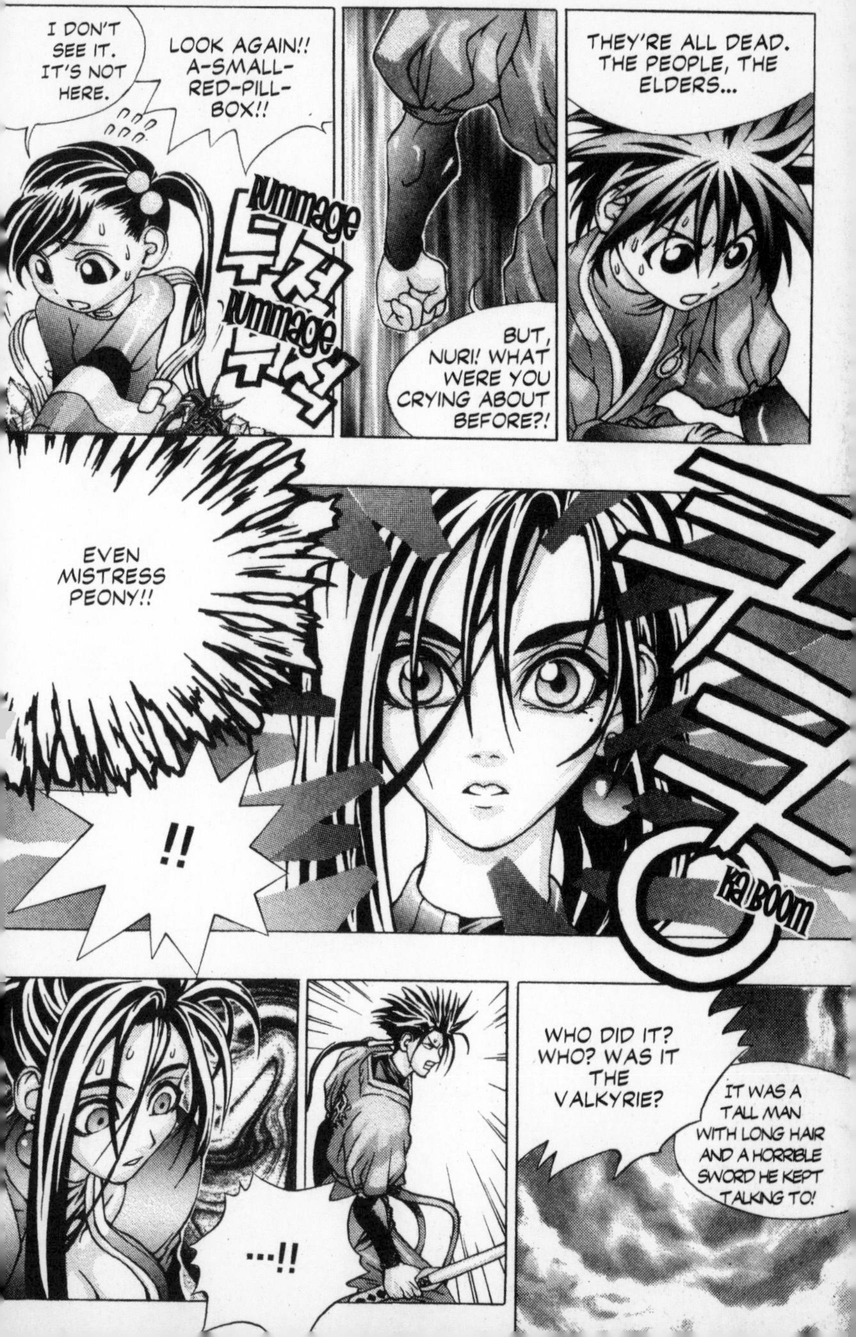
I DON'T SEE IT. IT'S NOT HERE.
LOOK AGAIN!! A-SMALL-RED-PILL-BOX!!
RUMMAGE
RUMMAGE
BUT, NURI! WHAT WERE YOU CRYING ABOUT BEFORE?!
THEY'RE ALL DEAD. THE PEOPLE, THE ELDERS...
EVEN MISTRESS PEONY!!
!!
KA BOOM
...!!
WHO DID IT? WHO? WAS IT THE VALKYRIE?
IT WAS A TALL MAN WITH LONG HAIR AND A HORRIBLE SWORD HE KEPT TALKING TO!

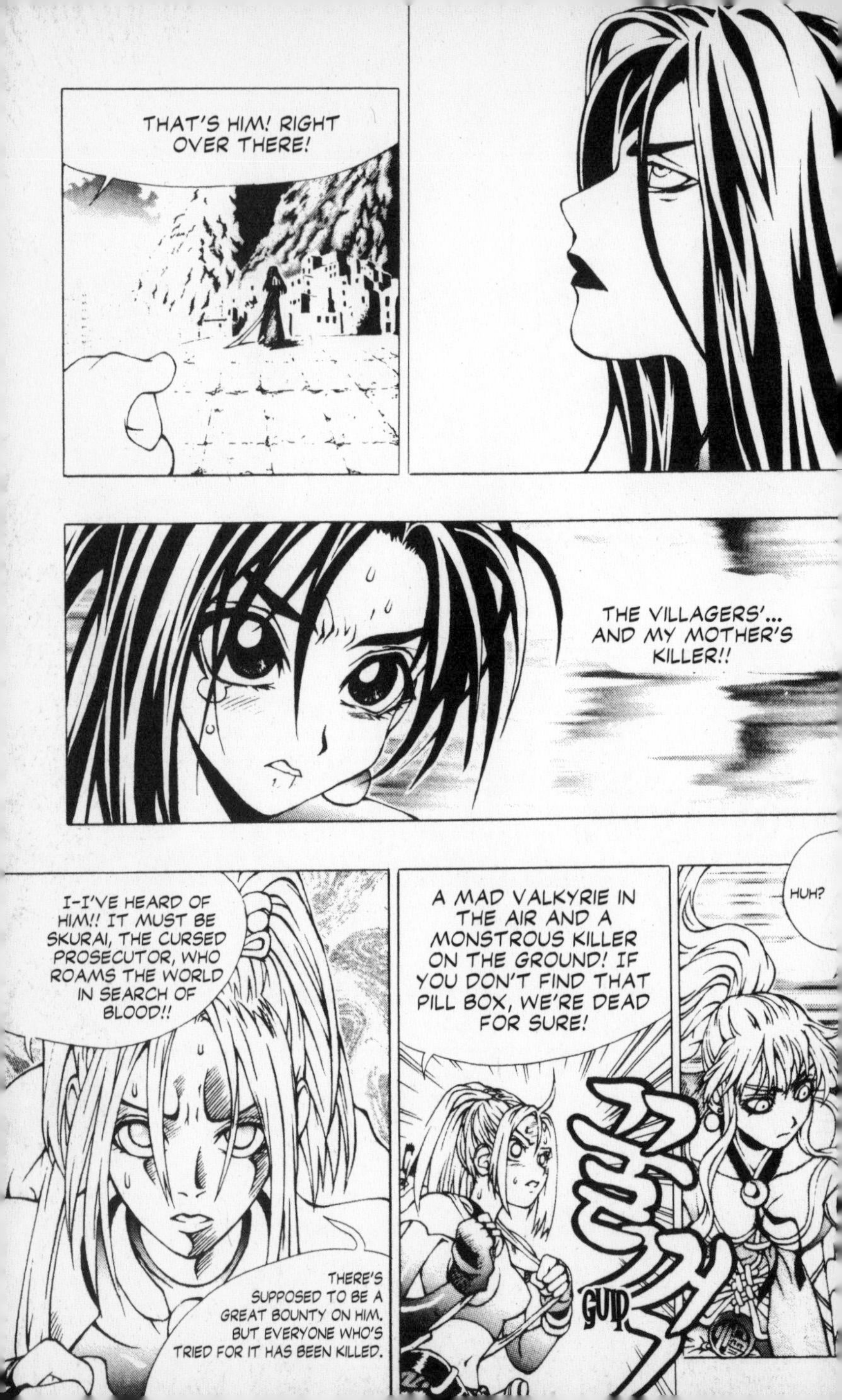
THAT'S HIM! RIGHT OVER THERE!
THE VILLAGERS'... AND MY MOTHER'S KILLER!!
I-I'VE HEARD OF HIM!! IT MUST BE SKURAI, THE CURSED PROSECUTOR, WHO ROAMS THE WORLD IN SEARCH OF BLOOD!!
THERE'S SUPPOSED TO BE A GREAT BOUNTY ON HIM. BUT EVERYONE WHO'S TRIED FOR IT HAS BEEN KILLED.
A MAD VALKYRIE IN THE AIR AND A MONSTROUS KILLER ON THE GROUND! IF YOU DON'T FIND THAT PILL BOX, WE'RE DEAD FOR SURE!
GULP
HUH?

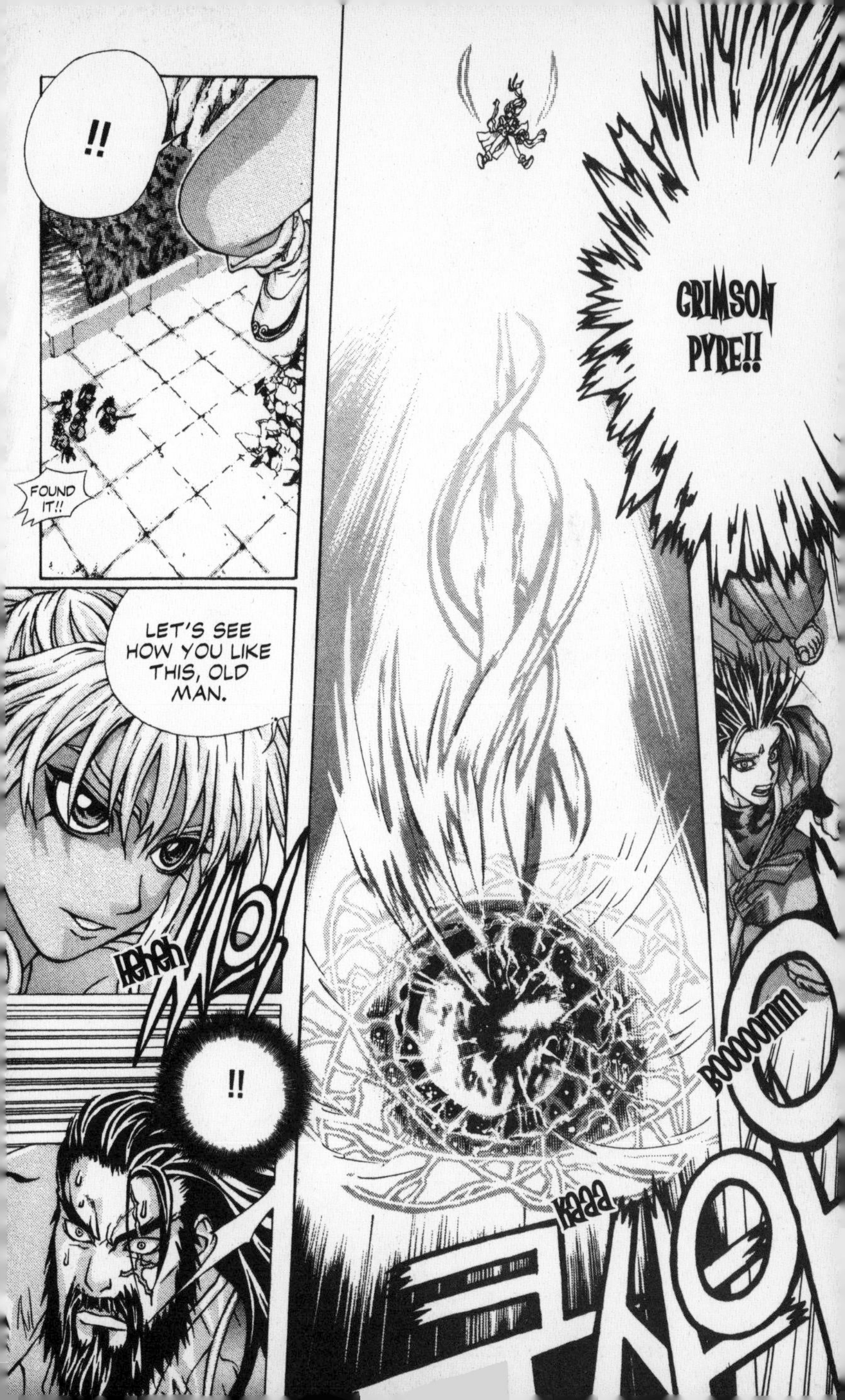
!!
FOUND IT!!
LET'S SEE HOW YOU LIKE THIS, OLD MAN.
HEHEH
!!
CRIMSON PYRE!!
BOOOOOMMM
KAAA

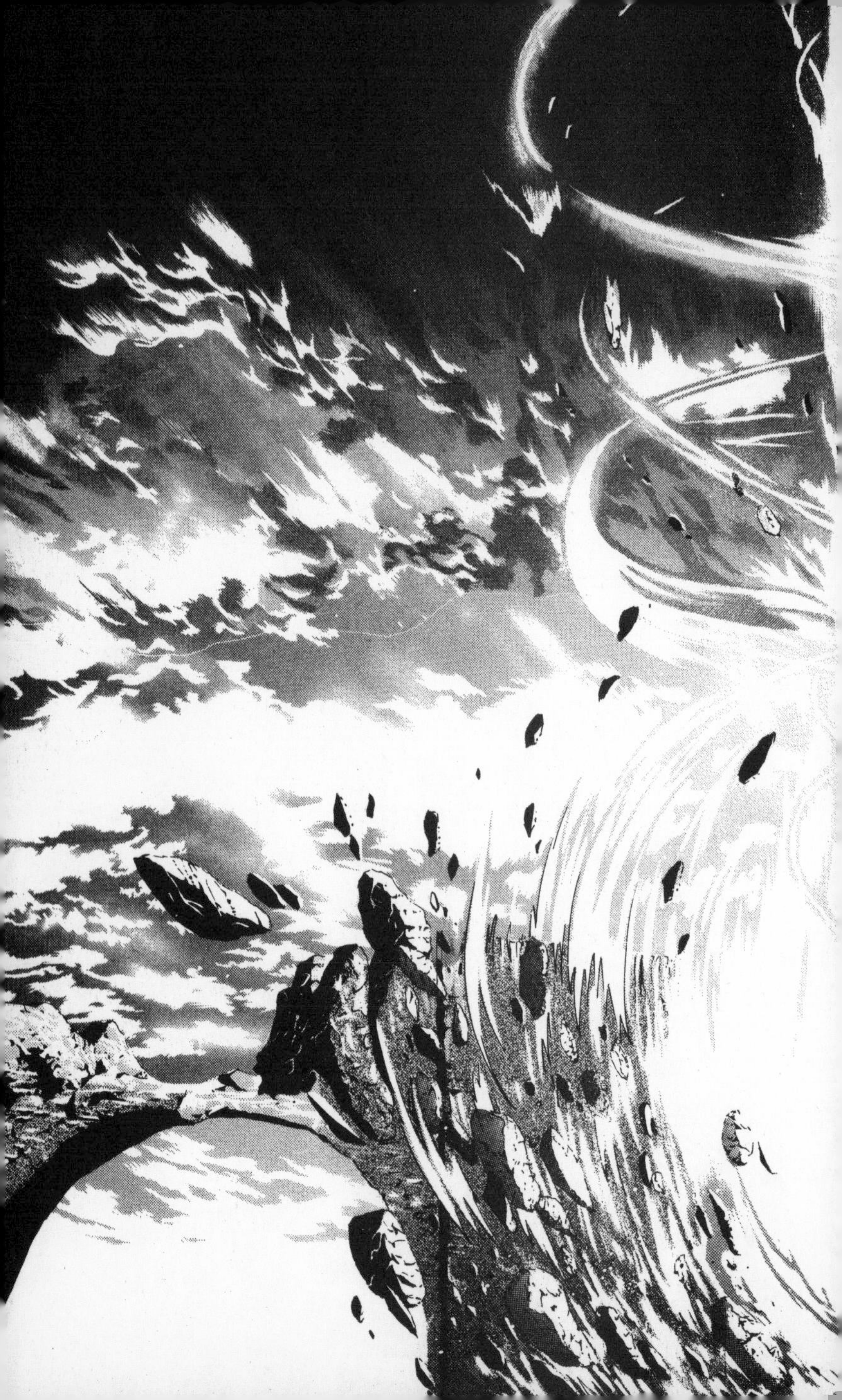

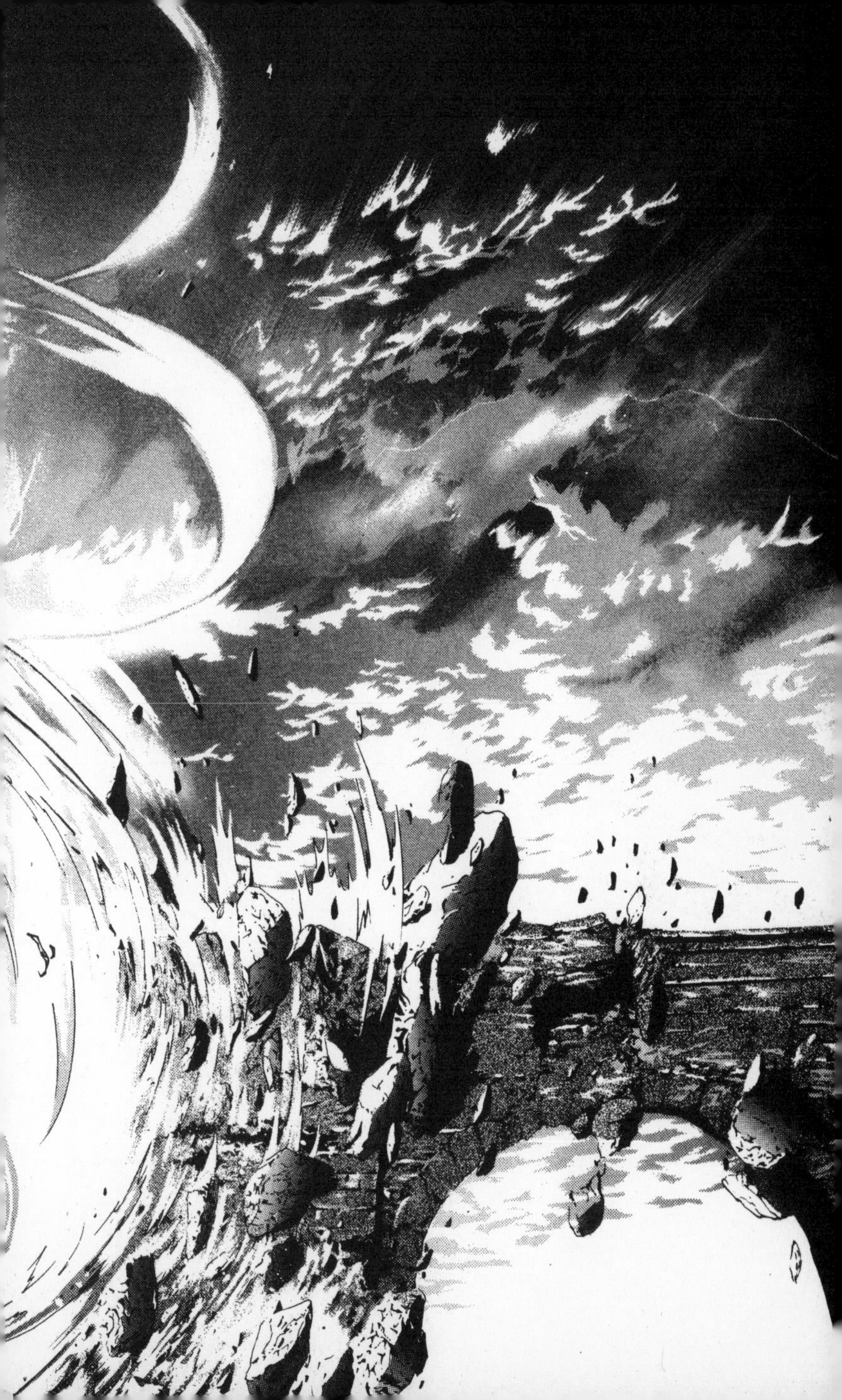

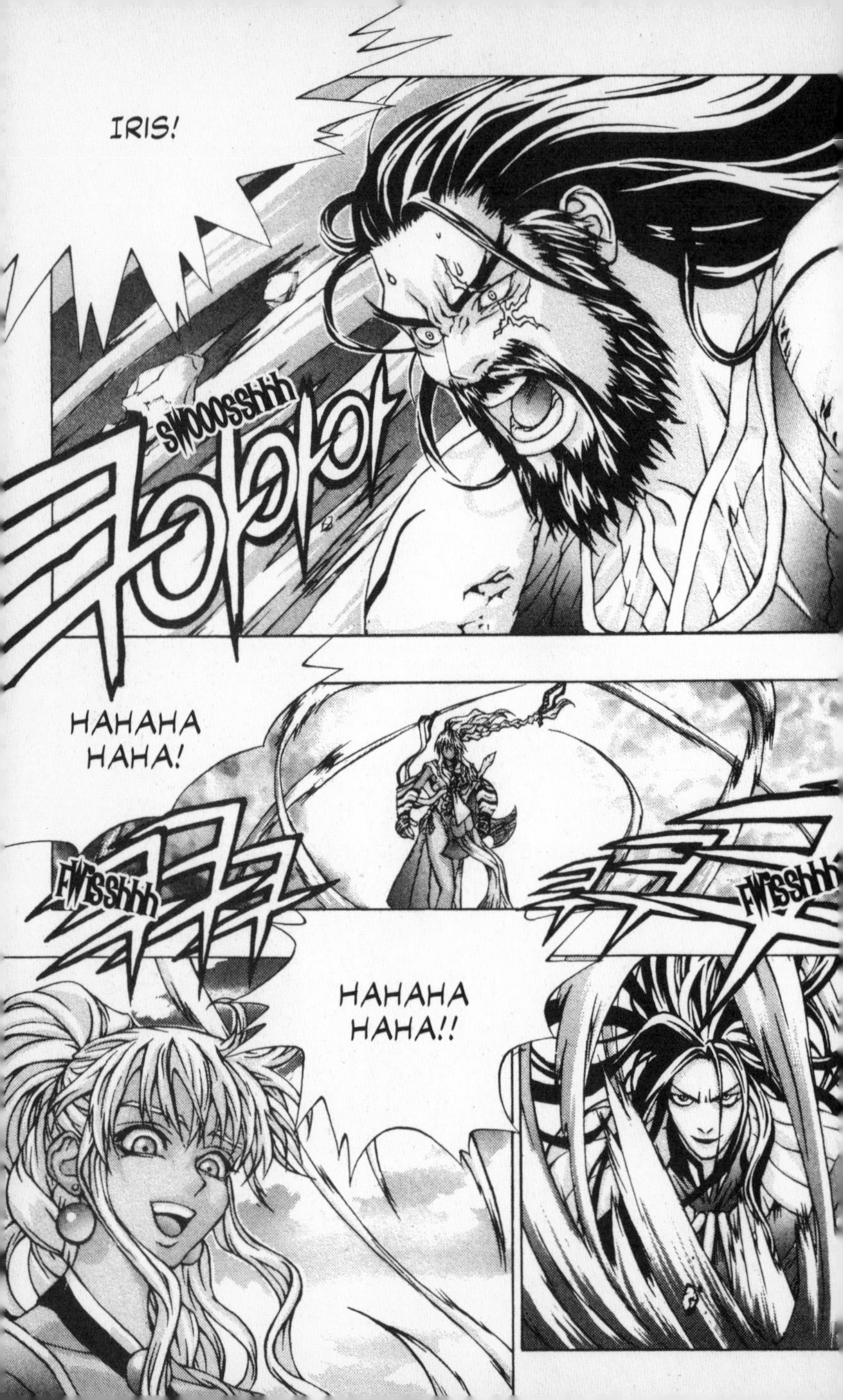
IRIS!
SWOOOSSHHH
HAHAHA HAHA!
FWISSHHH
FWISSHHH
HAHAHA HAHA!!

RAGNAROK
라그나로크
INTO THE ABYSS

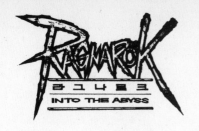

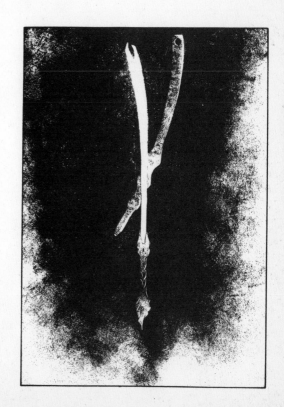

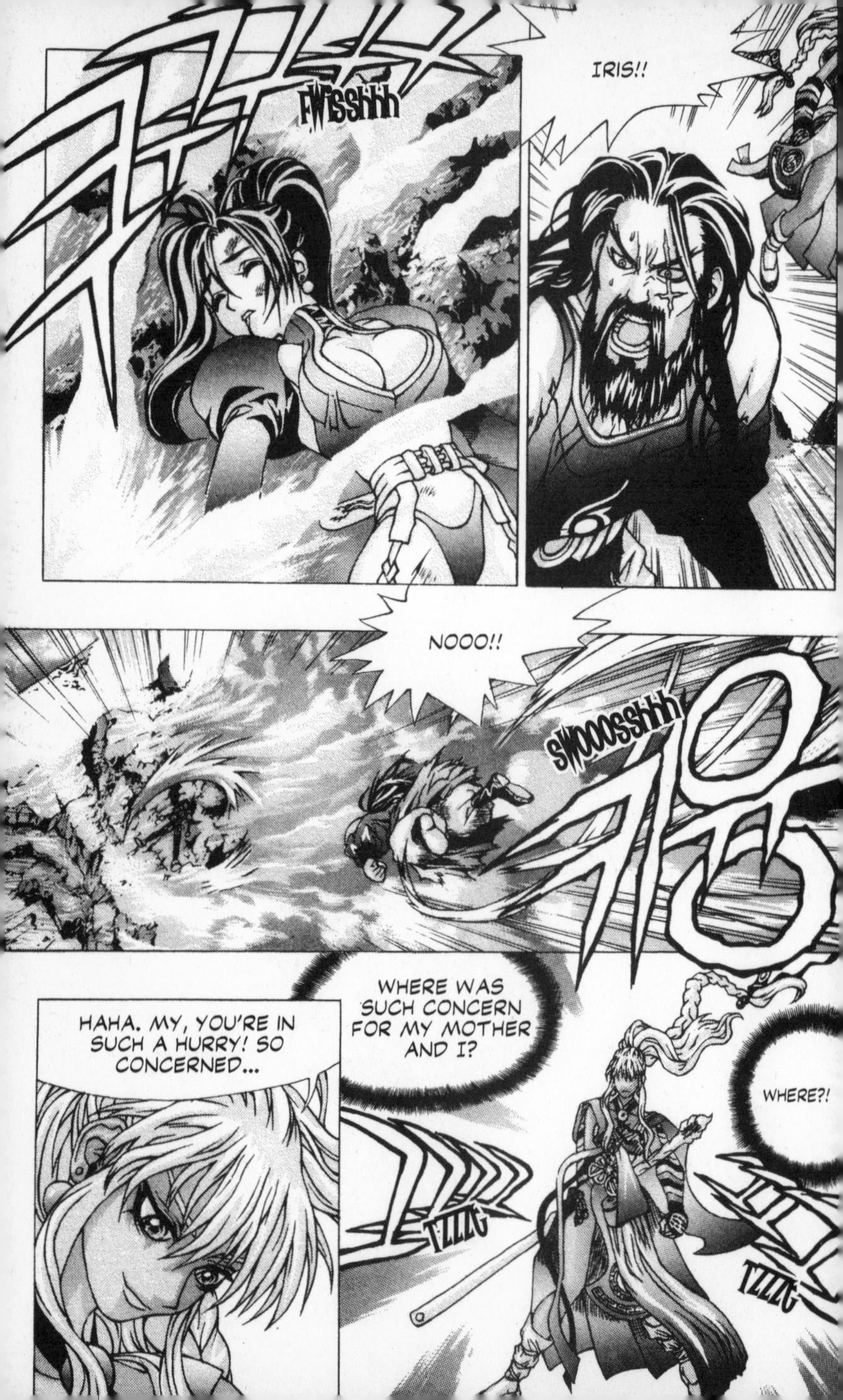
FWISSHHH
IRIS!!
NOOO!!
SWOOOSSHHH
HAHA. MY, YOU'RE IN SUCH A HURRY! SO CONCERNED...
WHERE WAS SUCH CONCERN FOR MY MOTHER AND I?
WHERE?!
TZZZG
TZZZG

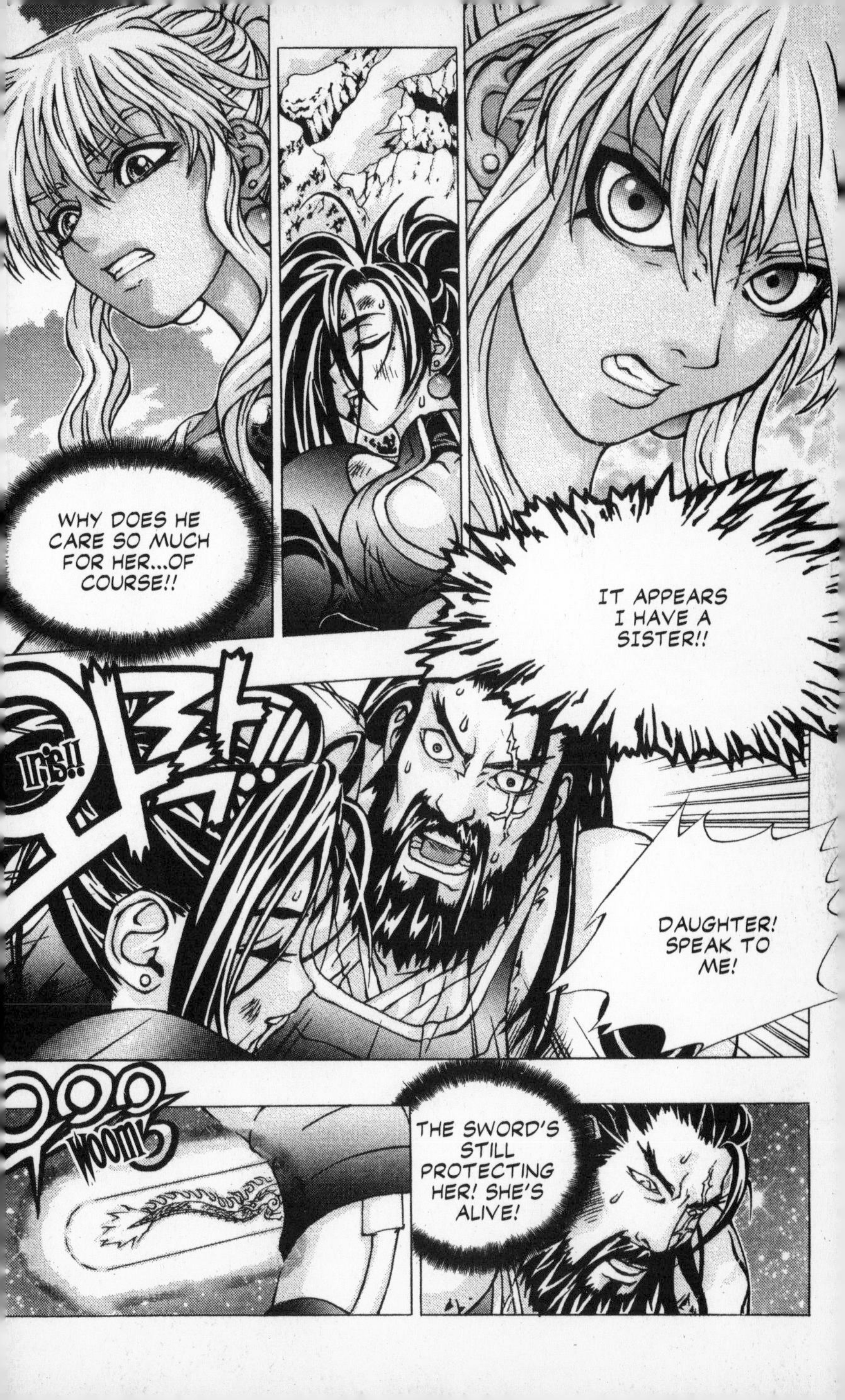
WHY DOES HE CARE SO MUCH FOR HER...OF COURSE!!
IT APPEARS I HAVE A SISTER!!
Iris!!
DAUGHTER! SPEAK TO ME!
WOOM
THE SWORD'S STILL PROTECTING HER! SHE'S ALIVE!

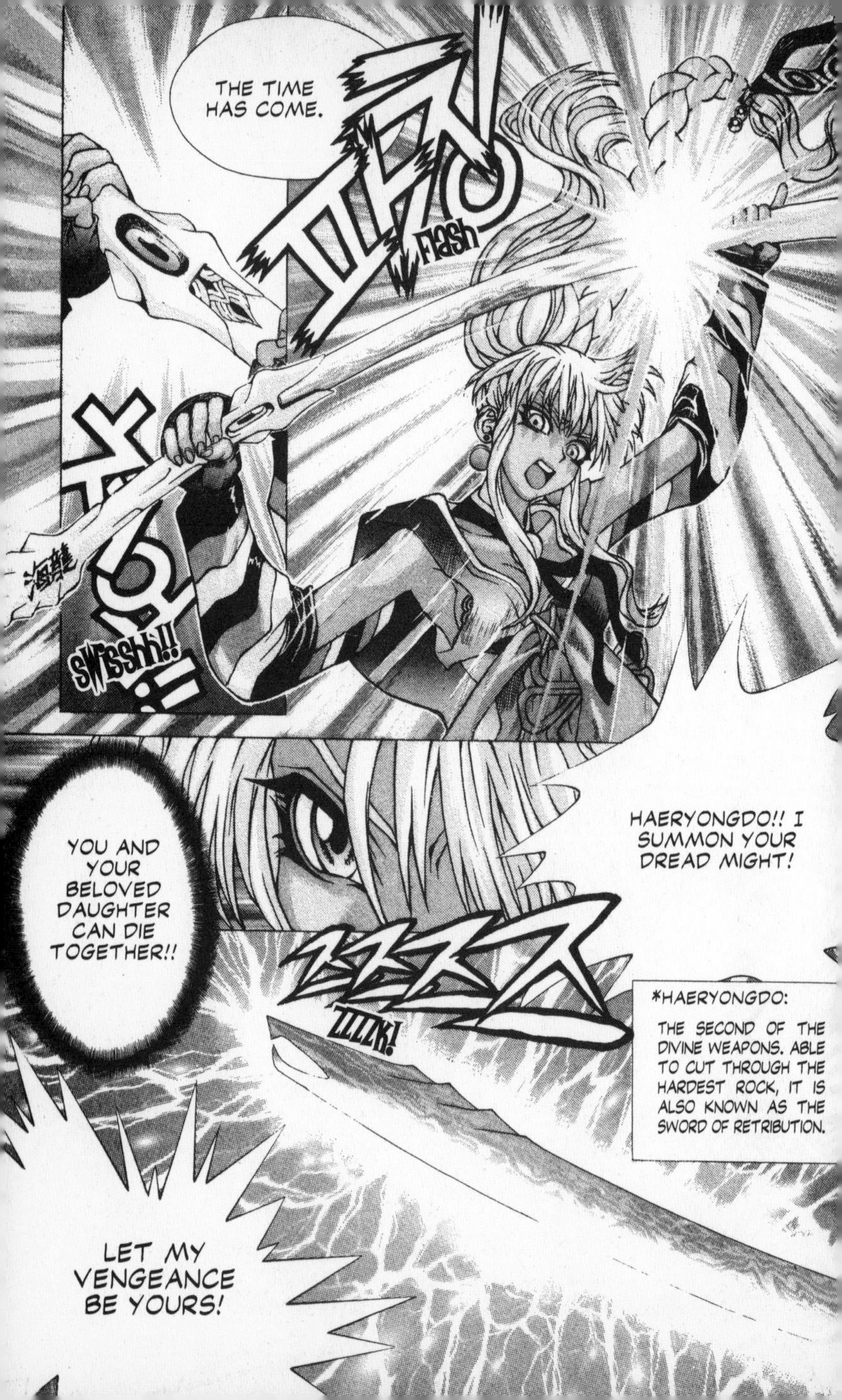

THE TIME HAS COME.
FLASH
SWISSHH!!
YOU AND YOUR BELOVED DAUGHTER CAN DIE TOGETHER!!
HAERYONGDO!! I SUMMON YOUR DREAD MIGHT!
ZZZZK!
*HAERYONGDO:
THE SECOND OF THE DIVINE WEAPONS. ABLE TO CUT THROUGH THE HARDEST ROCK, IT IS ALSO KNOWN AS THE SWORD OF RETRIBUTION.
LET MY VENGEANCE BE YOURS!

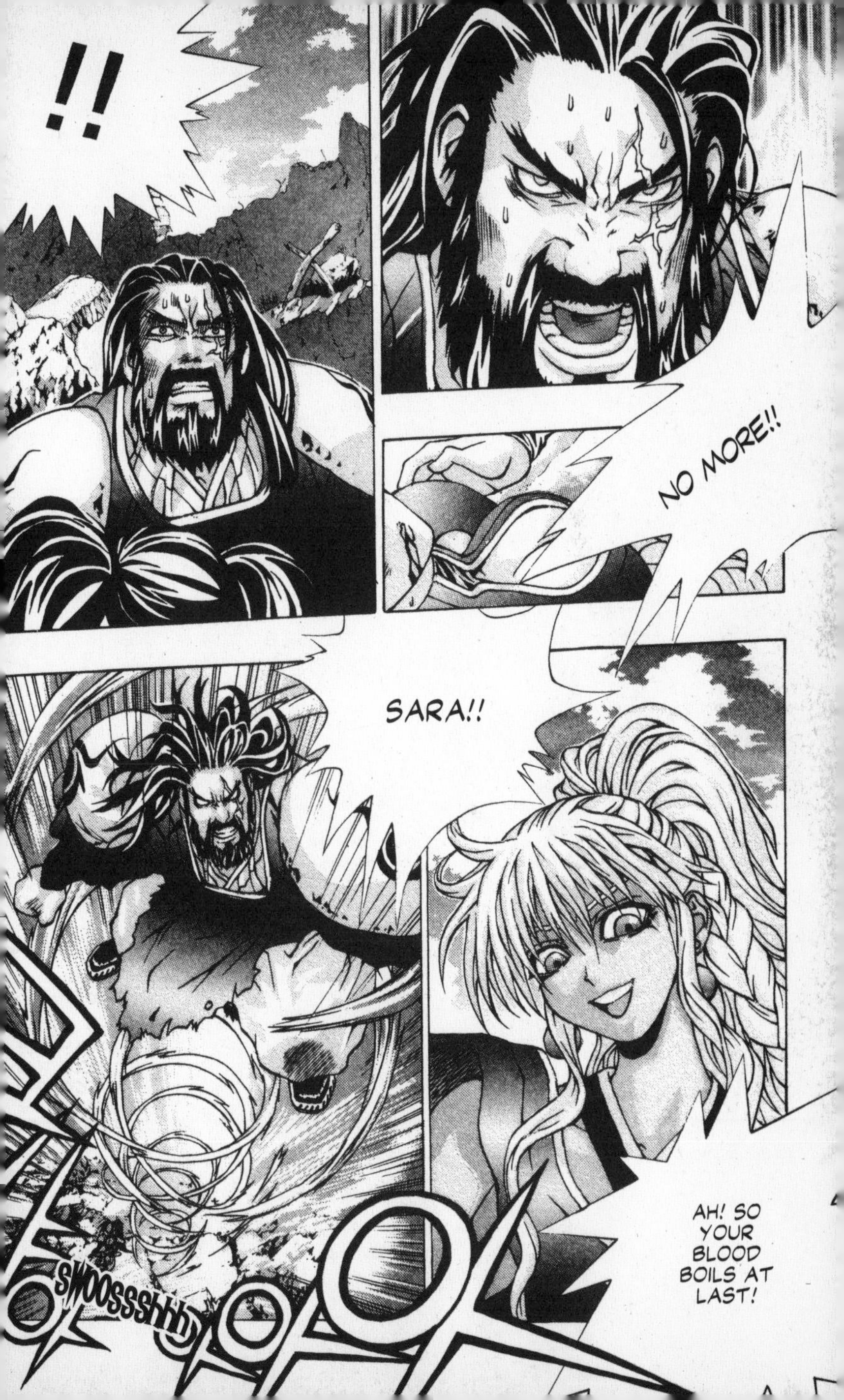
!!
NO MORE!!
SARA!!
SWOOSSSHHH
AH! SO YOUR BLOOD BOILS AT LAST!

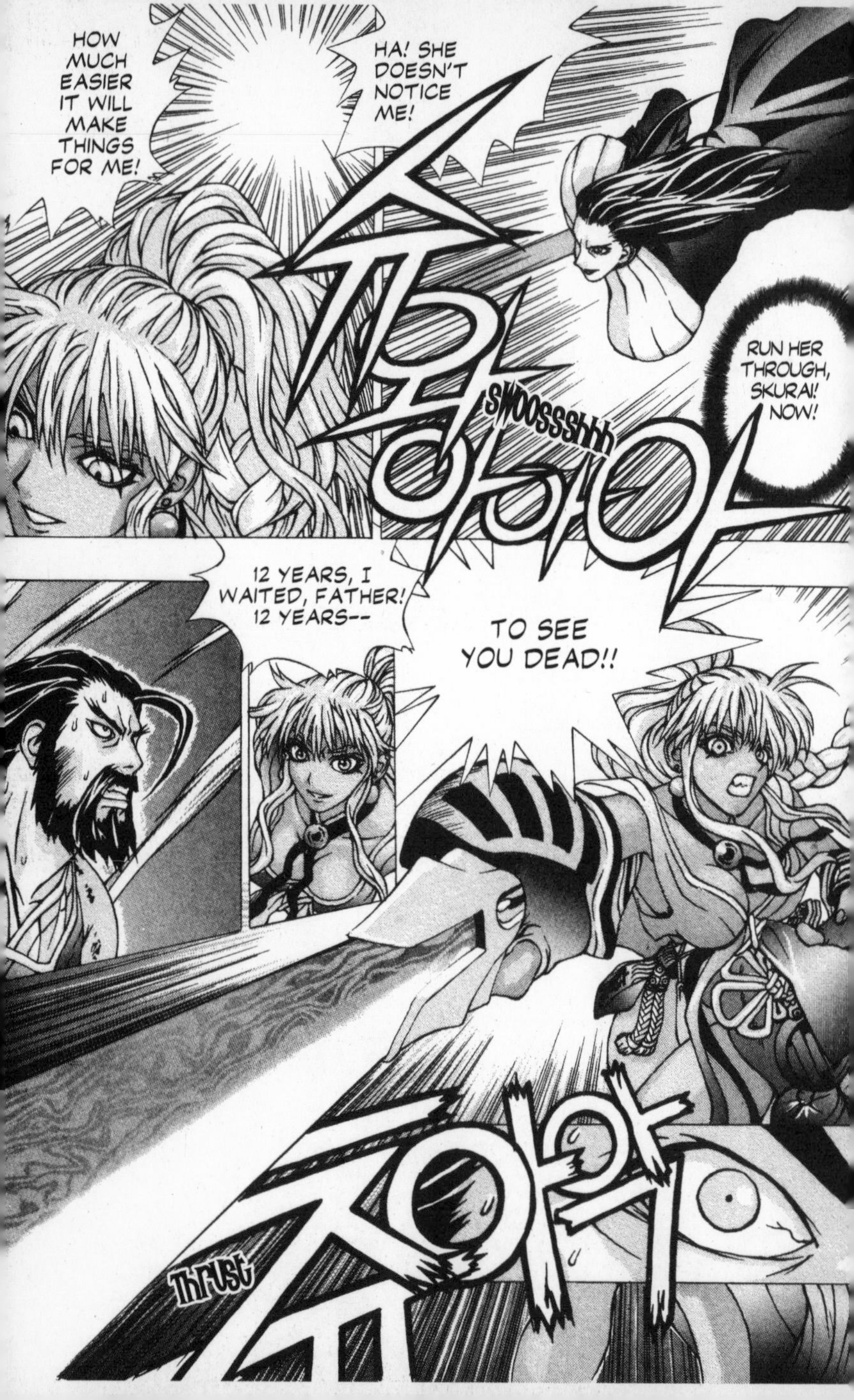
HOW MUCH EASIER IT WILL MAKE THINGS FOR ME!
HA! SHE DOESN'T NOTICE ME!
SWOOSSSHHH
RUN HER THROUGH, SKURAI! NOW!
12 YEARS, I WAITED, FATHER! 12 YEARS--
TO SEE YOU DEAD!!
THRUST

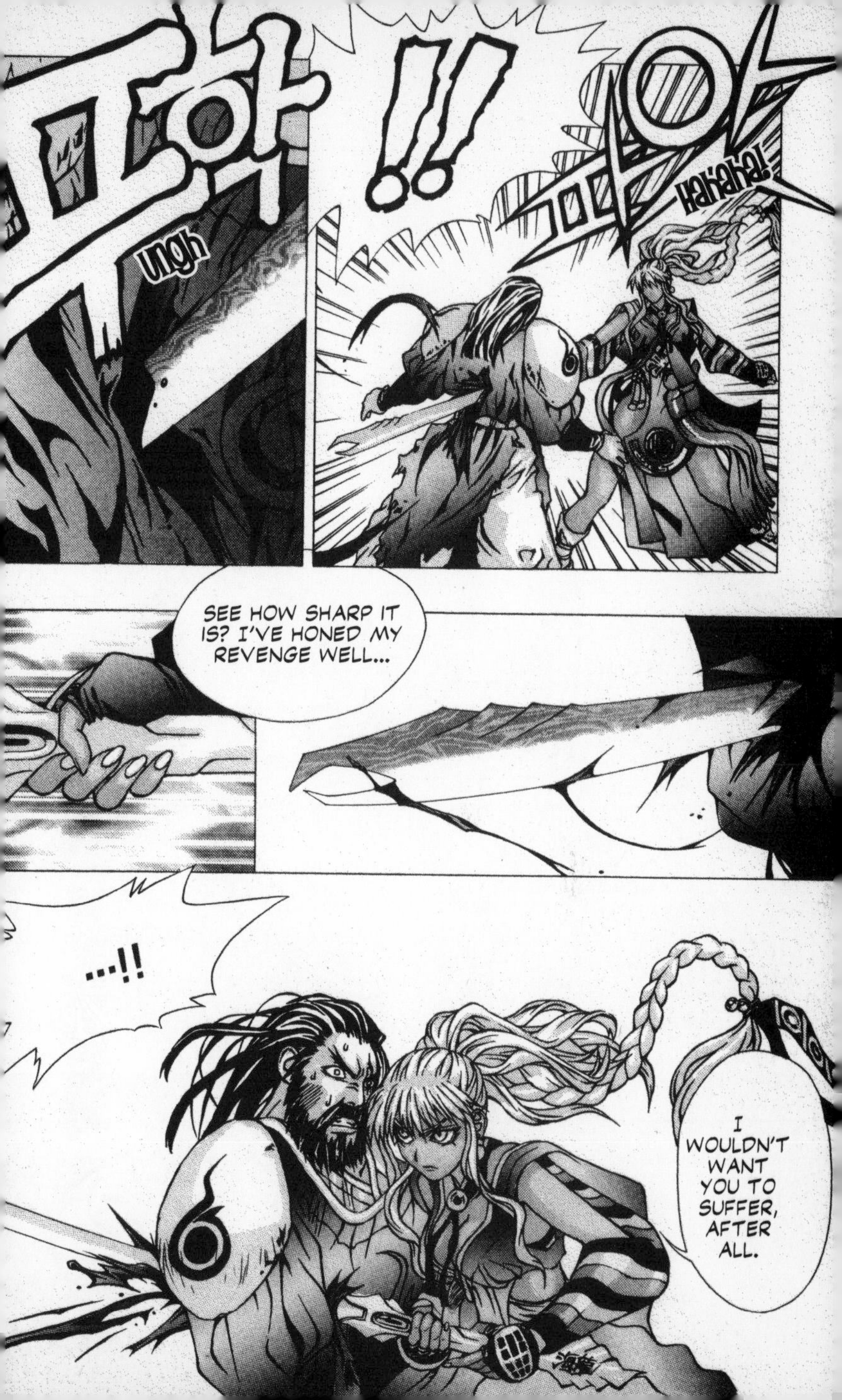
Ungh
HAHAHA!
SEE HOW SHARP IT IS? I'VE HONED MY REVENGE WELL...
...!!
I WOULDN'T WANT YOU TO SUFFER, AFTER ALL.

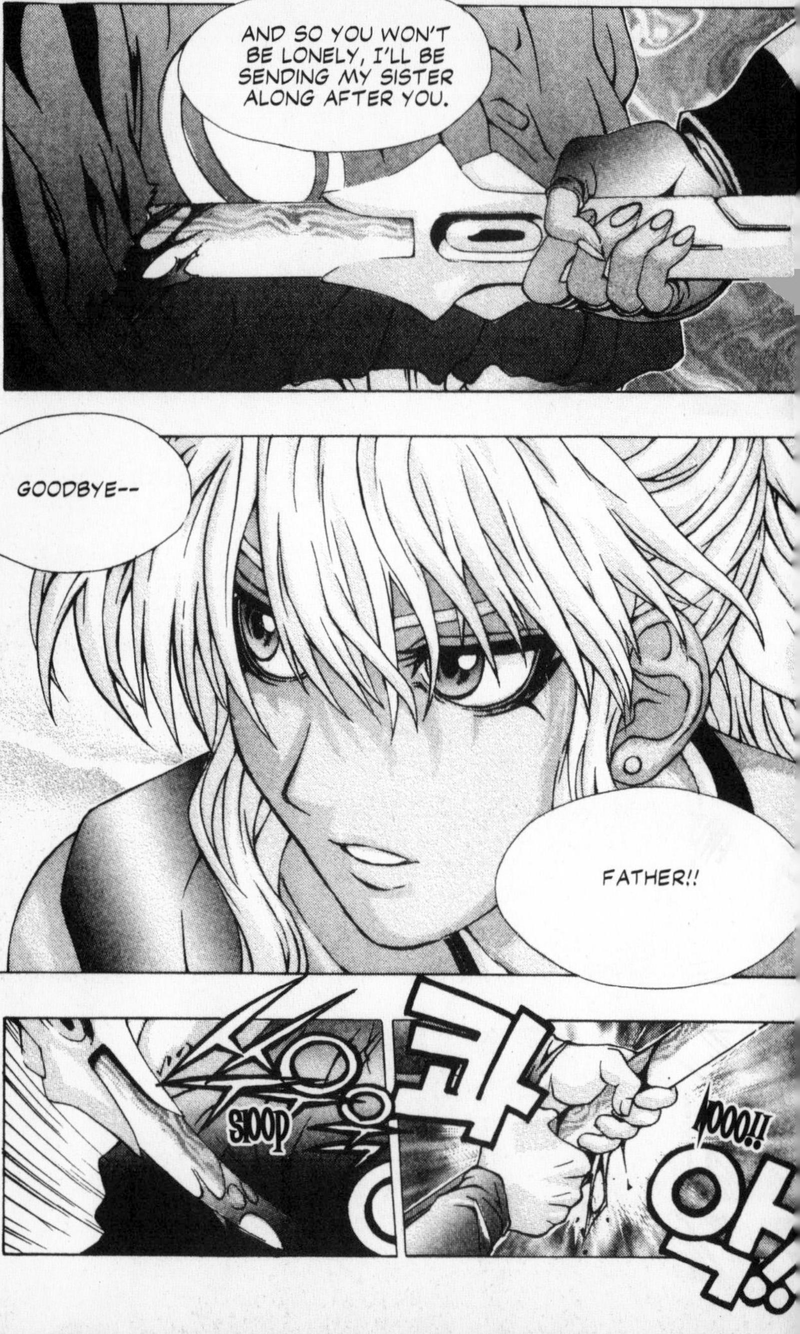
AND SO YOU WON'T BE LONELY, I'LL BE SENDING MY SISTER ALONG AFTER YOU.
GOODBYE--
FATHER!!
SLOOP
팍
NOOO!!
아..

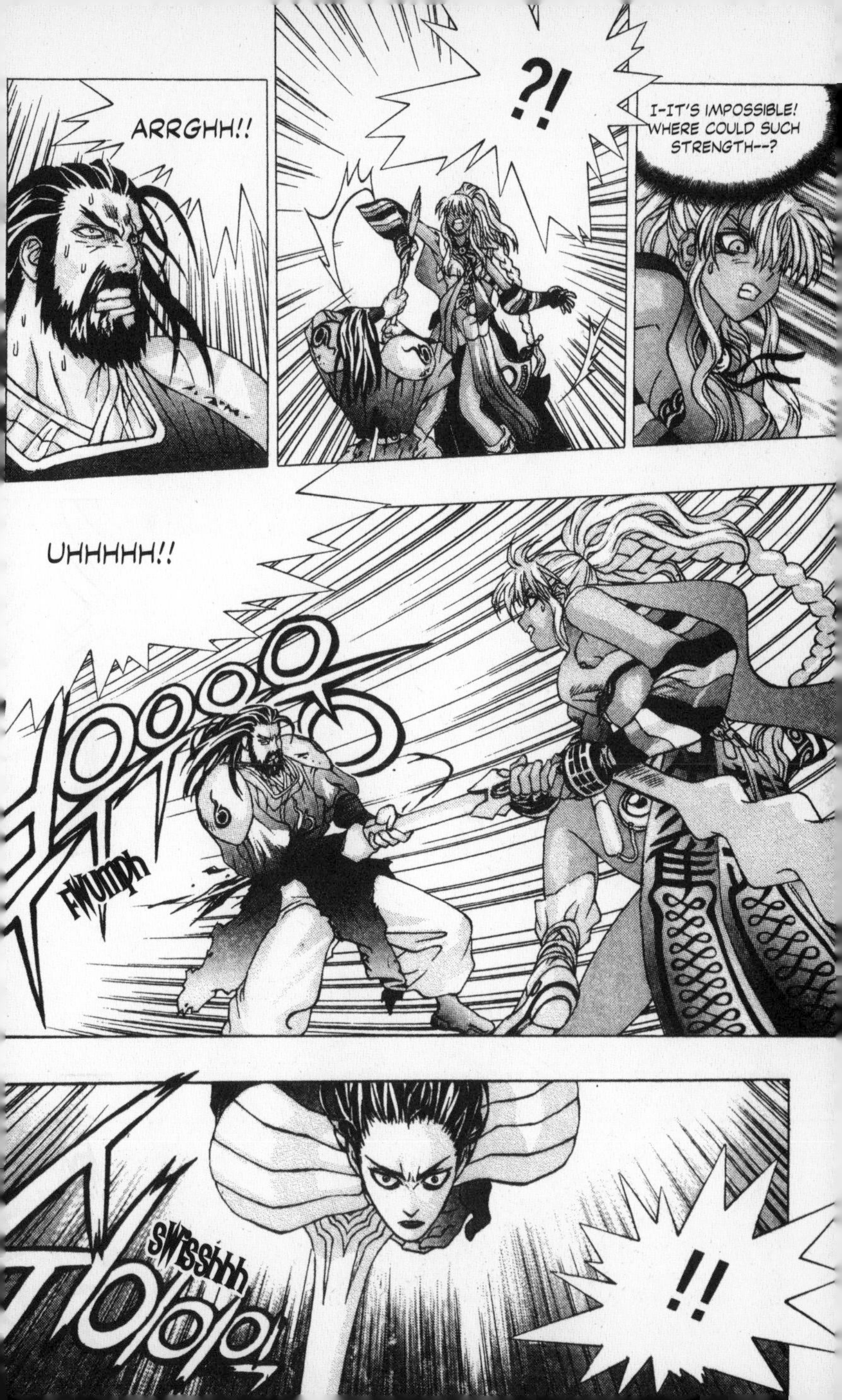
ARRGHH!!
?!
I-IT'S IMPOSSIBLE! WHERE COULD SUCH STRENGTH--?
UHHHHH!!
FWUMPH
SWISSHHH
!!

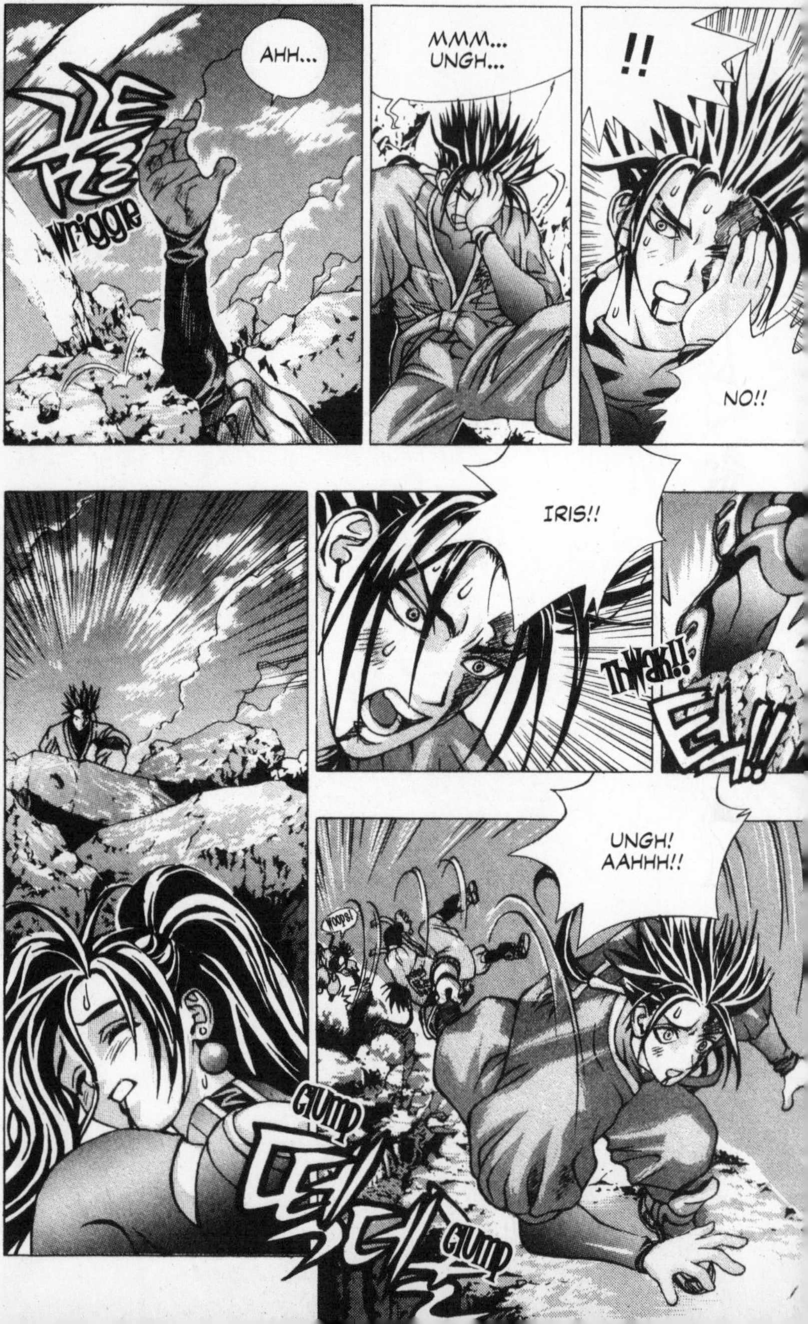

AHH...
wriggle
MMM... UNGH...
!!
NO!!
IRIS!!
THWAK!!
UNGH! AAHHH!!
GLUMP
GLUMP

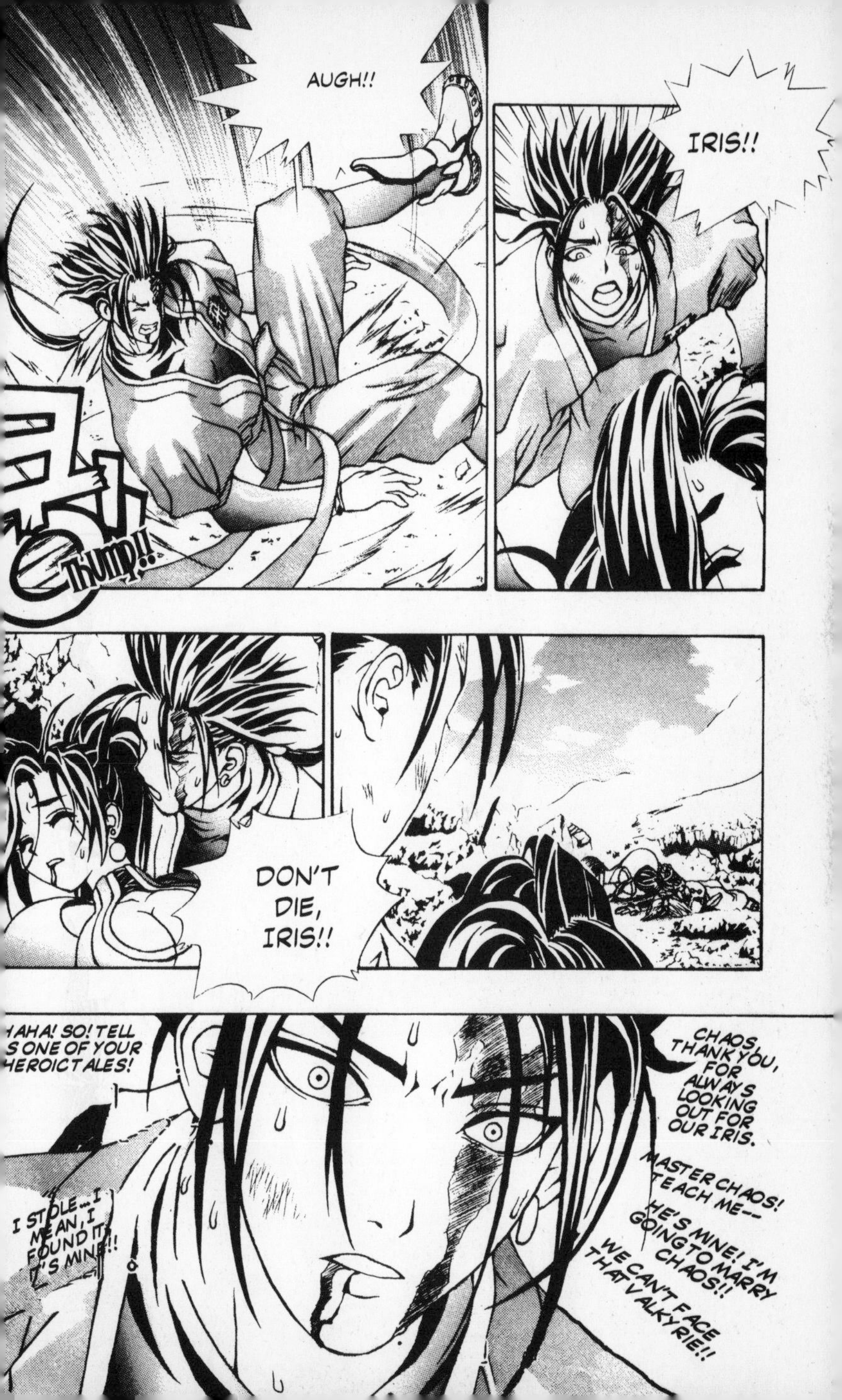
AUGH!!
THUMP!!
IRIS!!
DON'T DIE, IRIS!!
HAHA! SO! TELL S ONE OF YOUR HEROIC TALES!
I STOLE...I MEAN, I FOUND IT! IT'S MINE!!
CHAOS, THANK YOU, FOR ALWAYS LOOKING OUT FOR OUR IRIS.
MASTER CHAOS! TEACH ME--
HE'S MINE! I'M GOING TO MARRY CHAOS!!
WE CAN'T FACE THAT VALKYRIE!!

I CAN'T LET THIS GO ON.

I HAVE TO SAVE THEM! NO MATTER THE COST.

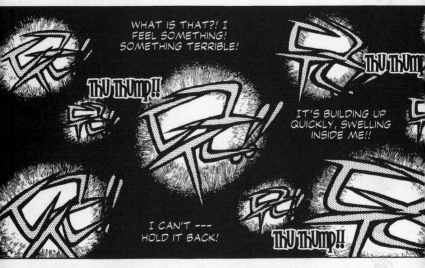

WHAT IS THAT?! I FEEL SOMETHING! SOMETHING TERRIBLE!

THU THUMP!!

IT'S BUILDING UP QUICKLY, SWELLING INSIDE ME!!

THU THUMP!

I CAN'T --- HOLD IT BACK!

THU THUMP!!

UNH... UNH

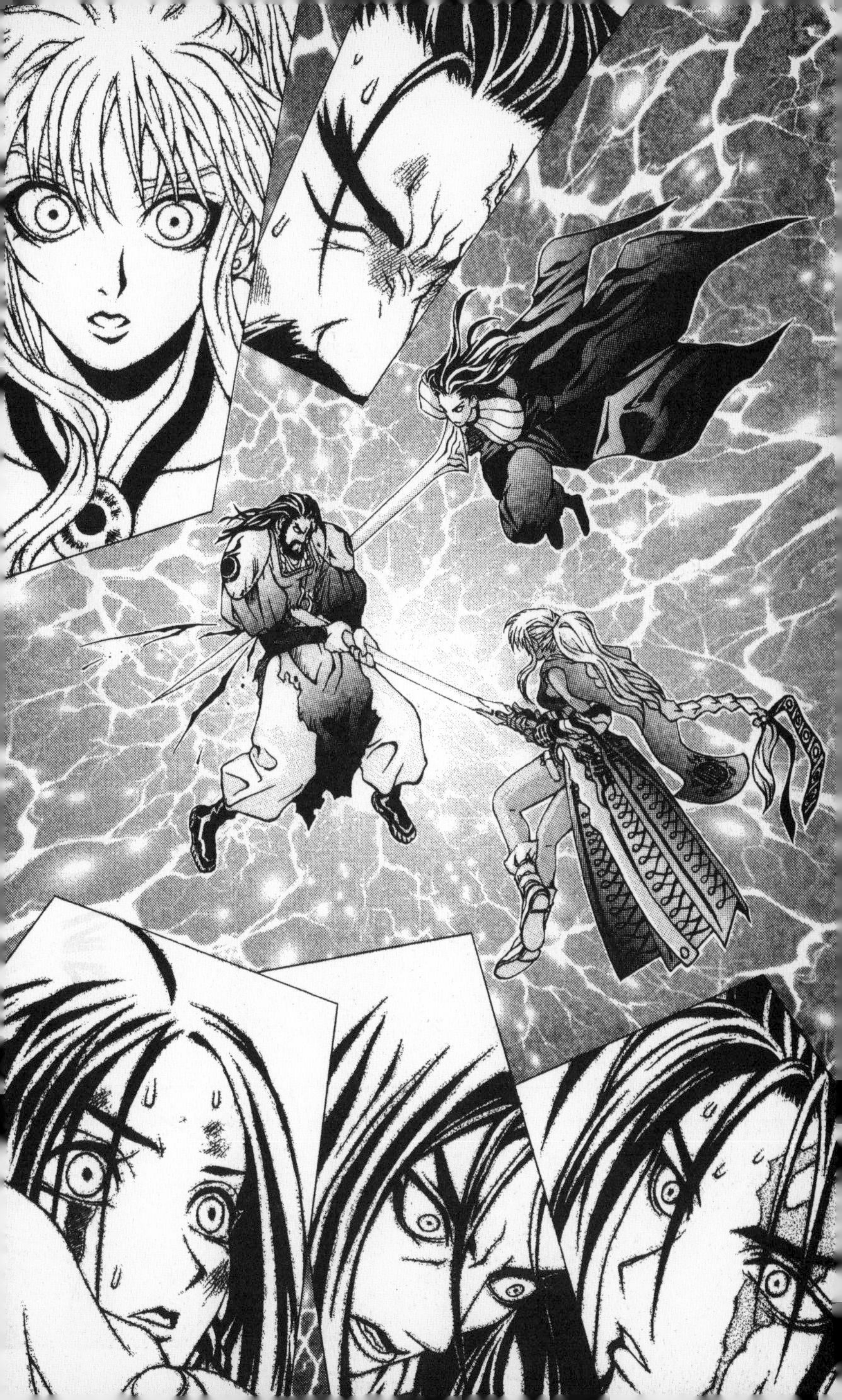

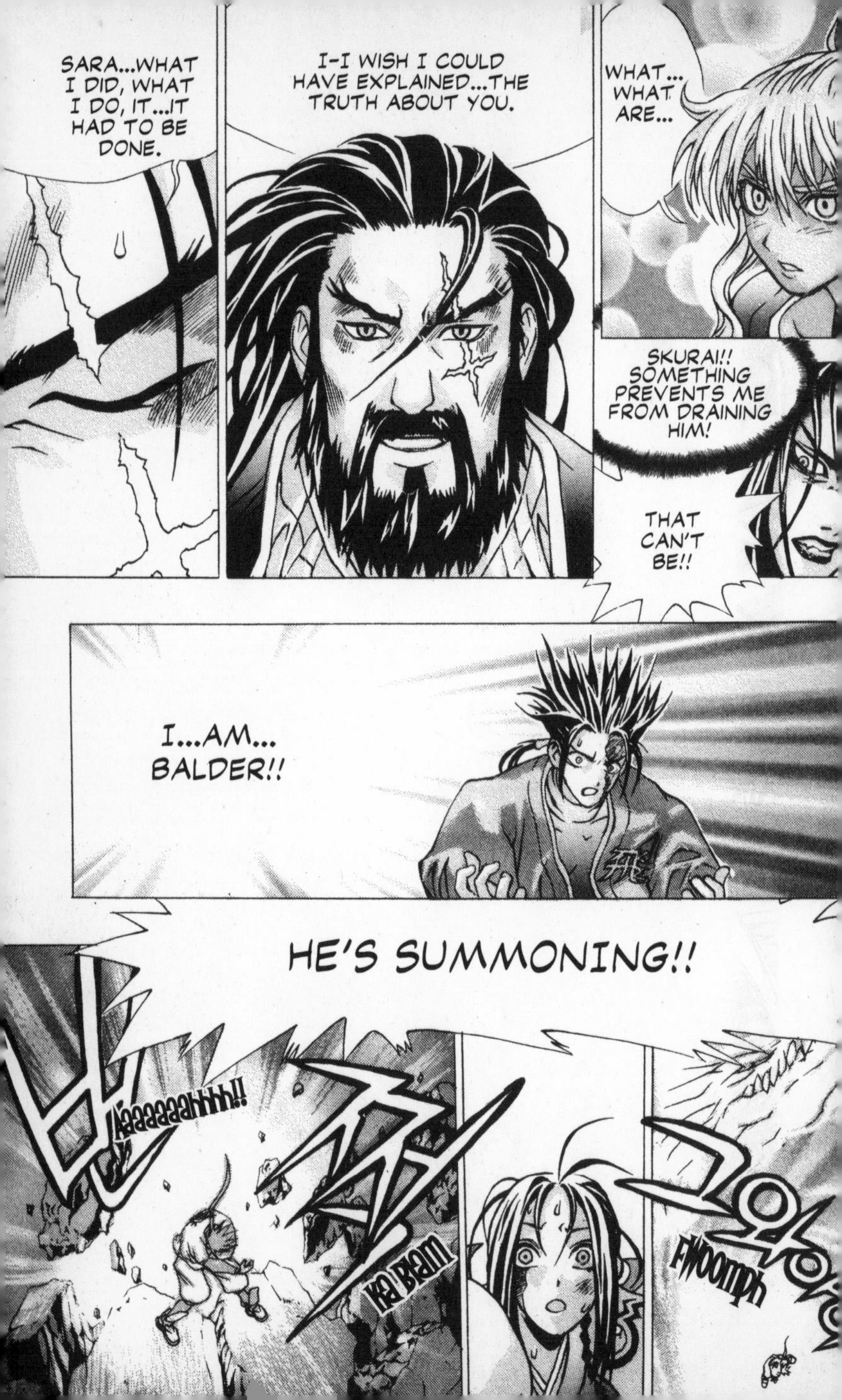

SARA...WHAT I DID, WHAT I DO, IT...IT HAD TO BE DONE.
I-I WISH I COULD HAVE EXPLAINED...THE TRUTH ABOUT YOU.
WHAT... WHAT ARE...
SKURAI!! SOMETHING PREVENTS ME FROM DRAINING HIM!
THAT CAN'T BE!!
I...AM... BALDER!!
HE'S SUMMONING!!
Aaaaaaaahhhh!!
KA BLAM
FWOOMPH

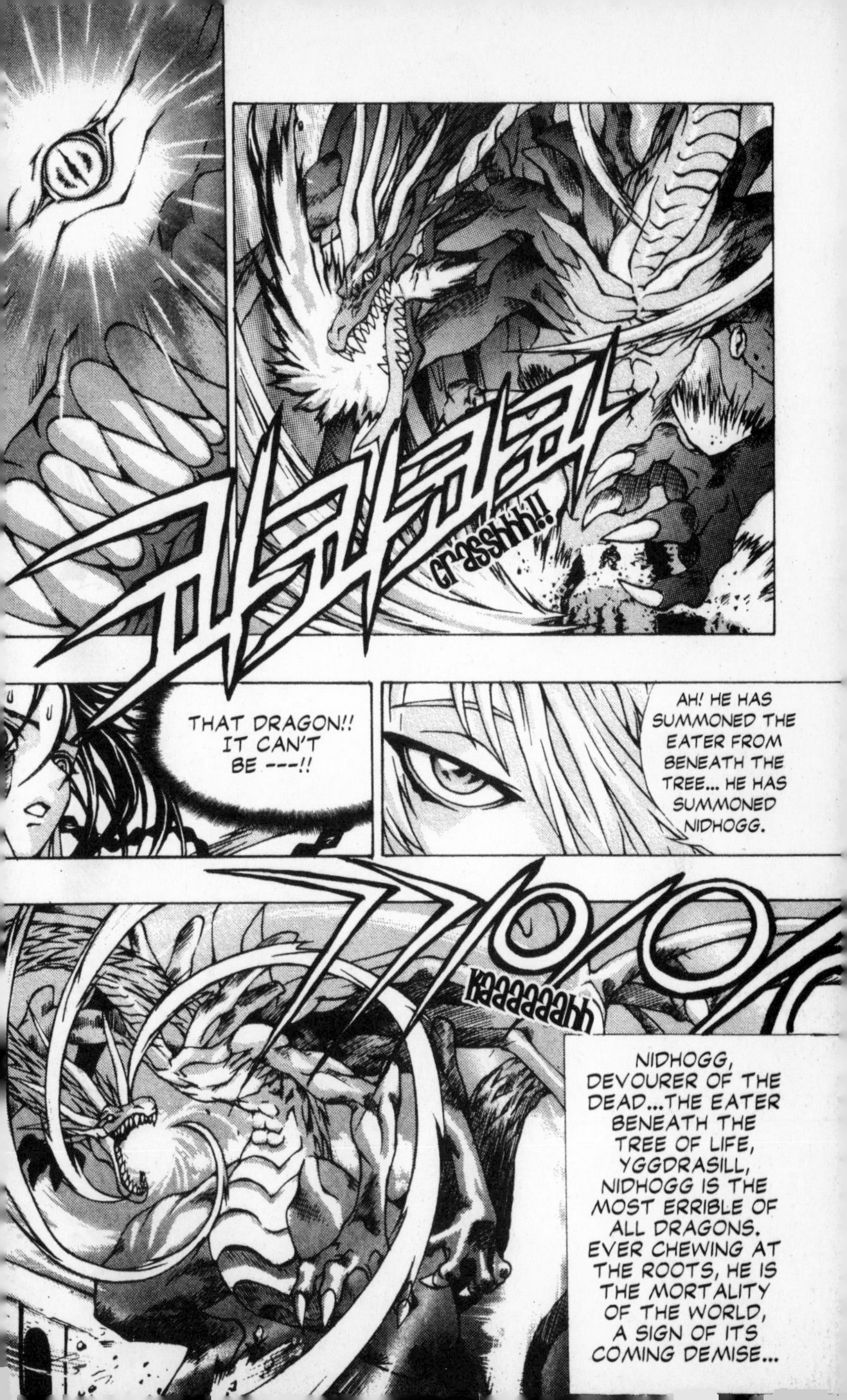
CRASSHHH!!
THAT DRAGON!! IT CAN'T BE ---!!
AH! HE HAS SUMMONED THE EATER FROM BENEATH THE TREE... HE HAS SUMMONED NIDHOGG.
KAAAAAAAHH
NIDHOGG, DEVOURER OF THE DEAD...THE EATER BENEATH THE TREE OF LIFE, YGGDRASILL, NIDHOGG IS THE MOST ERRIBLE OF ALL DRAGONS. EVER CHEWING AT THE ROOTS, HE IS THE MORTALITY OF THE WORLD, A SIGN OF ITS COMING DEMISE...

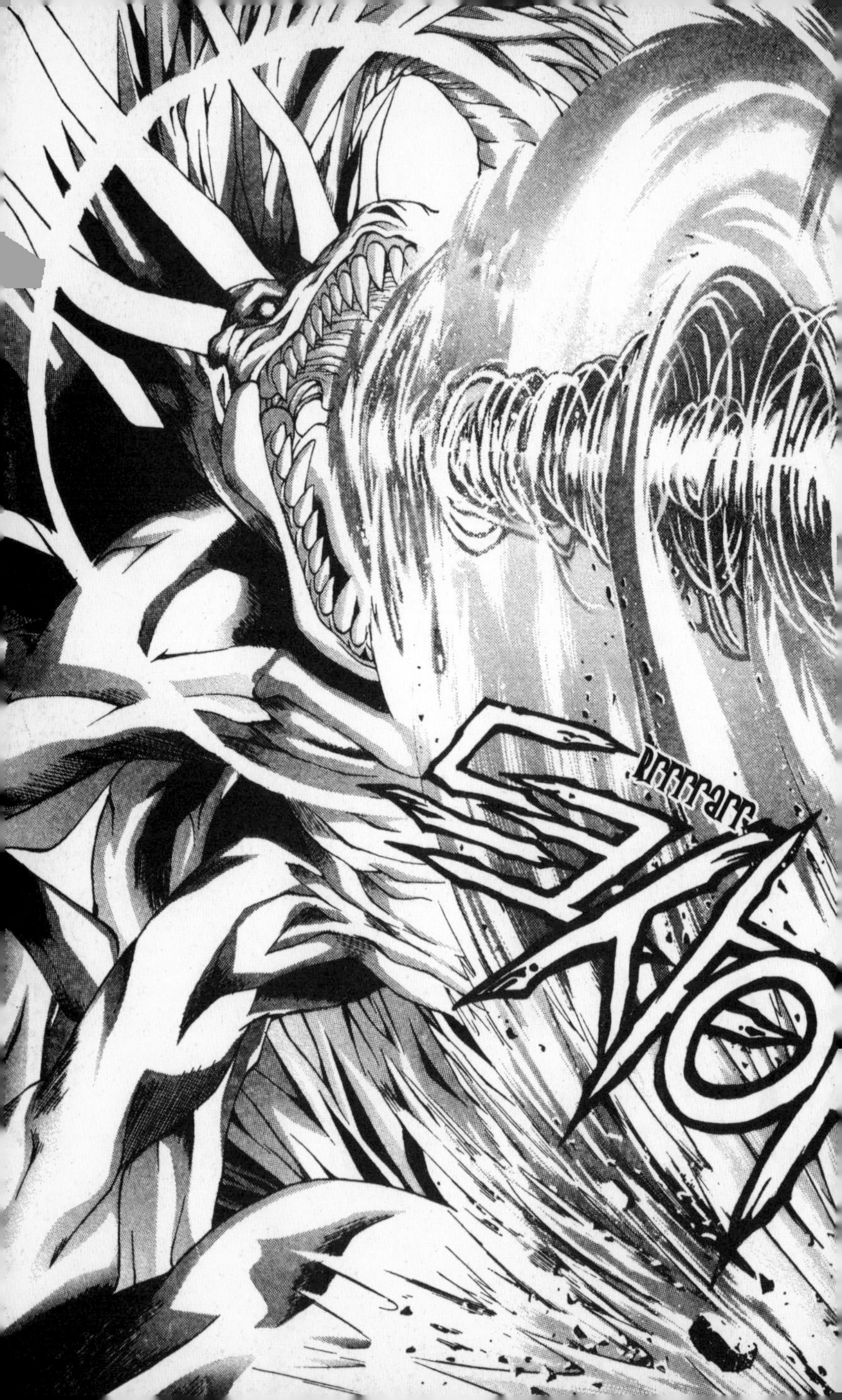
Rrrrarr

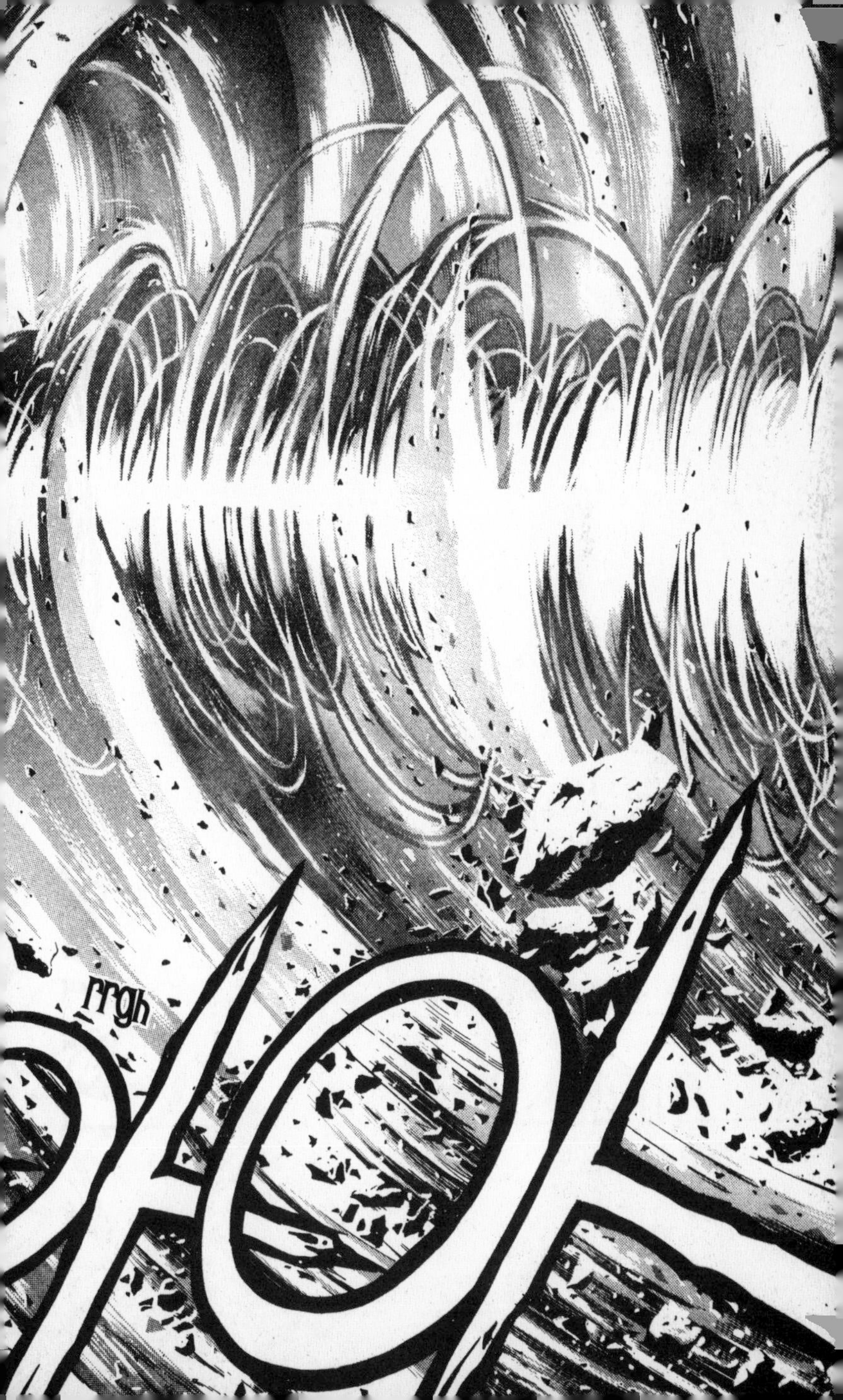
rrgh

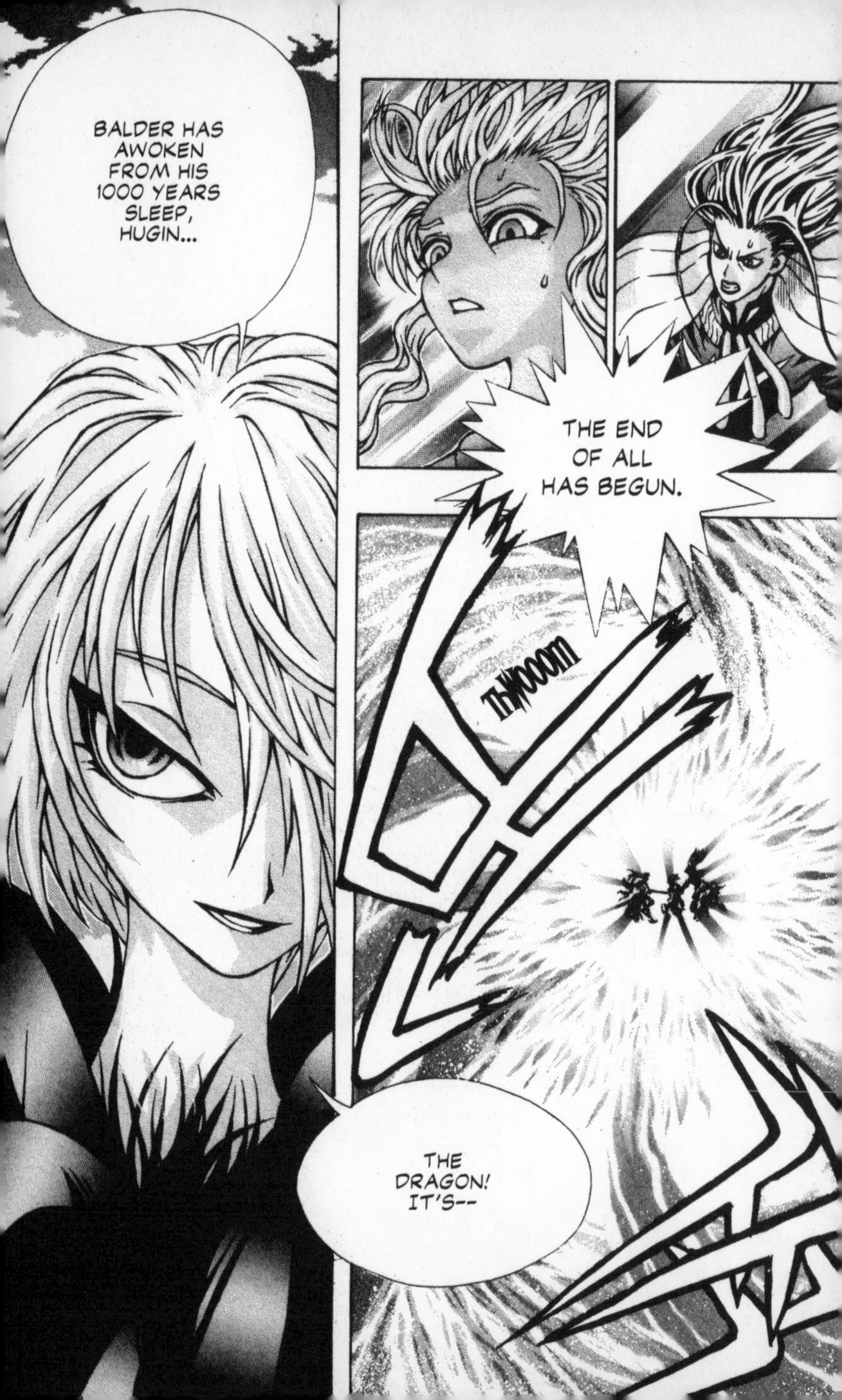
BALDER HAS AWOKEN FROM HIS 1000 YEARS SLEEP, HUGIN...
THE END OF ALL HAS BEGUN.
THWOOM
THE DRAGON! IT'S--

RAGNAROK
라그나로크
INTO THE ABYSS

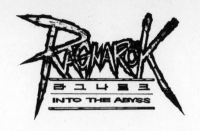

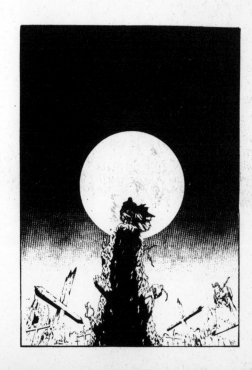

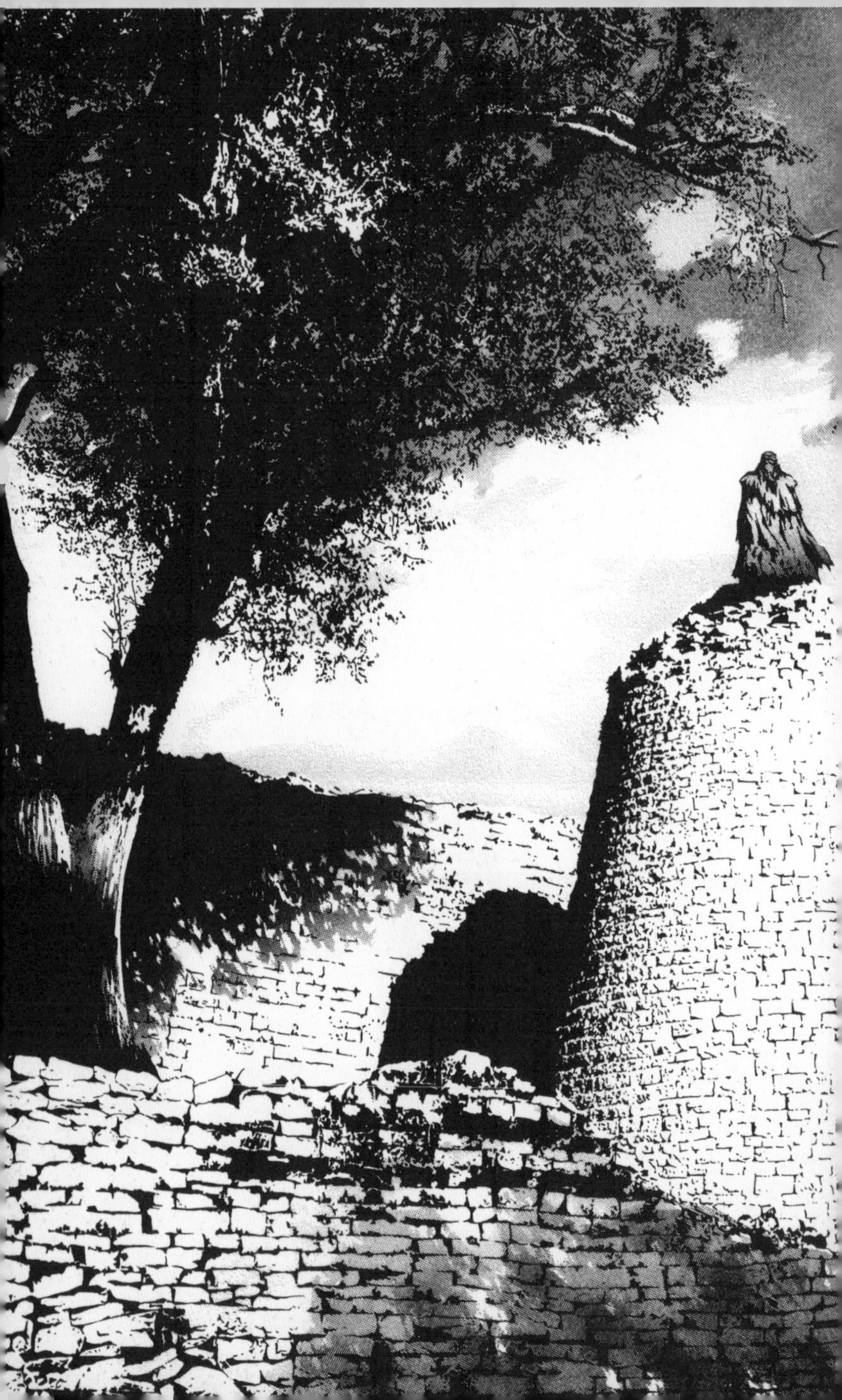

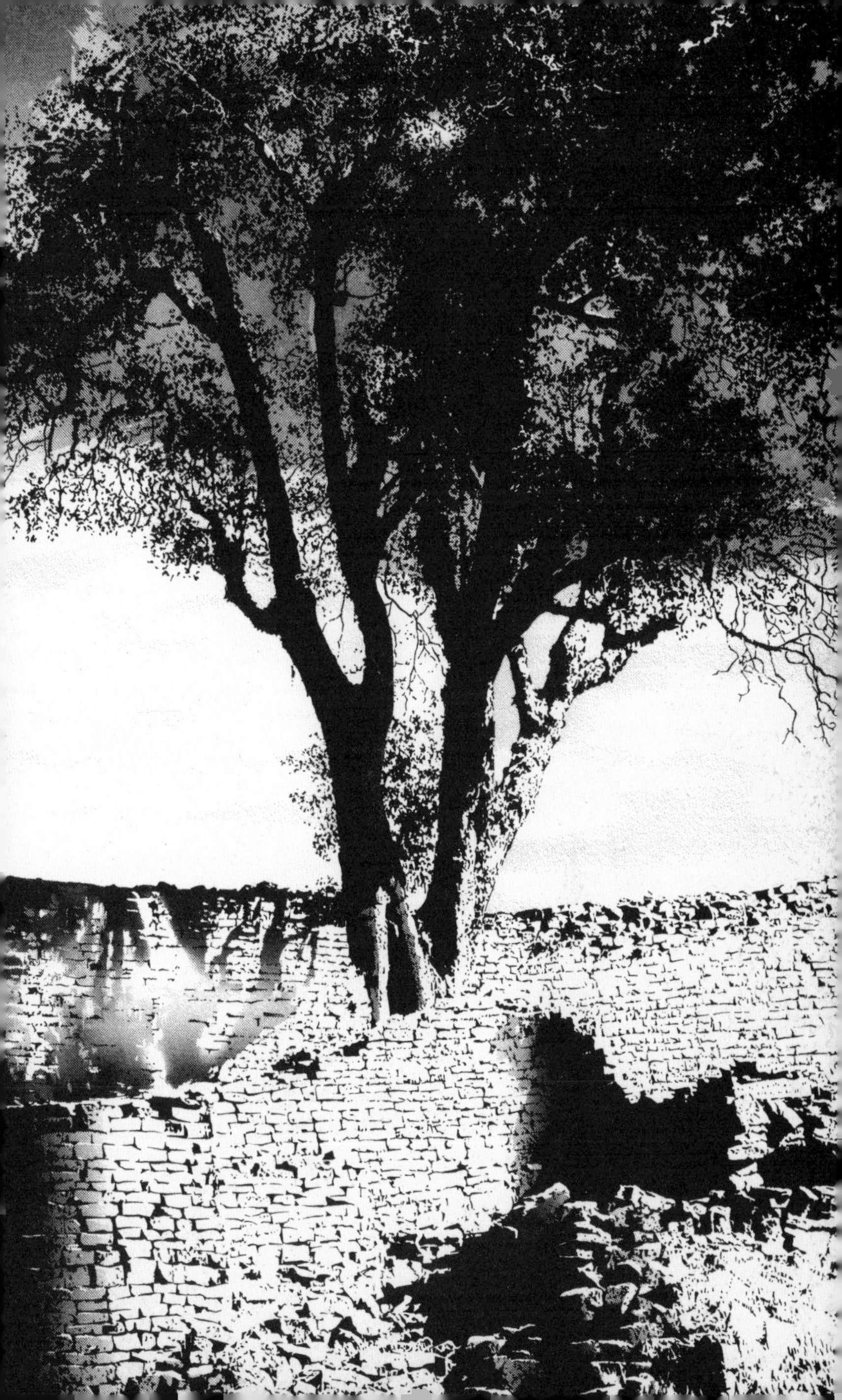

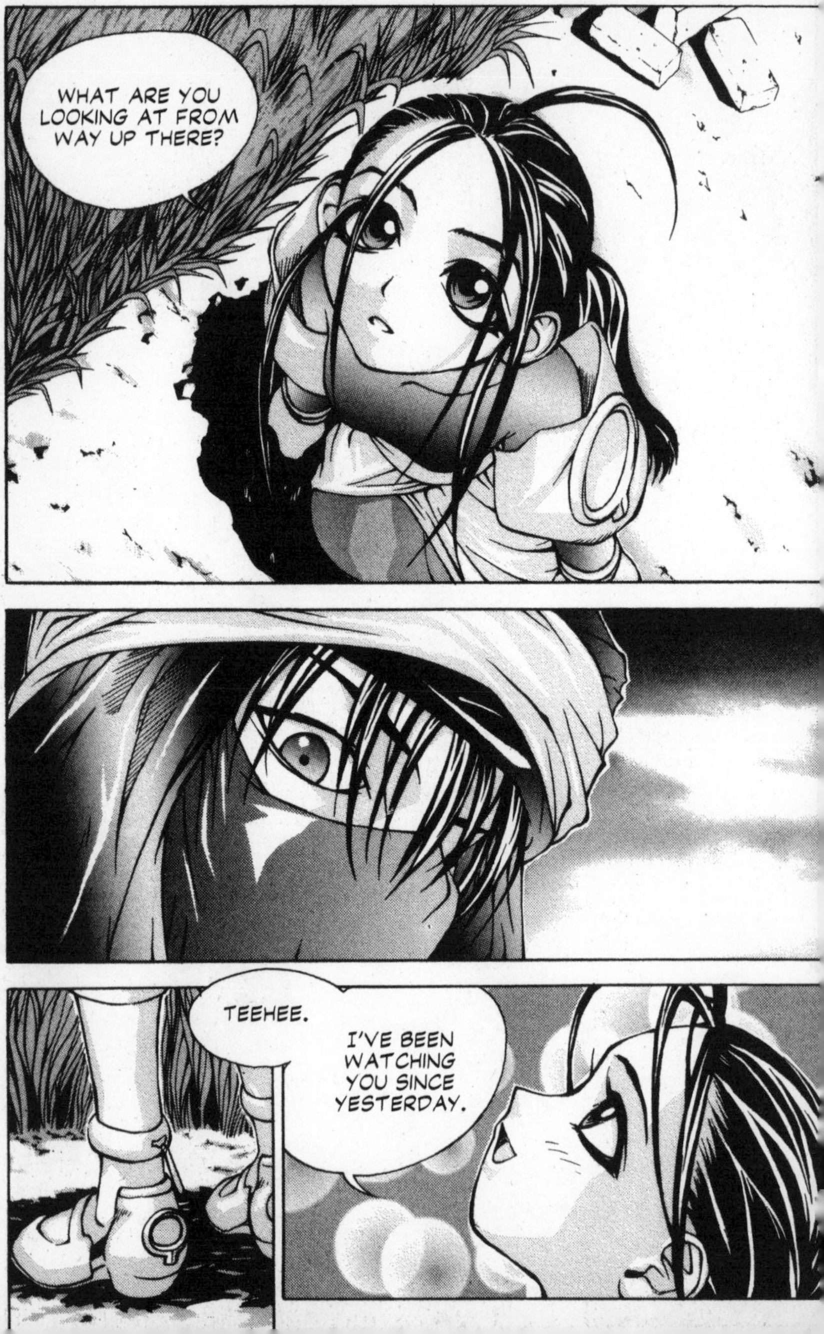
WHAT ARE YOU LOOKING AT FROM WAY UP THERE?
TEEHEE.
I'VE BEEN WATCHING YOU SINCE YESTERDAY.

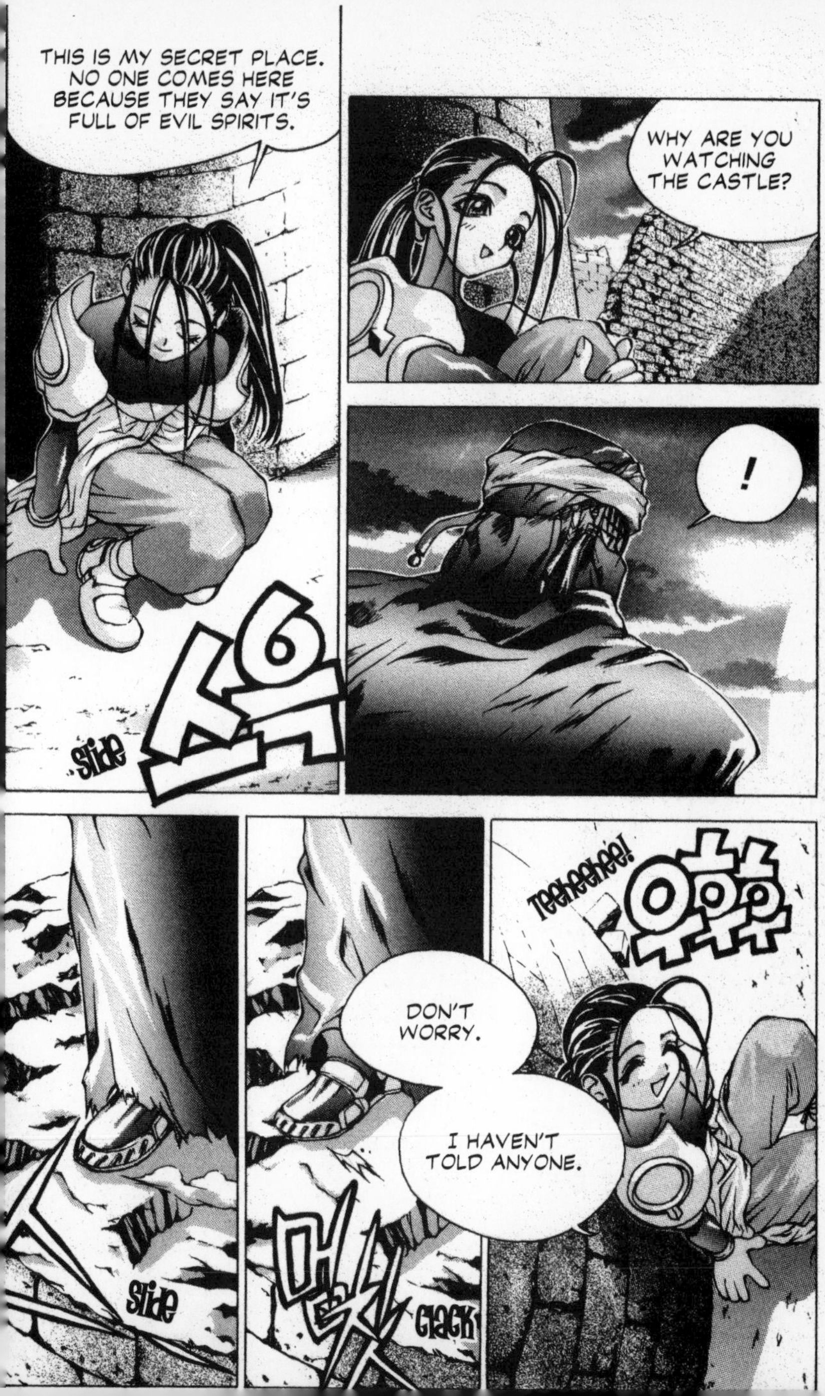
THIS IS MY SECRET PLACE. NO ONE COMES HERE BECAUSE THEY SAY IT'S FULL OF EVIL SPIRITS.
slide
WHY ARE YOU WATCHING THE CASTLE?
!
slide
DON'T WORRY.
CLACK!
TEEHEEHEE!
I HAVEN'T TOLD ANYONE.

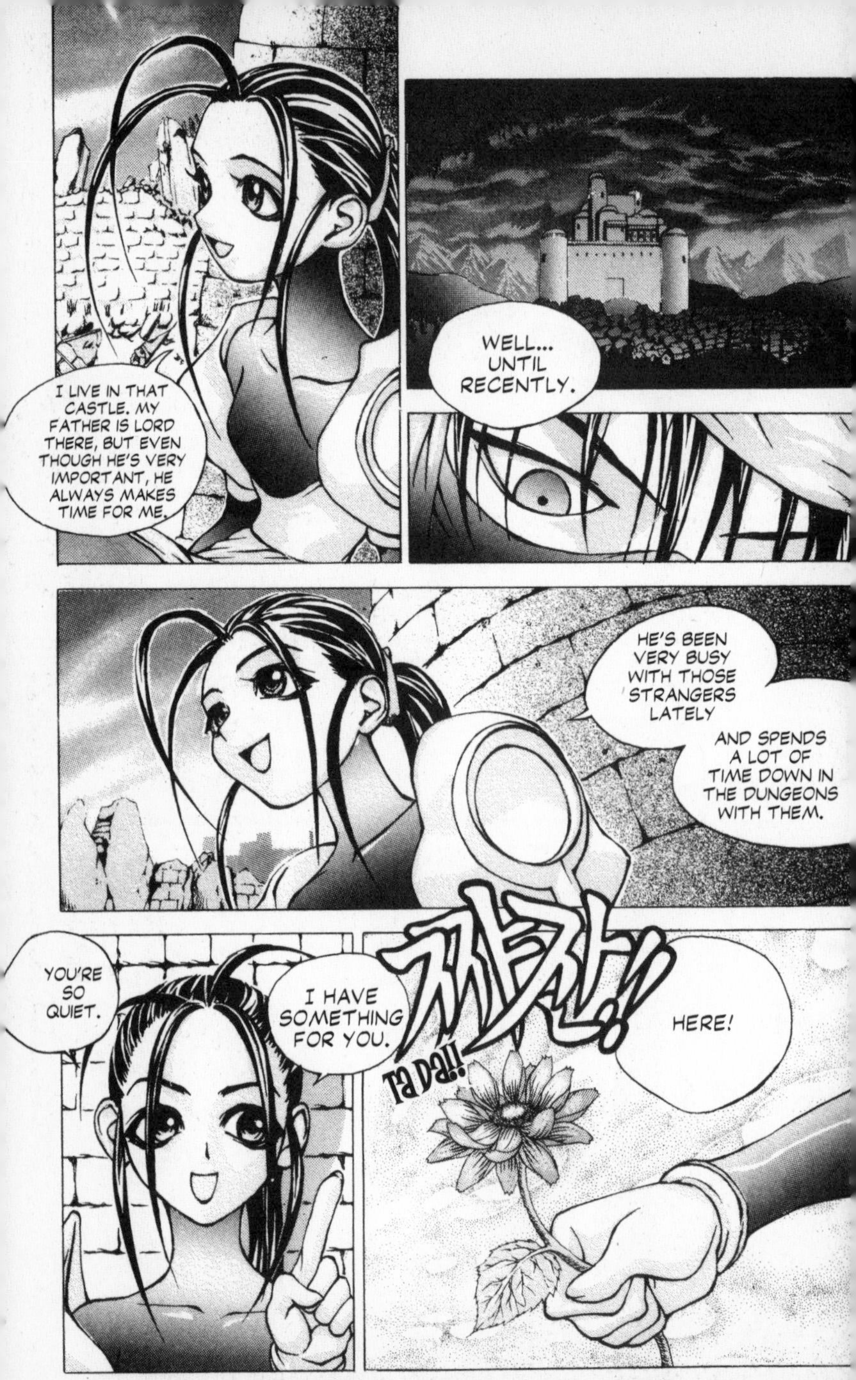
I LIVE IN THAT CASTLE. MY FATHER IS LORD THERE, BUT EVEN THOUGH HE'S VERY IMPORTANT, HE ALWAYS MAKES TIME FOR ME.
WELL... UNTIL RECENTLY.
HE'S BEEN VERY BUSY WITH THOSE STRANGERS LATELY
AND SPENDS A LOT OF TIME DOWN IN THE DUNGEONS WITH THEM.
YOU'RE SO QUIET.
I HAVE SOMETHING FOR YOU.
TA DA!!
HERE!

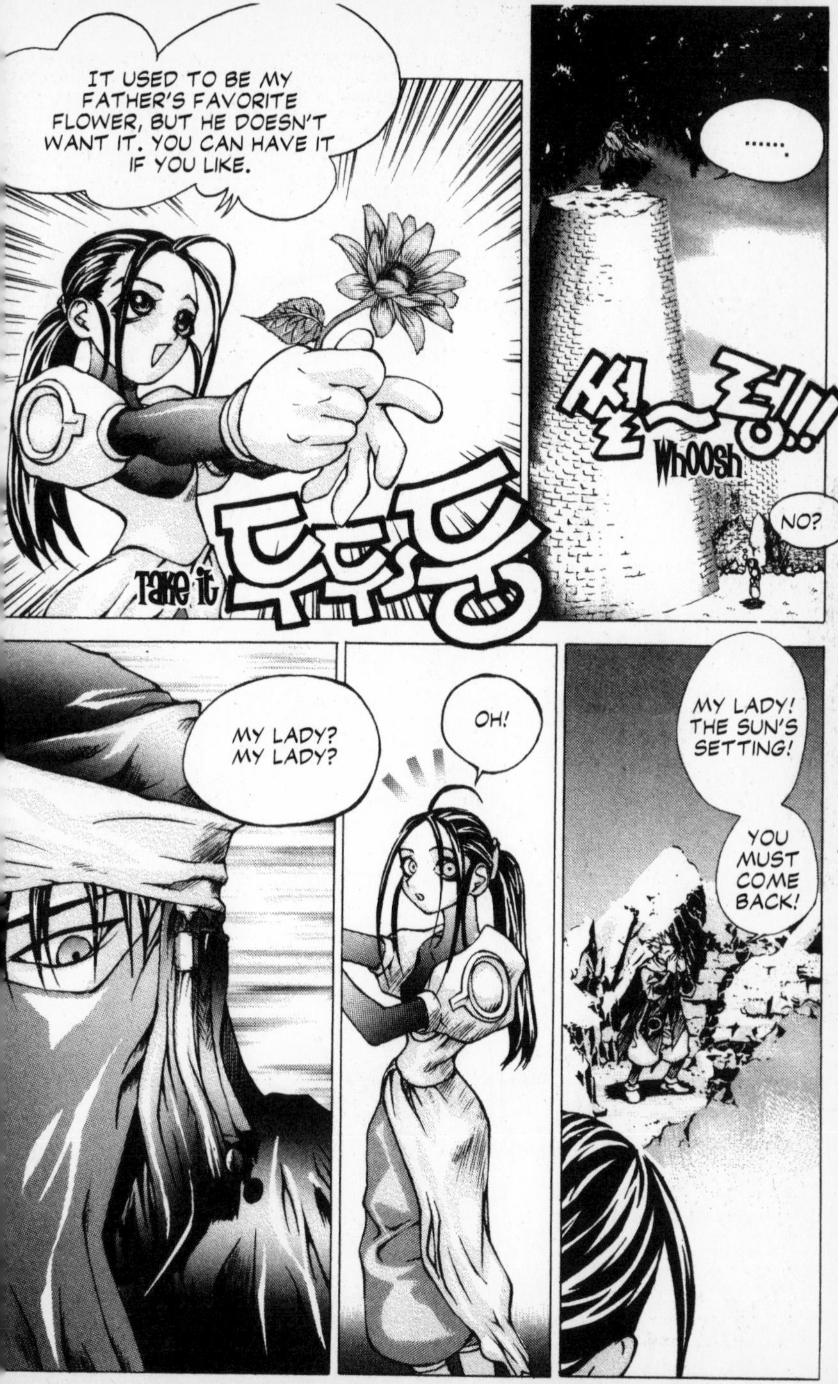
IT USED TO BE MY FATHER'S FAVORITE FLOWER, BUT HE DOESN'T WANT IT. YOU CAN HAVE IT IF YOU LIKE.
Take it
......
Whoosh
NO?
MY LADY? MY LADY?
OH!
MY LADY! THE SUN'S SETTING!
YOU MUST COME BACK!

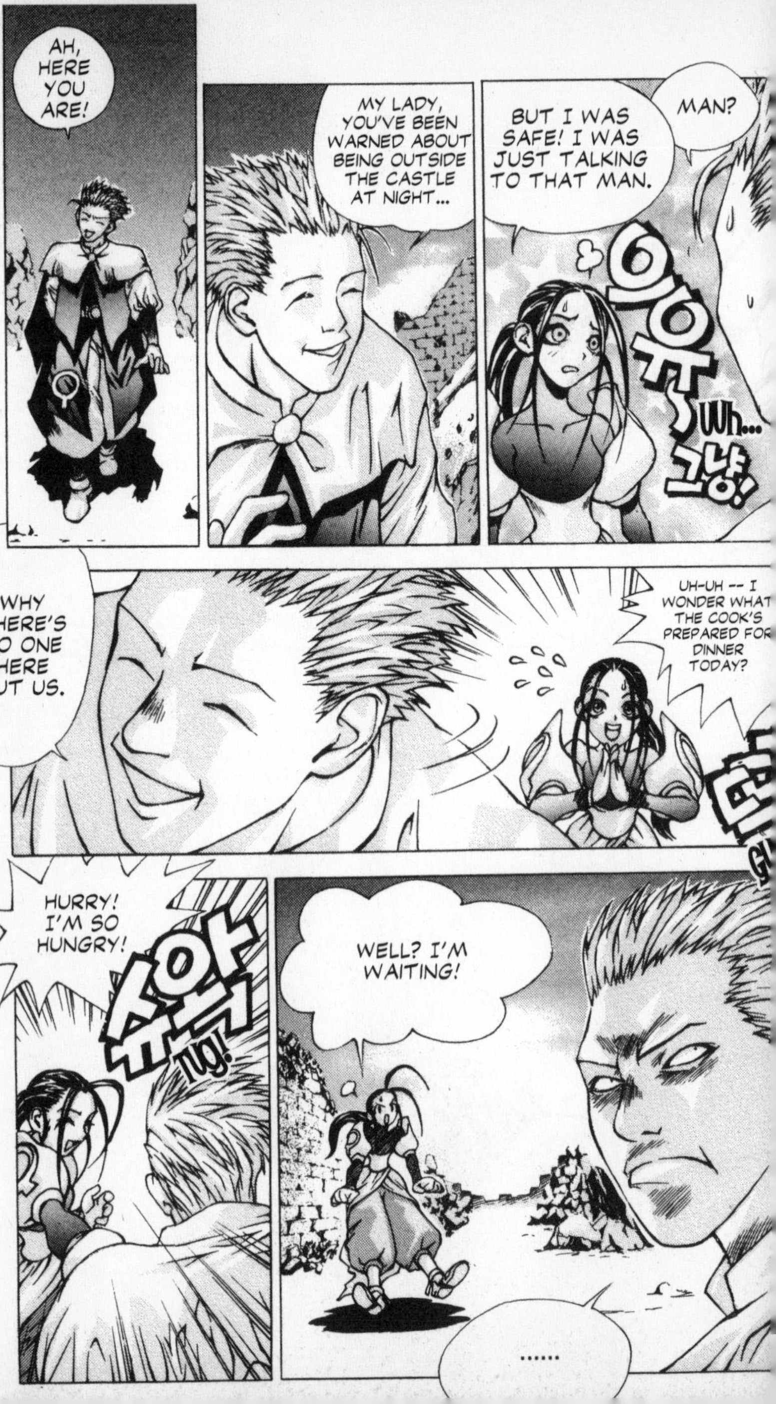

AH, HERE YOU ARE!
MY LADY, YOU'VE BEEN WARNED ABOUT BEING OUTSIDE THE CASTLE AT NIGHT...
BUT I WAS SAFE! I WAS JUST TALKING TO THAT MAN.
MAN?
uh...
WHY THERE'S NO ONE HERE BUT US.
UH-UH -- I WONDER WHAT THE COOK'S PREPARED FOR DINNER TODAY?
HURRY! I'M SO HUNGRY!
TUG!
WELL? I'M WAITING!
......

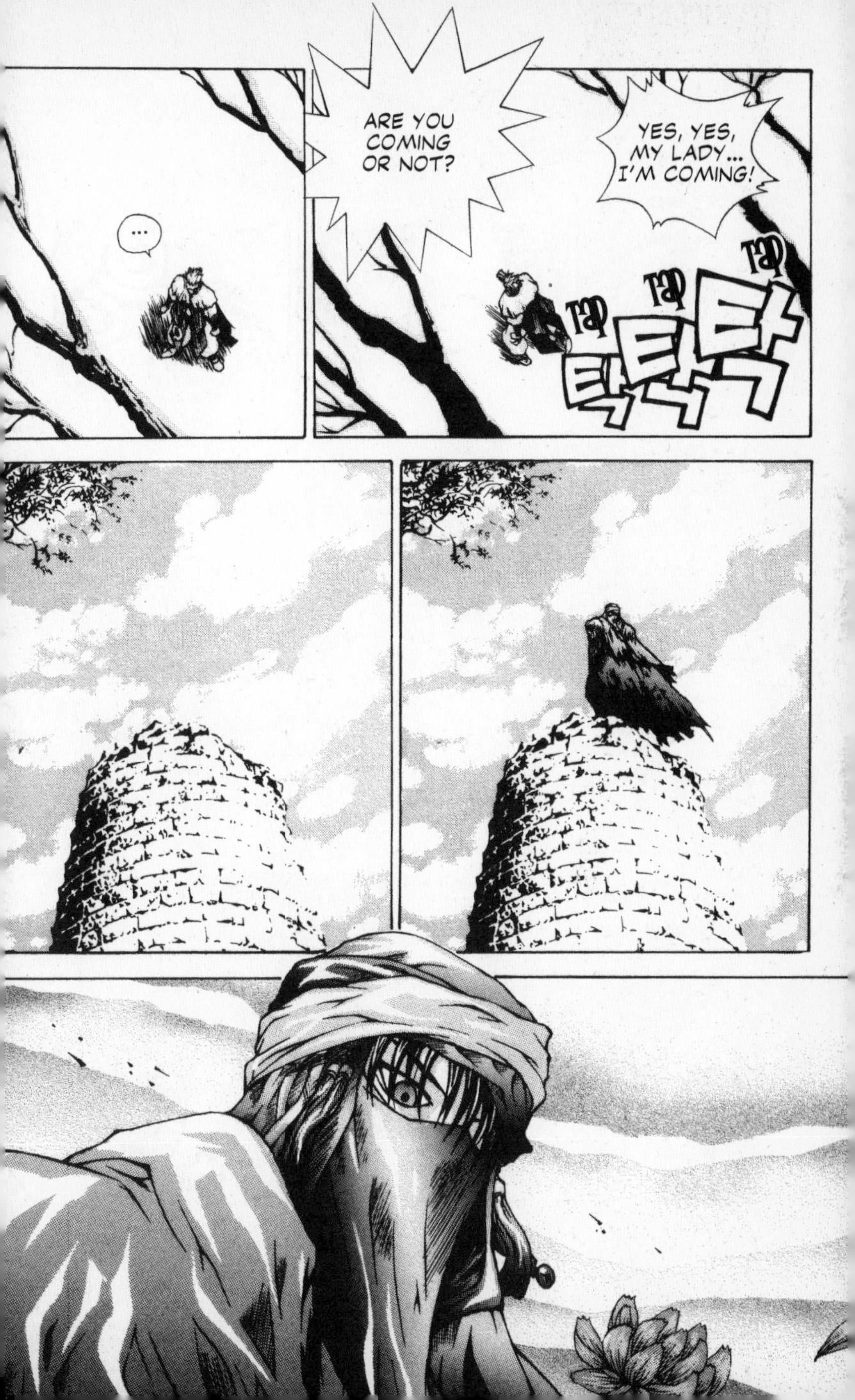
...
ARE YOU COMING OR NOT?
YES, YES, MY LADY... I'M COMING!
TAP
TAP
TAP

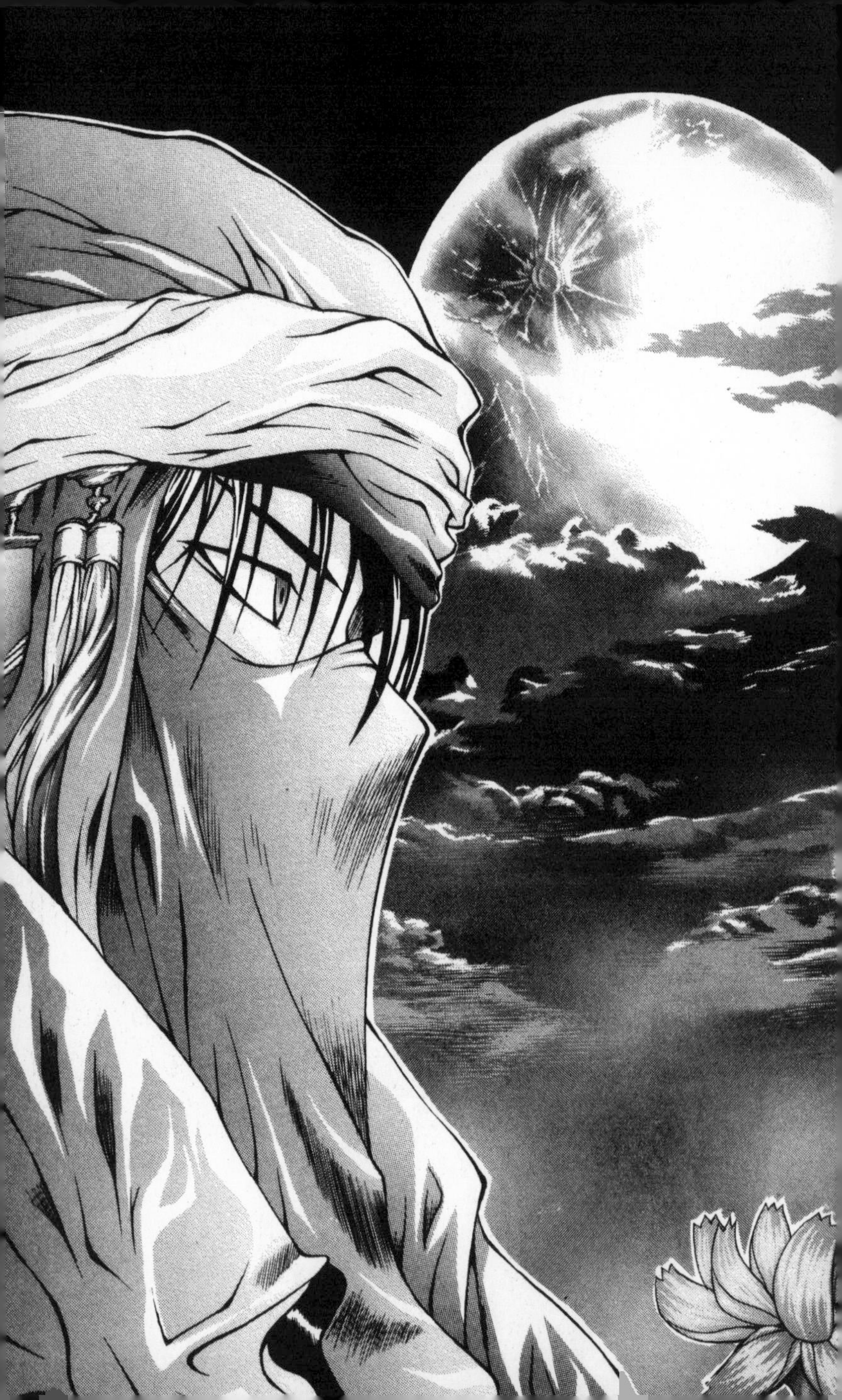

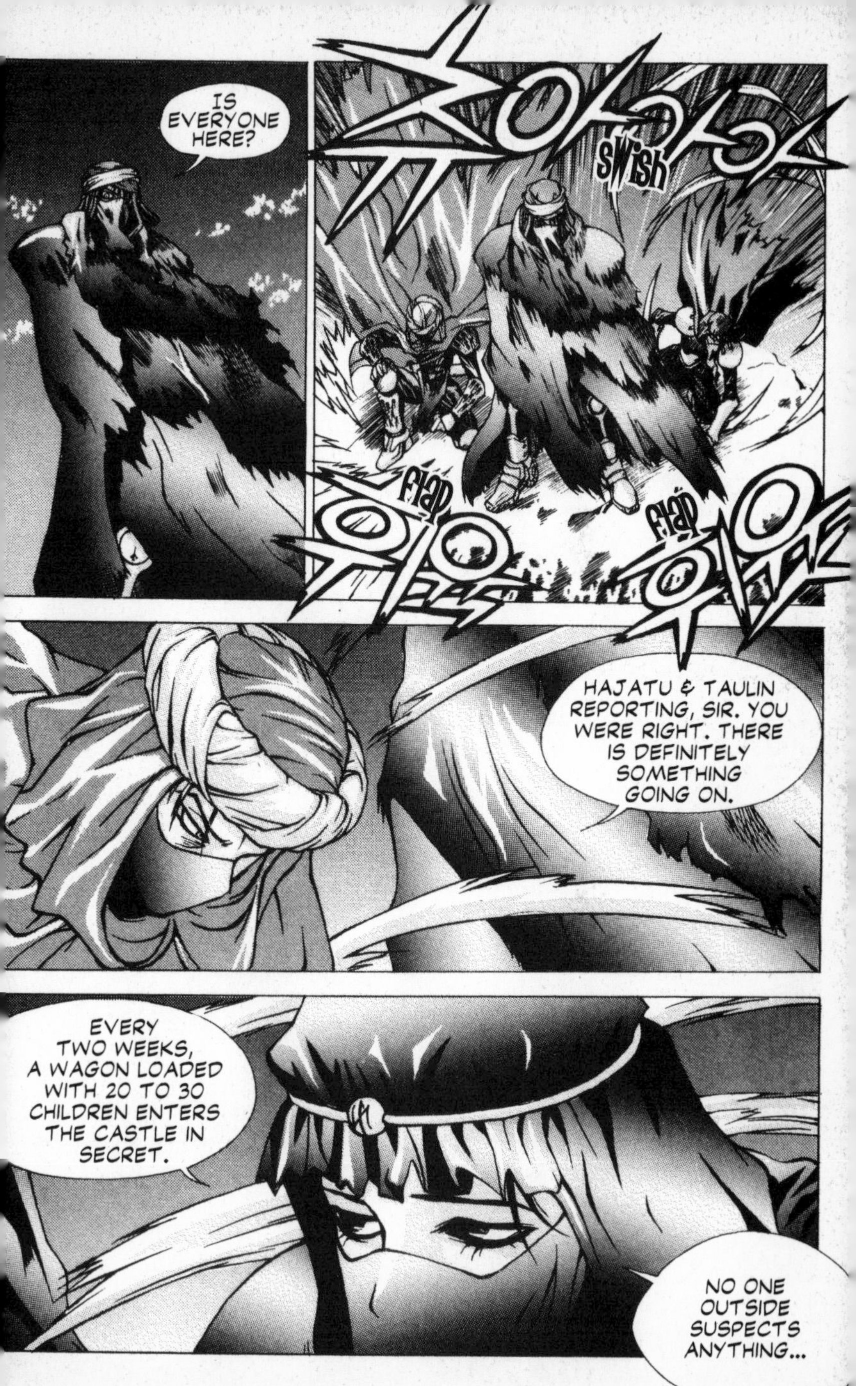
IS EVERYONE HERE?
SWISH
FLAP
FLAP
HAJATU & TAULIN REPORTING, SIR. YOU WERE RIGHT. THERE IS DEFINITELY SOMETHING GOING ON.
EVERY TWO WEEKS, A WAGON LOADED WITH 20 TO 30 CHILDREN ENTERS THE CASTLE IN SECRET.
NO ONE OUTSIDE SUSPECTS ANYTHING...

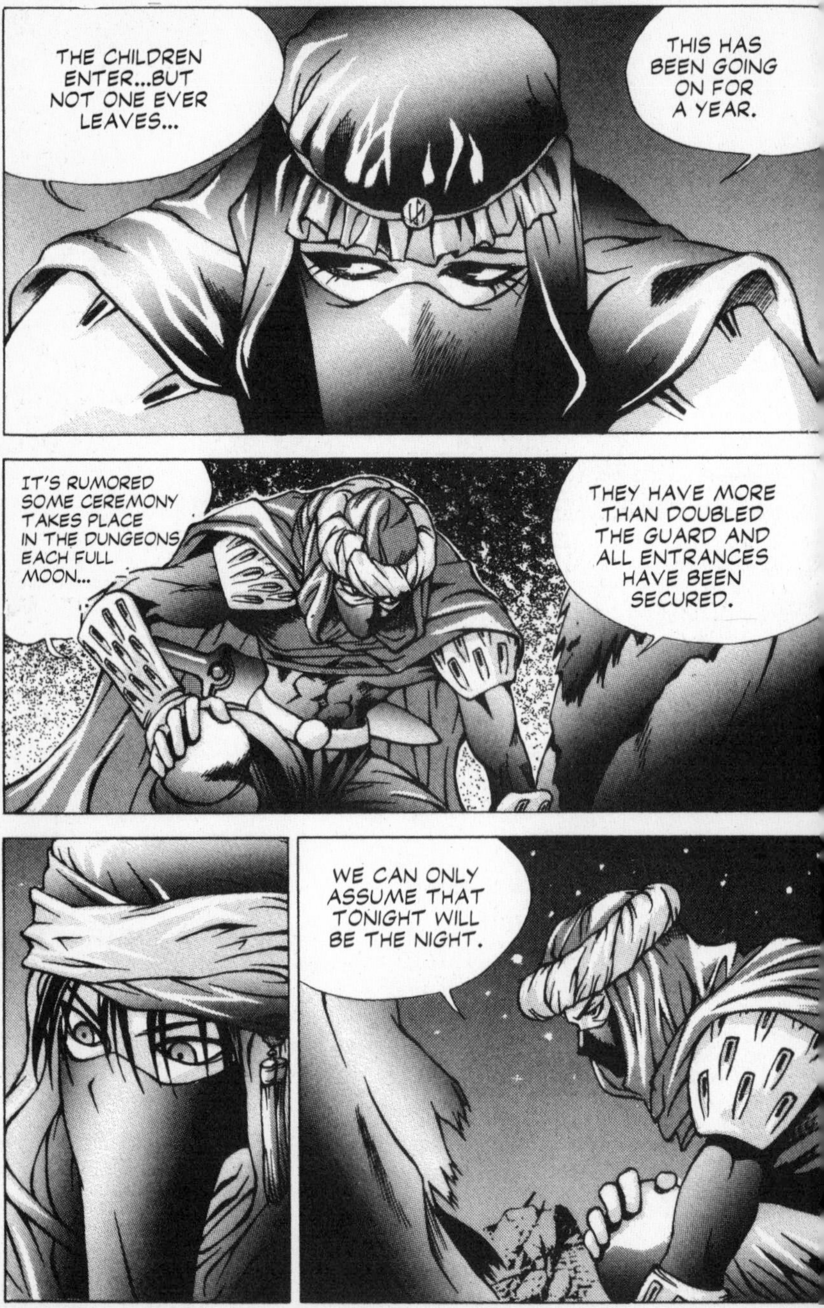
THE CHILDREN ENTER...BUT NOT ONE EVER LEAVES...
THIS HAS BEEN GOING ON FOR A YEAR.
IT'S RUMORED SOME CEREMONY TAKES PLACE IN THE DUNGEONS EACH FULL MOON...
THEY HAVE MORE THAN DOUBLED THE GUARD AND ALL ENTRANCES HAVE BEEN SECURED.
WE CAN ONLY ASSUME THAT TONIGHT WILL BE THE NIGHT.

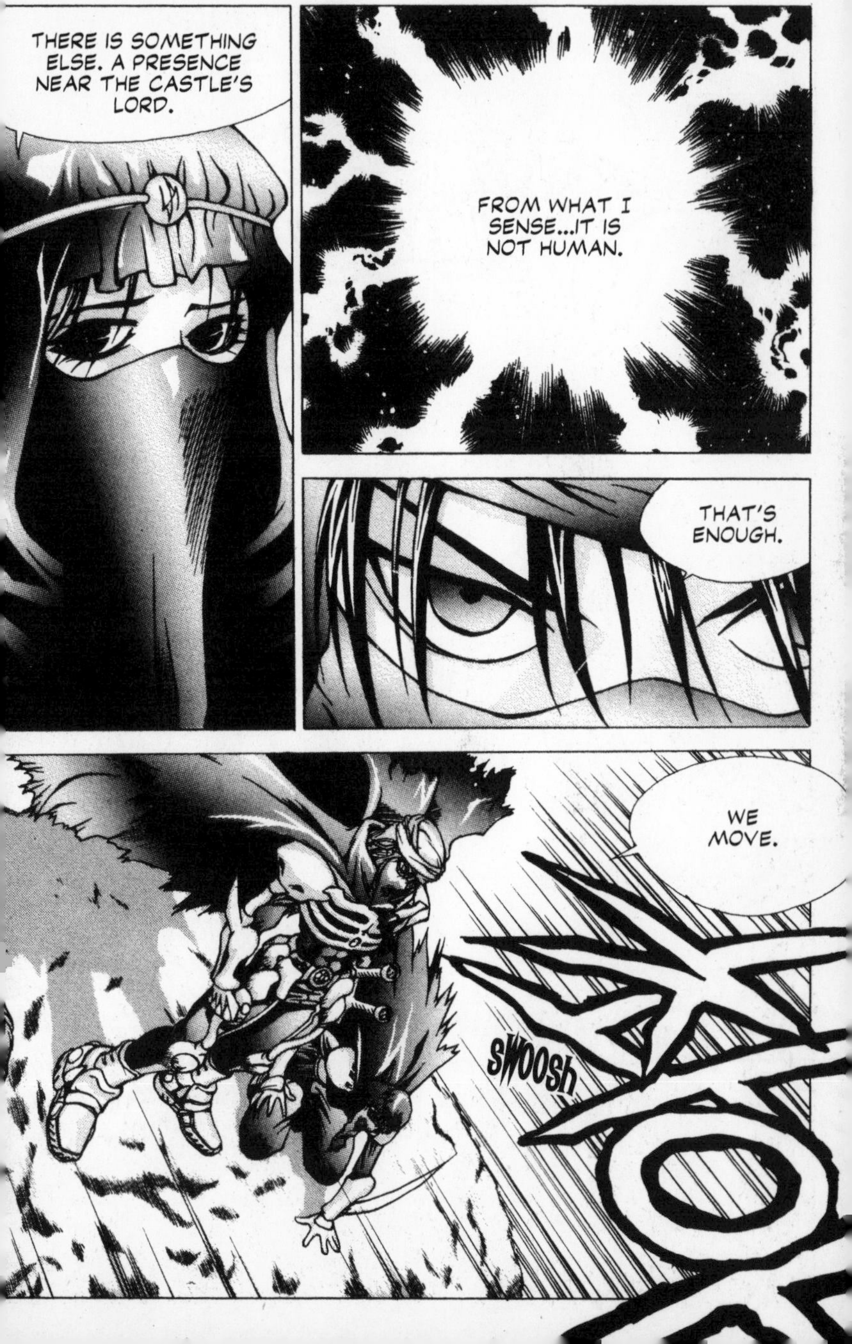
THERE IS SOMETHING ELSE. A PRESENCE NEAR THE CASTLE'S LORD.
FROM WHAT I SENSE...IT IS NOT HUMAN.
THAT'S ENOUGH.
WE MOVE.
sWOOSh

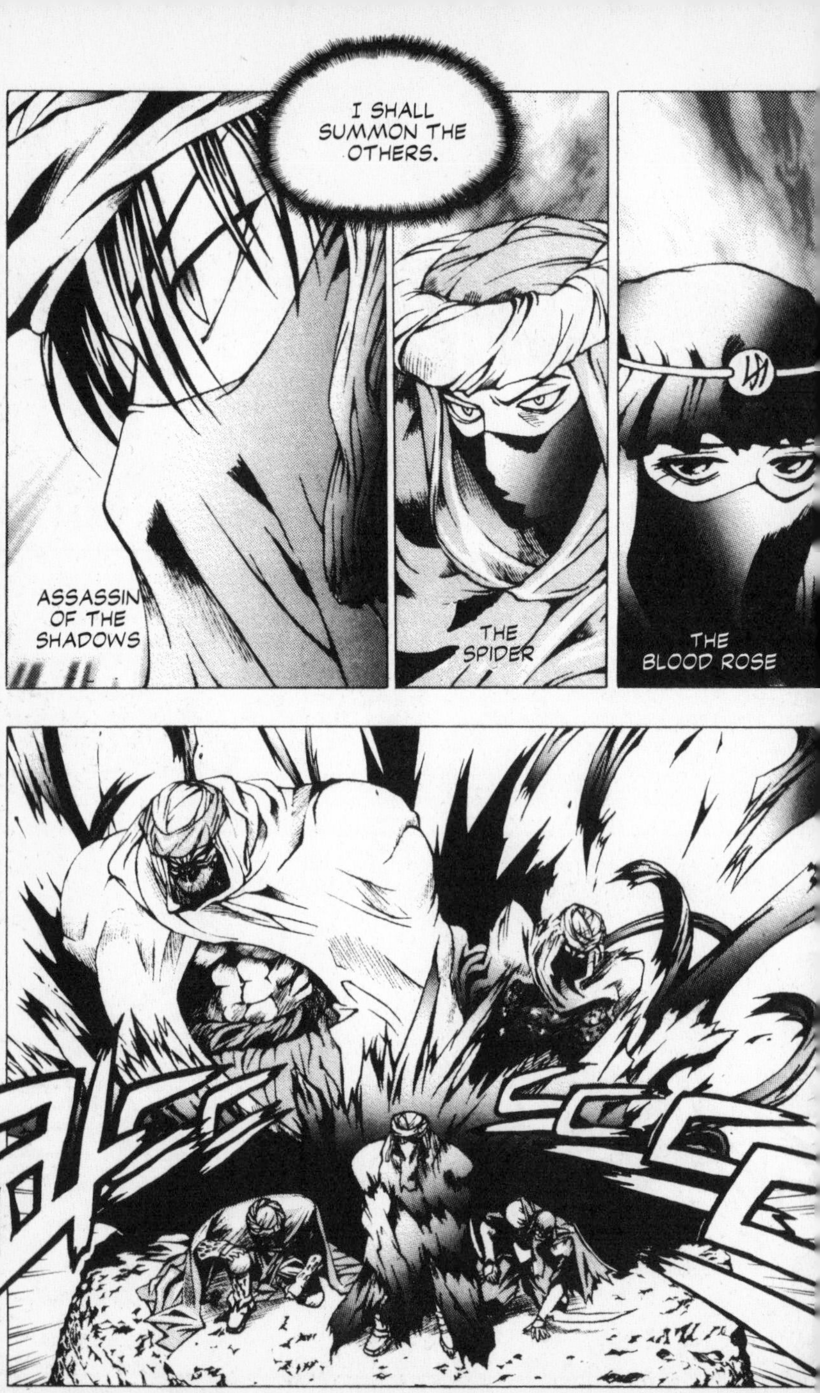
I SHALL SUMMON THE OTHERS.
ASSASSIN OF THE SHADOWS
THE SPIDER
THE BLOOD ROSE

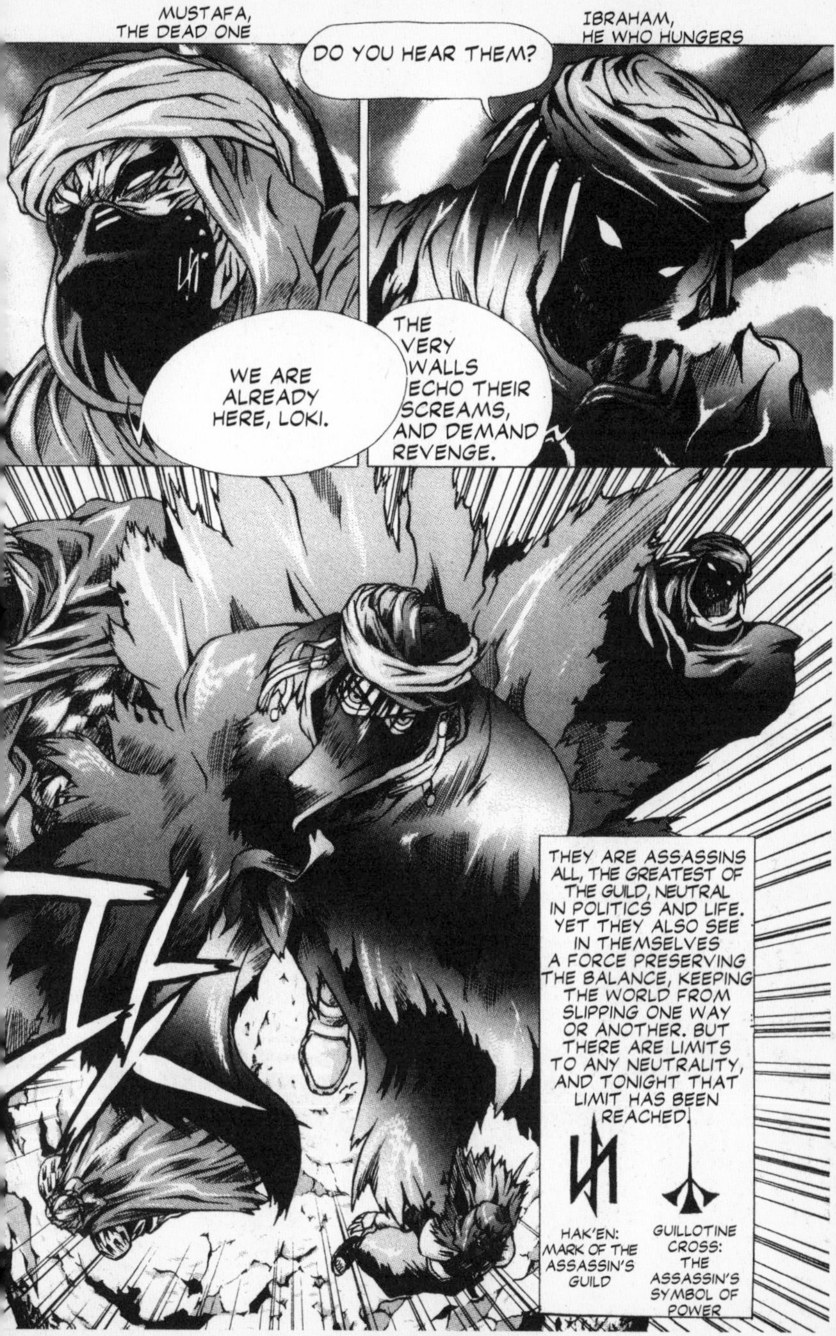
MUSTAFA, THE DEAD ONE
IBRAHAM, HE WHO HUNGERS
DO YOU HEAR THEM?
WE ARE ALREADY HERE, LOKI.
THE VERY WALLS ECHO THEIR SCREAMS, AND DEMAND REVENGE.
THEY ARE ASSASSINS ALL, THE GREATEST OF THE GUILD, NEUTRAL IN POLITICS AND LIFE. YET THEY ALSO SEE IN THEMSELVES A FORCE PRESERVING THE BALANCE, KEEPING THE WORLD FROM SLIPPING ONE WAY OR ANOTHER. BUT THERE ARE LIMITS TO ANY NEUTRALITY, AND TONIGHT THAT LIMIT HAS BEEN REACHED.
HAK'EN: MARK OF THE ASSASSIN'S GUILD
GUILLOTINE CROSS: THE ASSASSIN'S SYMBOL OF POWER

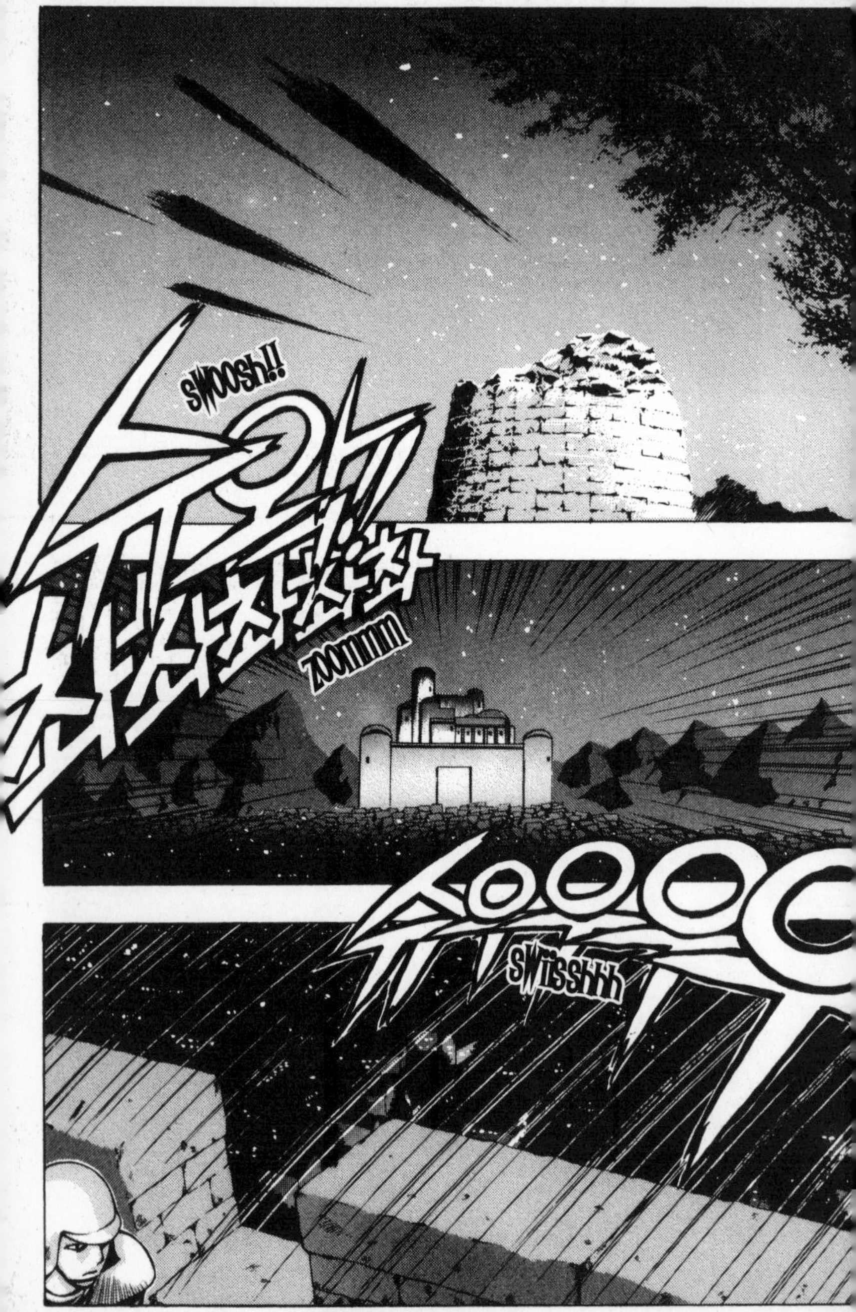
SWOOSH!!
ZOOMMMM
SWISSHHH

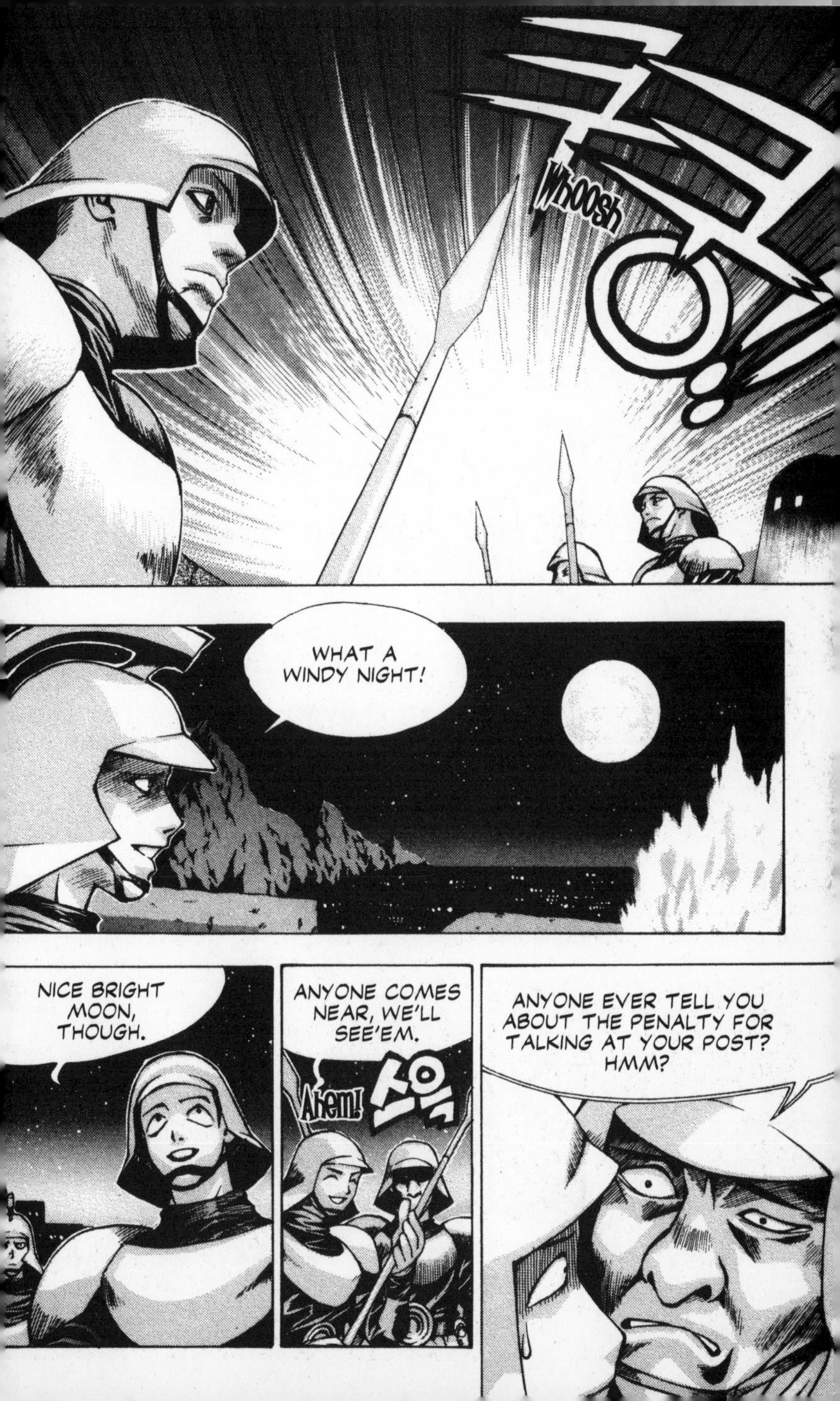

Whoosh
WHAT A WINDY NIGHT!
NICE BRIGHT MOON, THOUGH.
ANYONE COMES NEAR, WE'LL SEE'EM.
Ahem!
ANYONE EVER TELL YOU ABOUT THE PENALTY FOR TALKING AT YOUR POST? HMM?

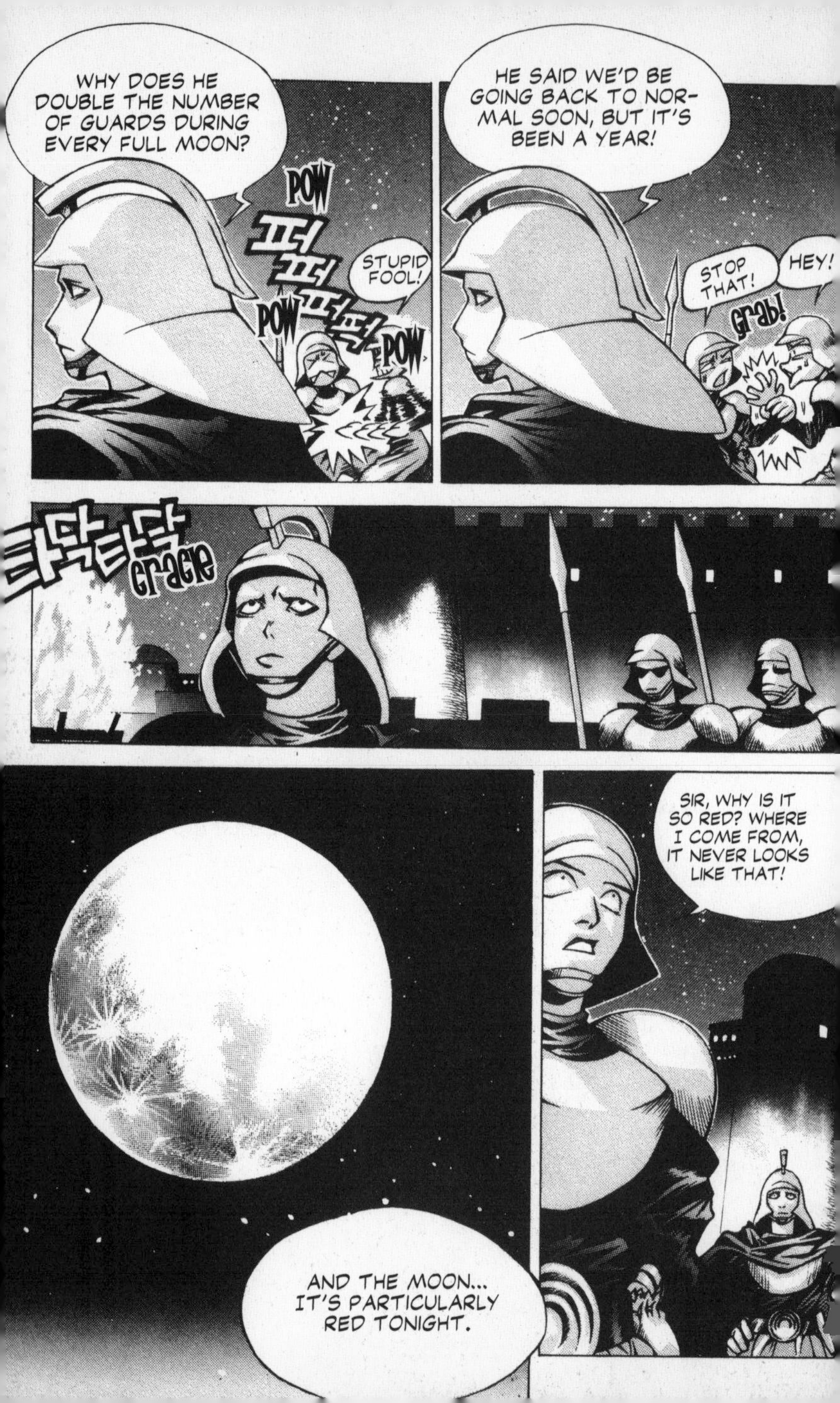
WHY DOES HE DOUBLE THE NUMBER OF GUARDS DURING EVERY FULL MOON?
POW
퍼!
퍼!
POW
STUPID FOOL!
POW
HE SAID WE'D BE GOING BACK TO NOR-MAL SOON, BUT IT'S BEEN A YEAR!
STOP THAT!
HEY!
GRAB!
타닥타닥
cracle
AND THE MOON... IT'S PARTICULARLY RED TONIGHT.
SIR, WHY IS IT SO RED? WHERE I COME FROM, IT NEVER LOOKS LIKE THAT!

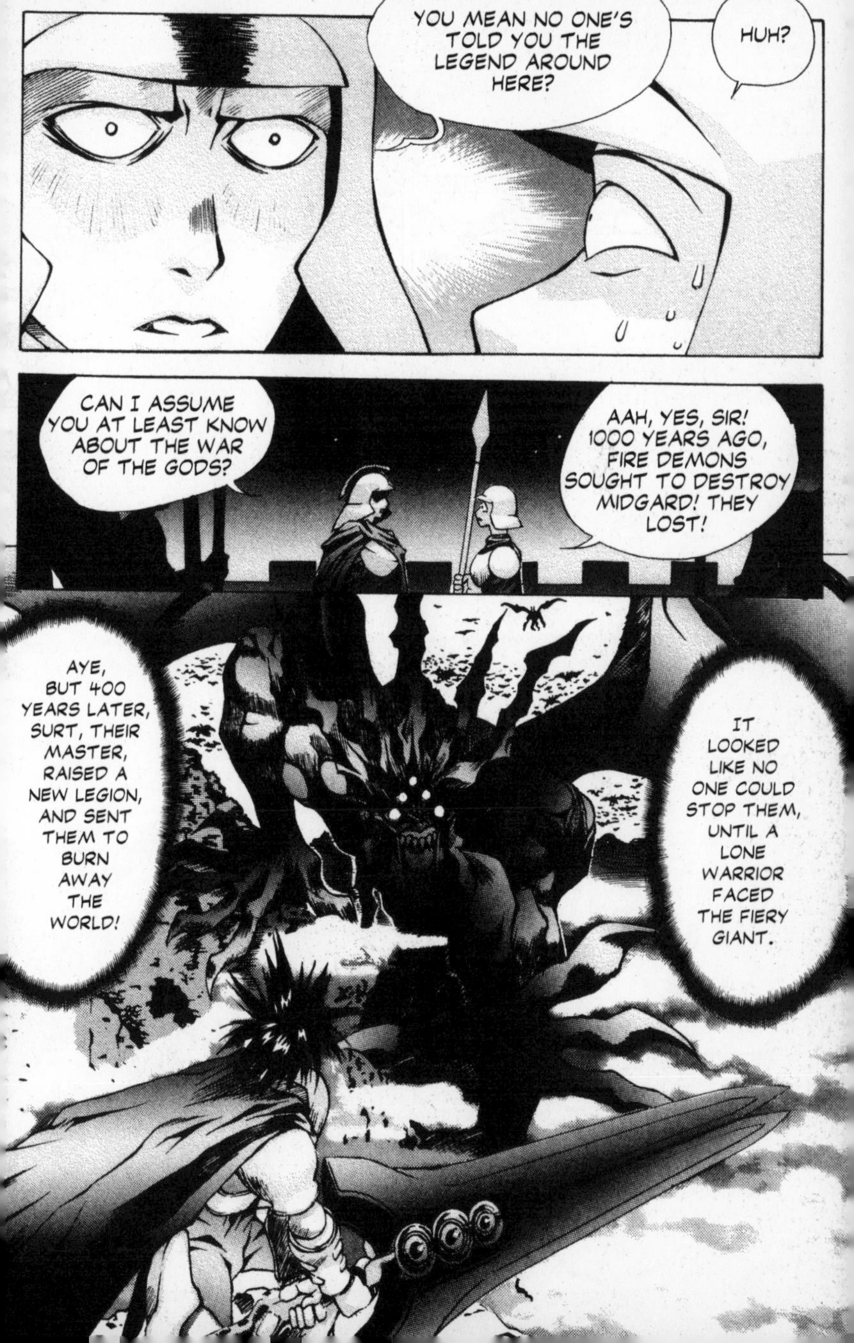
YOU MEAN NO ONE'S TOLD YOU THE LEGEND AROUND HERE?
HUH?
CAN I ASSUME YOU AT LEAST KNOW ABOUT THE WAR OF THE GODS?
AAH, YES, SIR! 1000 YEARS AGO, FIRE DEMONS SOUGHT TO DESTROY MIDGARD! THEY LOST!
AYE, BUT 400 YEARS LATER, SURT, THEIR MASTER, RAISED A NEW LEGION, AND SENT THEM TO BURN AWAY THE WORLD!
IT LOOKED LIKE NO ONE COULD STOP THEM, UNTIL A LONE WARRIOR FACED THE FIERY GIANT.

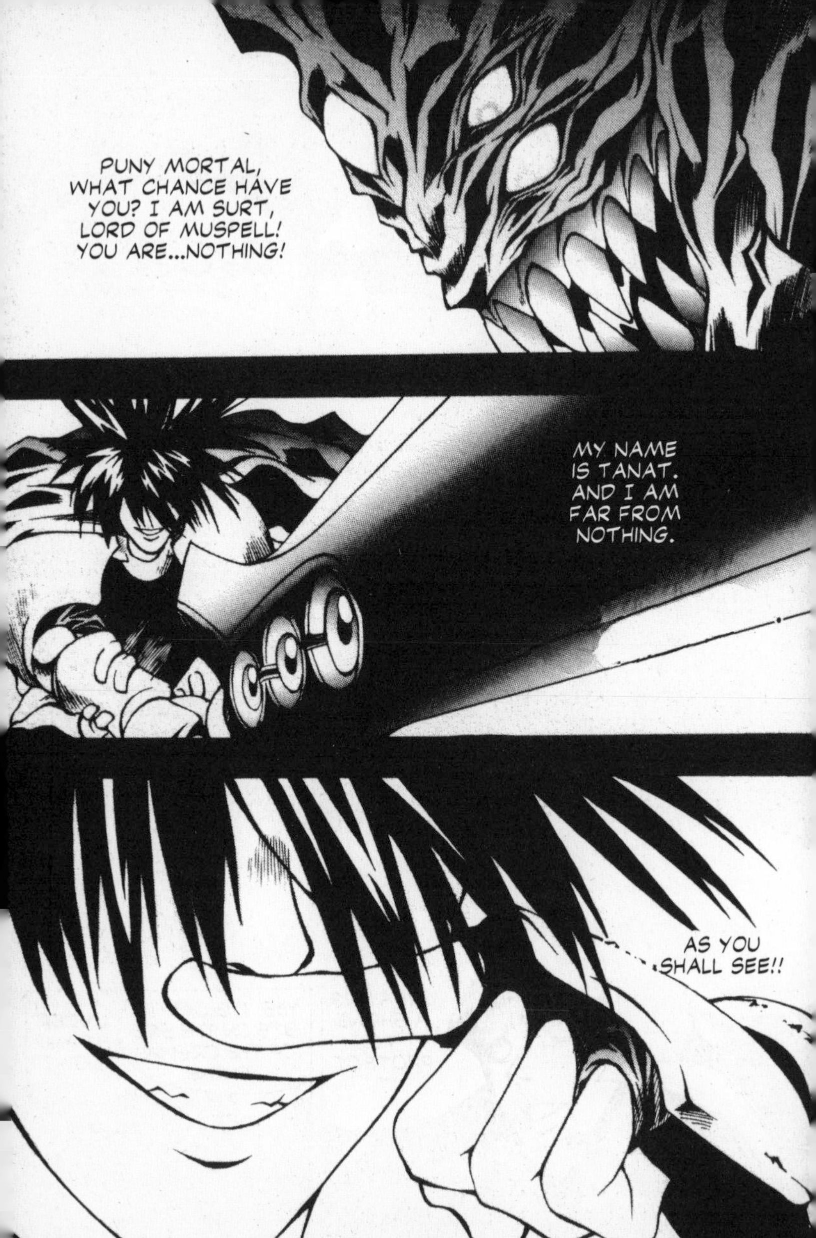
PUNY MORTAL, WHAT CHANCE HAVE YOU? I AM SURT, LORD OF MUSPELL! YOU ARE...NOTHING!
MY NAME IS TANAT. AND I AM FAR FROM NOTHING.
AS YOU SHALL SEE!!

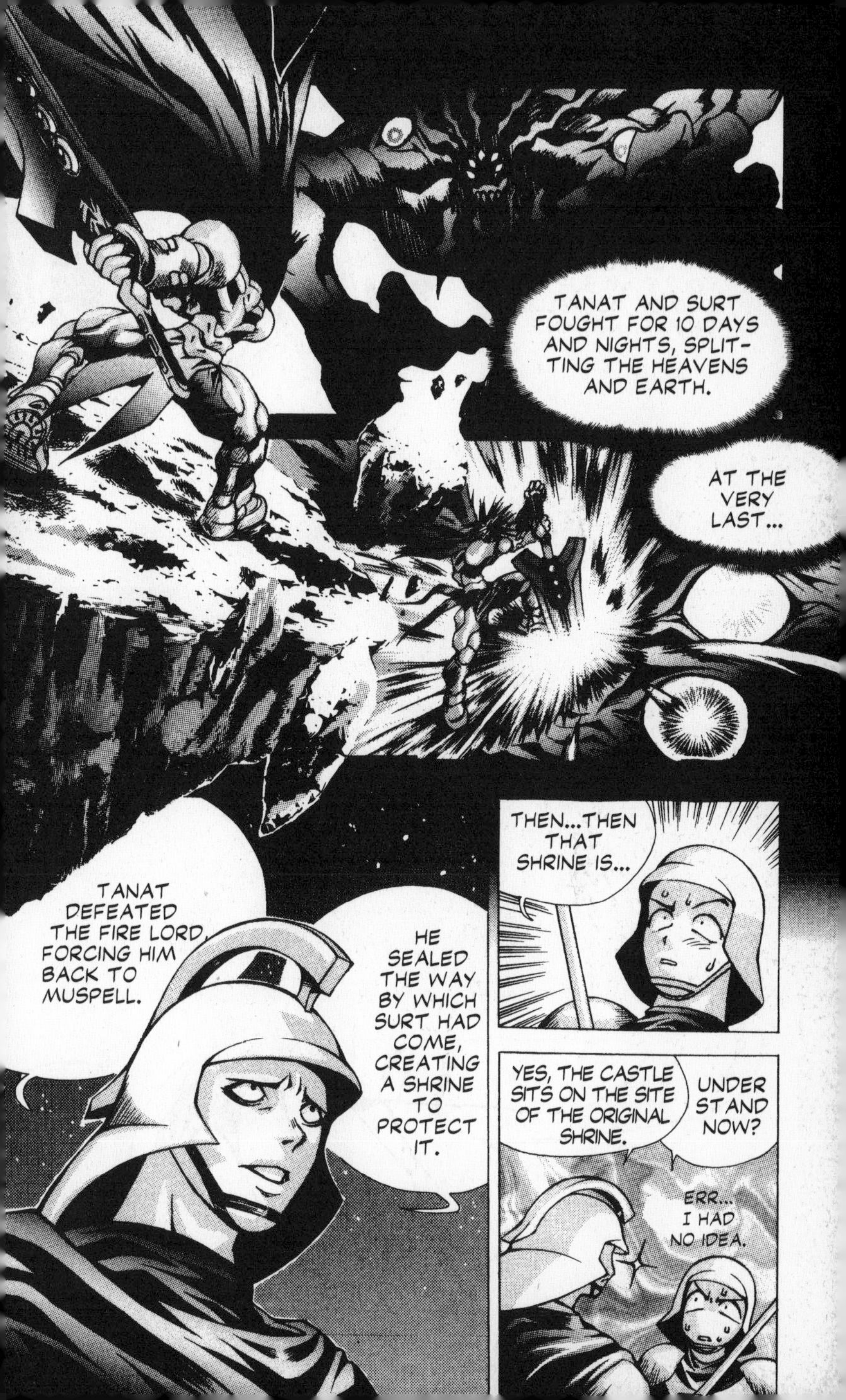
TANAT AND SURT FOUGHT FOR 10 DAYS AND NIGHTS, SPLITTING THE HEAVENS AND EARTH.
AT THE VERY LAST...
TANAT DEFEATED THE FIRE LORD, FORCING HIM BACK TO MUSPELL.
HE SEALED THE WAY BY WHICH SURT HAD COME, CREATING A SHRINE TO PROTECT IT.
THEN...THEN THAT SHRINE IS...
YES, THE CASTLE SITS ON THE SITE OF THE ORIGINAL SHRINE.
UNDER STAND NOW?
ERR... I HAD NO IDEA.

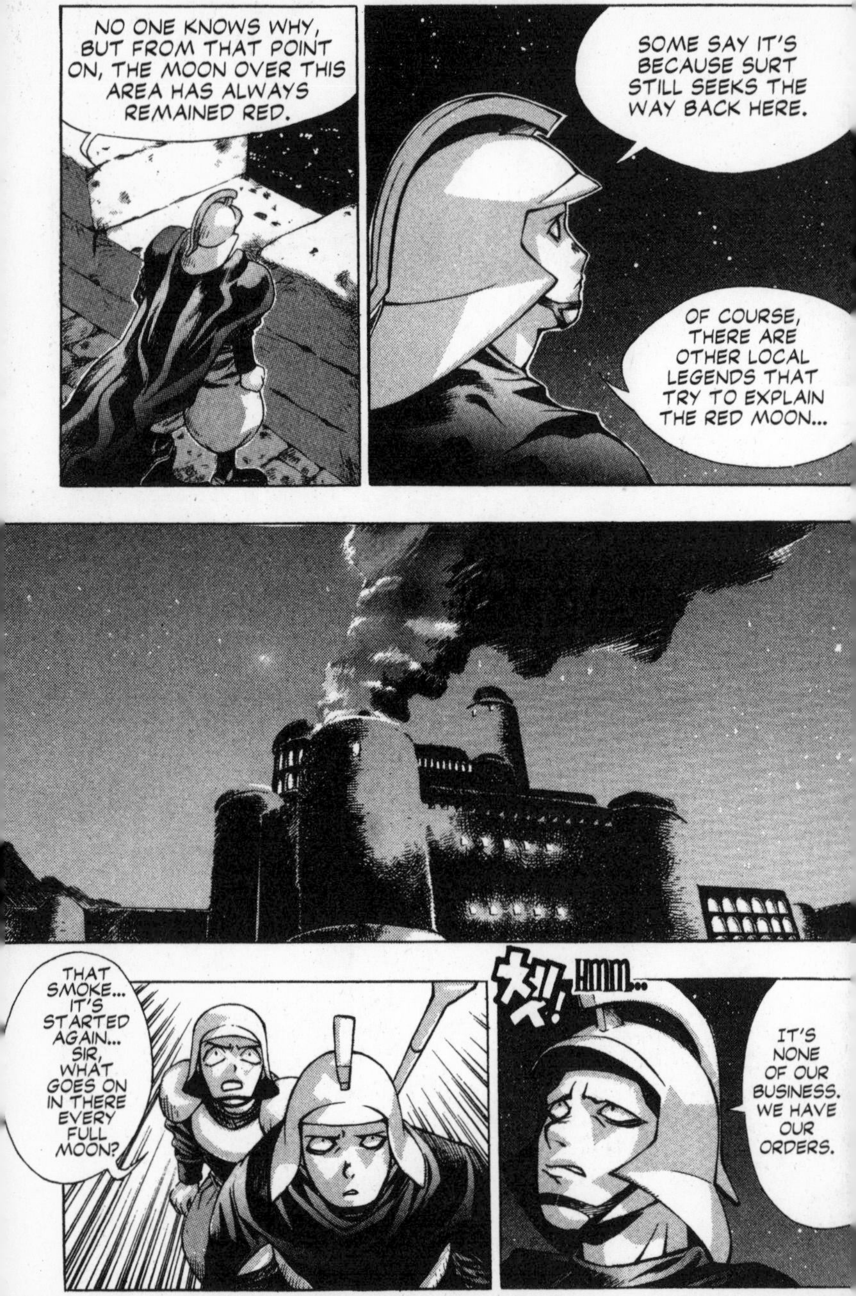
NO ONE KNOWS WHY, BUT FROM THAT POINT ON, THE MOON OVER THIS AREA HAS ALWAYS REMAINED RED.
SOME SAY IT'S BECAUSE SURT STILL SEEKS THE WAY BACK HERE.
OF COURSE, THERE ARE OTHER LOCAL LEGENDS THAT TRY TO EXPLAIN THE RED MOON...
THAT SMOKE... IT'S STARTED AGAIN... SIR, WHAT GOES ON IN THERE EVERY FULL MOON?
HMM...
IT'S NONE OF OUR BUSINESS. WE HAVE OUR ORDERS.

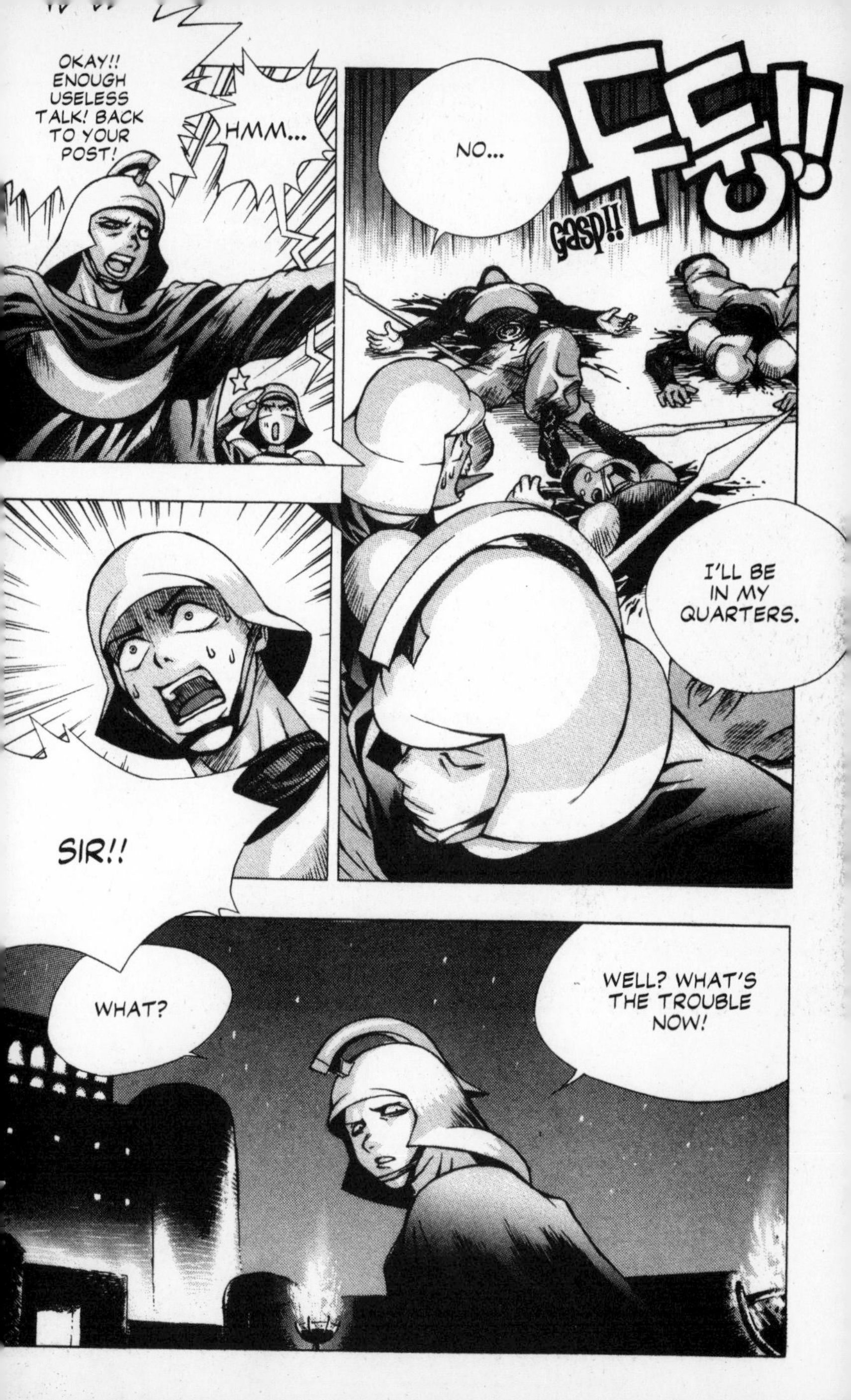
OKAY!! ENOUGH USELESS TALK! BACK TO YOUR POST!
HMM...
SIR!!
NO...
두둥!!
GASP!!
I'LL BE IN MY QUARTERS.
WHAT?
WELL? WHAT'S THE TROUBLE NOW!

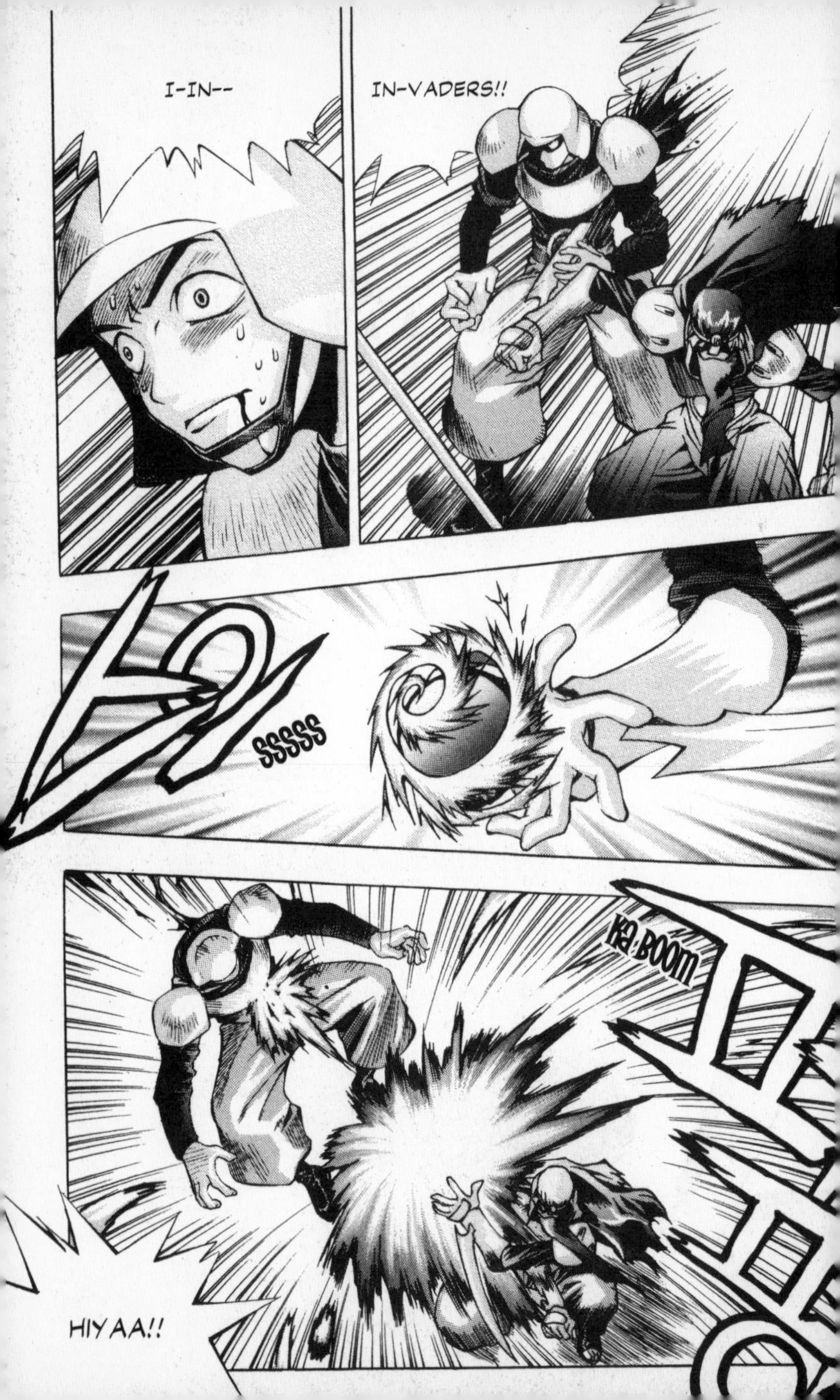
I-IN--
IN-VADERS!!
SSSSS
KA-BOOM
HIYAA!!

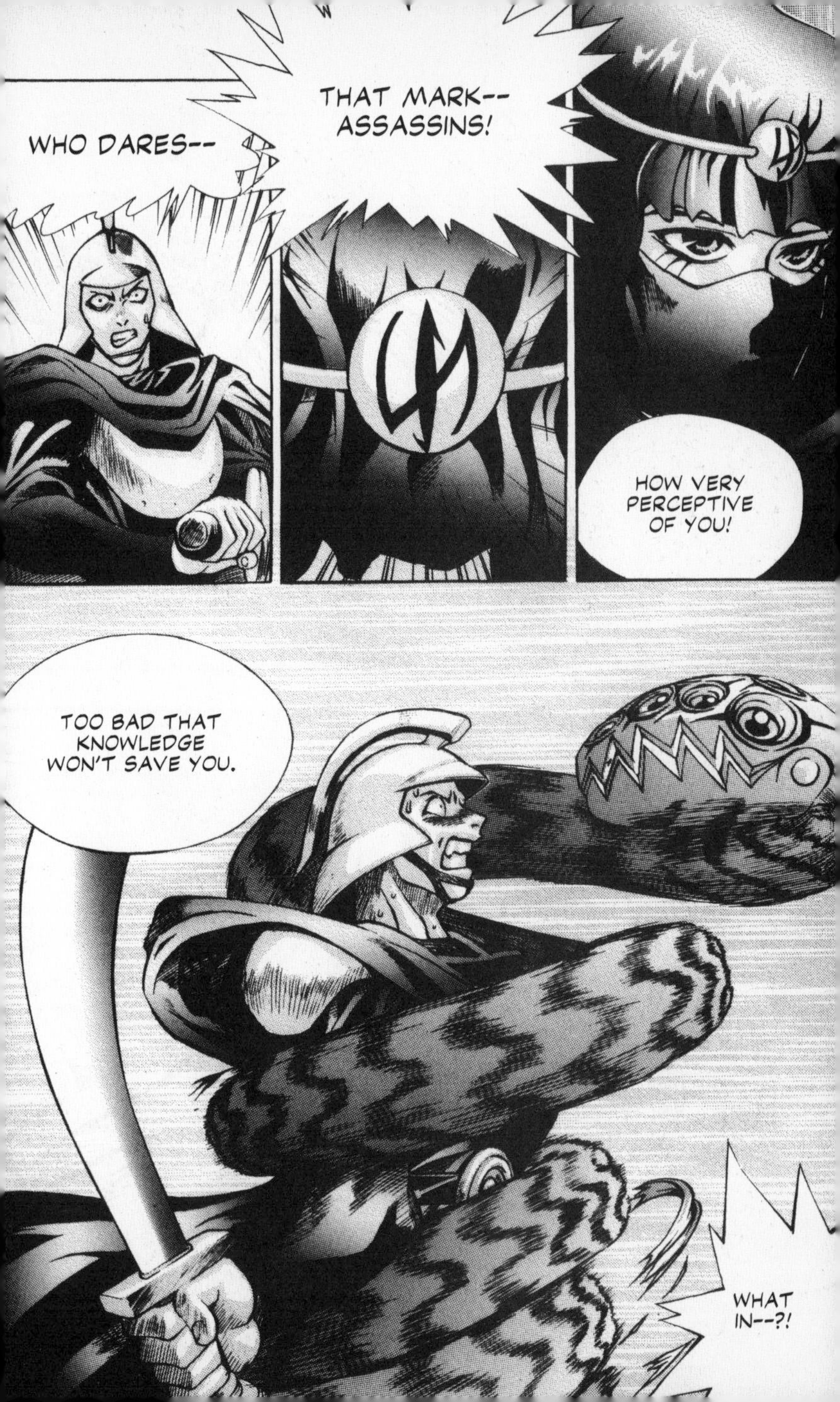
WHO DARES--
THAT MARK--
ASSASSINS!
HOW VERY PERCEPTIVE OF YOU!
TOO BAD THAT KNOWLEDGE WON'T SAVE YOU.
WHAT IN--?!

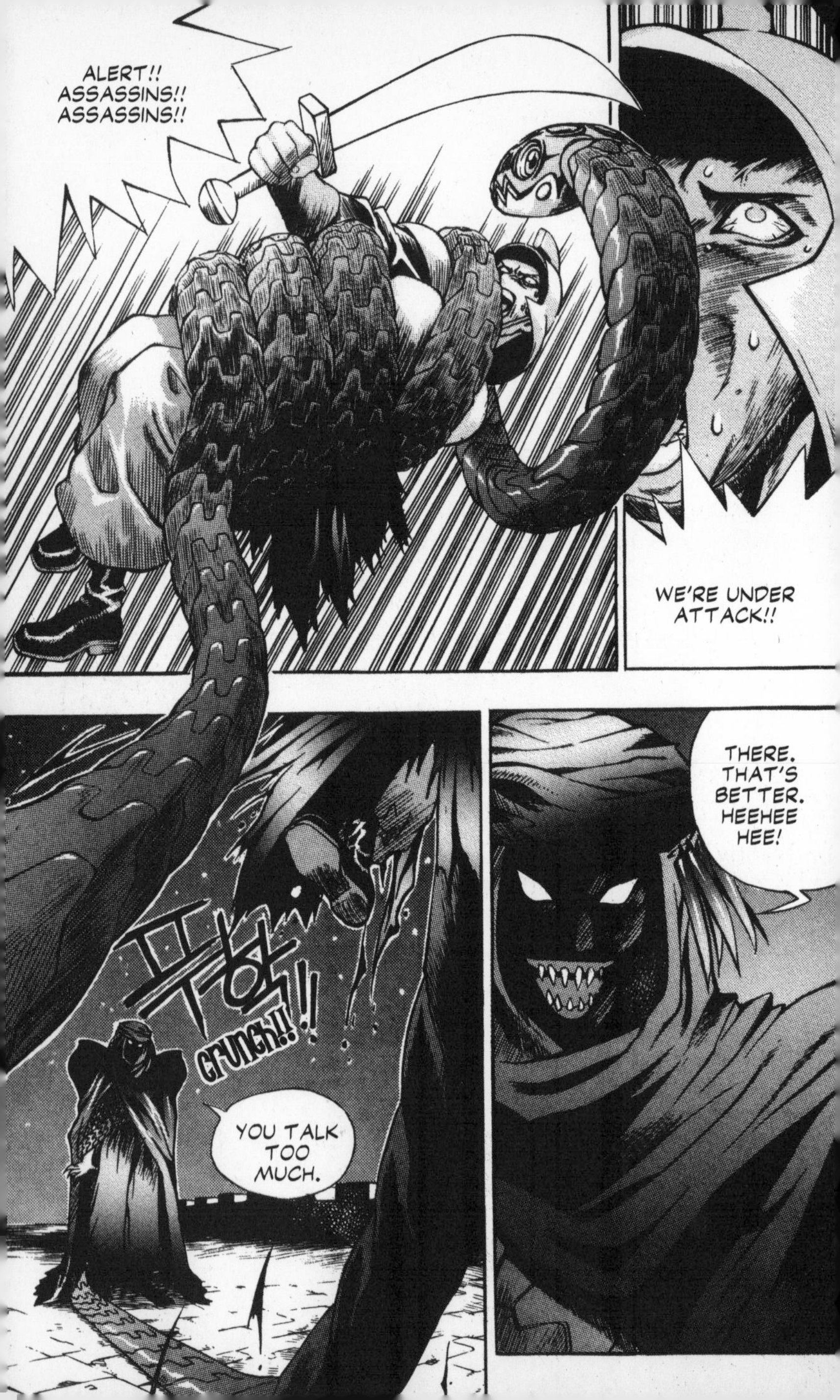
ALERT!! ASSASSINS!! ASSASSINS!!
WE'RE UNDER ATTACK!!
CRUNCH!!
YOU TALK TOO MUCH.
THERE. THAT'S BETTER. HEEHEE HEE!

RAGNAROK
라그나로크
INTO THE ABYSS

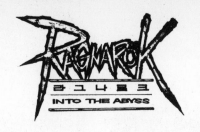

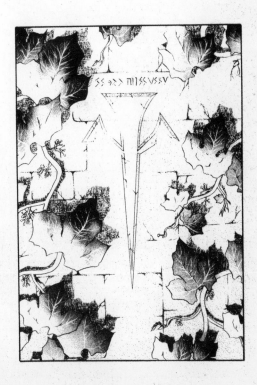

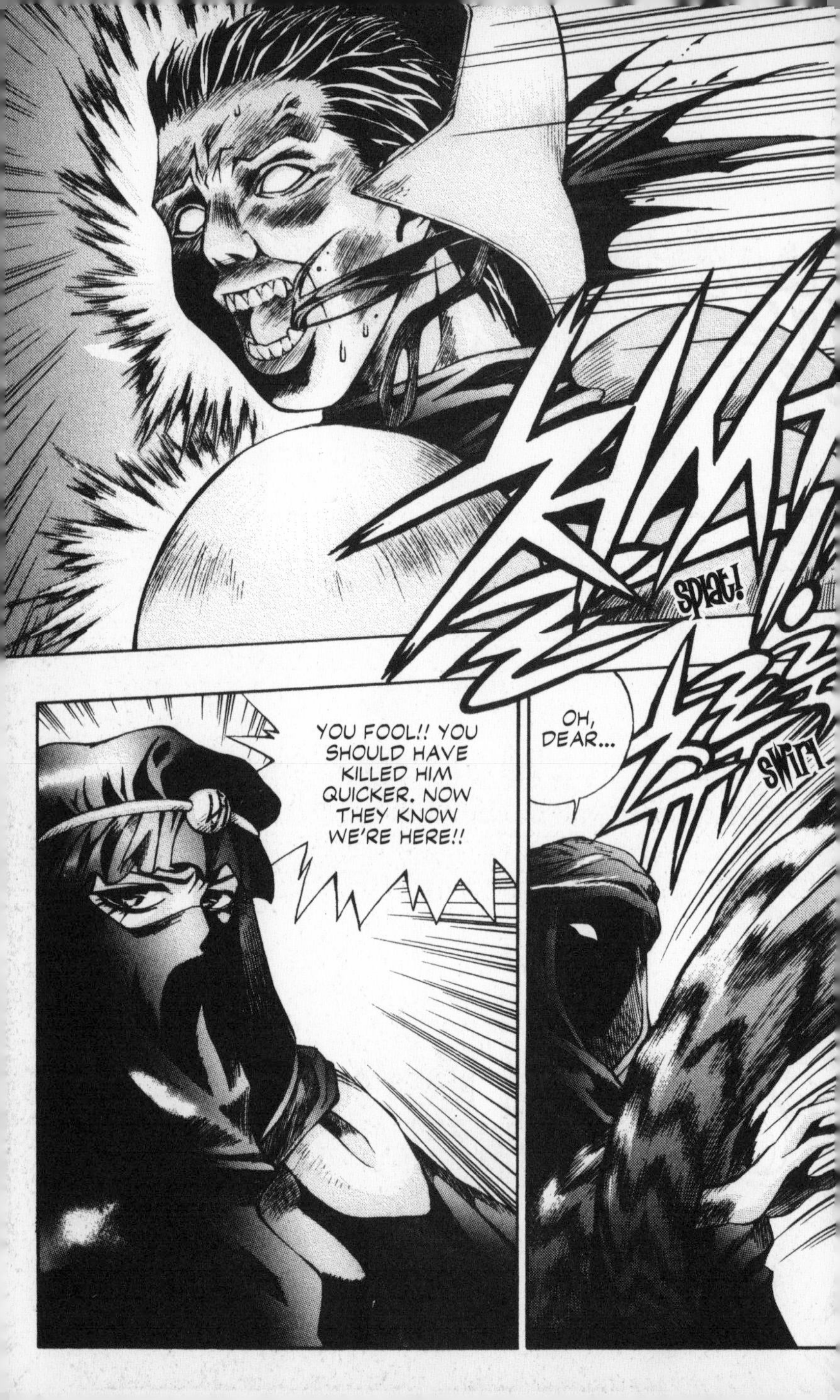
SPLAT!
YOU FOOL!! YOU SHOULD HAVE KILLED HIM QUICKER. NOW THEY KNOW WE'RE HERE!!
OH, DEAR...
SWIRL

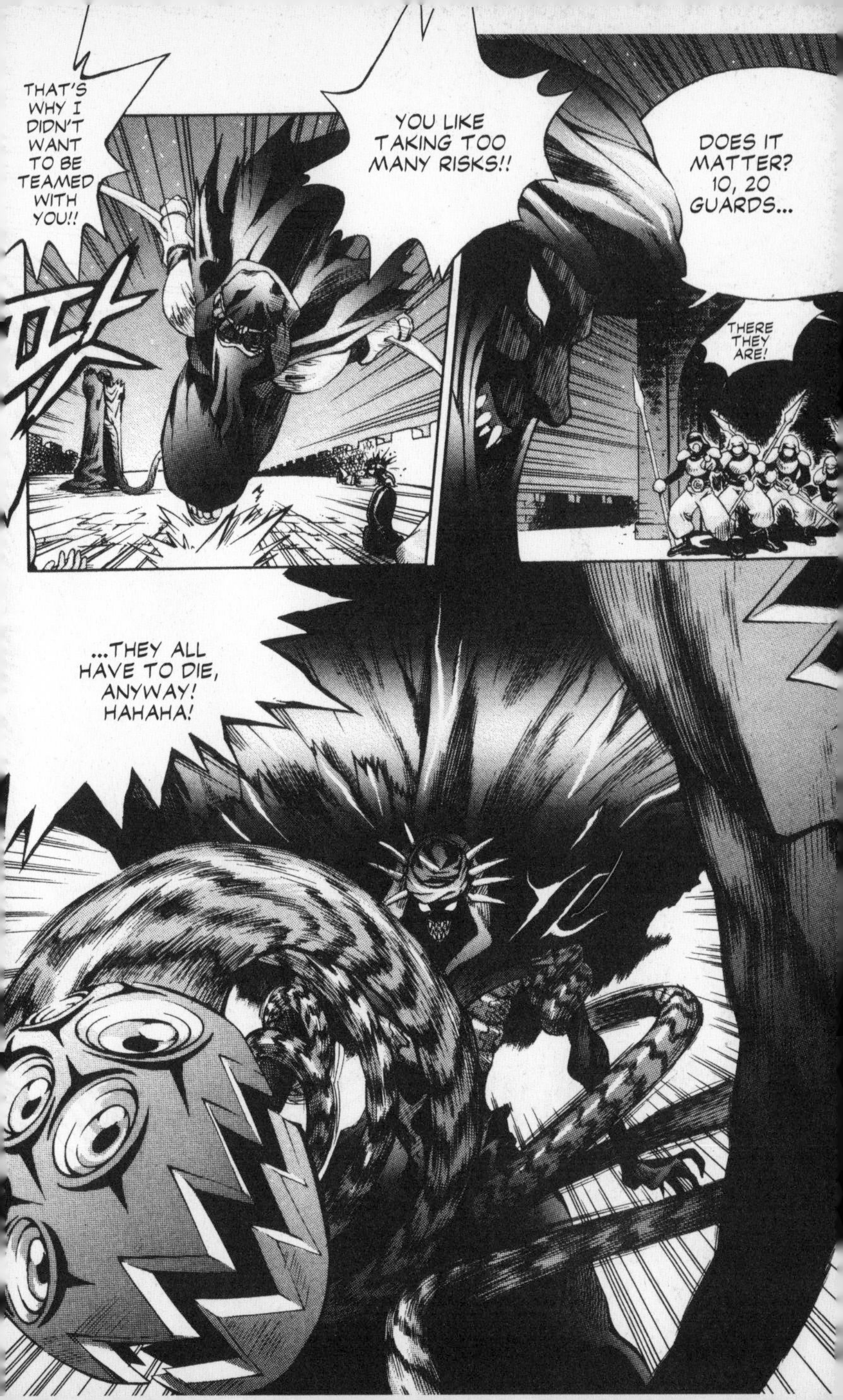
THAT'S WHY I DIDN'T WANT TO BE TEAMED WITH YOU!!
YOU LIKE TAKING TOO MANY RISKS!!
DOES IT MATTER? 10, 20 GUARDS...
THERE THEY ARE!
...THEY ALL HAVE TO DIE, ANYWAY! HAHAHA!

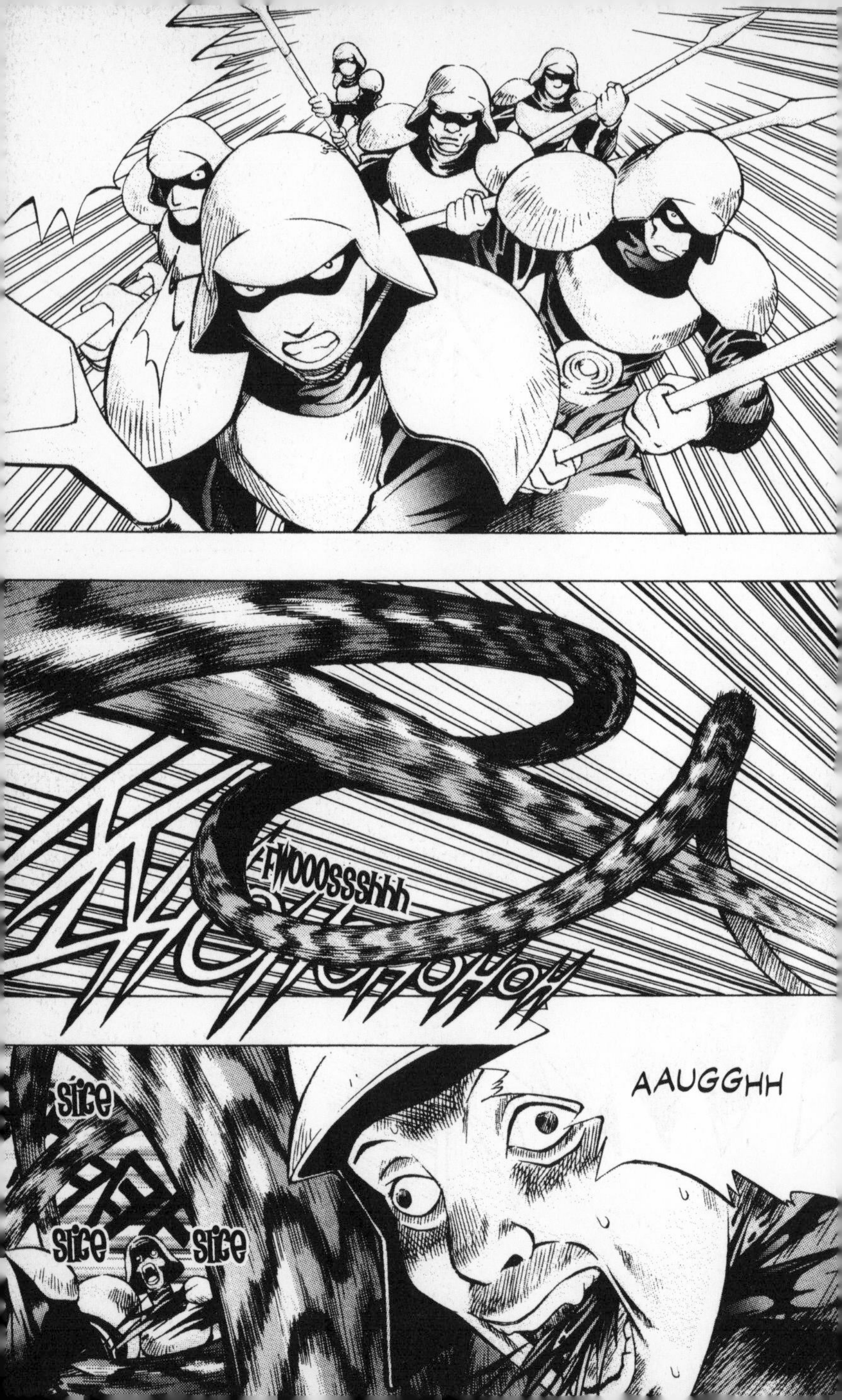
FWOOOSSSHHH
slice
slice
slice
AAUGGHH

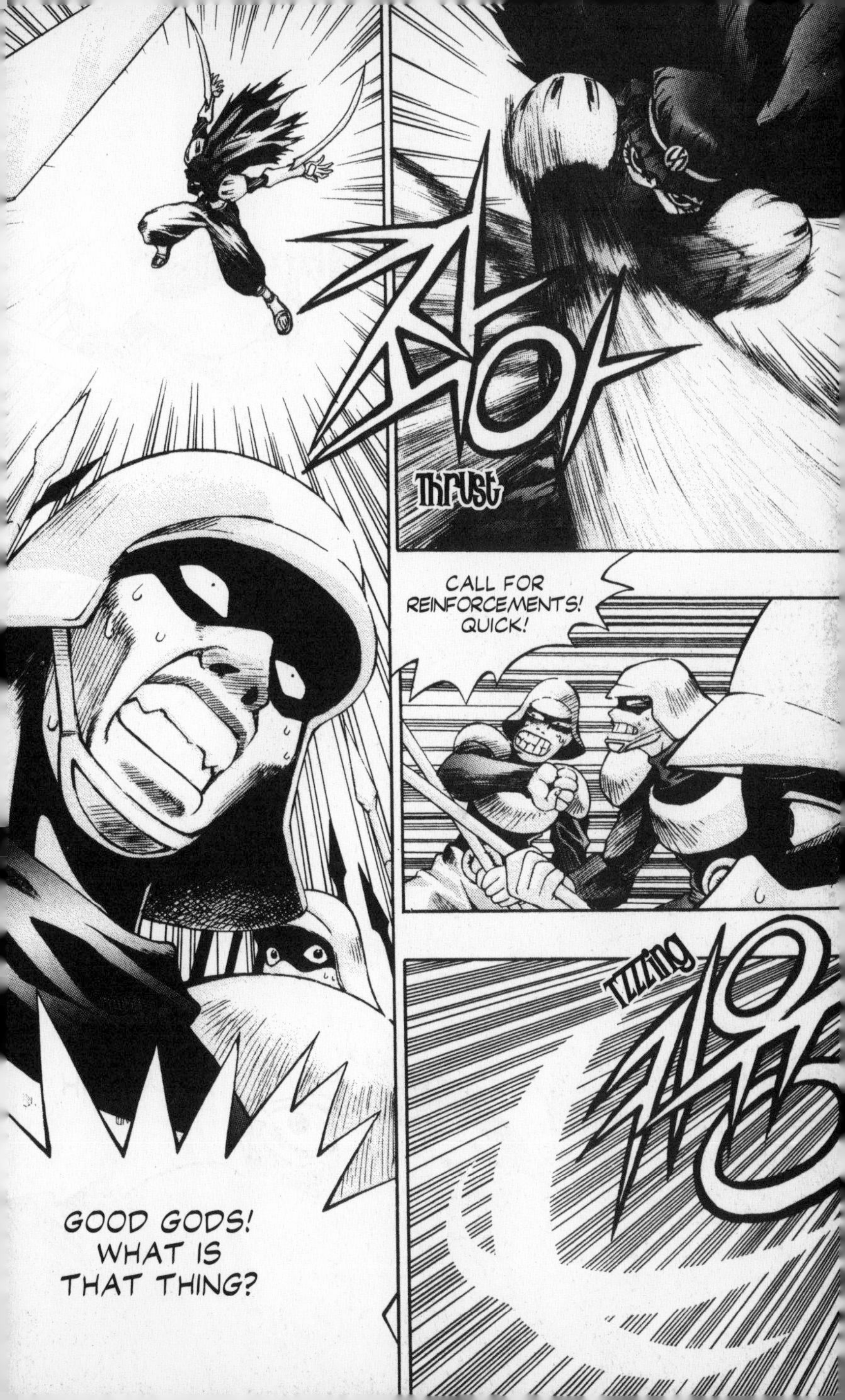
GOOD GODS! WHAT IS THAT THING?
Thrust
CALL FOR REINFORCEMENTS! QUICK!
Tzzing

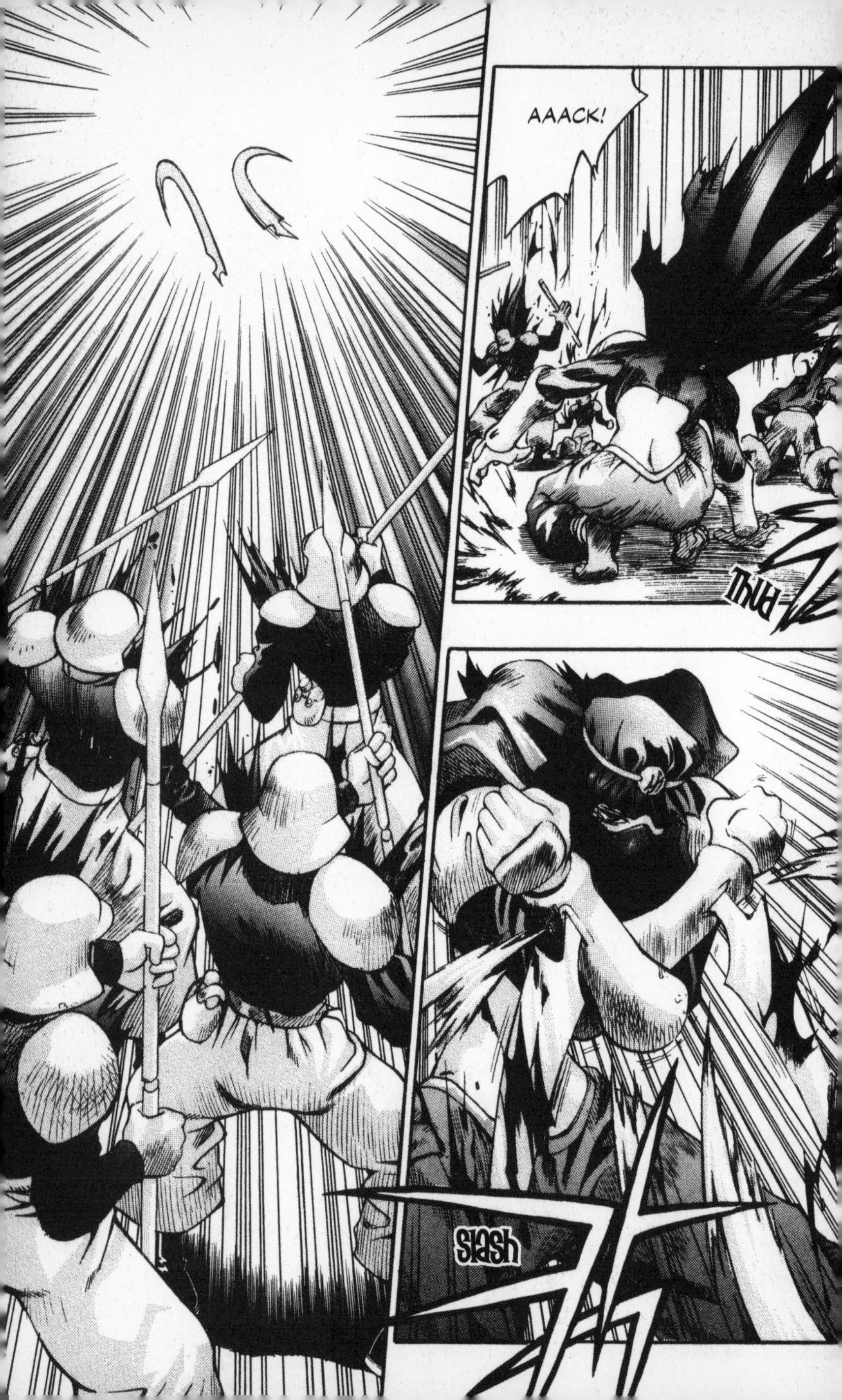
AAACK!
THUD
SLASH

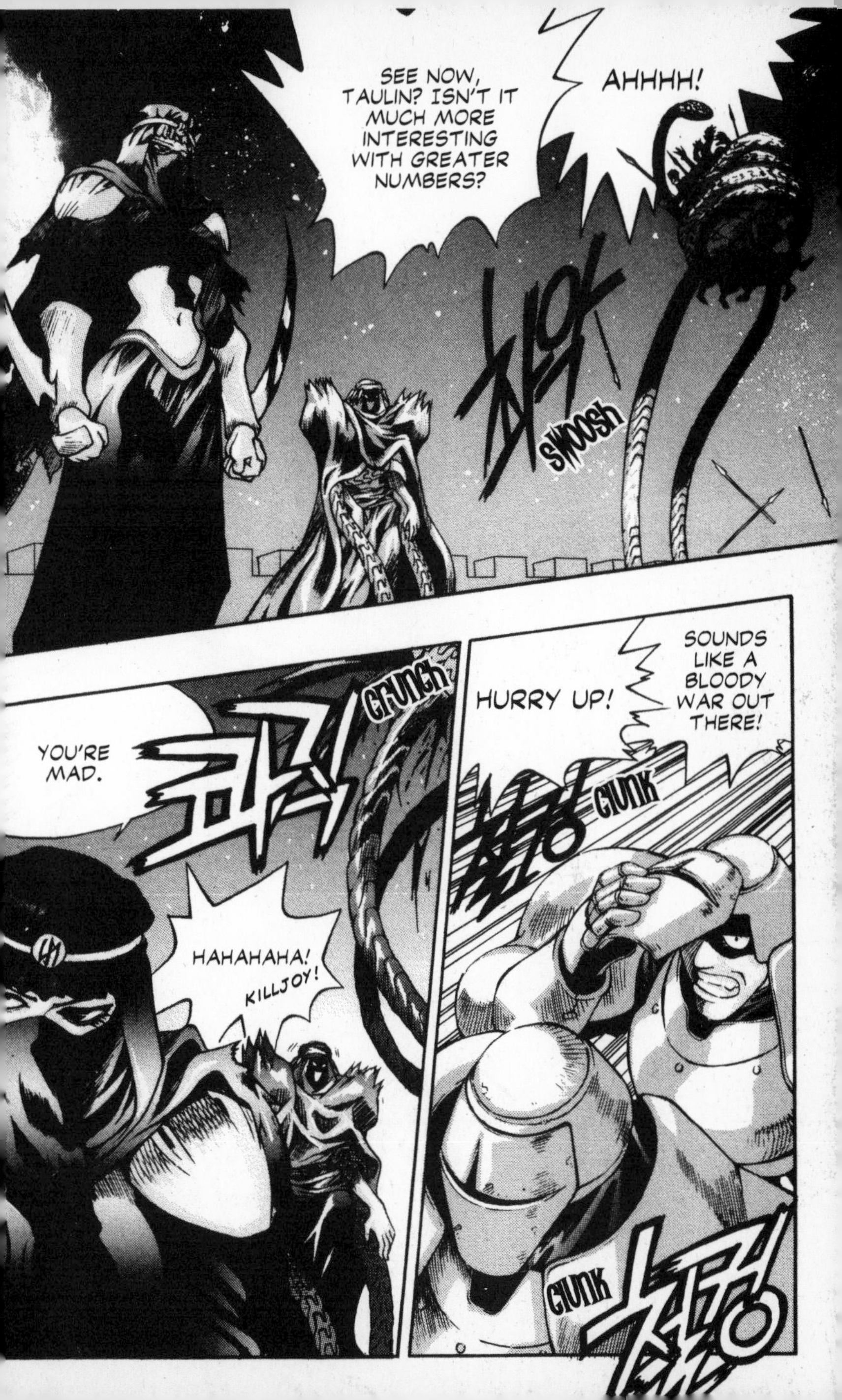
SEE NOW, TAULIN? ISN'T IT MUCH MORE INTERESTING WITH GREATER NUMBERS?
AHHHH!
SWOOSH
YOU'RE MAD.
CRUNCH
HAHAHAHA!
KILLJOY!
HURRY UP!
SOUNDS LIKE A BLOODY WAR OUT THERE!
CLUNK
CLUNK

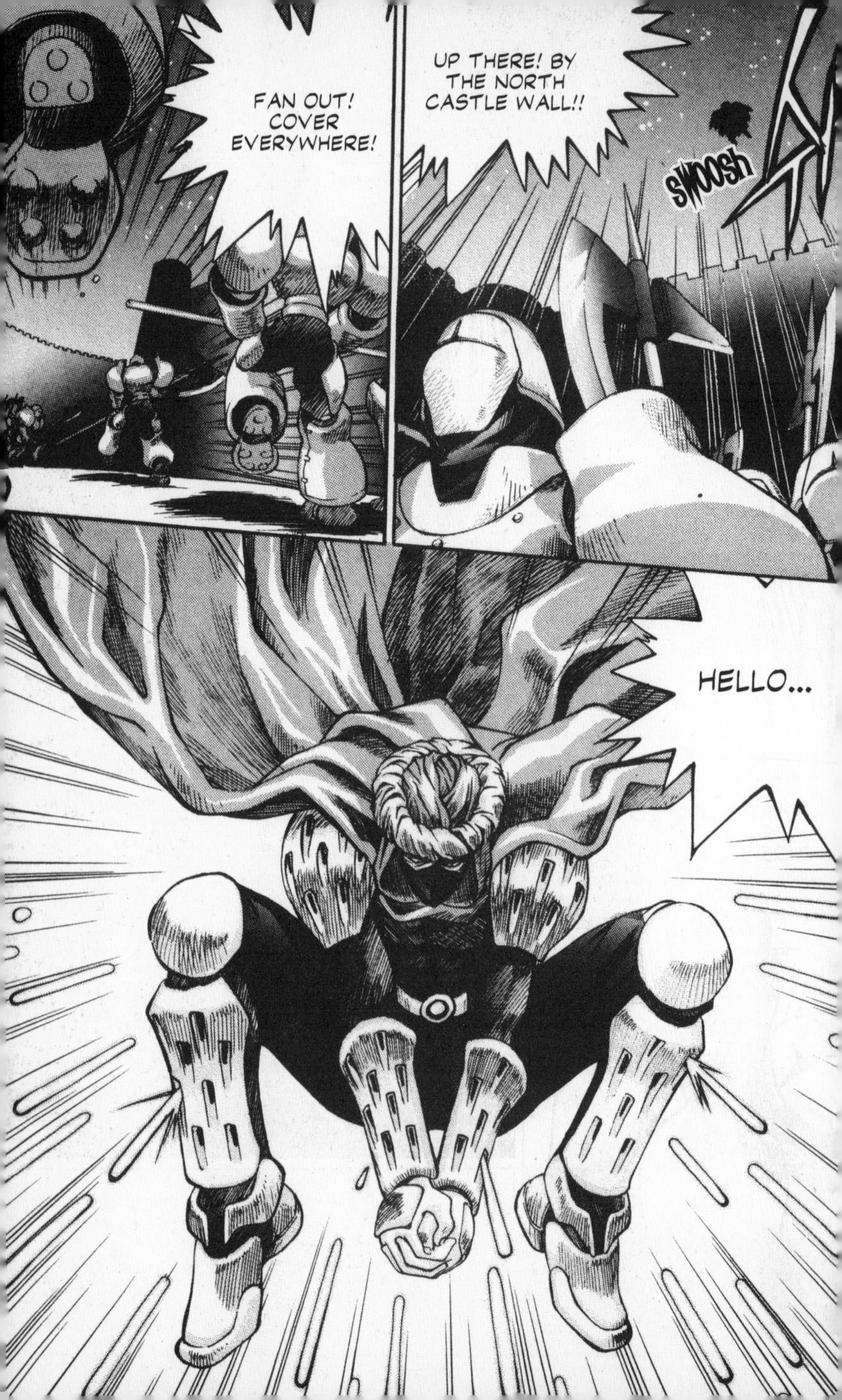
FAN OUT! COVER EVERYWHERE!
UP THERE! BY THE NORTH CASTLE WALL!!
SWOOSH
HELLO...

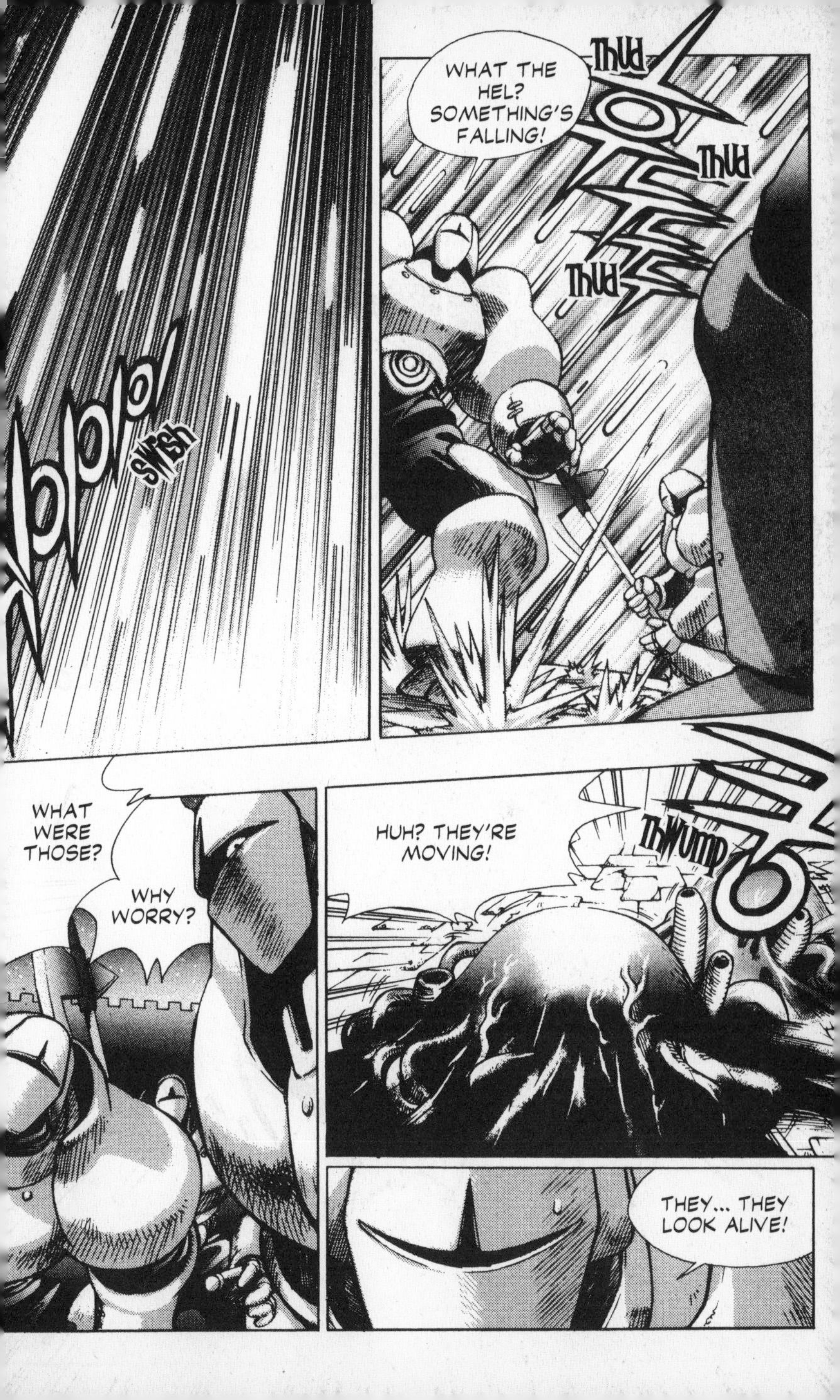

SWISH
WHAT THE HEL? SOMETHING'S FALLING!
THUD
THUD
THUD
WHAT WERE THOSE?
WHY WORRY?
HUH? THEY'RE MOVING!
THWUMP
THEY... THEY LOOK ALIVE!

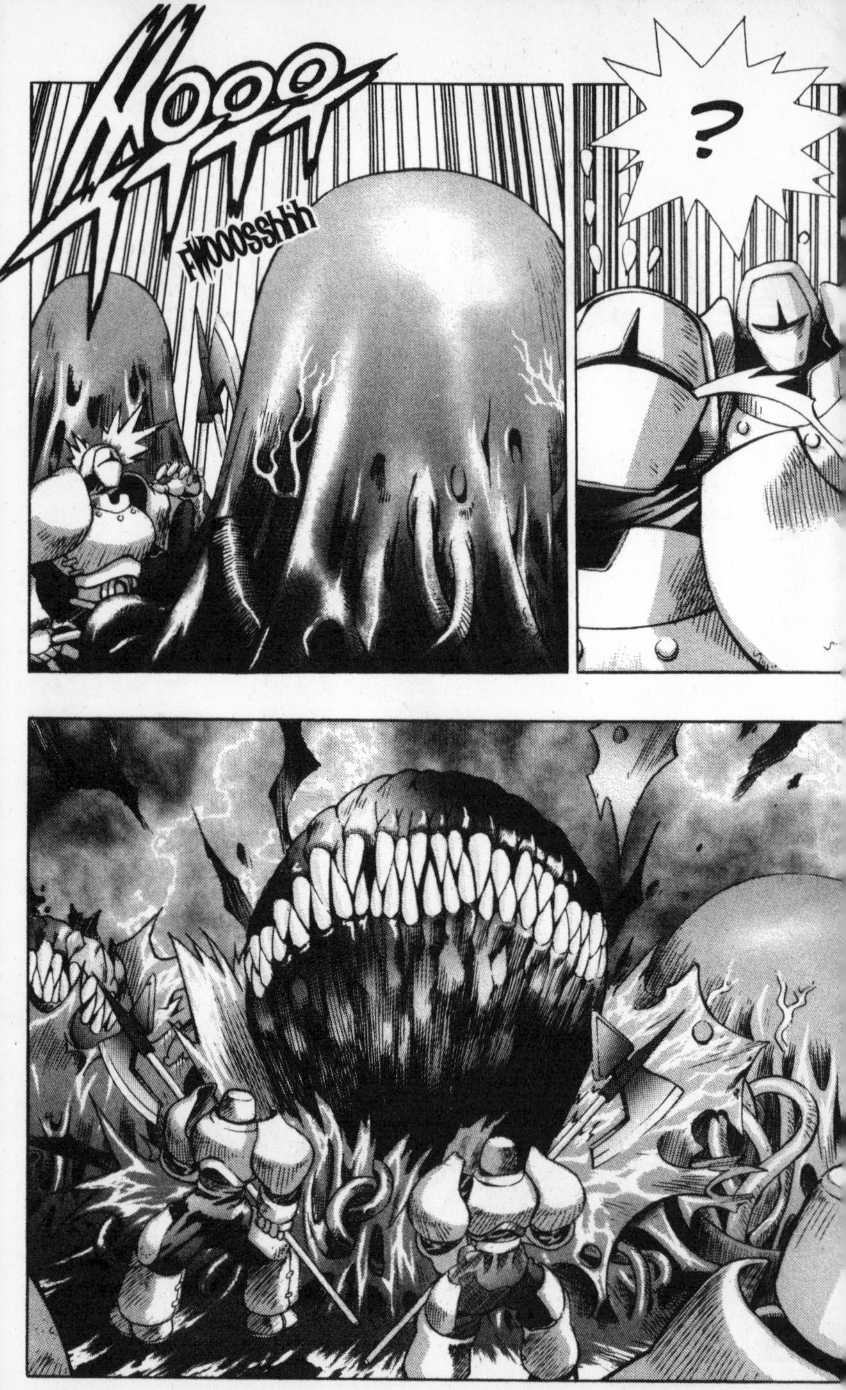
WOOOM
FWOOOSshhh
?

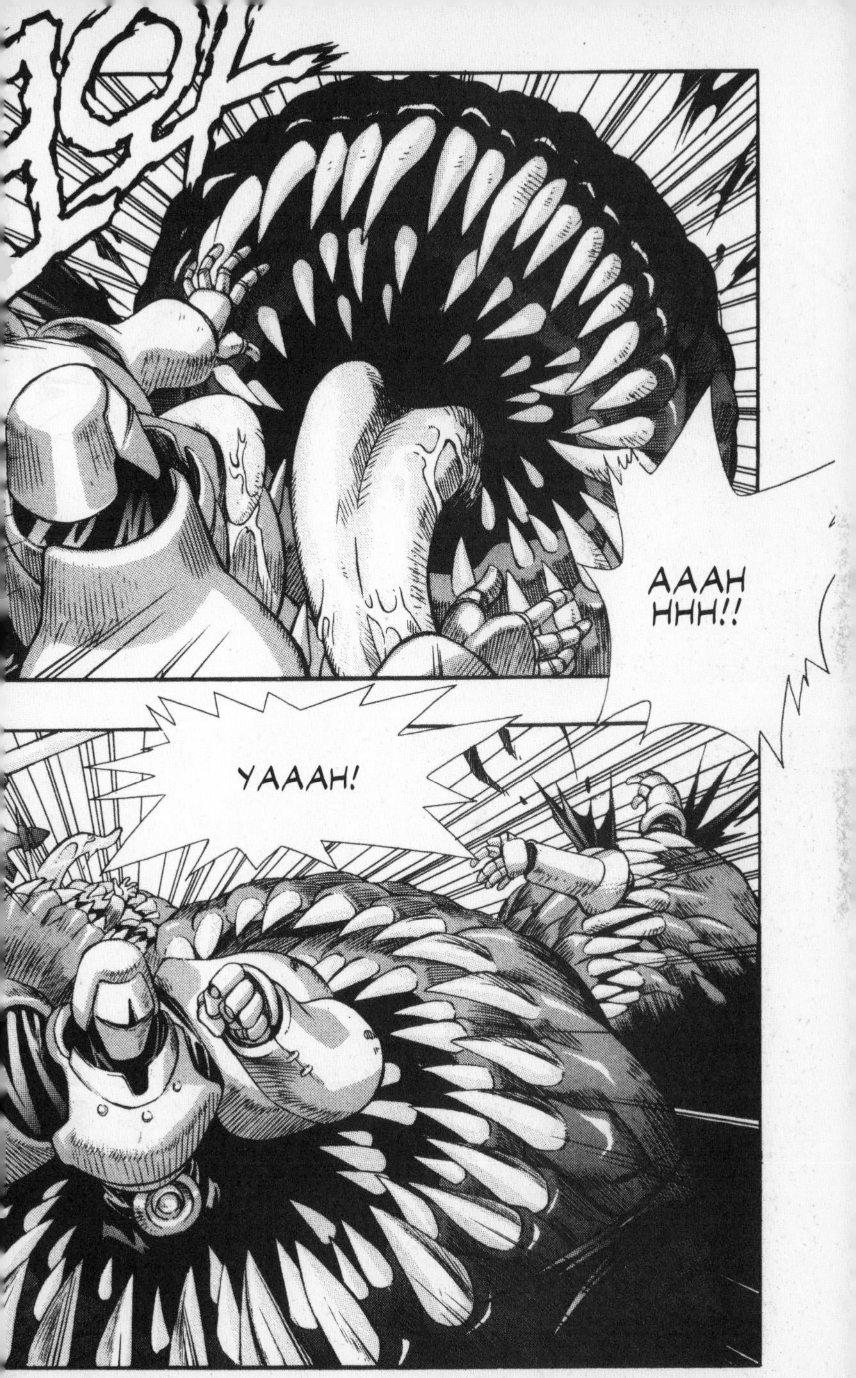
AAAH HHH!!
YAAAH!

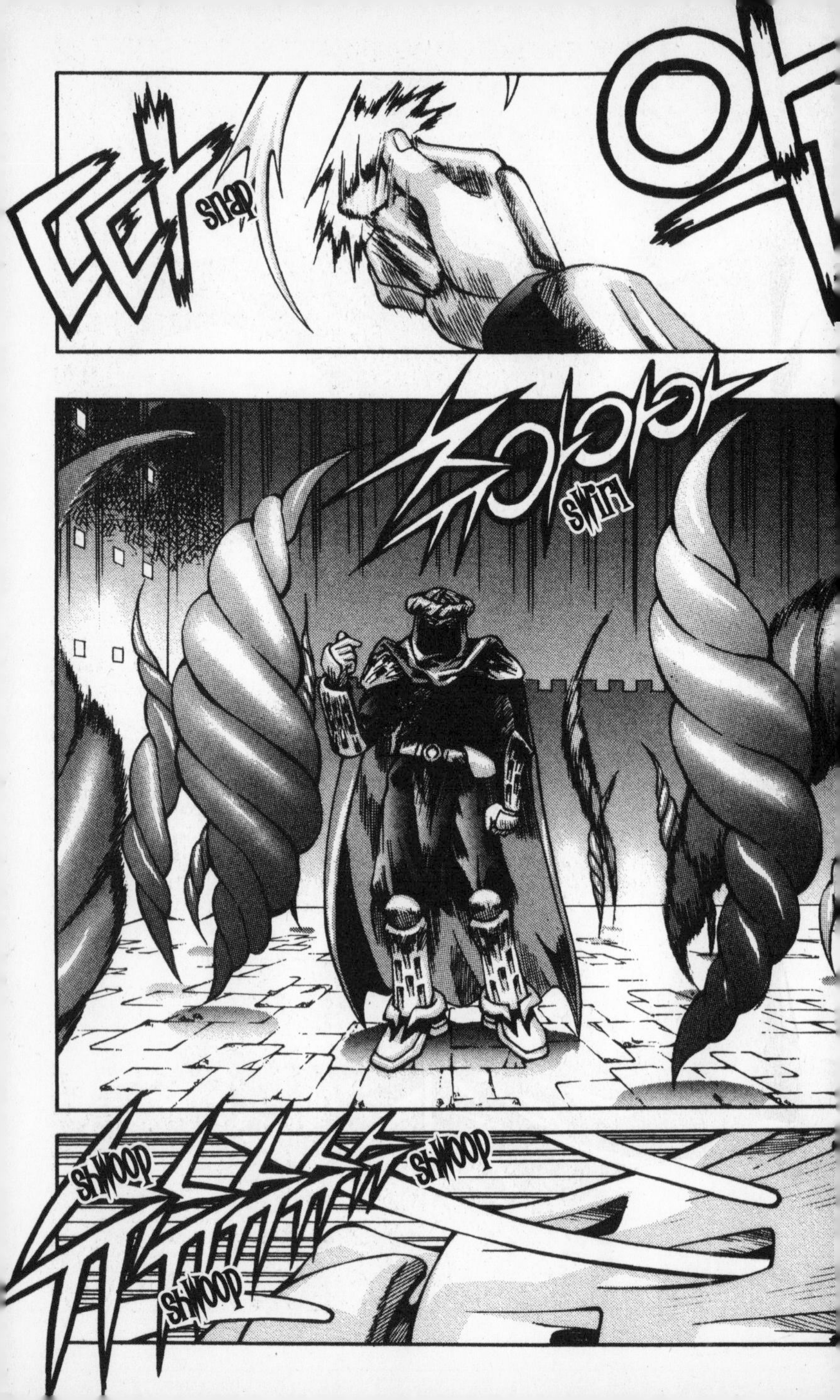
snap
swirl
shwoop
shwoop
shwoop

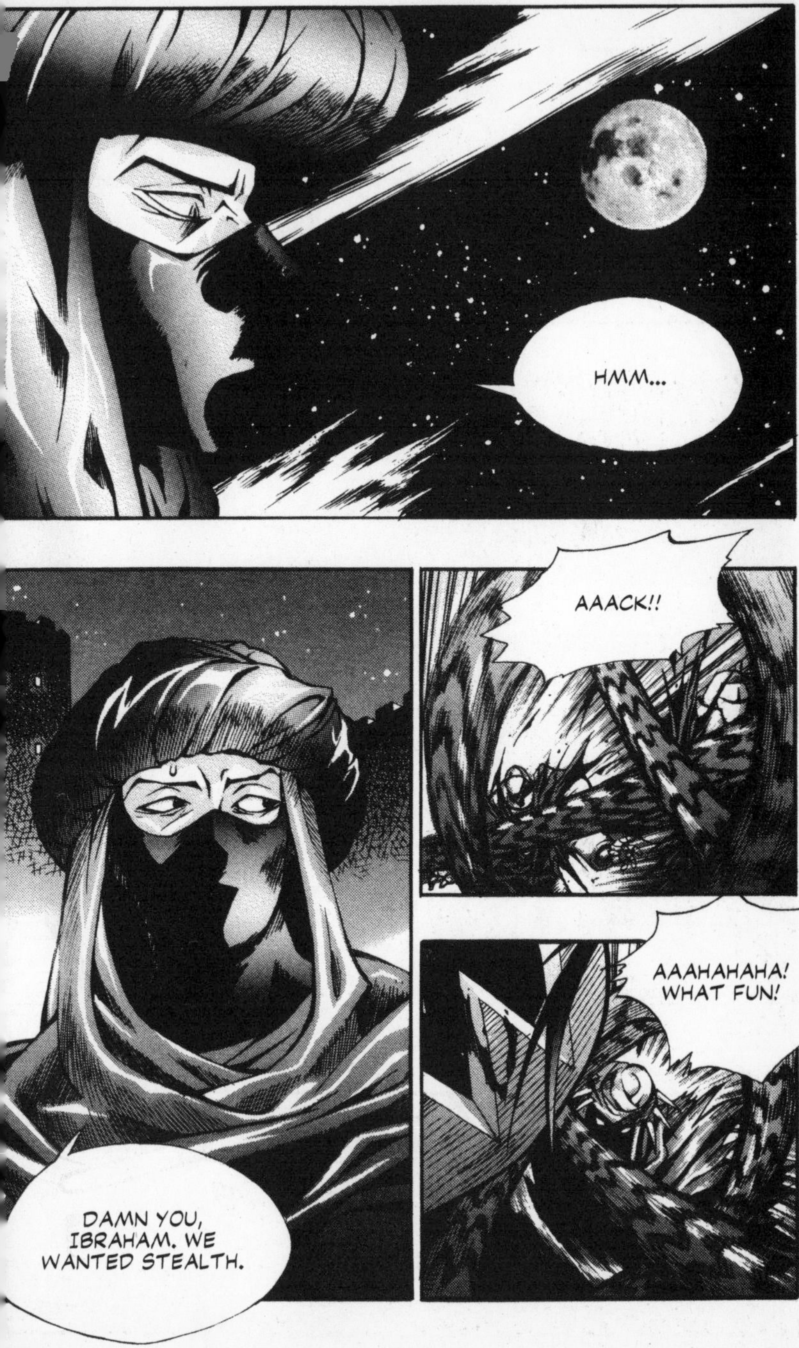
HMM...
DAMN YOU, IBRAHAM. WE WANTED STEALTH.
AAACK!!
AAAHAHAHA! WHAT FUN!

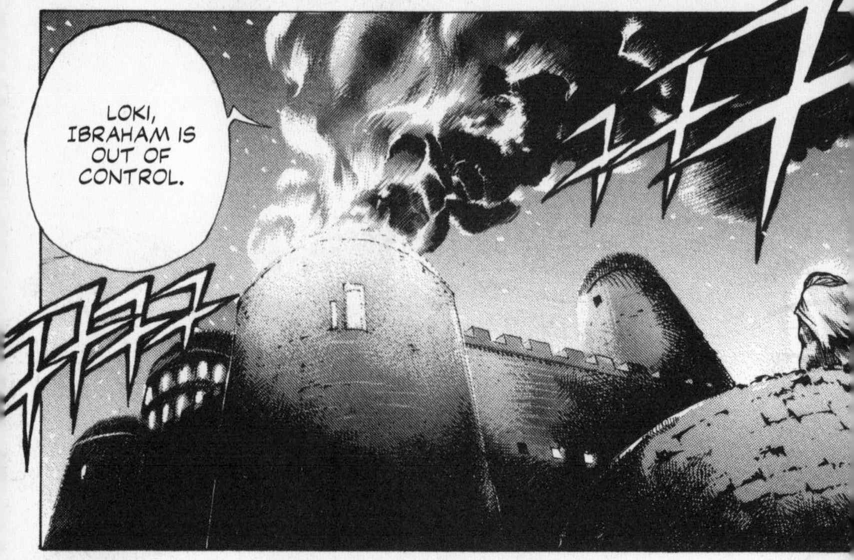
LOKI, IBRAHAM IS OUT OF CONTROL.

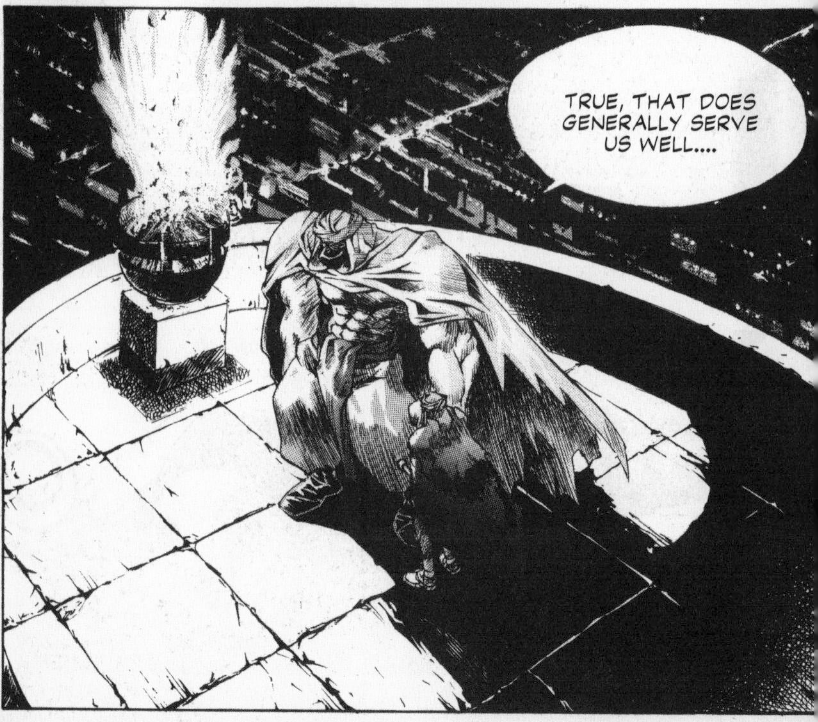
TRUE, THAT DOES GENERALLY SERVE US WELL....

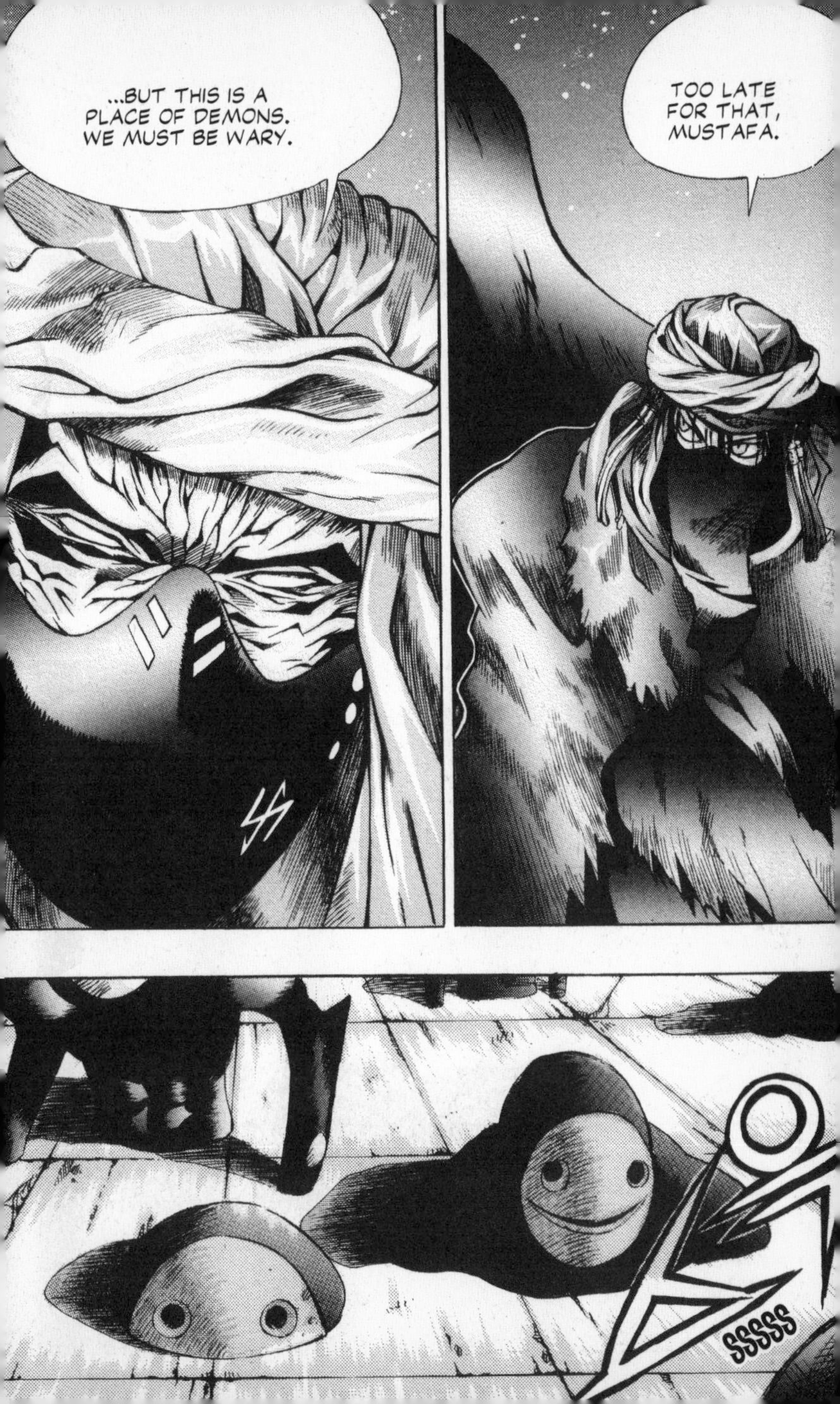
...BUT THIS IS A PLACE OF DEMONS. WE MUST BE WARY.
TOO LATE FOR THAT, MUSTAFA.
SSSSS

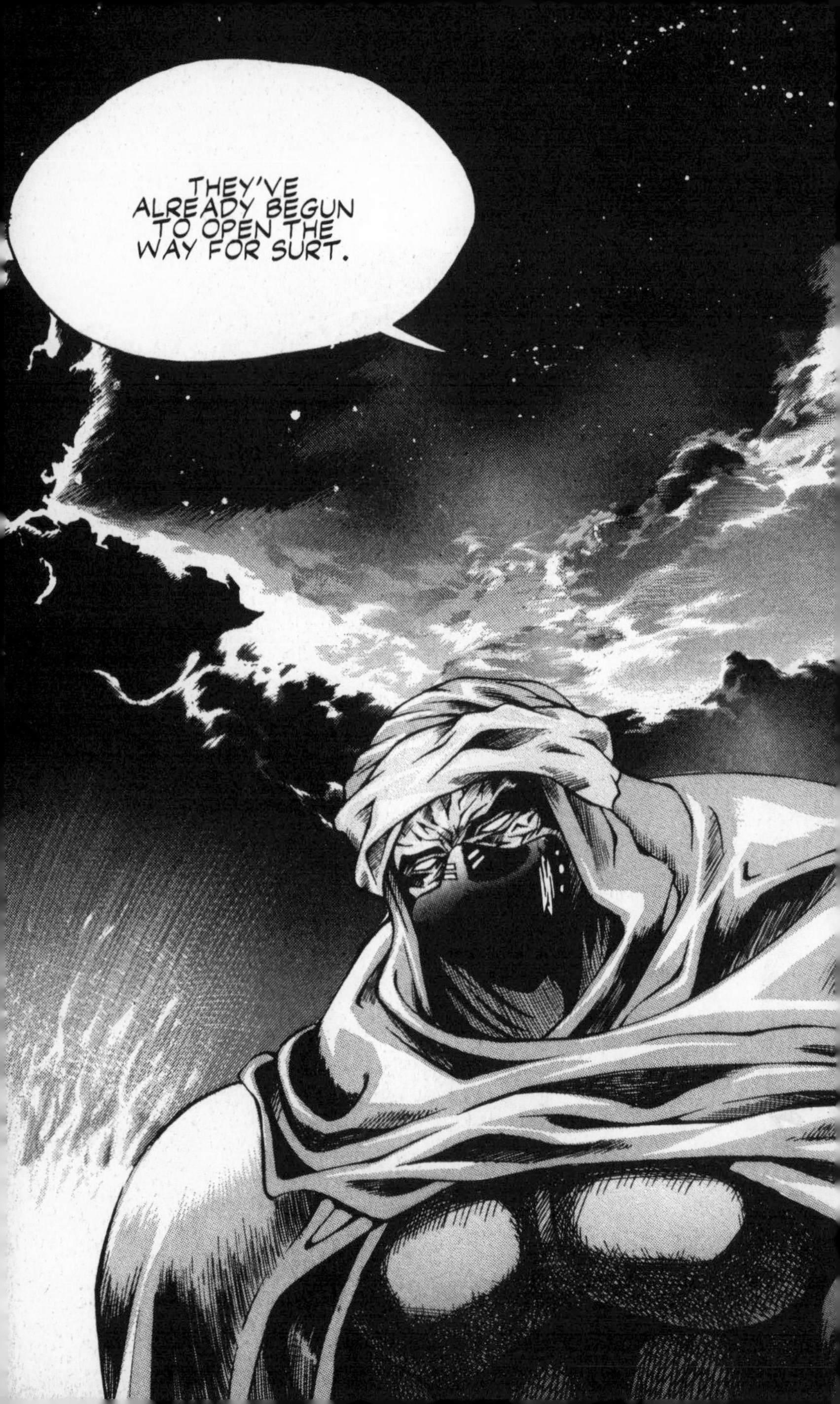
THEY'VE ALREADY BEGUN TO OPEN THE WAY FOR SURT.

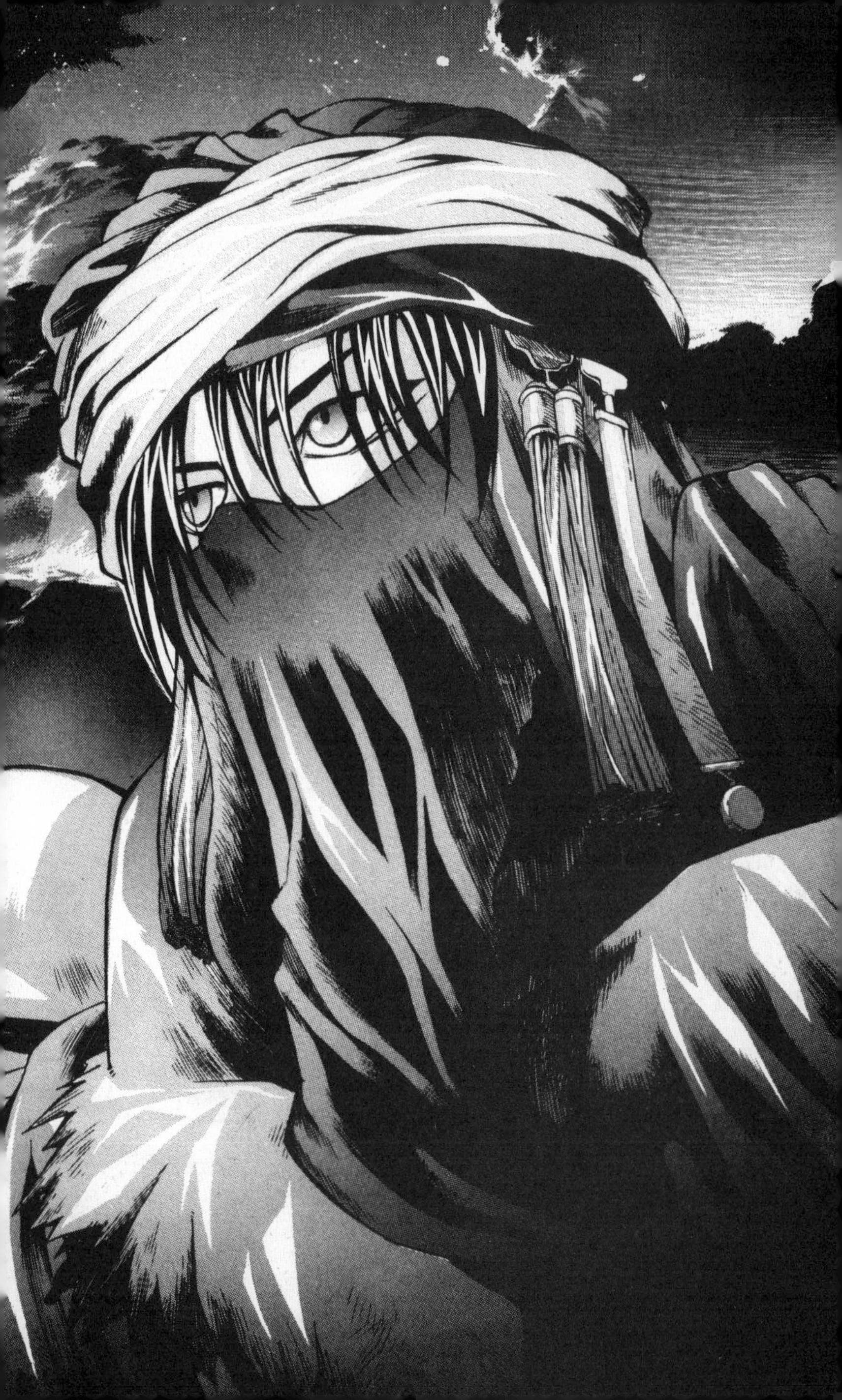

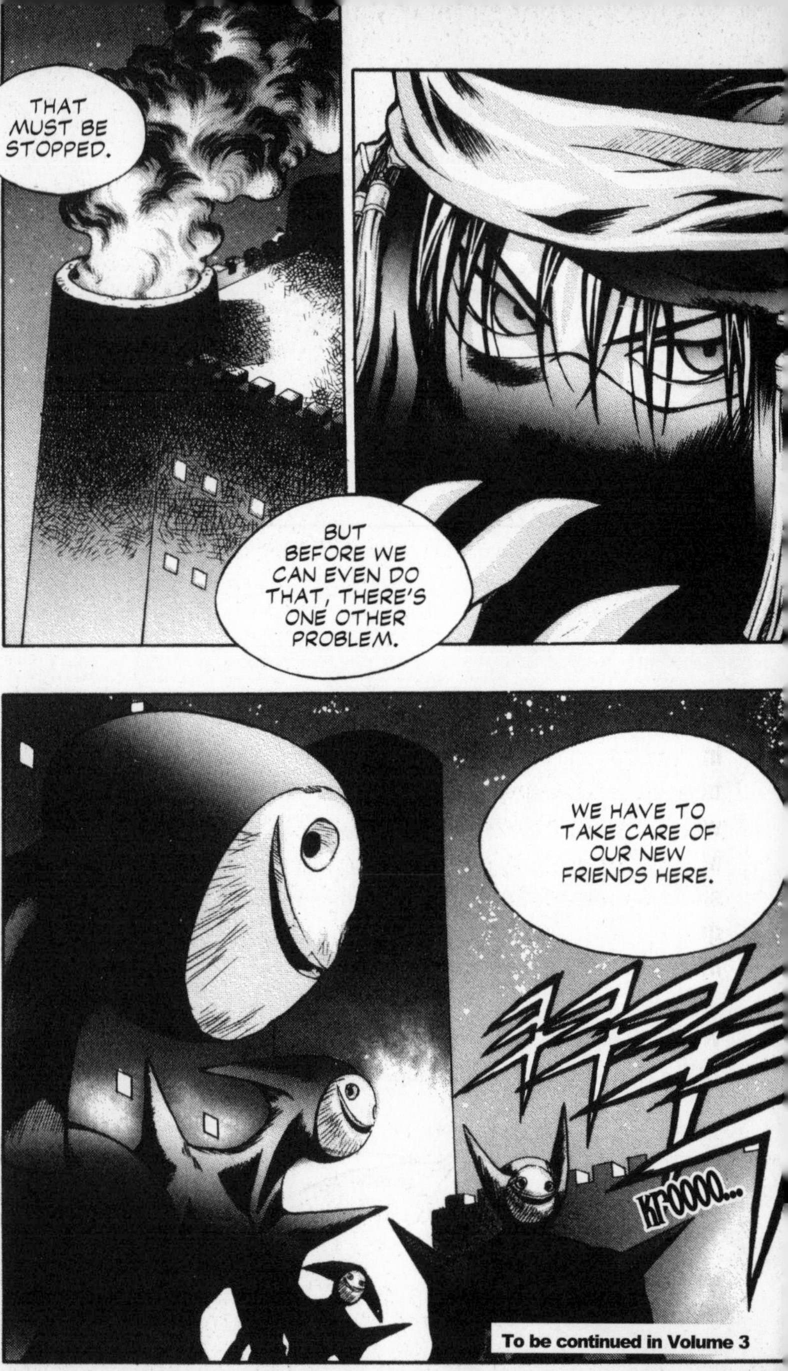
THAT MUST BE STOPPED.
BUT BEFORE WE CAN EVEN DO THAT, THERE'S ONE OTHER PROBLEM.
WE HAVE TO TAKE CARE OF OUR NEW FRIENDS HERE.
KI-OOOO...
To be continued in Volume 3

RAGNARÖK

An ancient evil threatens to return to Midgard and shroud the world in its shadow. The followers of the demon Surt have begun the rites to resurrect dark fallen lord, and when he returns the streets will run with blood. The Assassins Guild has sworn to keep the balance in Midgard, and they cannot allow Surt to return. Loki's team of assassins have infiltrated the Temple of Surt, but now that the human guards are out of the way, they must confront Surt's demon spawn in the temple's inner sanctum.

Witness the Mark of the Assassin in *Ragnarok Volume 3: Reign of Blood* available from Tokyopop.

3

By Myung-Jin Lee

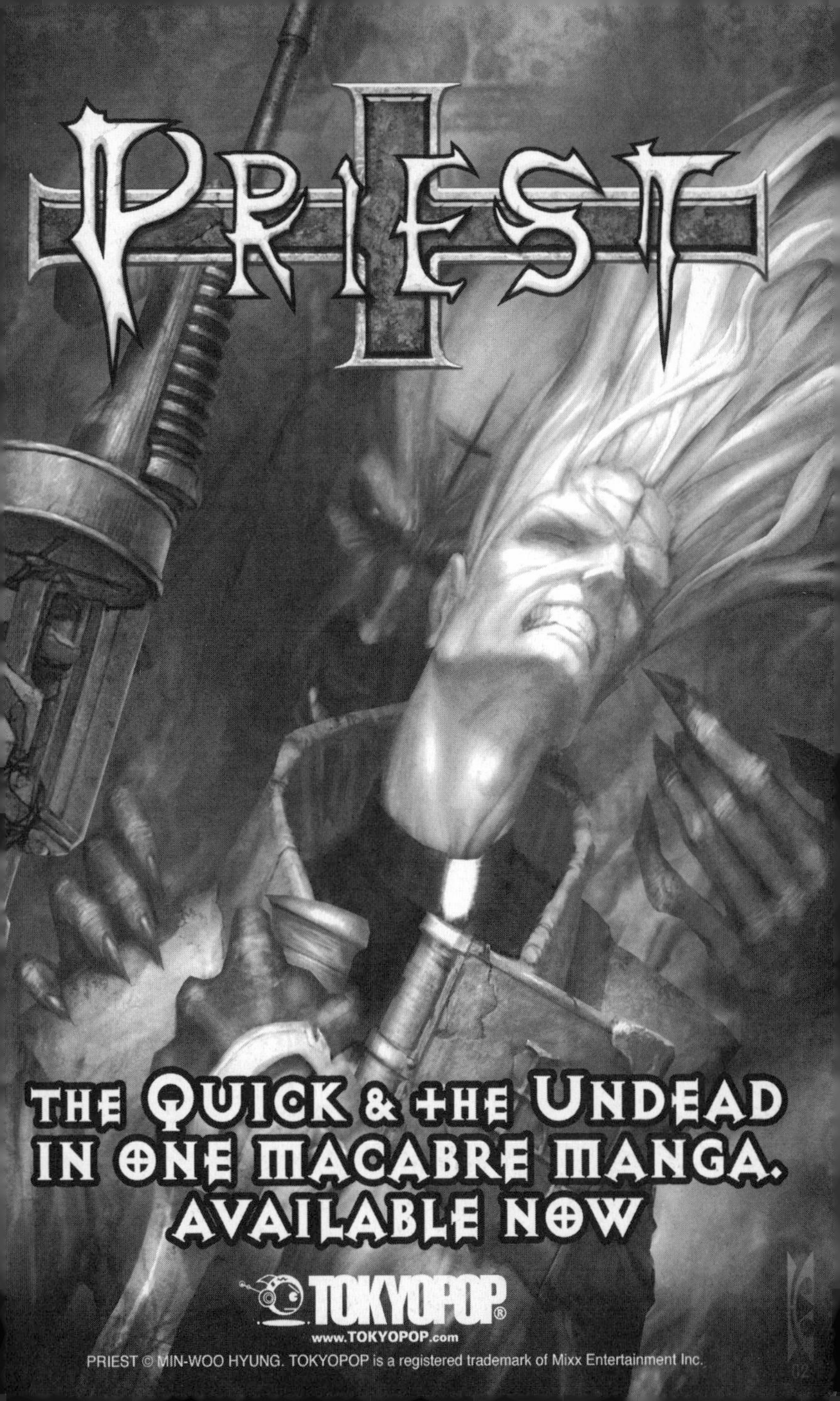

PRIEST
THE QUICK & THE UNDEAD
IN ONE MACABRE MANGA.
AVAILABLE NOW
TOKYOPOP®
www.TOKYOPOP.com
PRIEST © MIN-WOO HYUNG. TOKYOPOP is a registered trademark of Mixx Entertainment Inc.

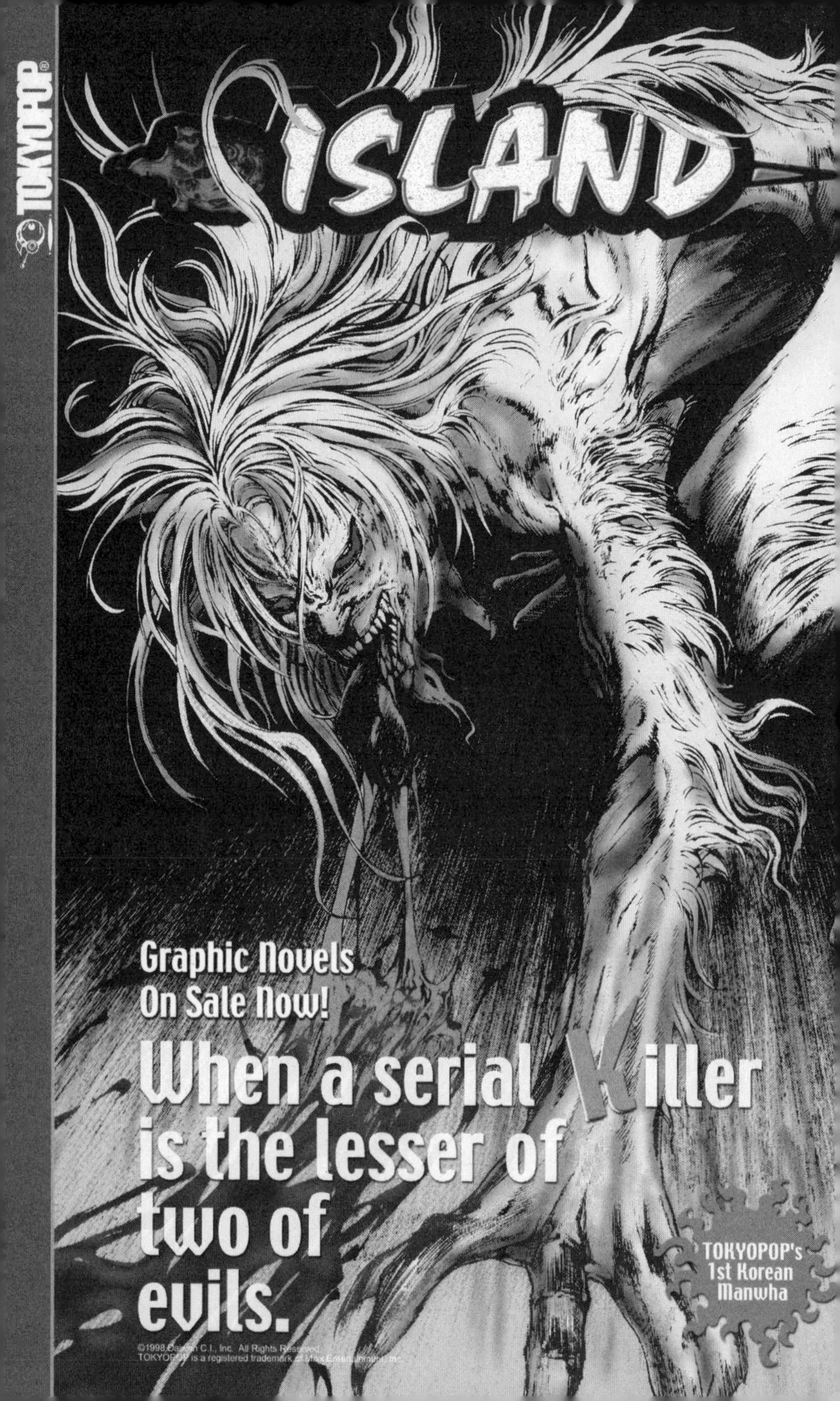
TOKYOPOP
ISLAND
Graphic Novels
On Sale Now!
When a serial Killer
is the lesser of
two of
evils.
TOKYOPOP's
1st Korean
Manwha